# THE RISE OF CHINGIS KHAN AND HIS
# CONQUEST OF NORTH CHINA

CHINGIS KHAN

# THE RISE OF CHINGIS KHAN
## AND HIS
# CONQUEST OF NORTH CHINA

BY

### H. DESMOND MARTIN

Introduction by Owen Lattimore
Edited by Eleanor Lattimore

1971

## OCTAGON BOOKS
*New York*

*Reprinted 1971*
*by special arrangement with The Johns Hopkins Press*

OCTAGON BOOKS
A DIVISION OF FARRAR, STRAUS & GIROUX, INC.
19 Union Square West
New York, N. Y. 10003

LIBRARY OF CONGRESS CATALOG CARD NUMBER: 70-120647

*Printed in U.S.A. by*
NOBLE OFFSET PRINTERS, INC.
NEW YORK 3, N. Y.

*For My Mother*

ELIZA FLORENCE MARTIN

# FOREWORD

DURING the last twenty years a number of biographies on Chingis Khan have been presented to the public, but though some contain excellent chapters on his rise to power and conquests in the Moslem West, none have dealt adequately or at any length with the conqueror's wars in China. This has, of course, been due largely to the very limited number of works on the subject available to those unable to consult Chinese records. Of late, the efforts of such renowned sinologists as Pelliot and Haenisch have done much to overcome this obstacle, but as yet it seems that there is still no full length account of Chingis Khan's wars in East Asia. This is the more to be regretted in that, not only during the reign of the great conqueror himself, but during those of his sons and grandsons, China was always the main object of Mongol arms. Surpassing any other country of that day in wealth and population, it naturally drew against it the most powerful armies at the disposal of the great Khans.

The primary object of the present study is to give as detailed and comprehensive a picture as possible of that phase of the Mongol conquest of China falling within the reign of Chingis Khan (1206-27). However, before embarking upon this, I have considered it advisable to include a portrait of the conqueror, and an account of the Mongol army, that astonishing war machine which played so large a part in making of the Mongols the greatest military power in history, and a brief survey of Chingis Khan's rise to power.

As is now generally known, the Mongol eruption, and others of the same kind, were due to political causes, not to desiccation in Mongolia as was once assumed. Within historic times there have been no climatic changes that permanently reduced the amount of grazing necessary to support the population that seems to have lived in Outer Mongolia up to the present

vii

day. At times, sudden droughts, or a series of droughts, must
have brought about small migrations from the poorer pastures
bordering the desert, but with the return of normal conditions
the desiccated areas appear to have soon received a fresh
population.

The imperialism of the Mongols and that of their predecessors and successors was the positive stage of a cycle of
centralization and decentralization which has characterized the
history of nomadic Asia just as it has that of China, Iran,
India and the Mediterranean, with whose destinies those of
the nomads were linked.

Regarding the material drawn upon, a look at the bibli-
ography will show that both Chinese and Occidental works
have been used, but when dealing strictly with Mongol activities in China, I have relied largely upon Chinese records. Of
these, those compiled during the 13th century have been
adhered to whenever possible, though I have kept in mind that
such works, e. g. the " Yüan Ch'ao Pi Shih," the " Yüan Sheng
Wu Ch'in Cheng Lu " and the " Yüan Shih " of Sung Lien,
naturally, tend to favor the Mongols. To avoid becoming
biased, I have paid considerable attention to the " Chin Shih,"
especially to the biographies, which are often much more infor-
mative than the main text, and to the " Li-tai T'ung-Chien
Chi-Lan." But over and above these, I owe much to certain
recent works, particularly to the commentaries of Wang Kuo-
Wei on the " Yüan Sheng Wu Ch'in Cheng Lu " and the
" Meng Ta Pei Lu," and to T'u Chi's great history, the " Meng-
wu-erh Shih." This last has proved invaluable in helping to
clear up many obscure political and military problems which
other works have merely recorded and left unclarified. Nevertheless, I have often been obliged to trust to my own judgment
and to resort to conjecture, but when doing so I have tried
to make this plain, either in the text or by means of footnotes.
Hazardous as such license may seem, it is unavoidable if one is
to present anything like an intelligible picture of the military
side of the subject involved. Hence, some may find much to
criticize in my solution and in my maps illustrating the various

campaigns of Chingis Khan and his generals. Moreover, not unnaturally, the drainage and general topography shown is that of the 20th century. In this instance, the map used has been the Hoku Shina Chizu (map of N. China), published in Dairen during 1936, but for the sake of clearness much topographical detail has been omitted and for the correct identification of places, several historical-geographical works have been consulted. Concerning the sites of certain battles and the routes to and from them followed by the Mongols, many of those falling within the Outer and Inner Great Walls, and in the regions where the Tanguts once held sway, have been seen at first hand by the author, who has consequently drawn on this experience to support or differ from the Chinese sources dealing with the events that took place in these areas.

For those not acquainted with Chinese names, it may be of help if the meaning of certain words that appear often in the text and maps are explained. Starting with the geographical terms, Ling means a range of mountains, Shan an individual hill or mountain, or at times an entire range, Ho and Chiang both stand for river, Hu is a lake and Pei, Nan, Tung and Hsi, North, South, East and West, while in the matter of place names, Ching is a capital city, e. g. Hsi Ching, The Western Capital. Fu indicates a large city which is the administrative center of a considerable area, usually at least half a province. Chou is next in order and controls the next administrative unit, though sometimes Chou cities are quite independent of Fu. Hsien is the smallest administrative unit, while Ch'eng simply indicates a walled town. For fortifications the Chinese have a number of terms, Ch'eng, as just mentioned, meaning a wall, Pao either fort or wall, Kuan a fortified pass, or simply a pass, K'ou the mouth of a pass, fortified or unfortified and Chai a stronghold perched on a more or less inaccessible elevation.

As in all works of this nature, the author owes much to the help of others. Hence I am greatly indebted to Professor Owen Lattimore and Mrs. Lattimore for many improvements in the arrangement of the text. To Professor C. C. Lingard and

The Canadian Social Science Research Council, who made possible the publication of this book, I cannot sufficiently express my gratitude. In this connection, I would do ill to forget the Reverend G. R. Taylor and Professor C. C. Shih of the University of Toronto who first brought my book to the attention of Professor Lingard. I have also to thank Captain B. H. Liddell Hart, the eminent British military critic, and Professor J. Hudson of All Souls, Oxford, who kindly read through the manuscript and tendered much valuable advice. Going back to the days when the Chinese material for this work was being collected, I take pleasure in thanking The Roman Catholic University of Peking for the use of their magnificent library, also for the assistance that Mr. Achilles Fang afforded Mr. Chang, Chien-chiang and myself in wrestling with the various texts used. Since I am not a Sinologist, I owe a great deal to the efforts of both in doing the heavy work of translation. Perhaps those to whom my debt is greatest, certainly to whom the success of my wanderings in the path of Chingis Khan north of the Great Wall is due, are George Karl Söderbom of the Sven Hedin expeditions to Sinkiang, and Torgny Oberg of Kuei-hua, Sui-yüan, who put me in touch with the ways and means so indispensable for such undertakings. Associated in my mind with both is the Ordos Mongol prince of Khangin, the A Wang, who so kindly provided me and two friends with an open letter to his brother princes. This, despite the tense political situation of 1936, overcame all obstacles and insured the success of our expedition. There are many additional names that should be included, to mention only a few, Miss Ida Pruitt who provided me with invaluable contacts, the late Henning Haslund, leader of The Royal Danish Central Asiatic Expedition, Professor Wada who threw open to me the Toyobunko Library in Tokyo, Professor John De Francis of the Johns Hopkins University and Commander Eric Purdon, U. S. Navy and my companion to Ala Shan, who left me a splendid set of photographs covering our trip. But here I must end, though there are many others, Occidental, Chinese and Mongol to whom I am indebted in one way or another.

# INTRODUCTION

BY

OWEN LATTIMORE

WESTERN scholarship has always been fascinated by
those campaigns of the Mongols that brought them
across the threshold of Europe. A note of horrified romanticism
runs through much of the Western writing on the subject. The
idea that the Mongols were some kind of mysterious natural
calamity, like a plague, was reinforced when they turned back
from Europe not because they had been defeated but because
their commanders had been summoned to attend an assembly
for the election of a new Khan in their distant homeland. I do
not know that any European writer has said so in so many
words, but the impression that seems to have been left behind
was that for these ferocious and invincible warriors the election
of a new Khan was more important than the plunder of Europe.
So great was their discipline that for this great ceremony they
must return at once on receipt of the word of command; the
sacking of Europe, it seemed to be implied, was something to
which they could return at any convenient time.

Because the Mongols were a threat that had withdrawn of
its own accord, not a challenge that had been turned back by
the arms of Europe, the Europeans appear never to have felt
that they had really taken the measure of the Mongols, or
fully comprehended the processes out of which grew the Mongol forms of military power and the political and economic
exploitation of conquest. Much European writing on the subject is, indeed, closer to legend and to subjective, speculative
interpretation than to analytical and perceptive history. Many
accounts dwell with fascination, insufficiently supported by
factual data, on the supposed processes by which conquerors
like Chingis and his predecessors among the Huns and Turks
arose, gathered together something vague and not very well
understood called a horde, overwhelmed all opposition by a

xi

combination of weight of numbers and animal ferocity, and swept westward.

Several marks are helpful in classifying this kind of writing: emphasis on the sweep westward; emphasis on the unpredictable quality of genius in the leader; emphasis on an assumed inborn martial quality in the pastoral nomad; and emphasis on irresistible numbers—though the fact is that the Mongols relied on skill, not numbers. Embellishments are often added, such as theories of climatic changes that supposedly caused nomads to migrate from desiccated lands toward greener pastures.

In recent years a more sociological approach to these problems of history has been developed which is less romantic but carries more intellectual conviction. The character of a conquest cannot be measured absolutely in terms only of the martial quality of the conquerors. It must be measured relatively by assessment both of those who conquered and those who were conquered. This assessment is the basic justification of the sociological approach, which undertakes to study not only those processes within a society which result, from time to time, in the emergence of a great man, but those relations between societies which explain why a society—like that of China, for instance—in contact for many generations with neighbors—as in Mongolia, for instance—whose social organization is of a different kind, is in one generation able to resist invasion but in another generation succumbs to invasion.

In this book Mr. Martin has made a valuable contribution to the further study of these problems. His account of the campaigns of the Mongols in China balances the better-known accounts of their westward campaigns, and makes possible a more panoramic view of the history of the period in China, in Inner Asia, and on the fringes of the Indian, Iranian, Slavic, and European worlds. He touches on the well-known problem of the alternating cycles of strength and decadence in the dynastic history of China, and the material he assembles in describing military operations supports the theory that there were similar cycles in other regions, such as Northern Iran and South Russia, where states based on revenues from settled agriculture and commercial cities were in close contact with societies of pastoral nomads. From the material on which he has drawn it can be seen that one explanation of the vast geographical sweep of the conquests of Chingis and his commanders is that at the beginning of the thirteenth century the agriculturally based empires of the Chin in North China, the Sung in South China, the empire of Khwarazm, and the partially agricultural kingdoms of the Khara Kitai in Central Asia and the Hsi Hsia in Northwest China were all simultaneously in the downward phase of the cycle of strength and decay. The Mongols were at no time forced to turn in one direction because of the strength of the resistance in some other direction. They were able to alternate their campaigns in any direction, to their own advantage, at their own choice.

In his account of how Chingis rose to be a great military leader in his own Mongol homeland Mr. Martin is dealing with material that has often been used before. Here his narrative, in combination with his accounts of the campaigns against " civilized " countries, supports the already well-known theory that in the rise of a nomad conqueror the early tribal wars between rather small armies, all drawn from within the nomad society, were critical. The nomad who could first conquer other nomads and then incorporate them in his own forces could thereafter not be checked by any " civilized " state unless that state were at a high point of centralized control and discipline.

Two factors explain the importance of wars within the nomad or " barbarian " society as an antecedent to war between the nomads and settled peoples. One—noted long ago by Gibbon in his *Decline and Fall of the Roman Empire*—was that the mobility of the nomad society was adaptable to war. The horse ridden in daily life was a cavalry mount that did not have to be separately bought by the state and provided for the trooper. The bow used all the time in hunting was the primary weapon. The cattle and sheep that had to be driven in normal seasonal migration could be mobilized, with a minimum of special measures, as a commissariat supply. And—a most important point—the women and children, since they also lived in tents and were used to migration as a normal seasonal procedure, could be moved into safe territory when a retreat was needed, or moved forward into a newly conquered territory, with no dislocation of normal social structure or economic activity.

These characteristics of the nomad society, through many centuries, were a permanent advantage in warfare against settled peoples. The settled farmer, especially the farmer living within range of nomad raids, had his whole life disrupted in periods of prolonged warfare. Spring raids interfered with plowing and planting. Autumn raids might deprive him of his harvested crop. If he fled, he had to abandon his farm and his poor possessions. A period of prolonged or chronic warfare tended, therefore to be profitable for the nomad and disastrous for the settled farmer; so much so that the border farmer, if the state behind him were not strong enough to protect him, was under great pressure to settle his own problems by placing himself under the protection of a nomad chief to whom he offered regular tribute. It was in this manner that the nomads first acquired, on a small scale, the experience in the administration of conquered territories and subject populations that enabled them, after later triumphs, to rule large empires.

The second factor is the cycle of alternating unity and dispersal in nomad society, corresponding to the cycle of imperial unification and regional autonomy in such countries as China. This nomad cycle requires a great deal more study. Indispensable pioneer work has been done by such great scholars as Vladimirtsov; but his extraordinarily rich source material needs to be gone over again, because he thought in terms of an evolution from tribalism into and through feudalism, rather than in phases of feudal unification alternating with relapses into tribal separatism.

Chingis made his first mark as a warrior in a phase when the separate tribes of Mongolia, weakened by war against each other, were falling apart and feudal unification lay within the reach of the most able contender. Because the tribal structure, during the youth of Chingis, did not give security to either life or property, tribal allegiances were weakening and men were willing to transfer their loyalties. It is this that explains the importance of the *nukur* or companion-at-arms who played such an extraordinary part in the fortunes of Chingis. These were men who detached themselves from tribe, clan, and even immediate family and attached themselves to a personal leader, such as Chingis. Their loyalty to him superseded all other loyalties, and from such men Chingis chose groups, as well as individuals, who detached themselves from old allegiances and, in joining Chingis, placed themselves under the standard of a new political loyalty.

It would not, in fact, have been possible for Chingis to create his armies and carry out his amazing conquests had he had to contend with an equivalent, in his own time and society, of what we now call nationalism. This lack of nationalism, making it possible to brigade together warriors from very different tribes and even peoples, was as important in the time of Attila as it was in that of Chingis. The sociological importance of this phenomenon is therefore not restricted to the career of Chingis, but is of general significance in nomad history and in the relations between nomad empires and settled empires.

Mr. Martin's method, in assembling his material, has been one of reconnaissance. His access to Chinese and Mongol sources was chiefly through Chinese colleagues with whom he worked in Peking. The material that they translated from dynastic histories, accounts of campaigns, and biographies he classified and compared according to date and subject matter and correlated with material already available in Western publications. This method often made it impossible to arrive at exact and final determination of a place, a date, or the spelling or meaning of a name. Such details often require a special philological training. On the other hand, Mr. Martin made the best of his reconnaissance by extending it as widely as possible in scope. Through his collaborators he sampled many sources not easily accessible to Western scholarship; sources that will not be translated in full for many years. Pending full translation, he has given the Western student who wants to understand better the general sweep and character of Mongol history an access to new material which, though not full, has the great merit of being presented here and now.

# CONTENTS

# Chapter I

# THE PORTRAIT OF A CONQUEROR

NEITHER in the past nor present has any historical figure excited greater admiration, fear and hate than Chingis Khan, but of few such men have we so exasperatingly little detailed and authentic information concerning their personality and appearance. This is partly attributable to the fact that many of those most closely in contact with him were illiterate and so unable to record their impressions. The Bilik or Maxims of Chingis Khan have indeed survived, and, if only in fragments, provide some interesting glimpses of this remarkable man, but being public utterances, are naturally of limited value. It is tempting to think that the conqueror's great Sino-Khitan minister Yeh-lü Ch'u-ts'ai, who knew him well, left a description of his master, but if he did it has been lost to posterity. In the absence of any such account we must make the best of what we have, and I shall open this chapter with the very little that has come down to us concerning Chingis Khan's appearance.

According to Juzjani, who spoke to various persons who saw him during the conquest of Khurasan, he was distinguished by his tall stature, vigorous build, strong constitution, the small amount of gray hair on his head—he was then in his fifty-sixth year—and cat's eyes. As for the remarks about his physique, we shall later see that his strength of body was astonishing.

It is generally supposed that Chingis Khan spoke no language except Mongol, but from a message sent to the celebrated Taoist sage Ch'iu Ch'ang-ch'un during December, 1223, it appears that he could muster a few phrases of Chinese.[1] This

---

[1] Waley, Ch'ang-ch'un, Appendix, pp. 158-159.

is by no means surprising, when one considers the numbers of Chinese-speaking officers and officials in his service.

In his personal life, as in his public life, he rarely allowed himself to go to extremes. Mongol tradition declares that he was passionately enamoured of the beautiful Mergid Kulan but, as Vladimirtsov remarks, it is hard to say if Chingis Khan ever really loved any woman. When at home he liked to be surrounded by good looking women, but his vigor of mind and body up to the last certainly indicates that he never indulged in sensual excesses.

The favorite pleasures of Chingis Khan were polo and the chase, at both of which he excelled. He was also by no means a stranger to the joys of wine, which was a taste he shared in common with his people, but unlike his son and successor Ugedei, he never let drinking become a vice. Giving voice to his feelings on the subject, he once said: " If unable to abstain from drinking, a man may get drunk three times a month; if he does it more than three times he is culpable; if he gets drunk twice a month it is better; if once a month, this is still more laudable, and if one does not drink at all, what can be better? But where can such a man be found! If such a man were found he would be worthy of the highest esteem." [2]

A born aristocrat, Chingis Khan met all with courtesy and confidence. On greeting the sage Ch'iu Ch'ang-ch'un in May, 1222, he openly expressed his delight at his arrival, saying, " Other rulers summoned you, but you would not go to them. And now you have come ten thousand li to see me. I take this as a high compliment." The sage replied, " That I, a hermit of the mountains, should come at your majesty's bidding was the will of Heaven." Chingis was delighted, begged him to be seated and ordered food to be served. Then he asked him, " Adept, what medicine of long life have you brought me from afar? " The Master replied, " I have means of protecting life, but no elexir that will prolong it." [3] Disappointed though

[2] This is from the " Bilik '" of Chingis Khan; see Riasanovsky, *Fundamentaı Principles of Mongol Law*, p. 88.
[3] Waley, *Ch'ang-ch'un*, pp. 100-101.

Chingis was by this answer, he praised Ch'ang-ch'un's candor, had two tents set up to the east of his own for the visitor and his disciples and continued to extend his unqualified favor to the great sage.

Able to master his fear of the unknown when necesary, Chingis nevertheless still subscribed to many of the popular superstitions of his day and frequently consulted those he believed able to interpret heavenly signs and omens. When, during the last days of July, 1219, he was preparing to leave the Altai Mountains, so much snow fell that the ground was covered to a depth of over two feet. Astonished, he turned to Yeh-lü Ch'u-ts'ai for an explanation and was told that it presaged the victory of the lord of the Northern climes (himself) over the lord of the Southern (the Khwarazm Shah).[4] Fortified, he went forward to one of the most spectacular and epoch making conquests in recorded history.

Just as he was superstitious, so did he believe that he was under the special protection of Heaven. This is well illustrated by the following anecdote. One day Bala Kharaja, a privileged commander, asked him, " You are called master of power and a hero; what signs of conquest are there to be seen on your hand? " " Before I assumed the throne of empire," replied the conqueror, " I was one day riding down a road. Six men, lying in ambush at a ford, attempted my life. When I drew near I unsheathed my sword and attacked them. They met me with a hail of arrows but all their arrows missed their mark and not one touched me. I delivered them to death with my sword and rode on unhurt. On my way back I passed the place where I had slain those men; their six horses were roaming riderless. I drove all those horses to my home." [5] Chingis thus cited an example of his valor such as Bala Kharaja demanded, but more important, affirmed his belief in Heaven's protection. " The Sky having decreed that he would not meet a chance death, he had killed all his enemies and taken their horses." [6]

[4] See Rémusat, " Vie de Yeliu Thsoutsai," *Nouveaux Mélanges Asiatiques*, Vol. II.
[5] Vladimirtsov, *The Life of Chingis Khan*, p. 168.
[6] Vladimirtsov, *The Life of Chingis Khan*, pp. 168-169.

Himself a very brave man, as proved by the courage and fortitude that he displayed in his early days, he admired courage in friend or foe. Valor being universal in a society like that of the Mongols, he had of necessity fought his way to power against men of exceptional bravery. Even so, on the occasion of his victory over the Khorezmian prince Jalal ad-Din on the Indus in 1221 he was so impressed by the latter's courage that, though chagrined at his escape over the river, he exclaimed, "Happy the father of such a son," and held him up as a model of valor to his own. The bravery of his officers he invariably richly rewarded and in the ensuing pages we shall encounter many instances of both their devotion and his generosity.

Not unnaturally in line with his admiration for courage went an equal admiration for personal loyalty. Hence, in accordance with the better instincts of the steppes, and whether an adversary were involved or not, he rarely failed to punish the followers of a nobleman for betraying their lord or to praise and reward those who had proved faithful.

Famous for his munificence, Chingis was nevertheless extremely jealous of all that he regarded as his property. Portraying this characteristic is a story related by the "Yüan Ch'ao Pi Shih." After the capture of Gurganj in 1221, the princes Juchi, Jaghatai and Ugedei divided all the spoil of the place without setting aside anything for their father. Consequently, when later they returned to imperial headquarters, they found him greatly angered and were unable to obtain an audience. At length Mukhali, Bugurji and Shiki Kutuku intervened and, remonstrating with the conqueror, spoke as follows: "We have vanquished the Moslems; your sons and all in the city are your property: with the help of Heaven and earth we have triumphed in this war and we your officers are full of joy; therefore, why, oh Khan, be so wrath? Your sons have acknowledged their fault and are afraid; they have been warned for the future so now let them come before you." At these words Chingis Khan's anger abated a little and he agreed to receive them, but on their appearance it once more returned and the sweat of fear covered the bodies of the princes. Thereupon three archers of the Guard, Khonghai, Khongtakhar and Chormaghan, interceded in their turn.[7] "Your sons," they declared, "resemble falcons who but begin their training; they are making their first campaign; if you treat them so, in the future their minds may turn from you. From the rising to the setting of the sun are foes; send us against them and we will attack them like Tibetan dogs. If Heaven prosper us and we are victorious, we will bring you all that they possess of gold, silver and silks; in the West is the Caliph of Baghdad; send us against him." This time Chingis Khan's anger was assuaged and he forgave the princes.[8]

The Mongol conqueror has been charged with the perpetration of terrible atrocities. It can not be denied that he was the author of many appalling butcheries, but in vilifying him for such deeds one should keep in mind the society to which he belonged and the day and age into which he was born. Throwing light on this side of his character is an excerpt from the Bilik (Maxims) expressing his opinion on the highest pleasure of man. "A man's greatest pleasure," he declared, "is to defeat his enemies, to drive them before him, to take from them that which they possessed, to see those whom they cherished in tears, to ride their horses, to hold their wives and daughters in his arms." [9] In giving utterance to such sentiments Chingis Khan was voicing the feelings of the majority of his people.

The carnage of his wars differed in degree, not in kind,

---

[7] After the death of Chingis Khan, it was Chormaghan who was charged with the final overthrow of Jalal ad-Din and the conquest of Iraq-i-Ajami and Azerbaijan (1230-31).

[8] This version of the anecdote is from the translation of the Yüan Ch'ao Pi Shih in Haenisch's " Die Letzen Feldzüge Cingis Han's und sein Tod nach der Ostasiatischen Ueberlieferung," *Asia Major*, Vol. IX, 1932.

Mukhali was at the time in China, while Juchi did not return with his brothers to the camp of Chingis Khan. However, during the siege of Gurganj the quarrels of the princes had greatly displeased their father and it is also quite possible that they thoughtlessly added to his anger by forgetting him in their division of the loot from the captured city.

[9] Vladimirtsov, *The Life of Chingis Khan*, p. 160.

from that which accompanied those of his contemporaries. Greater in size than the massacres perpetrated elsewhere, because the places taken were generally larger, his slaughters were not more cruel. Having captured the little Sung town of Tsao-chia Pao in 1218, the Chin general Wan-yen Arin had 15,000 of the inhabitants put to the sword.[10] In Europe during 1209 two terrible massacres took place in the Albigensian towns of Bézieres and Carcassone. Toward the close of the century, in 1291, Edward I of England slew 7,000 to 8,000 of the people of Berwick, while in India the succeeding century was opened in 1303 by the death of 30,000 Hindus at Chitor when the place was stormed by the troops of Ala ad-Din Khilji (1295-1315).[11] The age was one of exceptional violence and bloodshed and Chingis and his contemporaries, Asiatic and European, being products of their age, behaved accordingly.

If pitiless to his enemies, Chingis Khan was a steadfast friend to those who were loyal and served him well. This is nowhere better illustrated than in his dealing with his officers. In the realm of imperial policy he kept a jealous hand upon them, but in military matters he allowed them much freedom, and once a general was engaged upon a distant expedition, he rarely interfered. Sure that the commander of his choice was competent, and realizing that the man on the spot must have the best appreciation of local conditions, he never attempted to give any but the most general instructions.

A good instance of this is afforded by the words that the " Yüan Ch'ao Pi Shih " puts into his mouth when sending Subudei against the Mergids in 1216. " In order to come up with your quarry," he said, ' you will have to make your way over high mountain passes and across great rivers. As the road will be long, spare your cavalry and economize on your provisions. On the way you will encounter much game, but do not permit your men to hunt except for the purpose of replenishing your supplies; otherwise your horses will be worn

---

[10] De Mailla, *Histoire Générale de La Chine*, Vol. IX.
[11] Ishwari Prasad, *History of Medieval India*, p. 198.

out before you have overtaken the enemy. See to it that
neither cruppers nor snaffle bridles injure your mounts. Should
any man disobey you, send him back to me if I know him;
but if I do not, punish him yourself."

Since prince Juchi was with the army, so in nominal command, the conqueror's words may really have been meant for
him, especially those about hunting, for his son was inordi-
nately fond of the chase. However, there can be little doubt
that the true leader of the expedition was the great Subudei,
a tried captain and nearly ten years the prince's senior.

Besides showing trust in his subordinates, he was ever ready
to acclaim their successes. In 1223, Subudei was loudly
eulogized for the remarkable campaign that he and Jebe
(dead since the end of 1222)—had carried out from the
summer of 1220 to the winter of 1222 in Western Persia,
Georgia, the Caucasus, southeastern Russia and Greater Bulgaria. " Subudei," said Chingis Khan, " has slept on his shield,
he has prevailed in bloody battles and has exposed himself
for our house and we are deeply gratified." [12] Two years
earlier Mukhali, another great general, was even more highly
praised for his exploits in China.

Equally great minded was he when the unexpected happened
and one of his generals was defeated. Having inspected the
valley of Biruan in Afghanistan, where his adopted son Shiki
Kutuku had been beaten by the Khorezmian Jalal ad-Din,
he indulged in no recriminations, but merely criticized the
general's choice of battle-field. Then turning to those about
him he said, " Shiki Kutuku has always been accustomed to
victory and has never yet experienced fortune's cruelty; now
that he has he will be more cautious." [13]

Even infractions of discipline, usually severely punished,
were at times leniently dealt with. In 1220, when Subudei,
Jebe and Tokuchar were despatched in pursuit of the Khwarazm Shah, all three were enjoined to march through the
dominions of Khan Amir-ul-Mulk of Herat without molesting

[12] *Yüan Shih*, Biog. of " Subudei."
[13] Rashid ad-Din, Barthold, *Turkestan down to the Mongol Invasion*, p. 443.

them. Subudei and Jebe obeyed, but Tokuchar plundered part of the territory. When he received word of it, Chingis Khan at first intended to execute the disobedient general, but on second thought only delivered a reprimand and associated another officer with him in his command.

By his trust, gratitude, absence of jealousy—the presence of which marred the relations of both Alexander and Napoleon with their generals—and ability to master his anger,[14] Chingis Khan won for himself and his family the unbounded loyalty and devotion of those who served him. Fired with an almost fanatical determination to carry out his behests, they rarely failed to overcome all obstacles.

Some writers have contended that in purely military ability Chingis was surpassed by certain of his generals. Unquestionably the most outstanding of them conducted brilliant campaigns entirely on their own, and when present with the conqueror contributed greatly to those carried out under his immediate direction, but since in all the major operations of his reign the final decision fell to him, to him must go most of the credit for the resounding triumphs that have so justly made him famous. In support of this one has but to turn to the invasion of the Khorezmian empire. Then, from the spring of 1221 to the autumn of 1222 when his three greatest commanders were absent, one in the east, two in the west, he not only conquered the whole of Khwarazm and Khurasan, but marched victoriously through the formidable mountains of Afghanistan without his army once being in jeopardy. After his death, and not even when commanded by the most celebrated generals of his sons and grandsons, did the Mongols perform feats of arms that equalled their deeds under Chingis Khan.

That the conqueror was able to command the admiration of such men as Yeh-lü Ch'u-ts'ai, and, to mention only a few

---

[14] On occasions, however, he flew into fits of rage, and on being courageously censured by a certain Moslem Qahdi for the terrible loss of life his wars had cost Islam, he furiously flung down his bow and arrows and turned from his interlocutor in a state of intense emotion, but did the brave man no harm. (See Vladimirtsov, *The Life of Chingis Khan*, pp. 162-163.)

names in that peerless galaxy of captains that surrounded him, the Mongols, Bugurji, Mukhali, Subudei, Jebe and Samukha, the Tangut Chaghan and the Chinese Shih T'ien-hsiang shows not only that he himself was a very great man but that his judgment in choosing men amounted to nothing less than genius. Further proof of this is demonstrated by his selection of Ugedei, his third son, to succeed him.[15] Though the least talented of the great Mongol's sons—he had neither the military ability of Juchi or Tului nor Jaghatai's unbending sense of duty—Ugedei was a more attractive personality and was, therefore, the least likely of the four to antagonize the other members of the imperial family. At the same time he had sufficient firmness not to be swayed by irresponsible influences and was never too proud to take advice from those of greater ability and experience than himself. It was for these reasons that Chingis settled the succession on him.

A stranger to all foreign civilization, the conqueror nevertheless appreciated many of its exponents, particularly the Khitan Yeh-lü Ch'u-ts'ai to whom he extended his unbounded favor and confidence, and whom he counselled his son Ugedei always to consult on matters of state. Since he believed and hoped that not long after his death the Mongol aristocracy would become sufficiently conversant with the civilization of the conquered to be able to carry on the administration of the empire unaided by outsiders, it is not surprising to learn that he greatly favored Shiki Kutuku, who we are told was ever ready to receive new ideas; also Boru, the son of Mukhali, who was a gifted linguist and more conversant with Chinese culture than most of his Mongol colleagues.

To sum up, a great statesman and a superlatively great soldier, Chingis Khan's outstanding characteristics were an unbreakable determination and the ability, so vital in one wielding such power, never to over-reach himself. The first we shall see exemplified by his prosecution of the last Tangut war, despite severe internal injuries sustained while hunting;

---

[15] In Chingis Khan's time the Mongols did not adhere to the law of primogenitor.

the second by his refusal to embark upon the invasion of the Chin empire before striking an initial blow against the Tanguts. While a man of great ambition, he was careful to see that each new project was within the range of his power. Consequently he suffered no military catastrophe like Napoleon's retreat from Moscow, and left to his sons a vast empire and the most powerful army in the world.

Chapter II

# THE MONGOL ARMY

## Part I

A S WITH so many famous military forces, the size of the Mongol army has all too often been vastly overestimated. Even within the last fifty years writers of both acumen and learning have allowed themselves to accept and quote fabulous figures for the armies of Chingis Khan and his successors. Hence one reads that when the Mongol conqueror invaded the Korezmian empire he was at the head of 700,000 men, and his grandson Batu is reported to have overrun Russia and Central Europe with an army 500,000 strong. Such exaggeration arises partly from the inclination, common for many centuries, to give great soldiers great armies and naturally enough is most frequently encountered in the works of ancient and mediaeval historians. But in the case of the Mongols, as with nearly every barbarian invader who has overthrown the forces of more civilized states, there has also been a tendency among the vanquished to attribute defeat to the overwhelming numerical superiority of the enemy.

Of late, more careful examination of original documents and fuller knowledge of the means and military system of the Mongols has revealed the truth. Their triumphs were the outcome of splendid organization, discipline, leadership and morale, not of great numbers. Robert of Spolato, a contemporary of the Mongol invasion of Central Europe, speaking of them says: " There is no people in the world who know so well how to overcome an adversary in the open by skill in warfare." [1]

Whenever it is possible to obtain reliable information on the

[1] Fernand Grenard, *Gengis Khan*, p. 192.

11

strength of Mongol forces, one finds that often they were
heavily out-numbered by their enemies. We shall see that in
1211 Chingis Khan marched against the Chin with little more
than 110,000 men—decidedly less than a quarter of the forces
of his opponent. During 1219 he mobilized perhaps 150,000
effectives for the war against the Khwarazm Shah. On that
occasion, while the army opposed to him was neither quite so
large—aproximately 400,000—or as well organized as that of
the Chin, he had to march west nearly one thousand miles
from his last home base before reaching the enemy's border.
In 1216, three years before hostilities had officially begun with
the Moslem potentate, 20,000 Mongols under prince Juchi
and the generals Subudei and Tokuchar were attacked in the
present province of Turgai (north of the Aral Sea) by a Khorezmian army of 60,000 men.[2] Although so outnumbered, the
Mongols nearly won and nightfall put an end to an indecisive
battle. In the troops of Chingis Khan numerical inferiority,
both on the battlefield and on campaign, was common.

Since many Mongol expeditions were carried out far from
Mongolia and lasted a number of years—that against the
Khorezmian empire from 1219-22—there arises the question
of reinforcements. Recruits from Mongolia reached the various
armies from time to time, but they cannot have been numerous
and a considerable interval must often have elapsed before
they caught up with the forces to which they were sent.[3]
Generally, the Mongols had to make good their losses on the
spot. In Iran, Afghanistan and South Russia this was not
difficult. Once the main armies and central government of the
enemy had been broken, the Mongols were able to recruit

[2] Barthold, *Turkestan down to the Mongol Invasion*, p. 372. For information on
the numerical strength of the Shah's entire army; see Appendix A, n. 15 at end
of present volume.

[3] In a note on the *Meng Ta Pei Lu* of Meng Hung, the historian Wang Kuo-wei
says that Hsü Ting, when on an embassy to Ugedei during 1235 and 1236, reports
having met some troops in Mongolia about to start for the west against the Moslems.
Numbers of these were no more than 13 or 14 years of age, but he adds that as
they had with them livestock they may only have been a military colony and not
destined for active service. I think, however, that the younger ones were quite
likely intended for various noncombatant duties with some army until old enough
to take their place in the ranks.

numbers of auxiliaries from among those of the population leading a pastoral or semi-pastoral life. In many such regions remounts were also picked up.[4] One of the principal factors that enabled Jebe and Subudei, from 1220-21, to maintain themselves in northwestern Iran, to invade Georgia and to cross to the Caucasus, with but the smallest if any reinforcement from Chingis Khan, was that they were joined by bands of Kurds, Turks and Turkomans eager to share in the loot of captured towns and cities. In China, too, the same thing happened, but not to any extent until after three years of war. Then many of the troops that came over were infantry—the first to be employed by the Mongols. As the East Asian dominions of the Great Khans spread southward, Chinese soldiers played an increasingly important part in the Imperial Army. This naturally led to certain modifications in the organization and tactics of those forces operating in China and farther to the south, but these can not be dealt with here.

As the empire expanded this enrollment of non-Mongol troops constantly increased the size of the Army, but even then the largest field force of which we have any reliable record cannot have counted more than 200,000. This was the army placed under the great general Bayan in 1275 for the conquest of the Sung Empire.

The strength of the Imperial Army when the Mongol empire reached its zenith is a matter of conjecture, perhaps it totalled about 1,000,000; but on the Mongol army proper we have some definite information.[5] D'Ohsson, quoting Rashid ad-Din, says that at the death of Chingis Khan in 1227 it numbered 129,000 effectives, 62,000 in the Army of the Left-Wing, 38,000 in the Army of the Right-Wing, 1,000 picked men in the center, which was also the Imperial guard, 4,000 men in each of the guards of the princes Juchi, Jaghatai and Ugedei, and 16,000 divided

---

[4] Considering the foregoing exertions of the Mongol cavalry, it is highly probable that Jebe and Subudei pursued the Khwarazm Shah during the summer of 1220 on horses taken in Transoxiana.

[5] The military power of the Mongols reached its zenith under Mongkha Khaghan (1251-59), for after his death parts of the empire were intermittently torn by civil war.

among the other members of the Imperial family. Erdmann, drawing on a different edition of the same work, gives 230,000; the Khan's guard 1,000 men, the center 101,000, the Left Wing 52,000, the Right Wing 47,000, the guards of Juchi, Jaghatai and Ugedei, 4,000 men each, and the rest of the Imperial family 17,000.[6]

The Central, Left and Right Wing Armies, as will be shown later, here refer to territorial distribution and have nothing to do with order in the field.

As regards the troops of the three princes, the small forces mentioned were but a fraction of their troops at the death of Chingis Khan, the majority of which came from appanages conquered outside Mongolia before 1227. The fourth son Tului received by traditional right of inheritance the Central, Left and Right Wing Armies, that is the greater part of the Mongol Army proper, at his father's death.[7]

What is known of the population of Outer Mongolia makes it unlikely that in Chingis Khan's day the people were much more numerous than now. A relatively recent Soviet census estimates them at 800,000.[8] If to this is added the Mongols of Buriat Mongolia and former north Chahar, a total of about 1,000,000 is reached, which may well approximate to the population under Chingis Khan when his work of unification was completed. From this 129,000 men could have been drawn, but not 230,000. Adding together the units detailed by Erdmann, save the 101,000 for the Center, it is found that the total is also 129,000, so it seems that the figure for the center must be a mistake. Probably the center corresponded to The Guard or Keshik, numbering, says the " Yüan Ch'ao Pi Shih," 10,000 chosen men and including a specially picked 1,000 that

[6] These were divided as follows: Temuge Ochigin, youngest brother of Chingis Khan, 5,000; Kulgan, son of Kulan Khatun, 4,000; the sons of Juchi Khassar, first brother of Chingis Khan, 1,000; Aljigidei, son of Khachiun Ulchi, Chingis Khan's second brother, 3,000; the Queen Mother Oelun Eke (then dead) 3,000; and supernumeraries 1,000. With the exception of the last 1,000 D'Ohsson's enumeration is the same as that of Erdmann. (See D'Ohsson, *Histoire des Mongols*, Vol. II, pp. 3-5, and Erdmann, *Temudschin der Unerschschutterliche*, p. 455.

[7] See Barthold, *Turkestan down to the Mongol Invasion*, p. 404.

[8] See the *Chinese Year Book*, 1938-39.

only took the field when Chingis Khan went to war.[9] The Army therefore may have counted 138,000 effectives, 62,000 or 52,000 in the Army of the Left Wing, 38,000 or 47,000 in the Army of the Right Wing, 10,000 in the Guard (Keshik) or Army of the Center, 12,000 divided between Juchi, Jaghatai and Ugedei, and 16,000 or 17,000 distributed among the other members of the Imperial family.

By the time that Ugedei (1229-41) succeeded to the throne, these forces must have been considerably more than doubled by the addition of troops from the Solangs (Solons), Onguds, Khitans, Jurchids, Kirghiz, Tanguts and Chinese and by nomad tribesmen formerly subject to the empires of Khara Khitai and Khwarazm. Even so, an army of perhaps some 400,000 men was small for the control and extension of dominions as vast as those of Chingis Khan. The Mongol operational armies, while big when compared with those of Medieval Christendom, were at first often numerically inferior to the forces of the major powers encountered by them in Asia.

By far the largest and most efficient army of Christendom was that of the Byzantine Empire. From the time of its reorganization at the beginning of the 8th century until its disastrous defeat at Manzikurt by the Saljuks in 1071, it never exceeded 150,000 effectives and sometimes no more than 120,000. Of these, 24,000 were stationed in Constantinople, 70,000 in Asia Minor and the rest in Europe.[10] On the day of Manzikurt, one of the most decisive in history, the Byzantine army on the field numbered little over 60,000,[11] all cavalry, that of the Saljuks only 40,000.

[9] Barthold, " Chingis Khan," Encyclopaedia of Islam, Vol. I, pp. 856-862.

[10] Robert Byron, *The Byzantine Achievement*, pp. 273-74 and Charles Diehl, " Le Monde Oriental de 395-1081," *Histoire du Moyen Age*, Tome III, pp. 465-67.

[11] This was an exceptionally large army for the empire, and in the days of its greatest glory the biggest force ever to take the field was that with which the famous Basil II (976-1025) marched from Bulgaria to the relief of Aleppo during the winter of 994-95. Notwithstanding the fact that the enemy to be encountered was an army of the powerful Fatimite Caliph Al Aziz (975-995), the emperor was at the head of no more than 40,000 troops. (See Byron, *The Byzantine Achievement*, pp. 278-79).

Regarding the strength of the contending armies at Manzikurt; see Gibbon, *The Decline and Fall of the Roman Empire*, Vol. VI, p. 239, and footnote by the cele-

With some reason, certain modern writers, notably Léon
Cahun, have treated the Mongol army as something unique
in the history of war.[12] Better than any other mounted force
before or since, it demonstrated that cavalry need not rest
on a stable infantry base. "Although," says Liddell Hart,
"Cavalry was the decisive arm of both Alexander and Hanni-
bal, it formed merely the mobile wings hinged on an essentially
protective infantry center, which was the pivot on which it
manoeuvered." [13]

To the world of the Roman empire and the Near East, an
Army composed entirely of horsemen was something unknown,
but among the pastoral peoples dwelling north of the Black
Sea and in Central and Northern Asia, mounted forces had
long been used.

The Parthian army, reputedly so famed for its cavalry,
included no more than 40,000-50,000 mounted archers and
lancers. The only occasion on which the Hellenistic world
witnessed an engagement where one army was composed
entirely of horsemen was that of Carrhae in 53 B. C., where
the Parthian Suren utterly defeated a Roman army of from
28,000 to 35,000. Then, contrary to the usual Parthian practice of combining cavalry and infantry, Suren had nothing but
mounted troops. Tarn contends that his force did not exceed
11,000 effectives, 10,000 of which were light armored horsemen,
the remaining 1,000, cataphracts or heavily armored lancers.
In addition there were 1,000 camels for carrying spare arrows.
Despite the brilliant success of this new type of army, it disappeared with Suren who was murdered shortly after Carrhae
by King Orodes II (57 B. C.-36 B. C.).[14]

brated J. B. Bury, *Warfare* by Spaulding, Nickerson and Wright, p. 280 and Charles
Oman, *A Hist. of The Art of Warfare in The Middle Ages*, Vol. I, p. 219.

[12] Léon Cahun, *Introduction a l'histoire de L'Asie, Turcs et Mongols des origines
a 1405.*

[13] Capt. B. H. Liddell Hart, *Great Captains Unveiled*, "Jenghiz Khan and
Sabutai," p. 32.

[14] See G. Rawlinson, *The Sixth Great Oriental Monarchy*, pp. 403-7; Brigadier
Percy Sykes, *A History of Persia*, Vol. 1, pp. 376-79; Tarn: *Hellenistic Military and
Naval Developments*, pp. 89-92 and Appendix 1, Ferrero, *The Life of Julius Caesar*,
pp. 316-324, and Debevoise, *A Political History of Parthia*, pp. 83-93.

Chinese records show that from the rise of the Hsiungnu in the third century B. C. to the fall of the Jzungars in the 18th century, A. D., the armies of the steppes tended to resemble each other in organization, strategy and tactics. But with the formation of the Khitan empire (907-1125), there came into existence a variation of this military system that excelled any that had preceded it, and which, imitated by the Jurchids, finally passed to the Mongols under whom it attained its apogee. First introduced to western Asia by the Khitan Yeh-lü Ta-shih (1132-43), this eastern school of cavalry warfare speedily established supremacy over its western counterpart and under Chingis Khan swept all before it.[15]

## PART II

In most respects the Mongol of today resembles his forebears. Of middle height, but made to appear broader than he is by his riding boots and sheepskin coat, he possesses great powers of endurance. Just as in the 13th century he conquered Russia during the winter, crossing large rivers on the ice, the present day Mongol thinks nothing of travel in the bitterest cold; but though he can still remain in the saddle many hours without food or sleep, it is long since he has been required to endure the privations demanded of his ancestors in the days of conquest. Marco Polo tells us that the Mongol warrior often slept mounted and armed while his horse grazed and could go ten days without cooking food.[16] On such occasions he lived on

[15] See Wittfogel and Feng Chia-sheng, *History of Chinese Society: Liao* (907-1125), pp. 533 and 669. For a splendid account of the Khitan military system, see Section XV of this work.

A very brief but, nevertheless, useful study on the same subject is to be found in Rolf Stein's translation and comments on the *Liao Shih*; see Stein, "Leao-tche," *T'oung Pao*, Vol. XXXV, pp. 54-59.

In Western Asia the most powerful proponents of the western school were the Saljuks of Persia who in 1141, and under the celebrated Sultan Sinjar (1133-53), suffered a crushing defeat at the hands of Yeh-lü Ta Shih to the north of Samarkand. On the South Russian plains there were the Kipchaks, but they too can be said to have belonged to the western school and were later relatively easily defeated by the Mongols.

[16] See *The Book of Marco Polo*, Yule, Cordier, Vol. 1, Chap. LIV. Marco Polo says that the Mongols living in Cathay and the Levant had much degenerated from their forebears and those living in Tartary proper (Mongolia).

his iron ration, which consisted of ten pounds of dried milk curd, two litres of Kumis (fermented mare's milk) and a certain quantity of cured meat. According to some authorities, he would in necessity eat carrion and even use the blood of his horse by opening a vein in its neck. Then as now, Mongol sight and sense of direction were extraordinary and must have helped to make those marches over the wilderness without maps that have so amazed the world.

If the Mongol compels our admiration, so does the horse he rode. From thirteen to fourteen hands in height, watered once a day and for the most part grass fed, the Mongol pony is unsurpassed the world over for stamina. Capable of almost incredible journeys, it contributed in no small measure to the mighty conquests of its rider. Carruthers in his " Unknown Mongolia " says that a Mongol on a single pony will ride from Urga to Kalgan—by the shortest route 600 miles—in nine days.[17] If greater speed is necessary, one or more spare mounts are led. During the 13th century Mongol troops, with the use of spare horses, carried out marches unrivalled for speed by either ancient or modern armies. During September 1221, Chingis Khan, hoping to overtake the Khorezmian Jalal ad-Din, went from Bamian to Ghazna via Kabul in two days without allowing his men a single halt long enough to prepare food.[18] The distance covered was about 130 miles, an astonishing achievement since the country crossed was some of the highest and roughest in Afghanistan. In 1241 an army under his grandson, Batu, invaded Hungary and, in crossing the pass of Ruska in the Carpathians, the vanguard is reported to have marched 180 miles between March twelfth and fifteenth.[19] Such feats could only have been done by men and horses possessed of remarkable staying powers.[20]

---

[17] Carruthers, *Unknown Mongolia*, Vol. II, p. 133.

[18] Juwayni; D'Ohsson, *Histoire des Mongols*, Vol. I, pp. 305-306.

[19] Capt. B. H. Liddell Hart; *Great Captains Unveiled*, " Jenghiz Khan and Sabutai," p. 26.

[20] Batu's invasion was of course made largely on horses drawn from the Volga and the steppes north of the Black Sea, but in most respects these were much the same as those from Monoglia.

Of the training of the Mongol pony in the past, there is not much information. The Chinese general, Meng Hung, a contemporary of Chingis Khan, states that horses were never ridden until three years of age, which is still the practice today. When broken in, he continues, 100,000 could be assembled without difficulty and if left untied they never strayed.[21] Grenard—see " Gengis Khan "—asserts that they were obedient to the sound of the voice and were trained to permit the archer to shoot not only while in the saddle but from behind them when dismounted. Finally, from Friar John of Plano Carpini it is learned that whenever possible horses ridden one day were not ridden for three or four days afterward.[22]

As many a stricken battlefield bore witness, Mongol horsemanship and archery made the armies of Chingis Khan and his successors almost invincible. A fact that should be kept in mind is that the attainment of such qualities in the same degree was well nigh impossible for any but pastoral peoples. Taught to ride at the age of three by his mother, the young Mongol was tied onto the back of a horse. On reaching the age of four or five he was given his first bow and arrows and from then on was encouraged to spend as much time as possible hunting on horseback. Consequently, his riding and archery became superb.[23]

The saddle used by the Mongol was made of wood and was kept rubbed with sheep's fat to prevent swelling in the rain. Its weight, according to Meng Hung, was from seven to eight catties, or about nine and a half pounds to eleven pounds. High in the back and front, it enabled the rider to retain a rock firm seat, while shooting toward any point of the compass.

The bow was of the compound type, was very large and required a pull of at least 120 catties (166 lbs.), which was considerably more than that of the English long bow, and its

---

[21] See Meng Hung; the *Meng Ta Pei Lu.*

[22] See " The Journey of Friar John Plano Carpini," Chapters 15 and 16, Beazley, *Hakluyt.*

[23] See Meng Hung. Among the Hsiungnu, babies were taught to ride on sheep and to shoot rats and birds with small bows and arrows. (See Parker, *A Thousand Years of the Tartars,* p. 4).

destructive range was from 200-300 yards.[24] The arrows dis-
charged were, says Marco Polo, of two types, light ones with
small sharp points for long range shooting and pursuit, and
heavy ones with large broad heads for close quarters. In action
thirty of each were carried by every trooper. Plano Carpini
says that the Mongol carried two bows and that his arrow
heads cut two ways like a sword and were hardened by dipping
red hot into brine, after which they could pierce armor. Meng
Hung enumerates three types of arrow, the sounding arrow,
the camelbone arrow and the armor piercing, the shafts of all
being provided with eagle feathers.[25]

Other Mongol weapons were light sharp sabers imported
or copied from the Moslem Turks of the west, short and long
lances (according to Carpini provided with a hook for pulling
men out of the saddle), and a mace.

Mongol armor, besides a steel cap helmet with leather neck-
piece, was either of hide, lacquered to keep out humidity, or
of overlapping iron scales laced together, and burnished so
bright, says John of Plano Carpini, that one could see the
reflection of the face. Both kinds were used for men and horses
alike. The hide armor consisted of six layers tightly sewn, and
after being softened by boiling, was shaped to fit the body.

Meng Hung also mentions four kinds of shield, large skin
or willow wood shields—probably for sentry duty only—smaller
shields carried by front rank troops to ward off arrows when on
foot, a visor worn over the face, and large tortoise shields for
assaulting walls.

According to Meng Hung, the Mongols at the time of their
war with China were better equipped than any previous

[24] For the Mongol Bow, see: Meng Hung, the *Meng Ta Pei Lu*; Murdoch, *History
of Japan*, Vol. 1, Chap. 16; Grenard, *Gengis Khan*; Lamb, *Tamerlain*, note on bows
in the east and west and H. G. Creel, *Birth of China*, Chap. X. Creel says that the
Peking Guard used bows of 156 lb. pull, which was far greater than that of the
English long bow.

[25] Describing the equipment of the Khitan Army, which was very like that of
the Mongols, Parker says that each soldier had to keep in readiness four bows and
400 arrows. (See Parker, *A Thousand Years of the Tartars*, p. 258. For a full
dress account of Khitan equipment, see Wittfogel and Feng Chia-sheng, *History
of Chinese Society: Liao* (907-1125), section XV, p. 523.

invaders of China. This he attributed to their supplies of iron. Before the days of the Chin, he declares, there was an embargo on the sale of iron and weapons to the north, but subsequently both were exported in considerable quantities.[26]

The remaining field equipment of the Mongol included a hatchet, a file for sharpening arrow heads, a lasso, a rope for pulling wagons and engines of war, an iron cooking pot, two leather bottles, and a leather bag closed by a thong to keep clothes and other equipment dry when crossing rivers. Every man also had a fur helmet and a fur or sheepskin coat with the hide turned outward, while to every ten troopers a small tent was provided against rain. This was doubtless the Maikhan still used by the Mongols when travelling today.

## PART III

As among their Hsiungnu and Turkish predecessors, every able bodied Mongol from fourteen to sixty years of age was liable to military service.[27] In peace time too, all called upon to participate in the annual winter hunt were obliged to attend. These hunts, undertaken both as a military exercise and to provide a supply of meat, took the form of a campaign. During a whole month the steppes and the mountains were beaten and game was driven into a vast retreat selected before hand. Once all were gathered there, the beaters closed the area by a cordon, broken neither by ravines, rivers or marshes. Sentinels were posted, signal fires lit and every precaution taken to prevent the trapped animals escaping. At the same time it was forbidden under pain of death to use weapons against them. Finally the Khan opened the chase, the princes and nobles followed, and

[26] In the same notice Meng Hung asserts that most of the iron was in the shape of coins formerly circulated by the Sung (960-1279) in Ho-Tung (Shansi), but after the conquest of this province by the Chin the money was abolished and the inhabitants sold it to the Ta-ta.

[27] Meng Hung says from the age of fifteen to sixty-one, which would mean that boys of fourteen could be called up, for the Chinese regard a child as one year old at its birth. Parker, see *A Thousand Years of the Tartars*, p. 4, says that among the Hsiungnu, every male strong enough to draw an ordinary bow was liable for military service.

after they had killed their choice of game, the sport was thrown open to the surrounding troops. When all was over, the Khan criticized the operation as one would a campaign.

Adhering to the recognized usage of the steppes, the Mongol Army was divided territorially into three main forces, the Army of the Left Wing or East (Junghar), the Army of the Right Wing or West (Baraunghar) and the Army of the Center or Imperial Ordus (Khol). The organization of these was on a decimal basis, the strongest unit being the *tumen* of 10,000, which corresponded to a division and of which two or more grouped together formed an army. Each such tumen was divided into ten regiments of 1,000 (minghan), each regiment into ten squadrons of 100 (jagun) and each squadron into ten troops of 10 (arban). Transfer from one unit to another, Juwayni reports, was strictly forbidden.[28]

The individual clans and tribes of the empire were grouped or divided so that units of 1,000 to 10,000 men could be mustered at the shortest notice. " At the head of each unit," says Vladimirtsov, " Chingis Khan placed men he knew personally and trusted and who were as a rule kinsmen of the men under their command. This policy preserved the clan constitution from decomposition, while giving it at the same time a regular, if rudimentary, military skeleton. In place of men who had become chiefs by chance were placed commanders of the same aristocratic origin, but bound by their service to the Khan and by military discipline." [29] As a sign of authority the commander of an army was given a great drum which was sounded only at his order. If the Khan were present, all marched under his orders, which were issued from beneath the white nine tailed standard of the Imperial Ordus. Once, as will appear later, such a banner was given by Chingis Khan to the great general Mukhali, whom in 1217 he left as commander-in-chief of all forces in China for the prosecution of the war against the Chin, and whose orders were to be obeyed as his own.

[28] See D'Ohsson, *Histoire des Mongols.*
[29] See Vladimirtsov, *The Life of Chingis Khan,* p. 69.

Attached to the Imperial Ordus and organized for its protection was the Guard (Keshik), which I believe should be identified with the Army of the Center (Khol). Like the other military institutions of the Mongols, it was nothing completely new. Both Turk and Khitan before them had imperial guardsmen, while all Chingis Khan's rivals in Mongolia seem to have had bodyguards. In the biography of the Khitan Yeh-lü Tukha it is specifically stated that he was sent by the Chin emperor to enter the Kerait guard while residing at the court of Tughrul the Wang Khan.

The guard constituted the crack force of the Mongol Army and had precedence over all the other troops. The year 1203, in which Chingis Khan overthrew the Keraits, is the earliest date for which there is an account of its organiaztion. Then 70 men were selected for the day guard (turghaut) and 80 men for the night guard (kabtaut).[30] Besides these there were 400 archers (khorchin) and a personal guard of 1000 braves (baatut) who formed the advance guard in battle and part of the court guard in peace. Barthold also includes table-deckers (bawurchi), door-keepers ( perhaps egudenchi), grooms (akhtachi) and commissary officers of the imperial ordus (cherbi), all of whom held important posts in the guard.

During 1206, when Chingis Khan assumed supreme power, the strength of the Guard was augmented. " Formerly," he said, " I had only 80 night guards and 70 day guards, but since Heaven has ordered me to rule all nations, 10,000 men shall form my guard.[31] All must be chosen from the sons of nobles or of free men and must be well-built, agile and hardy. The son of a commander of 1000 shall bring with him a kinsman

[30] Turghaut and kabtaut, also baatut, are spelled in accordance with Pelliot's correction of Barthold. (See Pelliot, " Notes sur le Turkestan," T'oung-Pao, 1930, and René Grousset, Le Conquérant du Monde, pp. 218-219.)

Pelliot thinks it highly probable that the Torguts of today derive their name from the word turghaut, though, if as believed by some, the Torguts are the descendants of a branch of the Keraits, the turghaut in question must have been the day guard of some Kerait prince. In this connection, it is worth mentioning that according to various traditions, the Torgut rulers believe themselves to be descended from a brother of Tughrul, the last ruler of the Keraits.

[31] By the time of Kubilai (1260-94) the guard (keshik) seems to have been raised to 12,000. (See The Book of Marco Polo; Yule, Cordier).

and ten comrades, and the son of a commander of 100 shall bring a kinsman and five comrades, and the leader of 10, as well as *darkhat*, i. e. free men enjoying special privileges, a kinsman and three comrades. Should anyone oppose these regulations, he shall be punished and if any night guardsman refuse to stand watch, he shall be expelled. Whoever wishes to become a guardsman shall not be prevented."

In this way the turghaut were raised to 1000 men and the kabtaut first to 800 men then to 1000; the 400 khorchin to 1000, and on the model of the original 1000 baatut, another 6000 were formed. The Guard (Keshik), which was Chingis Khan's personal army, only took the field when he himself went to war. In camp, the original 1000 baatut were placed in front of his quarters, the khorchin and turghaut on the right and the kabtaut and remaining 6000 baatut on the left. The watches of the guard were divided into four shifts of three days each.[32]

For the guidance and protection of the guard, Chingis Khan issued the following rules:

1. The commander of the shift on duty must himself stand night watch.

2. The watch (kharawul) must be changed every three days.

3. The first failure of a guardsman to appear on duty was to be punished with 30 strokes, a second failure with 70

---

[32] After the Guard had been increased to 10,000, Chingis Khan made Bogelo Cherbi commander of the first thousand, Bukha of the second thousand, Alchida of the third thousand, Dodai Cherbi of the fourth thousand, Dokholka of the fifth thousand, Chana (perhaps Chaghan) of the sixth thousand, Akuda of the seventh thousand and Arkhai Khassar of the eighth thousand. This is the list given by Palladius who, however, fails to include the commanders of the remaining 2000. Perhaps Yekeneyurin was one, for we are told a little earlier in the text that he was put over the night guard, while one of the three officers Jelmei, Yisunta and Bugidei, who were set in charge of the original 400 archers, may have commanded the other 1,000. As will be seen later, some of these officers, notably Chaghan, held important posts outside the Guard.

All information on the organization, personnel and strength of the Guard, has come from Palladius' translation of the *Yüan Ch'ao Pi Shih*; from Vladimirtsov, *The Life of Chingis Khan*, pp. 67-68, and Barthold, *Turkestan down to the Mongol Invasion*, pp. 383-385.

strokes and a third failure with 37 strokes and expulsion from the guard.

4. Delinquent guardsmen were to be punished only after the Khan himself had given the necessary order.

5. All misdemeanors were to be reported to the Khan, and any officer punishing on his own initiative was himself to be punished.

6. A member of the guard was to rank higher than any soldier of the line.

7. The families of guardsmen were to be held superior to all others.

8. Any outsider quarrelling with a guardsman was to be punished.

9. The archers of the guard were to give up their bows to the night watch when it went on duty.

10. The night watch was to arrest all persons found prowling about after dark.

11. When the new shift went on duty, it must show an official stamp of authority.

12. Any person wishing an audience at night must first consult the commander of the shift on duty.

13. No one might mingle with the guard while it was on duty.

14. No one might enquire the day of duty of the guard; any one doing so was to be fined his clothing and a saddled horse.

15. The inner cherbi and the shepherds were to be subordinate to the night watch.

16. The guard was to have charge of the commissary of the inner tents (doubtless Chingis Khan's own household).

17. The guard was to examine carefully all persons passing in and out of the camp.

18. The camp was always to be guarded by members of the night watch.

19. The night watch was never to be absent from the Khan and were only to take the field when he went to war.

20. In the hunt the guard were always to be about his person.
21. In time of peace the camp and all in it were to be in their charge.
22. All legal cases were to be judged by Shiki Kutuku (an adopted son of Chingis Khan) —and one of the guard.
23. The distribution of clothes and military equipment was the duty of the cherbi and the guard. (The cherbi had by this time been raised to six).[33]

From these regulations, it is seen, that if the guard was subject to strict discipline and had great responsibilities, it also enjoyed considerable privileges and the unbounded confidence and gratitude of Chingis Khan. To further illustrate this, one need only quote the conqueror's words to his old guardsmen. " You are the body-guardsmen of the night watch for the peace of my body and soul; you mounted guard all round my tent on rainy and snowy nights, as well as on the clear night of alarms and of battles with the enemy. Owing to you I have attained to supreme power." Then to those about him, " My descendants shall look upon these body-guardsmen as a monument of myself and take care of them; they shall not excite their resentment, and shall regard them as good genii." [34]

But the Guard was more than a body of picked soldiers. It was also, as Vladimirtsov notes, an institution that, under Chingis Khan's personal direction and constant control, became a nursery of trusty lieutenants. " He knew each man personally and could give him tasks in accordance with his individual aptitudes." At the same time, by its aristocratic personnel, the Guard strengthened Chingis Khan's hold on the Mongol nobility.

### Part IV

Of paramount interest in the study of the Mongol Army are the strategy and tactics which played so large a part in

---

[33] These regulations are taken from the translation of the *Yüan Ch'ao Pi Shih* by Palladius.

[34] Vladimirtsov, *The Life of Chingis Khan*, p. 68.

its success. Most accounts of the major wars undertaken by Chingis Khan and his successors show that prior to any declaration of hostilities extreme care was taken to obtain full information on the political, economic and military situation within the state to be attacked. Before setting out against the Khorezmian empire in 1219, Chingis Khan knew nearly everything there was to know about it. Informed by the Moslem merchants, in whose hands was much of the trade of Central and Northern Asia and who benefited by the order and safety he had established along the caravan routes, he was well aware of the difficulties besetting his otherwise powerful enemy. Also on that occasion, as well as on others, much was learned from malcontents. Of the information gathered from such persons, and from scouts and spies sent out for the purpose, none equalled in importance that concerning roads, passes, river fords, fortified places, towns and cities, and the military forces likely to be encountered. On the basis of such knowledge the Mongol high command drew up its plans.

Once war had been decided upon, a great assembly (kuriltai) [35] was called, according to Meng Hung, usually during March or April. At this, the plan of campaign, the number of men to be called up, the number of horses to be used—at least two or three to each man [36]—and the necessary supplies— often live stock driven on the hoof—were discussed at length. Furthermore, the most suitable season for the impending campaign was carefully considered. Thus Russia was conquered during the winters of 1237-38 and 1238-39 when all the rivers were frozen; Iraq in the spring of 1258 when the heat and malaria were at a minimum. Neverthless, if necessary, operations were carried on even during the middle of summer and one rarely hears of an important siege being raised because of hot weather. When all had been settled, the main points of

---

[35] Kuriltai is the spelling favored by Pelliot, who thinks it preferrable to the form Kurultai of Barthold and Vladimirtsov. (See Pelliot's " Notes sur le Turkestan," T'oung Pao, 1930.)

[36] Meng Hung says that sometimes as many as six or seven spare horses were led.

concentration were fixed and mobilization orders were issued. A fact worth notice is that unlike so many armies of that and other days, the requirements demanded rarely failed to materialize. In 1299, when Ghazan (1295-1304), the greatest of the Il-Khans of Persia, was preparing to invade Syria, he sent out instructions for the mobilization of 90,000 troops— half of his entire army. These he ordered to come fully equipped and each man to have five horses. Six months' provisions were collected and for their transport 5,000 camels, all of which were ready at the appointed time.[37]

On distant campaigns or during long drawn out operations, the Mongols expected to extract a large part of their supplies from the country of the enemy. Indeed they can be said to have looked to the territory before them rather than to that behind to furnish their wants. But when camped for the summer or for the siege of city, town or fort, the whole of the surrounding area was combed.

Not infrequently the Mongols preceded expeditions by spreading abroad rumors exaggerating the numbers of the invading army. This was done during 1258 before Mongkha Khaghan (1251-59) invaded the province of Szechuan in the Sung Empire. The force under his immediate command actually numbered 40,000, but it was deliberately advertised as being 100,000 strong.

The Mongols also seldom failed to take advantage of dissension in the enemy ranks. After the fall of Samarkand in March 1220, Chingis Khan, knowing the Khwarazm Shah's distrust of those of his generals related to the queen mother Turkhan Khatun, forged letters ostensibly written by them, offering to betray their ruler. These he had secretly delivered to the Shah, who, his nerve already badly shaken, became convinced that a large part of his army was riddled with treachery. So instead of continuing to resist the Mongols in the east, he fled west to organize new forces in Iraq-i-Ajami (Persian Iraq) and so gave Chingis Khan a practically unopposed passage over the Amu Darya (R. Oxus).

[37] Howorth, *The History of the Mongols*, Part III, p. 435.

When preparations had been completed, the army of invasion was held in review to see that it was up to strength and a general inspection was made of horses and equipment. Orders were then given for the advance and the troops moved out from their respective concentration areas.

The Mongols nearly always entered a country in widely separated columns. In the face of a large enemy force or for the investment of a city, these could unite at unbelievable speed, their superior mobility giving them the same security that concentration gives slower moving armies. Such dispersion not only accelerated the army's progress, but the thrust of each column was planned so that it reacted to the advantage of the others. Thirty-five to seventy miles ahead of all such bodies there operated a mobile screen, its duty being to inform the commander concerning hostile troops in the area, towns and villages and their means of defense, localities containing provisions, good camping grounds and suitable sites for an engagement.[38] Beside these forward screens, Marco Polo informs us that similar screens were posted on the flanks and rear, while communication between all such troops and those they covered was maintained by couriers. Consequently it was almost impossible to surprise a Mongol army.

All evidence goes to show that the Mongols preferred to deal with the main field forces of the enemy before penetrating any distance into hostile territory, and in the years 1211 and 1213 we shall see them inflict crushing defeats upon the Chin armies before pressing south. But in the invasion of the Khorezmian empire they were favored by no such opportunity. For political and strategic reasons the Khwarazm Shah, despite numerical superiority, declined to give Chingis Khan battle in the open. Resolving to remain on the defensive, he distributed the greater part of his field forces among the towns and cities of Transoxiana and Khwarazm in the hope that the siege of so many strongly garrisoned places would wear the Mongols down. But in this he was disappointed. They reduced them all. Moreover, taking advantage of his opponent's passive

[38] See the *Meng Ta Pei Lu* of *Meng Hung*.

attitude, Chingis Khan was able to capture most of the
smaller places before launching an attack on the great cities
of Bokhara, Samarkand and Gurganj.[39] In this campaign, as
in that of 1213-14, it is clearly indicated that whenever possible
the Mongols left the most heavily fortified positions of the
enemy to the last. During both ancient and medieval times
sieges were tedious undertakings, and to the Mongols with
their original lack of technical knowledge in such warfare and
their limited manpower, the great cities of China and the
Moslem world might have proved irreducible. When Chingis
Khan invaded Hsi Hsia during 1209 he vainly besieged the
capital Chung-hsiung from July to the beginning of October.
Taught by this and other experiences the Mongols learned to
draw on the conquered for experts in such matters, and as early
as 1211, though to a greater extent by the end of 1213, several
Chinese soldiers versed in the technique of taking cities were
in their service.

According to the Sung envoy Hsü Ting, who was on an
embassy to Ugedei from 1235-36, the Mongols took over the
majority of their siege appliances from the Moslems. But even
before Chingis Khan turned west, the Chinese had provided
him with most of the engines of war commonly used by the
armies of ancient and medieval times,[40] and when he set out
against the Khorezmian empire, he took with him several
companies of Chinese soldiers versed in the art of operating
siege machines.

Some authorities believe that the Mongols employed gun-

[39] Since the conquest of Transoxiana is an example of Mongol military genius at
its best, and as of late the efforts of more than one soldier have thrown considerable
fresh light on the subject, I have included a brief account of it at the end of the
present volume. (See Appendix A)

[40] In a long note in *The Book of Marco Polo*, Vol. I, pp. 121-131 Colonel Yule
says that whereas in the Occident the largest trebuchets were operated by a
counterpoise, those in China were worked by man-power. Consequently, the largest
engines of this kind were built for the Mongols by Moslems. At the siege of
Hsiang-yang and Fan Ch'eng (1268-73), one of the longest in history, two engineers,
Ala ad-Din of Mosul and Ismail of Hilla, built machines that hurled 166 pound
projectiles with such force that they penetrated the beaten clay walls to a depth
of seven or eight feet. And during the invasion of Europe the Mongols are
reported to have used Mangonels having a range of 400 yards. (See " The Great
Tartar Invasion of Europe," *Slavonic Review*, Vol. 5, 1926-27.)

powder, and from accounts of the siege of K'ai-feng (1232-33) one gathers that both sides used crude mortars and bombs.[41] Beside heavy artillery, the Mongols had light catapults for use in the field, and at the battle of the Sajo in Hungary on April 10, 1241, they captured the bridge over the river by the fire of catapults and archers.

However, the outstanding thing about Mongol siegecraft was not the size or variety of their weapons, but the numbers in which these were used and the ruthless employment of captives. The siege of Nishapur in Khurasan is a good example of both. Reaching the city sometime in March 1221, the Mongols found the inhabitants ready to oppose a desperate defense. Among the preparations made to resist them were 3,000 ballistae (heavy javelin throwers) and 500 heavy catapults mounted on the walls. But the Mongols made even greater efforts, and forcing their captives to erect siege engines under fire from the city, set up 3,000 ballistae, 3,000 catapults and 700 machines for hurling burning naptha over the walls. Besides this, 4,000 scaling ladders were made and 2,500 loads of rock were brought down from the neighboring mountains. Their labor done, the wretched captives were forced to head the storming parties. Careless of the losses that befell these, the Mongols maintained an almost ceaseless assault, and after the moat had been filled and seventy breaches made in the walls, the 10th of April saw Nishapur carried by storm and every living thing in it put to the sword.[42]

Meng Hung reports that in all areas containing towns and cities the Mongols purposely began operations with the reduction of the small surrounding places in order to provide themselves with sufficient man power to help in the capture of the larger ones. Tardiness on the part of such impressed labor

[41] See Schlegel, " The Invention of Gun-powder and Fire-arms in China prior to the Arrival of the Europeans," the *T'oung Pao*, 1902. In 1219 the Sung used gun-powder to help defend Tsao-yang which the Chin vainly besieged for ninety days. (De Mailla, *Histoire Générale de La Chine*, Vol. IX). The Sung, however, had employed it still earlier against these same Northerners when the latter vainly tried to cross the Yangtse in 1161. (See Goodrich, *A Short History of The Chinese People*, pp. 148-49.)

[42] See D'Ohsson, *Histoire des Mongols*, Vol. I, pp. 288-291.

was visited with instant death. The Mongols however were not the first to resort to this inhuman practice, and the Khitans of the 10th century frequently made unlimited use of captives to take towns and cities and exterminated the population when this was accomplished.

In very mountainous countries, such as Afghanistan and the Elburz, forts were often perched on heights that no assault could reach. In such localities blockading forces were left in front of the place until starvation had done its work. But in the mountains, as well as before well fortified towns and cities, the Mongols frequently resorted to a ruse to lure the garrison into the open. When successful this sometimes enabled them to seize the place without a regular siege, but even if not so fortunate, the losses sure to be suffered by the garrison were likely to have a disheartening effect and ultimately shorten the investment.

Regarding the wholesale massacre of the inhabitants of certain towns and cities, it should be noted that, fearful as these were in reality, they have frequently been exaggerated and often did not extend beyond the slaughter of the garrison. When carried out the Mongol command generally had two motives in view; (1) to prevent the revolt of a hostile population in their rear; (2) the intimidation of other places into submission. The latter ambition was of course not always realized and on more than one occasion clemency paid better dividends. But once submitted, woe betide the city that rebelled. When retaken its people could look for nothing but extermination.

Realizing how dangerous it was to place Mongol troops in towns where their small numbers and limited experience of such places put them at the mercy of a possible uprising, the high command usually assigned garrison duty to auxiliaries accustomed to such work. In the open country, however, regular camps were established to keep the surrounding region in order and to repel hostile attacks. These, Meng Hung affirms, were located far enough apart to ensure adequate grazing for the horses and, whether permanent or temporary, were invariably situated on high ground. Protected night and day from surprises by outside patrols, the different camps were in constant touch with each other. Inside, at least two horses always stood saddled and ready to carry messages or orders, and at night all going to and fro must use the password, which was the name of the officer on duty. As an additional precaution, in hostile or semi-hostile country, areas containing such camps were frequently surrounded by a belt of desolation.

## PART V

Turning to the field tactics of the Mongol army, our chief source of information is again the Chinese general Meng Hung. According to him, as soon as the scouting screen of a Mongol army made contact with the enemy, the main body extended its front over as great a distance as possible so as to overlap the flanks of the hostile force.[43] On closer contact and the approach of action, skirmishers went forward, and scouts were called upon to bring in reports about local topography, lines of communication, and the strength and disposition of the opposing troops.

Reports on the battle formation of the Mongol army are most imperfect but apparently it resembled that of the Jurchids or Chin in their early days and consisted of five ranks, two clad in iron scale armor and three in lacquered hide armor. According to Ma Tuan-lin, the army of Akuda (1113-23) was drawn up for battle in squadrons of 50 horsemen, 20 with heavy cuirasses and long lances in front and 30 with light cuirasses and bows behind.[44] A Mongol squadron numbered 100 men and from Plano Carpini one learns that these were arranged at intervals with the heavily armored troops of each stationed in front. Meng Hung omits to give the ratio between

---

[43] Meng Hung affirms that on occasions 1000 men would stretch across a front of 100 li (approximately 35 miles) but probably one should read 10,000 men instead of 1000 men.

[44] Ma Tuan-lin, 'Le Nu-chih,' "Ethnographie des peuples étranges à la Chine," trans. par Stanislaus Julien, *Journal Asiatique*.

the heavy and light troops in a squadron but makes a point
of saying that such action was the duty of the front ranks.[45]
Throughout an engagement, all manoeuvers were directed from
the position taken up by the senior commander and his staff,
who rarely if ever participated in the melée. Orders were
transmitted by flag signals and bugle calls or at night by lamp
and fire signals.

Battle begun, the light troops, one body in support of
another, advanced through the squadron intervals in the two
front ranks and poured volleys of arrows into the opposing
lines. Simultaneously one or both the wings began an
enveloping movement to take the enemy on the flanks and
rear.[46] If the first storm of arrows succeeded in disordering
his array, the shock troops received the command to charge.
At times the whole army supported the assault when, says
Meng Hung, even if the enemy numbered 100,000, it was
almost impossible to escape defeat. Should the light troops
be repulsed by a charge, they retired shooting backward from
the saddle, which they could do with deadly effect, and other
detachments took their place and repeated the arrow storm.
If these in their turn were unsuccessful, the remaining light
troops took up the assault. It was rare that the third onset
failed, for by that time the wings of the army were probably
launching a simultaneous drive on the flanks and rear of the
foe and the way was paved for a decisive charge.[47]

[45] B. H. Liddell Hart, in his study of " Jenghiz Khan and Sabutai " in *Great
Captains Unveiled,* reports that the Mongol battle formation was comprised of five
ranks, the squadrons being separated by wide intervals. The troops in the two front
ranks wore complete armor, with sword and lance, and their horses also were
armored. The three rear ranks wore no armor and their weapons were the bow and
the javelin, p. 10.

[46] Plano Carpini reports that such enveloping manoeuvers frequently misled
opponents into believing that the Mongols were far more numerous than they really
were. But King Hayhon of Armenia, remarking on the close and regular order of
the Mongol ranks, says that their numbers were often underestimated.

[47] In one of his commentaries to the *Meng Ta Pei Lu,* Wang Kuo-wei includes a
note on the Khitan method of fighting a battle. The army of the Khitans, he tells
us, was built up on a decimal basis. Five hundred or 700 men constituted a
squadron, 10 squadrons a division and 10 divisions an army corps, this last being
under the orders of a senior commander.

When a general action was expected, scouts were sent out to make a careful

Although we have no very detailed description of any pitched battle fought by the Mongols, enough is known to show that these tactics won some of their greatest victories. When dealing with their first attack on the Chin in 1211, we shall see this combination of fire and shock action at Huan-erh-tsui defeat the most powerful army in the empire. Nearly one hundred years before at the battle of Hu-pu-ta-kang, fought in 1115 to the east of the Liao River, the Jurchids themselves used just such a combination to defeat the great army—100,000 strong—of the last Khitan emperor Yeh-lü Yen-hsi (1101-23), and in 979 the Khitans employed similar tactics in their victory over the emperor Sung T'ai Tsung (976-97) on the Kao-liang River outside Yen Ching (modern Peking). The battle procedure favored by the Mongols was therefore long tried and proven.

At Huan-erh-tsui the Mongols apparently remained in the saddle throughout the whole engagement and from start to finish took the offensive. Sometimes, however, if numbers of their horses were in poor condition, the riders were dismounted and waited for the enemy to make the first onslaught. Thus on December 22, 1299, at Salamiyet (30 miles northwest of Hims in Syria) Ghazan Khan (1295-1304) ordered part of his army to fight on foot. Standing behind their horses as a rampart, they awaited the attack of the heavily armored Mamluks, and when these came within range, poured storm after storm of arrows into their ranks. Surprised and broken, the charging horsemen tried to reform, but Ghazan threw his

reconnaissance of the local topography and lines of communiaction. This done, the army formed its ranks and covered its advance with skirmishers. As soon as contact was made with the enemy, the attack was begun by the first of the ten squadrons. If this was successful, the other nine squadrons were launched to its support and a charge was pressed home. But if the first squadron failed, it was called to the rear to rest and water its horses, while the second took its place. If necessary, this tactic was repeated until all 10 squadrons had charged forward and retired, when the first again resumed the attack and the whole procedure was carried out once more. Were a day of this insufficient to break the enemy, the same thing went on for two or three days. Finally, when the opposing troops had become tired, the Khitan commander instructed his men to tie grass to the tails of their horses and set in motion yet another series of charges. At the end of it, the enemy were almost sure to be overcome with dust and fatigue and would collapse before a determined onset by all ten squadrons.

still mounted troops upon them and swept the cavalry of Egypt from the field.[48] On this occasion the dismounted men were never in jeopardy of being ridden down, but Meng Hung implies that whenever this seemed likely the men left on horseback charged forward to engage the enemy.

Like the Mongols, the Mamluks also used the bow, but their archery was inferior to that of the Mongols; hence their preference for close action so as to use their magnificent shock cavalry. At Salamiyet the army of Ghazan was undoubtedly the larger of the two, perhaps 50,000, another reason for the Mamluks staking all on a charge, whereas the Egyptian force, according to Wassaf, Novari and Makrizi respectively, numbered 40,000, 25,000 and 20,000.[49]

Referring to the devastating effect of Mongol archery, a chronicler present at the battle of the Sajo (April 10, 1241), says that the men of the Hungarian army " fell to the right and left like the leaves of winter." Against the armies of Christendom, Islam and China, such archery was overwhelming and generally the succeeding charge carried all before it. But in Chingis Khan's wars of unification in Outer Mongolia every action was between armies composed entirely of mounted bowmen. Even from the scanty information at our disposal, it is evident that these early battles were among the fiercest ever fought by the conqueror. Since he had no advantage in the matter of fire power, victory depended upon better generalship, and on the superiority of his shock troops.

Besides the heavy troops normally composing part of the Mongol battle array, there was frequently a crack force held in reserve. This was used either to strike a decisive blow if victory were hanging in the balance or to repulse a particularly formidable enemy charge. In the battle between Chingis Khan and Jalal ad-Din near the Nilab ferry on the river Indus (late September or early October, 1221) the Khorezmian right nearly broke the Mongol center, but the Guard (Keshik) delivered a tremendous counter-attack that turned the tide of battle.

[48] Howorth, *The History of the Mongols*, part III, p. 438.
[49] *Ibid.*

Mention has been made of the Mongol practice of enveloping the flanks and rear of the enemy. This they generally did by extending and advancing their wings behind clouds of dust or in the cover of valleys and hills until they turned those of their adversary. At times this manoeuver was assisted by throwing an advance guard far forward to make contact with the enemy. As soon as this was effected, a retreat began and was carried on until the pursuing troops had been drawn within the grip of the encircling Mongol wings and escape made impossible. The retreating force then turned about and joined in a general attack upon the doomed enemy. On the 8th or 9th of April, 1241, Prince Henry of Silesia at the head of 20,000, some say 30,000, Germans and Poles fell into such a trap at Wahlstadt near Leignitz and perished with 10,000 men. Though the facts are obscure, it seems that part of the allied army pressed on in advance of the rest to pursue what they thought to be a retreating Mongol force. Suddenly they found themselves surrounded and subjected to a storm of arrows that paved the way for a crushing charge. Seeing their plight, Prince Henry and Popo von Osternau, who was leading the Teutonic Knights, hurried to their help, only to be overwhelmed in the same disaster.

The defeat at Leignitz was one of those that mediaeval historians ascribed to the overwhelming numbers of the Mongols. Actually the troops of the invaders on the field cannot have exceeded those of Prince Henry.

Of all the ruses employed by the Mongols none has attracted greater attention than their feigned retreats. After the trick became well known, it still succeeded. It is probable that neither Prince Henry nor his associates knew much about Mongol warfare, but even if they had it would have been difficult for their much slower moving composite force of infantry and heavy cavalry to have interfered with a Mongol flank movement. But for many of the armies so defeated no such excuse can be made. An outstanding instance is the great battle fought outside Delhi in 1299 where Zafar Khan, general of the celebrated Sultan Ala ad-Din Khilji (1295-1315), was slain. Despite a wealth of experience in fighting the Mongols, Zafar Khan, seeing their left wing give way, rushed forward to complete its destruction. Retreating before him, the Mongols fell back until 36 miles were between them and the Sultan who was engaged with the rest of their army. Troops were then detached from this to take the general in the rear, and Zafar Khan and the Moslem right were surrounded and annihilated. However, the Moslem center and left remained intact and the next day the Mongols broke off the engagement and withdrew with their plunder.[50]

The Moslem chroniclers of this battle believed or pretended to believe that the Mongol left was broken by Zafar Khan and only rallied afterward, but a critical examination of the action convinces one that the Mongols carried out a deliberate retreat to draw the general after them. The recorded numbers of the two armies are fantastic, the figure given for that of the Mongols being 200,000, while the Sultan is said to have been at the head of 300,000 cavalry and 2,700 elephants. Neither force employed infantry. However, since the Mongol leader, Kutlugh Khoja, was only governor of Kabul and as his father, the great Jaghatai Khan Duva (1276-1301), required the greater part of his troops for his incessant wars in the north, it is unlikely that the Mongols present exceeded 50,000 or 60,000. As for the army of the Sultan on the field, it may have numbered as many as 70,000 cavalry and perhaps 700 elephants, certainly little more.

Well appreciating the demoralizing effect of attacks in the rear, the Mongols themselves took good care to guard against them, and at Salamiyet (December 22, 1299) Ghazan posted a special force to deal with any such attempt by the enemy. Consequently, when the Mamluks detached 5000 Arabs to come up behind the army, the force was heavily repulsed.[51]

But to return to the Mongol use of retreats, on occasions these lasted for days. In such withdrawals their practice of

[50] See Sir Wolseley Haig, *Cambridge History of India*, Vol. III, "Turks and Afghans," p. 102; also Ferishta, *History of Hindustan*, Vol. I, pp. 248-250.
[51] See Howorth, *History of the Mongols*, Part III, p. 439.

leading spare mounts gave them a great advantage over non-pastoral peoples whose cavalry and infantry were sure to become exhausted. This happened in May 1222, when they met the combined Kipchak and Russian armies near the River Khalkha. Perceiving that they were heavily outnumbered, the Mongol commanders Jebe and Subudei ordered a retreat. After nine days (according to some eleven) the better mounted troops of the Prince of Galich and his Kipchak allies had forged ahead of the forces of Kiev. Meanwhile the Mongols had worked round onto both flanks, and launching a sudden attack surrounded and destroyed the Kipchak and Galichian forces before the slower moving troops of Kiev could come to their aid. These were then attacked in their turn. So swift was the Mongol onslaught that the men of Kiev had no time to recross the Khalkha, but taking up position on a neighboring hill were surrounded and compelled to surrender. At times the Mongols simply lured their victims into a prepared ambush and we shall find this a favorite ruse during their conquest of China.

Besides the information already provided by him, Meng Hung informs us of some less known practices of the Mongols. When an enemy stood on the defensive with spears planted to impale charging horses, the Mongols would withdraw the main body of their troops and leave detachments to harrass the spear-held lines. At length lack of rest, food, water and fuel compelled the enemy to move, whereupon the main force of the Mongols reappeared and attacked them on the march. At times this was not done until the enemy was further wearied by the road.

Still drawing on Meng Hung, we learn that on coming up against numerically superior forces the Mongols often sent troopers to stir up dust behind their own lines by means of branches tied to the tails of their horses. On seeing this the enemy sometimes believed that large reinforcements were at hand and fled.

A trick more novel, but not mentioned by Meng Hung, was that of placing stuffed dummies on spare horses. This was done in 1221 by the Mongol general Shiki Kutuku when he engaged Jalal ad-Din at Biruan between Kabul and Ghazna.[52] However, the Khorezmian prince was either undeceived or unafraid, for he charged and scattered the Mongols. But in Hungary during the spring of 1241, the trick met with complete success. Having sacked the town of Agria (modern Eger), an advance detachment from the principal Mongol army learned that a numerically superior force under the Bishop of Varadin was trying to overtake it. Therefore, while part of their troops took up a position out of sight with a number of such dummies, the rest waited for the enemy to catch up. After a slight skirmish the decoy troops retreated in haste toward the surprise force. Suddenly the pursuing Hungarians saw what seemed to be a large reinforcement and, falling into a panic, broke and fled. Whereupon the Mongols turned to the attack and drove the Bishop's men before them in utter rout.[53]

If the strength of the enemy or some other emergency made a retreat necessary, the Mongols, when possible, waited until dark. Then, leaving their camp fires burning, they retired at speed and were far on their way before the hostile army knew of their departure.

From time to time opponents were encountered, who even though surrounded fought with such courage that the Mongols purposely opened a path of escape, in order to achieve their destruction in the confusion of the retreat. It is not too much to say that never in history has an army understood so well the importance of pursuit or been so tireless in carrying it out. From the disastrous battlefield on the River Sajo (April 10, 1241) the Hungarians were harried for two days. Rogerius, an eye witness, says: "During a march of two days thou couldst see nothing along the roads but fallen warriors, their

---

[52] Some authorities believe that this battle was fought in the valley of the Panshir to the south of the Hindu Kush, but Raverty, followed by Barthold, thinks that it really took place not far from the sources of the Lugar, a tributary of the Kabul, and for a variety of reasons this seems the more probable site. (See Barthold, *Turkestan down to the Mongol Invasion*, p. 441, n. 6.

[53] See D'Ohsson, *Histoire des Mongols*, Vol. II, pp. 141-142.

dead bodies lying about like stones in a quarry." [54] At the end of it an army of 50,000 to 60,000 had been virtually destroyed.[55]

Far longer was the pursuit of the Mamluk army defeated at Salamiyet (December 22, 1299), when Mongol soldiers were seen as far south as Jerusalem and Gaza (over 250 and 300 miles from the scene of battle).[56] By pursuits of this nature the Mongols dealt such staggering blows to the field forces of their opponents that generally they were able to ravage the country of the defeated at will. Many armies have won great battles, but failing to carry out a proper pursuit have given the enemy time to reform and have had their work to do over again. This the Mongols never permitted, and unless their losses had been particularly heavy, or their horses were worn out, or some other good reasons were against it, they invariably followed up victory by a relentless and annihilating pursuit.

## Part VI

To form a complete picture of the Mongol army, a copy of the famous Yasa or Code of Chingis Khan would be invaluable, but even the fragments at our disposal are of great assistance. By the standards of today, discipline was very severe. But to maintain the solidarity of a people at the social and cultural level of the Mongols, rigorous punishments, especially in the army, were essential. A few examples must serve. No matter what his rank, a noble was obliged to give himself up to the messenger sent by the Khan to punish him, even if the messenger was the lowest of his servants, and he had to prostrate himself before the man until the punishment was carried out, even if it meant death.

All officers were responsible for the training of their men. On active service they had personally to inspect their troops

---

[54] See Vambéry, *Story of Hungary*, p. 139.

[55] For this estimate see Lukinich, *A History of Hungary*, pp. 70-72 and Vambéry, p. 138.

[56] See Howorth, *History of the Mongols*, part III, p. 446.

and to supply them with everything, even to needle and thread. If any soldier lacked a necessary part of his equipment his officer was punished.

During battle, in attack or retreat, if any one let fall his pack or bow or any baggage, the man behind him must alight and return the thing to its owner; should he not do so he was put to death.

In action, flight before the order to retire, plundering before the word of command and the desertion of a comrade were punished by death.

Stringent as such regulations may seem, they were less severe than those reputedly enforced by the Jurchids during the 12th century. Ma Tuan-lin states that among them should the leader of five perish in battle, the four men under him were punished by decapitation; should the leader of ten fall, the two officers of five were slain, while the loss of a leader of 100 was punished by the execution of all the leaders of ten under him.[57]

Accustomed to render absolute submission to his superiors, the obedience of the Mongol soldier often astonished his contemporaries. The Moslem historian Mirkhwand tells us with surprise that after the defeat of the Mongols at Merj-es Suffar in Syria during December 1303, 5000 men who had lost their horses were obliged to make a two months' journey home on foot and at the end of it immediately set out on another expedition without a murmur.[58]

If discipline was harsh and much was expected of him, the Mongol soldier was at least justly treated and better cared for than the men of most armies until very modern times. True he received no pay; on the contrary, he paid taxes on any livestock he owned, but in the matter of loot, which was often immense, each from the Khan down received his prescribed share and a special portion was allotted to those doing garrison work, holding lines of communication, or acting as the home guard.

[57] Ma Tuan-lin, 'Le Nu-chih,' "Ethnographie des peuples étranges à La Chine," trans. par Stanislaus Julien, Journal Asiatique.
[58] Howorth, History of the Mongols, part III, p. 473.

Often in the wars of Chingis Khan one encounters instances of the conqueror's concern for his men. One of the best examples of this comes from an excerpt from his Bilik (Maxims), also extant only in fragments. Referring to one of his officers, he said: " There is no hero equal to Yisun Beg, and no man as skillful, but not knowing fatigue and hardships on campaign, he thinks that everyone has his endurance. Yet others cannot stand so much. Therefore Yisun Beg is not fit to be chief over his troops. Only a man who feels hunger and thirst, and by this estimates the feelings of others, is fit to be a commander, as he will see that his warriors do not suffer from hunger and thirst and that the four-footed beasts do not starve. The meaning of this is that the campaign and its hardships must be in proportion with the strength of the weakest warriors." [59]

I have already said that command of the Mongol army was in the hands of the nobility. This consisted of an aristocracy of birth (baatut, noyat and nukut) and of a class of freemen (darkhat) who had been granted special privileges for outstanding services.[60] From both of these Chingis Khan personally chose the majority of his officers. Later, owing to the expansion of the empire, those of his successors who became Supreme Khan (Khaghan) were obliged to share this privilege of selection with other members of the Imperial Family.

Besides the generals and officers of Mongol blood, there were several from other nations, for neither race nor creed overinfluenced the Mongols in the choice of lieutenants. Jurchid, Khitan, Tangut, Turkish, Chinese and Arab soldiers commanded Mongol and auxiliary troops. When Mukhali was assigned the task of carrying on the war against the Chin, two of the ablest soldiers left to assist him were the Chinese generals Shih T'ien-ni and Shih T'ien-hsiang. In the reign of Ugedei (1229-41), it was a general from far off Tangut who was entrusted with the final reduction of the Alans in the

[59] Riasanovsky, *Fundamental Principles of Mongol Law*, p. 88.
[60] Owen Lattimore, author of *Manchuria Cradle of Conflict, Inner Asian Frontiers of China*, etc., believes that Chingis Khan regarded the Darkhat as a valuable means of counterbalancing the hereditary aristocracy.

Caucasus during 1239. To any man of ability, Mongol or otherwise, the road to command lay open. It was this broad-minded policy that accounts for the high standard among the generals of the Mongol army. Youth was never a bar to promotion. In 1208, Subudei, when no more than thirty-one or thirty-two years of age, was given independent command of an army to pursue the Mergids.[61] Again, years later in 1275, Kubilai Khaghan (1260-94) made the thirty-nine year old Bayan commander of the great army mobilized for the conquest of the Sung Empire. There were many older generals whom he might have chosen, but impressed by the outstanding capacity of Bayan, he raised him over their heads. Under such commanders the Mongols achieved a series of triumphs without parallel. Never before nor since has an army won so many battles, taken so many cities or conquered so many kingdoms.

Consequently, not only did most of the vanquished regard the Mongols as invincible and a visitation from Heaven, but the Mongols believed it themselves. Before the battle of Kuzadagh in Armenia (June 26, 1243), a Georgian officer serving with them apprehensively pointed out that the Saljuk army was much larger than their own. Unperturbed, the commander Baiju answered him: "You know not our Mongol people; God has given us the victory and we count as nothing the number of our enemies; the more they are the more glorious it is to win and the more plunder we shall secure." [62] Surely the morale of the Mongol army has rarely been equalled and never surpassed.

On the eve of the invasion of Mesopotamia and Syria in 1259, Chingis Khan's grandson Kulagu (1255-65) sent an

[61] Subudei was born in 1176 and died in 1248—see René Grousset, *L'Empire des Steppes*, p. 263, n. 3. This famous soldier belonged to the Uriangkut tribe, then a steppe dwelling people, but one which later moved to the upper Yenisei where it took on a primarilly reindeer economy. *Ibid.*

[62] In this famous battle, which gave them Asia Minor, the Mongols are reported by King Haython to have numbered 30,000, while Malakia says that the army of the Saljuks was 160,000. Friar Rubruk gives the Mongols only 10,000, but reduces the Saljuks to 100,000. The figures for the Saljuk army are of course preposterous. (See Howorth, *History of the Mongols*, part III, pp. 45-46.)

envoy to the Ayubid Sultan al Nasir (1236-60) with a message stating the divinely appointed mission of the Mongols and demanding that all thought of resistance be put aside. The Sultan, however, returned a defiant reply, and having mobilized an army reputed to have numbered 100,000—certainly a vast exaggeration—prepared to fight. But shaken by the sack of Baghdad and the murder of the Caliph in 1258, his troops became panic stricken. Instead of marching to relieve Aleppo, they successively abandoned to their fate Hama, Hims, Balbek, and Damascus. Reduced by daily desertions, the remainder at length reached El Arish where they sought assistance and protection from the Mamluk government of Egypt. The Sultan himself, being a bitter enemy of the Mamluks, fled to Trans-jordania, where he was eventually captured by the Mongols, who put him to death in 1260.

Today it is difficult to appreciate the terror inspired by the Mongol army. As it approached Damascus on the heels of the retreating Ayubid troops, so great was the panic that all who could flee, escaped, and the demand for camels was such that a single one sold for 700 pieces of silver. Not even after the defeats inflicted on the Mongols by the Mamluks at Ain Jalud (September 3, 1260) and al Bistan (April 18, 1277), did their prestige wane.[63] Referring to the Mongol mercenaries in the service of the Mamluk Sultan Baibars (1260-77), Makrizi wrote as follows: " Egypt and Syria became filled with Mongols, and their customs spread everywhere. The terror before the name of Chingis Khan and his successors was so strong that respect towards the Mongols and fear of them entered into the flesh and blood of the people of Egypt.[64]

[63] See Grousset, *Histoire Des Croisades*, pp. 603, 694, and Stevenson, W. B., *The Crusaders in The East*, pp. 334, 341.

[64] A caricature further illustrating the fear and horror inspired by the Mongols has come down to us from the pen of the Persian poet Amir Khuzru who was a refugee at the court of Ghiyath ad-Din Balban (1266-87) sultan of Delhi. De-scribing several hundred Mongol prisoners taken by the Moslems, he says: " Their eyes were so narrow and piercing that they might have bored a hole in a brazen vessel, and their stench was more horrible than their color. Their heads were set on their bodies as if they had no necks, and their cheeks resembled leathern bottles full of wrinkles and knots. Their noses extended from cheekbone to cheekbone.

These Mongols, having adopted Islam, united the dictates of their religion with their own customs. All that was connected with religion was left to the Qadhi al Qudhat, but all that concerned the Mongols personally was regulated according to the laws (Yasa) of Chingis Khan—for that purpose a special officer was appointed."

Victorious over the Chin and Khorezmian empires—until the coming of the Mongols the two greatest military powers of their day—the reputation of the Mongol army naturally became extraordinary. Impressed and alarmed by its strength and efficiency, first Delhi and then Cairo greatly improved the organization and discipline of their own forces, while Mongol mercenaries were always welcome if dangerous recruits. Though saved from ultimate destruction by the internecine wars that shook the Mongol empire from 1260 on, these two Moslem states beat off assaults that would have crushed their predecessors. In this connection it is worth mentioning that Dr. Mahdi Husain in " The Rise and Fall of Muhammed bin Tughluk," draws special attention to the deterioration that overtook the army of Delhi after the decline of the Jaghatais relieved India from the fear of Mongol invasion.

Subsequently in both Transoxiana and Iran the descendants of Chingis Khan were supplanted by the great Timur (1370-1405), but the army with which he marched from victory to victory was in all essentials a copy of that of the Mongols.

With the progessive development of fire arms the bow became obsolete and the Mongol, whose archery and horsemanship had played so great a part in raising him to a pinnacle of military power equalled by no other people in history, passed from the stage of world politics. To the Occident this

Their nostrils resembled rotting graves, and from them the hair descended as far as the lips. Their moustaches were of extravagant length, but the beards about their chins were very scanty. Their chests, in color half black, half white, were covered with lice which looked like sesame growing on a bad soil. Their bodies, indeed, were covered with these insects, and their skins were as rough-grained as shagreen leather, fit only to be converted into shoes. They devoured dogs and pigs. . . . The sultan marveled at their beastly countenances and said that God had created them out of hell fire." See Sir Wolseley Haig, *Cambridge History of India*, Vol. III, " Turks and Afgans," p. 84.

greatest of conquering armies is still little known, but in its successful application of the principles of war—(economy of force, concentration, co-operation, security, mobility, surprise and offensive action)—it remains unrivalled in East or West.

With this sketch of the Mongol army it is hoped that the military operations to be dealt with will be more intelligible. Often the details of battles are exasperatingly meagre, but with the facts provided above it is possible to visualize at least some of those of major importance. As regards Mongol strategy we are more fortunate, for when our sources fail the map often comes to the rescue. So despite certain shortcomings in the material available, our knowledge of the Mongol army, plus reliable information concerning the topography involved, make it possible to construct a comparatively clear picture of their activities.

CHAPTER III

# TEMUCHIN THE VASSAL OF THE KERAIT

IF AN understanding of the Mongol military system is vital
for a proper appreciation of the campaigns fought by the
Mongols, of equal if not greater importance is a knowledge
of the events which led to the rise of this remarkable people.
Only with such knowledge can one view their empire in its
true relationship to the powers that surrounded it.

When the 13th century dawned neither the so-called Mongols
themselves nor their associated tribes were well known outside northeastern Asia. For three centuries no tribe nor confederacy of tribes had succeeded in uniting all the peoples
beyond the Gobi. In 840 the powerful and relatively civilized
Uighurs had lost the hegemony of Outer Mongolia to their less
civilized Kirghiz vassals from the Yenisei. This new imperium
lasted little beyond the opening of the tenth century, and
gradually losing power, moved its capital back from the River
Orkhon to the Yenisei from where it exercised a varying degree
of authority south of the Tannu Ula.

In eastern and central Mongolia the Kirghiz were succeeded
by a loose confederacy called the Tsu-pu, whom certain
authorities identify with the Tatars.[1] It was they who were
masters of the Orkhon valley when in 924 the founder of the
Khitan empire, A-pao-chi (907-26), occupied Khara Balghasun,
capital of the Uighur and Kirghiz empires. From 924 to about
1100 the Tsu-pu, despite revolts, recognized Khitan suzerainty,[2]

[1] This is the opinion of the late and eminent Mongolist Wang Kuo-wei. See
Wittfogel and Feng Chia-sheng; *History of Chinese Society: Liao* (907-1125), pp.
101-102 and 528. As for the Mongols, it is generally thought that they were a
branch of the Shih-wei, who from relatively early times inhabited the most north-
easterly portion of present Outer Mongolia (*Ibid.*, pp. 42 and 90, also end map).
[2] See Wittfogel and Feng Chia-sheng, *History of Chinese Society: Liao* (907-1125),
pp. 573-598.

48

but after the latter date seem to have become independent, only to fall into a state of dissolution a few years later.

After their collapse, the principal nation to arise north of the desert was that of the Naimans (Eight Clans), whose dominions extended from the Tarbaghatai in the west to the upper reaches of the Selenga and Orkhon in the east, and from the Tannu Ula in the north to the eastern limits of the Altai in the southeast. They thus fall heir to the ancient Uighur and Kirghiz capital of Khara Balghasun and until the close of the 12th century were the most powerful people in Outer Mongolia. Bordering them on the east were the Keraits whose main habitat was the valley of the Tola, but whose possessions also included the middle Orkhon and the Ongin to the south. North of the Keraits were the three confederate Mergid tribes of the Uduyit, Qaat and Uwas, who ranged along the Selenga, and still further north the Durben Oirads or Four Oirads settled between Lake Khobsögöl and Lake Baikal. Eastward, and living for the most part on the Onon and Kerulen rivers, were the Mongols,[3] and stretching beyond them to the northern Khinghan (Hsingan) the Tatars, whose main camps centered on the Bur and Kulun Nor. With the exception of the Jalairs, who dwelt near the junction of the Kilok and Selenga, and who were sometimes subject to the Mongols, these six nations or confederacies divided Outer Mongolia between them.

It would be a mistake to think of their territories as having fixed boundaries comparable to those of the settled states to the south. In such times of disorder and conflict as preceded the final triumph of Chingis Khan, territorial and tribal or national identity were loosely fixed and nomad nations were often permanently or temporarily displaced from their original grazing lands. As will later be seen in pursuing the rise of the Mongol conqueror, the size of a chief's following was of more

---

[3] After the triumph of Chingis Khan it was customary to divide the clans of the Mongol nation proper into two groups, the Nirun Mongols and the Durlukin Mongols. The former, who were held superior to the latter and who were related to the Kiyad-Borjigin, which was the conqueror's own clan, consisted of the Kiyads, Taijiuds, Uruds, Manguds, Jajirads, Barlas, Baarins, Durbens. Saljiuds and Khatakins; the latter of the Arulads, Bayauds, Khorolas, Suldus, Ikiras and Khongirads. (See René Grousset, *L'Empire des Steppes*, p. 248.)

importance than any specific territory he might conquer or inherit. Still further illustrating the turbulent conditions of the day are the struggles and rivalry that constantly broke out within the various confederacies themselves. These arose among the baatut and nakut, who comprised the nobility subject to the greater chiefs. Sometimes these quarrels resulted in the transference of a clan or sub-clan from one powerful leader to another, at others merely in the desertion of discontented subjects from one petty chief to a rival. Both processes were characteristic of steppe society in the early days of Chingis Khan.

Of the six great nomad nations the Naimans and Keraits were the most civilized and many of their subjects were Nestorian Christians.[4] Followers of the same persuasion were also found among the Mergids.

Northeast, east and south of the Gobi were three other tribes of considerable importance; the Solangs (Solons) living beyond the Khinghan along the Nonni and the T'ao-erh, the Khongirads occupying the northern Chahar of today and often included among the Mongols, and the Onguds of present west Chahar and Suiyüan. All three were subject to the Jurchids or Chin, but each from time to time participated in the various wars fought beyond the desert. The Solangs (Solons), a people of Tungus extraction, were comparatively backward, but the Khongirads and Onguds, especially the latter, who were Nestorian, were decidedly the most civilized of the Turko-Mongol peoples of Mongolia and were known to the Chinese as the Pai Ta-ta or civilized Tatars to differentiate them from the so-called Hei Ta-ta or uncivilized Tatars of the north[5] Equally civilized, and even more important, were the Khitans, but as they dwelt along the upper Liao in southwestern Manchuria,

[4] According to the report of the Syrian chronicler Bar Hebraeus, the Khan of the Keraits and 200,000 of his subjects were baptized in the year 1011; see Grousset, *L'Empire des Steppes*, p. 254.

[5] Owing to their proximity to China and their great reputation as soldiers, the Ta-ta or Tatars became the best known of the nomad peoples of the north and their name came to be used for many neighboring tribes. In Europe the word Tartar arose from the identification of the Mongols and their associated tribes with the legendary people of Tartarus. See Matthew Paris, *Chronica Majora*, Vol. IV.

they had less intercourse with Outer Mongolia than their neighbors.[6]

Being in close touch with these southern and eastern tribes, who were in direct contact with northern China, it was natural that the Keraits, Mongols and Tatars should be conversant with political events in the Middle Kingdom. Moreover, they were in the habit of receiving subsidies and recognizing the suzerainty of the imperial government. These factors, thinks the American expert Owen Lattimore, made such tribes especially fitted to produce the kind of leader able to unite the different peoples of Outer Mongolia. Chingis Khan, he points out, was a poor aristocrat of such a subsidy-drawing tribe and was therefore admirably adapted to play the role that was to make him world famous.[7] A wealthy " subsidy-eating chief," such as Tughrul Khan of the Keraits, was too conservative, a powerful non-subsidy-eating chief of the type of Tukta Biki the Mergid, too unsophisticated. Chingis Khan, conversant with both types and understanding their aspirations, but at first enjoying the wealth and position of neither, had the experience, and as it proved, the ability, courage and genius, to make of him the man to resurrect the empire of the steppes.

To the south and west of this nomad world lay four powerful states, Khara Khitai, Hsi Hsia, Chin and Sung. The first of these was created by the great Yeh-lü Ta-shih (1124-43) who, flying westward before the Jurchid conquerors of the Khitans, eventually established himself on the Imil near modern Chugu-chak.[8] From there, taking advantage of the general political

[6] The Kharluks and Uighurs to the west and southwest of Outer Mongolia were equally civilized, but have not been mentioned here as they were outside the orbit of Mongolia proper.

[7] See Owen Lattimore, Review of Grenard's " Gengis-Khan," *Pacific Affairs*, 1937; " The Geographical Factor in Mongol History," *Geographical Journal*, Vol. XCI, No. 1, Jan., 1938, and *Inner Asian Frontiers of China*, pp. 540-542 and pp. 544-545.

[8] Had this remarkable man commanded the Khitan army from the outset of the Jurchid revolt it is possible that the latter might have been crushed. Conversant with Chinese civilization—(he was holder of a Han-lin degree)—he proved himself an extremely able soldier long before his departure for the west. In 1122, when the empire of Liao was at its last gasp, the Sung sent north a powerful army, but near Cho Chou sustained a crushing defeat at the hands of Yeh-lü Ta-shih and a numerically much inferior Khitan army. However, after falling into the hands of

instability to the south, he speedily made himself master from the Tarbaghatai on the north to the K'un-lun Mountains on the south and from the edge of the Gobi in the east to the Syr Darya (Jaxartes) in the west. This vast realm, which included the Uighur Kingdom of the T'ien Shan and the Moslem Khara Khanid principalities of the western Tarim, he ruled with the title of Gur Khan from Balasagun on the upper Chu.[9] Since his conquests in the Tarim and on the Chu had been made at the expense of the Khara Khanids, it was inevitable that hostilities should break out with the remaining branch of that family who were the rulers of Farghana and Transoxiana. The first collision occurred in 1137, when the Khara Khanid Rukn ad-Din Mahmud Khan was disastrously beaten at Khojend. But in 1141 a far more serious clash took place. At Khatwan to the north of Samarkand both Mahmud and his suzerain the Saljuk Sultan Sinjar (1133-53) were defeated with such crushing losses that everything north of the Amu Darya (Oxus) fell to the Khitan, and Khwarazm to the west was compelled to submit.[10]

Yeh-lü Ta-shih's victory was more than the triumph of one power over another; it was a definite setback for the world of Islam, whose northward advance was stopped and whose rule in Central Asia was replaced by that of a heathen. But the conqueror proved a tolerant ruler, and if, as thinks Barthold, the official language of the administration became Chinese,[11] the Uighur and Khara Khanid vassals of the empire enjoyed a considerable degree of autonomy and none of their possessions

the Jurchids, escaping from them and rejoining Yeh-lü Yen-Hsi (1101-25), he decided that the Khitan cause in the east was lost. Flying northwest through the present province of Suiyüan, he first set up his headquarters on the Orkhon from where he unsuccessfully attacked the Kirghiz during 1128. Then in 1130 he set off for the west and established himself on the Imil near present Chuguchak, but three years later moved to Balasagun on the upper Chu. (For a most complete account of Yeh-lü Ta-shih and Khara Khitai; see Wittfogel and Feng Chia-Sheng, *History of Chinese Society: Liao* (907-1125), Appendix V.)

[9] Gur Khan means Universal Lord.

[10] The Moslems lost 30,000 killed in the battle and subsequent pursuit. See Barthold, *Turkestan Down to The Mongol Invasion*, pp. 326-27.

[11] Besides Chinese, Uighur and Persian were also employed in the administrative work of the government. (See Wittfogel and Feng Chia-Sheng, *History of Chinese Society: Liao* (907-1125), pp. 669-70.

were made over as fiefs to Ta-Shih's relatives.[12] Religion too was left free and untouched.

Beyond Khara Khitai's eastern frontier lay China which since the beginning of the 12th century had been divided between the national dynasty of Sung (960-1279), ruling in the basin of the Yangtse River, the Tangut Kingdom of Hsi Hsia (1101-1227) in the northwest and the powerful Jurchid empire of Chin (1113-1234) in the north and northeast. The Sung empire does not here concern us but a word must be said about the other two, and in the case of Hsi Hsia it is necessary to hark back several hundred years.

During the second half of the seventh century the Tibetans conquered the Kokonor and Tsaidam which was the original home of the Tanguts. Ever since the beginning of the fourth century this region had been ruled by the Tukuhun, so when in 672 they were overthrown, rather than bow to the Tibetans, many, with numbers of their Tangut subjects, fled to the borders of China.[13] There both were given an asylum by the T'ang (618-907) who settled them in the southern Ordos and the Alashan. From that time on the Tukuhun gradually lost their identity, perhaps they were absorbed by the more numerous Tanguts, but the latter appear more and more frequently, and employed by the imperial government as cavalry, proved invaluable soldiers and faithfully served the dynasty until its fall.

Throughout the succeeding period of The Five Short Dynasties (907-60), they made no overt attempt to assert their independence, but after the rise of the Sung there was a revolt under Li Chi-ch'ien (1001-1003) who established the kingdom of Hsi Hsia.[14] Under this prince and Chao Yüan-hao (1032-

[12] See " Kara Khitai," Barthold, *Encyclopaedia of Islam*, Vol. II, pp. 737-739.

[13] The Tanguts were akin to the Tibetans, but the Tukuhun were of Turko-Mongol stock and had arrived in the Kokonor during the early years of the fourth century when they established a considerable dominion. For their exodus to China; see Kervyn, *L'Empire Chinois et Les Barbares*, p. 27.

[14] Most of what is known about Hsi Hsia has come down to us in Chinese so is largely from the pens of enemies. Their own script was until comparatively recently little known, but lately considerable progress has been made due to the labors of Wylie, Devéria, Chavannes, Bushell, Morrisse, Ivanov, Pelliot and B. Laufer. As

48), the greatest of the Tangut rulers, Hsi Hsia extended its power over present Ning-hsia, the Ordos and all but the most easterly and southerly parts of Kansu. In this last area Kan Chou fell with its Shara Uighur masters in 1028, while Su Chou and the valley of the Shu-lo were taken from the Tibetans in 1036. Northward the Tanguts became masters of the Etsin Gol and adjoining stretches of the Gobi, and on the south controlled the ranges of the Nan-Shan but failed to conquer the Kokonor. Having an advantageous geographical position, and resorting to force or diplomacy as the circumstances demanded, they held their own against all comers until the advent of Chingis Khan.

Dwelling within the boundaries of this state, with its capital at Chung-hsing, were a mixed population of Tanguts, Tibetans, Shara Uighurs and Chinese, the last, numbering nearly 10,000,000, collected in the valley of the Yellow River and in the towns of Kansu.[15] The economic life of Hsi Hsia was divided between agriculture, commerce and pastoralism. Lying as it did athwart the trade route passing west from China into the Tarim basin, i. e., on the eastern stages of the famous silk road, it also drew considerable profits from taxes levied on itinerant caravans.

In the days of Chao Yüan-hao (1032-48) and his immediate successors the Tanguts were frequently at war with the Sung, the Khitans and the Tibetans of the Kokonor and Tsaidam,[16] but after 1165, when the Jurchids were firmly established as the paramount power of eastern Asia, an era of comparative peace set in.

Beyond the desert the nearest neighbors of Hsi Hsia were

for Li Chi-ch'ien, also known as Chao Pao-chi, the year 1001 is the date of his capture of Ling Chou from the Sung, but the Khitans recognized him as early as 990 when he was first a refugee among them. (Cordier, *Histoire Générale de la Chine et ses relations avec les pays étrangers*, Vol. 11, pp. 79-86; Grousset, *L'Empire des Steppes*, p. 185.)

[15] This figure for the Chinese population is from René Grousset's *L'Empire des Steppes*, p. 315.

[16] The Kingdom of the Kokonor and Tsaidam only rose after the fall of the Tibetan empire, which took place about 904 on the murder of Lang dar ma. (See Sir Charles Bell, *Tibet Past and Present*, pp. 30-31.)

the Naimans and Keraits, and with them relations were alternately hostile and friendly.

The Jurchids whose borders bounded those of the Tanguts on the east, had appeared much later on the scene. A people of Tungus extraction from the Hurka and upper Sungari, they had practicd a mixed economy of hunting, agriculture and stock-breeding, and had been more than a little influenced by their civilized Korean neighbors. Up to the opening of the 12th century, they had recognized Khitan suzerainty, but with the appearance of Akuda (1113-23) they revolted, and after vanquishing their overlords, found themselves masters of Manchuria, northern Korea, the country of the Khongirads and Onguds, and the most northerly districts of Shansi and Hopei. There the Jurchid conquest might have stopped. But the Sung, having participated in the final overthrow of the Khitans and having been given the long coveted city of Yen Ching (modern Peking) decided to break with their allies and attempted to drive them from China. The result was disastrous. Not only did the southerners lose everything north of the Yellow River and the Wei, but their capital K'ai-feng, with the emperors Hui Tsung (1101-26) and Ch'in Tsung (1126-27), fell into the hands of the Jurchids.[17] Another sovereign mounted the throne, but despite the temporary reoccupation of the capital and several successes by his generals, the emperor moved the seat of his government to Lin-an—modern Hang Chou—and resigned himself to the loss of the north. In 1141 peace was made. By it the line of the Huai Ho and Ts'in-ling Shan became the boundary between the two powers, a heavy tribute was exacted from the Sung and their emperor obliged to recognize the suzerainty of the conquerors. Twenty years later the Jurchids recommenced the war and made a supreme effort to extinguish the southern empire, but on the lower Yangtse sustained a terrible reverse. Hostilities continued until 1165 when a lasting peace was made and the former tribute was

---

[17] After the first and unsuccessful siege of K'ai-feng by the Jurchids, the emperor Hui Tsung abdicated in favor of his son who ascended the throne as Ch'in Tsung. For the history of the Chin conquest, see De Harlez, *L'Histoire de l'Empire du Kin.*

somewhat reduced. To the Chinese the Jurchid empire was known under its dynastic name of Chin (Gold) by which we shall henceforth call it. In proclaiming himself emperor, Akuda (1113-23) had named his house Aisin Khioro or Aisin Khuren, i. e., the Golden Court, which in Chinese is rendered by the word Chin.

Though they maintained their dominant position in China by means of military colonies composed of Jurchid tribesmen,[18] the newcomers were quick to appreciate Chinese methods of organization and as early as 1126 appointed a Chinese official head of the civil administration set up in their Chinese possessions.[19] Perhaps due to the same influence, they also organized the Ussuri, lower Sungari and Amur into administrative districts, as today there are to be seen the remains of towns and forts abandoned after the Mongol conquest of the 13th century.[20] As first they held their main capital at Hui-ning to the south of the middle Sungari, but in 1153 moved to Yen Ching (Peking) which they greatly enlarged and renamed Chung Tu. This became the principal seat of their government, but in addition they established four subsidiary capitals; Ta Ting or Pei Ching in present Jehol, Liao-yang or Tung Ching to the east of the Liao River, Ta-t'ung or Hsi Ching in northern Shansi and K'ai-feng or Nan Ching on the Yellow River. These five cities were the chief military and civil centers of the Chin empire.

In Manchuria the conquered Khitans[21] were confined to their original habitat on the upper Liao, but like the Onguds in the west and the Mukri in the east served in the imperial

---

[18] See Wittfogel (Dynasties of Conquest), "China," p. 117, *United Nations Series*, also Goodrich, *A Short History of the Chinese People*, p. 165.

[19] This was Han Chi-hsien, a native of Ho-pei; see Li-Chi, *Manchuria in History*, p. 28.

[20] Shirokogorof contends that besides these administrative districts along the Ussuri, Sungari and Amur, others were established as far northwest as the Argun and Shilka; see Shirokogorof, *Social Organization of Northern Tungus*, p. 158.

[21] A relatively small number of Khitans had migrated west with Yeh-lü Ta-shih (1124-43), who recruited the bulk of his troops from Outer Mongolia and the country around Lake Balkash. (See Wittfogel and Feng Chia-sheng, *History of Chinese Society: Liao (907-1125)*, p. 634.)

army. Although vassals, their status was still high, and despite an unsuccessful revolt in 1161-62, they held many positions of trust and importance. With the Onguds they were largely responsible for the northern and western frontier of the empire.

Masters of Inner Mongolia and Manchuria, it was natural that the Chin, like their Khitan predecessors, should wish to see their suzerainty recognized by the nomads of the north. But in this they were only partially successful and their pretensions were often disputed and their authority never extended beyond the eastern half of Outer Mongolia. To attain their ends they alternately resorted to punitive expeditions, intrigue, subsidies and the bestowal of honorary titles. During the days of Akuda (1113-23) and his brother Wukimai (1123-35) both Tatars and Mongols must have acknowledged Chin supremacy, for on the accession of Holoma (1135-49), the Mongol Khan Khabul visited the imperial court. It was this prince, a member of the Borjigin clan or Omuk, who after uniting a number of neighboring clans, took the name of Mongol for his nation or Ulus and so founded the original Mongol state.[22] Evidently the emperor felt that Khabul Khan, or Khabul Khaghan as he is styled by the " Yüan Ch'ao Pi Shih," would become a danger, for having first permitted him to return home, he sent to recall him. Overtaken, Khabul pretended to obey, but on the road escaped. The Chin then sent a representative to live at his camp, but realizing that he was a spy, Khabul had him murdered. Holoma thereupon despatched a powerful army to crush the Mongols. Setting out in 1137, it advanced from Hui-ning, and doubtless marching via the Nonni, penetrated a considerable distance into the enemy country. There a shortage of provisions compelled a retreat and the Mongols pursued and defeated it at Hai-ling— probably the Hailar Gol. Shortly afterwards Khabul died and was succeeded by his cousin Ambakai. Early in the reign of this prince war broke out with the Tatars, whose help Holoma

---

[22] Vladimirtsov says that Khabul took this name for his Ulus in commemoration of a powerful people of that name in ancient times. (Vladimirtsov, *The Life of Chingis Khan*, p. 7.)

had bought to counter the rising Mongol power, and during a truce Ambakai and Okin Barkhak, Khabul's son, were treacherously seized and delivered to the Chin, who put both to a hideous death. As soon as news of this reached the Mongols, they made Okin Barkhak's brother, Kutula, Khan, and began preparations for an invasion. While these were still underway an envoy arrived from an important official in southwestern Manchuria [23] who was in revolt against the Chin. Encouraged and aided by this rebel, Kutula marched south, crossed the Chin border and completely defeated the forces sent against him. He then proceeded to ravage the frontier and, after amassing a great booty, returned north.

There can be little doubt that Kutula's success was largely due to the fact that the majority of the best Chin troops and their ablest general Wu Chu were heavily engaged with the Sung, but after the conclusion of peace, the Chin were able to give their undivided attention to the Mongols. Consequently, Wu Chu was called north and, perhaps in 1143, undertook a second punitive expedition, but though this was more fortunate than its predecessor and met with no disaster, the war dragged on without success to either side. At length, in 1147, on the advice of Wu Chu himself, a treaty was arranged. According to one report this was a humiliating affair for the Chin.[24] By it they were to give up twenty-seven fortified places north of the Kerulen River [25] and to send annually a specified quantity of sheep, oxen, beans and rice. In reality an agreement was probably arrived at whereby in return for military service the Chin promised the Mongols a subsidy of livestock and food.

Apparently the Tatars were not included in the peace, for one next learns that Kutula set out against them to avenge the death of Ambakai and Okin Barkhak. The Chin thus

---

[23] Actually Liaohsi, the region west of the lower reaches of the Liao river.

[24] De Mailla, *Histoire Générale de la Chine*, Vol. IX. The report probably comes from the " T'ung-chien Kang-mu."

[25] T'u Chi, see the *Meng-wu-erh Shih*, says the Hsi-p'ing Ho, also known as the Lu-ch'u Ho, which was another name for the K'e-lu-lien Ho or Kerulen river. The forts in question were perhaps posts along the rampart today known as the Wall of Chingis Khan, which lies between the Kerulen and the Uldja.

achieved by diplomacy what they had failed to do by force of arms. Their two most dangerous neighbors in the north were left at loggerheads, while one of them, the Mongols, had agreed to act as an advanced frontier guard.

Despite their triumphs under Kutula, the Mongols fell into civil war: Kutula and four of his brothers were slain and the Mongol nation declined. Nevertheless they must again have begun hostilities with the Chin, for in 1161 a combined Chin and Tatar army inflicted upon them a crushing defeat near the Bur Nor.[26] This definitely put an end to their power, which was still further wasted by internal quarrels, and struggles with the Tatars. After this victory, Chin suzerainty was not only recognized by the Tatars, become the premier nation of Eastern Mongolia, and by the débris of the Mongol confederacy, but also by the Keraits to the west. Continuing to encourage warfare among these turbulent vassals, the Chin found it unnecessary to make another punitive expedition in the north for over thirty years.

Among the rival Mongol chiefs to emerge after the disaster of 1161, the most outstanding was Yisugei, the son of the Kiyad-Borjigin prince Bartan, only surviving brother of Kutula. Like his father, Yisugei never assumed the title of either Khan or Khaghan, but contented himself with the much humbler appellation of Baatur. While there can be no doubt that at his death he controlled other clans and sub-clans besides his own of Kiyad,[27] it seems equally certain that he was a vassal of the Kerait Khan.[28]

It was to Yisugei that in the year 1167 the future celebrated Chingis Khan was born.[29] Returning home one day to his

---

[26] See the *Chin Shih.*

[27] René Grousset, *L'Empire des Steppes,* believes that his authority was confined to the Kiyad Clan.

[28] Other Mongol clans—The Durbens, Saljiuds and Khatakins—appear to have become subject to the Tatars.

[29] The date of Chingis Khan's birth is variously given; the Moslem authorities favor 1155, the " *Yüan Shih,*" probably following the " *Yüan Sheng Wu Ch'in Cheng Lu,*" the year 1162, but M. Pelliot in a communication to the Asiatic Society, on December 9, 1938, reports that reliable and recently investigated Chinese sources of the year 1340 date the conqueror's birth in 1167. In accepting the year 1167

camp at Deliun-boldak [30] on the right bank of the Onon, he found that his wife Oelun Eke had given birth to a son. Since at the time he had just made a successful raid on the Tatars and captured the chief Temuchin, he followed the old Turko-Mongol custom of naming the newborn after some conspicuous event and gave his son the captive's name. Beside Temuchin, Oelun Eke presented her husband with three other sons, Juchi Khassar, Khachiun Ulchi and Temuge Ochighin and one daughter, Taimulun. By his second wife, Yisugei had two more sons, Belgutai and Bekter.

When Temuchin was nine years old, i. e., during the year 1176, his father betrothed him to Burte, the daughter of the Khongirad chief Dai Sechen, and again in accordance with the Turko-Mongol custom of the day, left him to spend several months with his future father-in-law. But Temuchin's sojourn in the house of Dai Sechen was short. On his way home to the Onon, Yisugei stopped to dine with some Tatars. Resuming his journey he soon realized that he had been poisoned and, hurrying home, despatched a retainer to fetch his son. But Temuchin arrived too late and when he returned Yisugei was dead.

The hand of the strong man removed, the clans (omuk) and sub-clans (yasun) united by Yisugei lost no time in breaking away. Under the leadership of the Taijiud-Borjigin chiefs, sons of Ambakai, the greater part of Yisugei's followers deserted his family. A handful were held together by the heroic Oelun Eke, but even they finally went their way and left the widow and her children to survive as best they could.

Unable to maintain themselves on the open steppes, the deserted family sought refuge in the Burkhan Khaldun, an eastern spur of the present Kentei Khan mountains where the Onon, Kerulen and Tola rivers rise. There they were reduced

---

I have been influenced not only by the apparent preference for the date of so outstanding an authority as Pelliot, but by the fact that it makes it far easier than the earlier dates to account for the remarkable energy displayed by the conqueror in his last days. (See Addendum, René Grousset, *L'Empire des Steppes*, p. 639.)

[30] Deliun-boldak is today in Russian territory and is approximately on the 115° longitude.

to fishing, the hunting of small game and the collecting of garlic, wild onion and other roots. " From the point of view of the pastoral nomad of the steppes such an existence was the most wretched imaginable." [31] But throughout it all Oelun refused to despair and brought up her sons in the belief that they would eventually emerge from their adversity and recover the power that was rightfully theirs. But worse was in store for the refugees. First, a family quarrel broke out and Temuchin and Juchi Khassar murdered their half brother Bekter. Then Temuchin was captured by the Taijiuds and only escaped through the bravery and kindness of a Suldus nobleman and his sons. No sooner had he returned to his camp than some thieves drove off most of his horses, but this time his ill fortune was to bring him some good. Going in search of the stolen animals, he fell in with a young Arulad Mongol named Bugurji. The two boys instantly took a fancy to each other and together recovered the lost horses. From that time on Bugurji remained with Temuchin and lived not only to become one of his most outstanding commanders but his closest friend.

From then on Temuchin's luck gradually improved, and after gaining a few other adherents, he went to the Khongirads in search of his betrothed Burte. True to the pledge made to Yisugei, her father Dai Sechen gave her to the young chief and as a dowry a coat of black sables. His position greatly improved by this marriage, Temuchin now repaired to the Tola, where the Keraits pitched their main camp, and presented himself, with the coat of sables, to his father's old friend Tughrul Khan. Given a hospitable reception and promised protection, Temuchin, like his father, became a vassal of the Kerait. Such were the beginnings of the man whose armies were to shake Asia from the Pacific to the Black Sea.

Tughrul Khan rather undeservedly became a famous personage, especially in mediaeval Europe where, owing to the tales spread by the Christians of the Near East, he was

[31] Vladimirtsov, *The Life of Chingis Khan*, p. 16.

identified with a mythical Nestorian Christian king of great power called Prester John. The legend of Prester John, however, was older than the late 12th and early 13th centuries and first occurs in 1145 when mention of it is made by Bishop Otto von Freisingen. He reported that at Rome the bishop of Djibal in Syria had spoken to him of a John who was priest and king of a Nestorian-Christian people living far in the east beyond Persia and Armenia. For purposes of propaganda the Nestorians would seem to have carried the legend on into the 13th century when the fable attached itself to the Kerait ruler.

Sir Henry Yule says that the story of Prester John arose as a result of the Khara Khitan Yeh-lü Ta-shih's victory over the Saljuk Sultan Sinjar in 1141.[32] The Khara Khitans were mostly Buddhists, but in the West, Buddhists and Nestorians were frequently mistaken for one another. Though Yule omits to mention it, Ta-shih's army must have included many Nestorians.

Far from resembling the great Yeh-lü Ta-shih, Tughrul was a comparatively insignificant person and already his cruelty had nearly cost him his throne. After the death of his father he had succeeded to the chieftainship of the Keraits by murdering two of his uncles and several cousins, but his surviving uncle fled to the Naiman Inanch Bilkha Khan who gave him an army with which to attack Tughrul. The latter was speedily overthrown and was only reinstated by Yisugei, to whom he appealed for help. It was doubtless the memory of this signal service that made Tughrul look so favorably upon his faithful vassal's son.

Temuchin soon had need of his patron's help. Scarcely had he returned home than a band of Mergids made a sudden descent upon him. Temuchin and his brothers escaped, but Burte and the mother of Belgutei fell into their hands. Unable to recover his wife without aid, Temuchin went to Tughrul, who took the field on his behalf, defeated the Mergids on the

[32] Yule, *Cathay and The Way Thither*, Vol. III, pp. 15-22.

Buura, a tributary of the Uda, and restored Burte. A little after, perhaps in 1184 or 1185, Burte bore a son, Juchi, but due to the fact that she had been some time among the Mergids before her rescue, there was always some doubt as to whether or not Juchi was really Temuchin's son.[33] Nevertheless, Burte remained his principal wife and subsequently presented him with three more sons, Jaghatai, Ugedei and Tului.

During the expedition against the Mergids, Temuchin had been brought in touch with another Borjigin chief, Jamukha the Jajirad, who like himself was a vassal of the Kerait Khan. As boys they had been made anda or sworn brothers and now renewed their old relationship. At the same time, on the request of Tughrul, Jamukha sent back certain clansmen who had deserted Temuchin at his father's death. The young Mongol thus became the leader of a sizeable following.

But the friendship of the two chiefs lasted no more than a year and a half. One day while moving to their summer grazing, Jamukha, who was riding ahead with Temuchin, turned to the latter and said, " today if we camp on the hill-slope, those who tend the horses will get tents; if we camp by the stream, those who tend the sheep and lambs will get food." Uncertain what to answer, Temuchin waited for his mother Oelun to ride up and repeated Jamukha's words, but before she could say what she thought his wife Burte interposed: " Of Jamukha, people say that he loves the new and despises the old; now he has had enough of us. Do not his words conceal some hostile intention against us? We must not stop; we must march on through the night, it is better to be parted from him." [34] Feeling that Burte was right, Temuchin went on and the next morning found that he had been followed by men from both the Jalair and Baarin clans who had left Jamukha for him. He thus increased his power but made an

---

[32] Barthold believes that in 1225 Juchi was at least forty years of age, so he must have been born during either 1184 or 1185. (Barthold, *Turkestan down to the Mongol Invasion*, p. 458.)

[34] For this celebrated passage, see Vladimirtsov, *The Life of Chingis Khan*, pp. 23-24.

implacable enemy of Jamukha who was to prove one of the ablest opponents of his early days.

This quarrel is a good example of the rivalry that continuously went on within the great confederacies. Both Temuchin and Jamukha were vassals of the Kerait Khan but this did not prevent various clans and sub-clans from transferring their allegiance from one to the other. Although hereditary prestige played a great part in furthering and upholding the authority of a chief, it was equally important that he prove capable of promoting the fortunes of his followers. Jamukha and Temuchin were both of the same noble lineage, but even then the latter was showing himself the more stable and reliable leader. Until recently in Mongolia the peace imposed by the late Manchu regime (1644-1911) enabled quite mediocre and often very incompetent princes to retain unchallenged authority as rulers, because of their descent from Chingis Khan or one of his brothers. In the days with which we are here dealing this would have been impossible and such chiefs would soon have disappeared from the scene.

On the strength of Jamukha's words concerning those who tend horses and those who tend sheep, and Burte's criticism about his loving the new and despising the old, Vladimirtsov once saw in him a leader of a " democratic " faction opposed to the aristocratic leadership of Temuchin, but later he withdrew this contention. According to Lattimore, Jamukha's words were in the nature of an indirect question, the answer to which would show how Temuchin felt. " Sheep and horses," he points out, " do not necessarily distinguish commoners from nobles; but the choice of pasture, when mixed tribes are travelling with mixed herds, may indicate whether nomads, in such a period as this, are on the warpath or not. Are they to favor sheep, which means their supply of meat and milk, of skins for clothing and wool for making tents, or are they to favor their horses, in preparation for war and raiding? It is apparent that the two chiefs differed in judgment." [35]

Léon Cahun for his part believed that Jamukha was a

---

[35] See Lattimore's review of Grenard's " Gengis Khan," *Pacific Affairs*, 1937.

champion of clan autonomy as opposed to the unification of all in a great state.[36] But it is plain that what we really have is the rivalry of two exceptionally able and ambitious chiefs.

Even before the break with Jamukha, Temuchin had lent a willing ear to those of his own and the Jajirad's followers who forecast for him a great future and saw in him the man who would restore the former power and glory of the Mongols. Hence, it was not strange that when, shortly after his separation from his sworn brother, still more people flocked to him, he agreed to be made Khan. Among those who chose him for this position were some with a better claim than himself, notably Altan Ochigin, the son of the famous Kutula Khan. After some hesitation he accepted. In the words of the "Yüan Ch'ao Pi Shih," "Altan, Kuchar (the son of Yisugei's elder brother) and Sacha Biki (chief of the Jurkin clan), announced to Temuchin: 'We have decided to proclaim thee Khaghan— (probably only Khan). When you are Khaghan we shall be in the front in every battle against your foes and if we capture beautiful girls and women we will give them to you. We will start earliest for the chase and the animals we catch we will give to you. If in battle we disobey your commands, or if in time of peace we do any injury to your interests, then you will take from us our wives and chattels and leave us to our fate in the empty wilderness.' Having taken this oath, they proclaimed Temuchin Khaghan and gave him the name of Chingis." [37] In reply to the assembled aristocracy and warriors around him, the new Khan said: "You, that are assembled here, you parted with Jamukha and decided to join me. If the Sky (Heaven) preserves me and helps me, all of you, my old friends, will ultimately become my happy companions." [38]

Temuchin, though belonging to a junior branch of the Bor-

[36] See Léon Cahun, *Introduction à l'histoire de l'Asie, Turcs et Mongols des Origines à 1405.*

[37] It is unlikely that Temuchin assumed the title of Chingis until later, and Pelliot, see "Notes sur le Turkestan," *T'ung-pao*, 1930, believes it is doubtful if he ever took the appellation of Khaghan which was borne by his successors. At the time of his election the title either of Khaghan or Chingis would have been an affront to his overlord Tughrul Khan of the Keraits.

[38] See Vladimirtsov, *The Life of Chingis Khan*, p. 39.

jigin clan, had been elected with the full consent of the older and nobler members of the family and, come what might, would have customary law and right on his side in punishing any breach of obedience or loyalty on their part if they should regret their choice and rebel.

Among those who assisted at his election was a man of less exalted stock than some, but destined to make a far greater mark in the world than any one present save Temuchin. This was Mukhali the Jalair who at the time—perhaps about 1190— was some twenty-one years of age. One hears too that the later celebrated Uriangkut Subudei was also present, but if the history of the Yüan dynasty is correct in dating his birth in 1176, this seems a little early.

When Tughrul learned of the election he said: " It is very good that Chingis (Temuchin) should have been made Khaghan; for how indeed could you Mongols do without a Khaghan. So mind that you do not undo what you have done by common consent." [39]

But if the Kerait Khan was a short sighted statesman, Jamukha was not. Though he remained outwardly calm he bided his time. Before long, taking advantage of a border incident, he attacked Temuchin. Perhaps he was supported by the Taijiuds, but at all events he defeated the new Khan at Dalan Baljiut near the sources of the Onon and made prisoner several nobles whom he had the barbarity to boil alive.[40] Far from furthering his cause, this cruelty had the opposite effect, and while Temuchin's reverse forced him to retreat down the Onon, he was there joined by still more of

[39] See Vladimirtsov, *The Life of Chingis Khan*, p. 39.

[40] For the location of Dalan Baljiut; see Grousset, *Le Conquérant du Monde*, p. 111.

The *Yuan Ch'ao Pi Shih*, Rashid ad-Din and the *Yüan Sheng Wu Ch'in Cheng Lu* all three include the Taijiuds in Jamukha's army, but whereas the first reports a reverse for Temuchin, the two latter give us a victory. This is to be explained by the fact that Rashid ad-Din's history and the *Yüan Sheng Wu Ch'in Cheng Lu* were written at the order of the Mongol conqueror's descendants who wished to conceal any humiliation suffered by their famous ancestor. (See Grousset, " L'Empire Mongol " (1re phase), *Histoire du Monde*, Tome VIII, pp. 566-567.)

The date of this engagement is unknown, but it could have occurred any time between 1190 and 1194.

Jamukha's followers. The most important of these were the Uruds,[41] Manguds, and Khongkhotats, the last coming over under Munglik, an old retainer of his father, to whom he now married his mother Oelun. He also allied himself with the chief of the Khorolas who was given his sister Taimulun. Despite his defeat at the hands of Jamukha, his power had become equal to if not greater than that of either his sworn brother or the Taijiuds.

He was soon, however, to see a further and quite unexpected development in his fortunes. During 1194, if Rashid ad-Din is correct, Tughrul was deposed and driven from his throne by his brother Erke Khara who called in the Naimans. Flying to the west via Hsi Hsia, Tughrul made for the court of the Gur Khan Yeh-lü Chiluku (1178-1211), grandson of the great Yeh-lü Ta-shih, and begged for help.[42] But, supposedly not wishing to become involved in a war with the Naimans, the Khara Khitan turned a deaf ear to the refugee's plea for succor.

For several months Tughrul led the life of a vagrant and not until 1196 did he return to the east, from where the Naimans had withdrawn, and appealed to his former vassal Temuchin. Though their positions were completely reversed, the Mongol Khan, as his father Yisugei before him, received Tughrul with every mark of respect and shortly restored him to power. Further, he sent an escort to bring back his brother Djagambo who had sought an asylum in the Chin empire.[43]

[41] The Uruds were one of the most powerful clans of the Mongol group and, according to the *Yüan Ch'ao Pi Shih*, their troops numbered 4,000.

[42] The date of Tughrul's flight—1194-95—is from Rashid ad-Din. The same authority is responsible for the dating of the events here recorded for 1196, 1197 and 1198. Lest it may be thought I have relied solely on the Persian in so debatable a matter, I should add that Wang Kuo-wei, one of the greatest Chinese experts on Mongol history, is in agreement with Rashid ad-Din—see his commentary to the *Yüan Sheng Wu Ch'in Cheng Lu* for this period as quoted by Wittfogel, *History of Chinese Society: Liao*, p. 648, n. 21.
After 1198 we reach firmer chronological ground since Rashid ad-Din is in close agreement with the *Yüan Shih*. For the whole subject; see Grousset, " L'Empire Mongol " (1re phase), *Histoire Du Monde*, Tome VIII, pp. 84-87, 97-98.

[43] Djagambo or Gambo is a Tibetan title denoting considerable position and authority and had been bestowed upon the Kerait prince by the Tanguts, whom he had formerly served for a number of years when captured by them during a raid. Grousset, " L'Empire Mongol " (1re phase), *Histoire Du Monde*, Tome VIII, pp. 86-87, also p. 440.

By this demonstration of loyalty, Temuchin was able not only to pose as the trusty vassal who refused to forget his vows of fealty, but by reinstating so important a personage as Tughrul, also greatly to enhance his own power and prestige among the people of the steppes who would be more inclined than ever to see in him a strong and promising leader.

The next year (1197) he had yet another opportunity of showing himself. Thinking that the recently restored Kerait Khan would still be weak, Tukta Biki,[44] chief of the Mergid confederacy, decided to make a descent upon Tughrul. But in the valley of the Mandja or Manza, an affluvent of the Chikoi, he was unexpectedly attacked and defeated by the ever alert Temuchin. Not content with this, the Mongol Khan sent his overlord all the booty taken from the enemy. The following year (1198) Tughrul, now much strengthened, undertook an expedition on his own against Tukta Biki. This was a complete success, the Mergids were severely defeated, one of Tukta's sons was slain, two others captured and the chief and his people obliged to flee and seek refuge in the country of Barkuchin to the east of Lake Baikal. But of all the prisoners, livestock and loot seized, Tughrul gave nothing to Temuchin. Such behavior could not fail to exhibit him in a most unfavorable light, but before long he was to commit a graver blunder in the perpetration of an outstanding piece of treachery.

In the meantime important events were developing elsewhere. To the east the Tatars had become restive and were giving trouble to the Chin. Therefore in the year 1198 the reigning emperor Madaku (1190-1208) [45] sent north an army under Wan-yen Hsiang. Setting forth, the general called upon the Kerait Khan to help. Seeing an opportunity to strike a blow at a dangerous and warlike neighbor, Tughrul gladly marched

---

[44] Biki was the title borne by a shaman who was also the secular leader of a clan or tribe and was most commonly encountered, as with the Mergids and Oirads, among those of the steppe people bordering the forest country to the north where it was in frequent use. Tukta Biki belonged to the Uduyit clan of the Mergids.

[45] To the Chinese the emperor Madaku was known under his reign title of Ming Ch'ang.

east and with him Temuchin, who was no less delighted to be able to attack the traditional enemies of his house. Reaching the Uldja, which flows between the Onon and Kerulen, they learned that the Tatars had already suffered a reverse at the hands of the Chin who were pursuing them to the river. Dividing their forces, Tughrul and Temuchin now advanced down both banks of the Uldja, and coming up with the already weakened Tatars, inflicted upon them a crushing defeat in which their chief was slain and a great number of his people captured.[46] The Tatars thus sustained a disaster comparable to that which they had helped inflict upon the Mongols in 1161.

Grateful for their signal service, the general conferred upon Tughrul the appellation of Wang, which was henceforth joined to his title of Khan, and upon Temuchin that of Jaukhuri (Military Commander of the Frontier).[47] The acceptance of these titles by Tughrul and his vassal makes it quite clear that both recognized the overlordship of the Chin whose authority in the north was then at its apogee.

Before setting out on this expedition, Temuchin had summoned the Jurkins to join him, but their chiefs Sacha Biki and Taichu, the former prominent at Temuchin's election, refused to go. Both were finding that the new Khan intended to be ruler in fact as well as in name and were planning to secede. But they acted too late, and no sooner had Temuchin returned from the Uldja, than he fell upon the Jurkins and seized and executed the recalcitrant chiefs.

It was a little time after this that the Naiman Khan, Inanch Bilkha died. Under him the Naimans had been the most

---

[46] The name of the Tatar chief, a prince of considerable power, was Megujin Seultu; see Grousset, *L'Empire des Steppes*, p. 259.

D'Ohsson dates this expedition in 1194 but does not give his authority. On the other hand Grousset draws attention to the fact that the *Yüan Shih* informs us that it was the two Jurkin chiefs Taichu and Sacha Biki, killed by Temuchin after the Tatar war, who conducted Djagambo back from Chin territory. That happened in 1196, and since 1197 and 1198 saw two expeditions against the Mergids, it seems unlikely that the struggle with the Tatars could have taken place earlier than 1198, by which time Tughrul's power had been completely restored. See Grousset, " L'Empire Mongol " (1ʳᵉ phase), *Histoire Du Monde*, Tome VIII, pp. 86-87.

[47] See Grousset, *Le Conquérant du Monde*, p. 120; also Vladimirtsov, *The Life of Chingis Khan*, p. 42.

powerful nation on the steppes, but with his death civil war
broke out between his two sons, Bai Bukha and Buyuruk,
who divided the kingdom between them.[48] The former, known
as the T'ai-yang or Ta Wang, ruled the northern half, and so
held the anicent Uighur and Kirghiz capital of Khara Balghasun, while the other controlled the Altai and river valleys
of the Khara Irtish and Urungu. Since Bai Bukha bore the
Chinese title of T'ai-yang, it is evident that the Chin, even
if they exercised no authority so far west, regarded him as
the premier nomad ruler of the north.

   According to the historian Rashid ad-Din, the quarrel
between the two princes arose over one of their father's con-
cubines and was still in progress in 1199.[49] Resolved to take
advantage of the situation, Tughrul, Temuchin and Jamukha,
the last still Temuchin's enemy but nevertheless the vassal
of the Kerait, marched against Buyuruk. Attacked on the
lower Khobdo before he was able to assemble all his troops,
the Naiman ruler fell back over the Altai, perhaps via the
Ulan Pass and retreated down the Urungu River to Lake
Kizil Bash (present Lake Ulungur). There he was severely
defeated,[50] but escaping from the field, made for the basin of
the Yenisei and sought refuge among the Kem-kemjiuts,
vassals of the Kirghiz dwelling on the present Kemchik River.
Triumphant, the victors recrossed the Altai and pitched camp
in the vicinity of Bayidarah Belchir near the Baidarik River
which flows south from the Khangai Mountains. In the meantime Bai Bukha, the enemy of Buyuruk but alarmed at this turn
of events, mustered his forces which came down on the allies
under Koksu Sabrak, his general-in-chief.[51] Battle was joined

   [48] Buyuruk is a title, not a name, and means simply Commander. (Rashid ad-
Din; see D'Ohsson, *Histoire des Mongols*, Vol. I, p. 57.)
   [49] Rashid ad-Din, D'Ohsson, *Histoire des Mongols*, p. 57. Perhaps the concubine
in question was Gurbésu who is sometimes referred to as the favorite wife of Bai
Bukha, but at others as his mother.
   [50] For the identification of the localities mentioned; see Grousset, *Le Conquérant
du Monde*, p. 126.
   [51] In this instance the *Yüan Ch'ao Pi Shih* speaks of Koksu Sabrak as the
general-in-chief of Buyuruk's army, but subsequent references to him make it
nearly certain that he was the commander of Bai Bukha's forces. Hence, I have

and a fierce encounter took place, but before victory was declared for either side, darkness put an end to the conflict. It was then that Jamukha struck. Realizing that here was an unrivalled opportunity for destroying Temuchin, and having taken stock of the weak and vacillating character of Tughrul, he persuaded him that Temuchin was preparing to join the enemy. Alarmed by Jamukha's words, and already jealous of his talented lieutenant, the Kerait Khan left his camp fires burning and beat a hasty retreat. When dawn broke, Temuchin immediately saw what had happened and instantly retired before the Naimans had a chance to renew the engagement. Conducting his withdrawal with consummate skill, he crossed the Khangai, and going by way of the Sari, probably the present Khodasin River, marched unmolested toward his own grazing lands.

It fared otheriwse with the Keraits. Seeing both his opponents in retreat, Koksu Sabrak decided to pursue the Wang Khan. Pressing after the Kerait army, he came up with it in a defile in the Khangai, and there trapped and crushed the rearguard under Djagambo and the heir apparent Ilkha (Nilkha), better known as the Sangun.[52] Thrusting forward, he next fell upon the main army and drove it before him in such tumultuous rout that not only did the Keraits lose all their baggage but the two lately captured sons of Tukta Biki escaped. Notwithstanding these disasters, Ilkha, who was a spirited and courageous soldier, begged his father for command of all the troops that he could gather together to try to hold up the Naiman advance. Tughrul for his part besought his recently betrayed ally for help. Appreciating the danger to himself as well as to the Wang-Khan, Temuchin lost no time in detaching a force under his four best commanders, Bugurji, Mukhali,

---

here treated him as the T'ai-yang's general and assumed that the battle of Bayidarah Belchir was fought against the army of Bai Bukha and not that of Buyuruk.

[52] Sangun is a title, not a name, and is probably a corruption of the Chinese appellation Chiang-Chün, meaning a general. (See Pelliot, " Notes sur Le Turkestan," T'ung Pao, 1930.) Barthold calls Ilkha, Ilakha. (See Turkestan down to the Mongol Invasion, p. 362, n. 4.)

Jelmei [53] and Chilaun.[54] These came up with the Naimans just as they had a second time defeated Ilkha, and taking advantage of the confusion of the pursuit, fell upon the victors, who, taken by surprise, were in their turn defeated and obliged to relinquish all their plunder.

Overcome with shame and gratitude, Tughrul generously rewarded the four Mongol generals and publicly entered into a pact with Temuchin that made clear to all that he regarded the Borjigin as the mainstay of his power.

The losses suffered by the Naimans must have been considerable, for immediately afterward another expedition was made against them and Juchi Khassar, who was in command of the army, won a decisive victory.

While these events were taking place, the lately vanquished Tukta Biki had been in touch with the Taijiuds whom he persuaded to join him in an attack on Temuchin. Accordingly, a combined Mergid and Taijiud army took the field, but early the next year, in 1200, sustained a terrible reverse at the hands of the Wang Khan and their intended victim.

Several tribes now became thoroughly alarmed and decided to enter into a coalition to crush the Kerait Khan and his formidable vassal. These were the Taijiuds, Khatakins, Saljiuds, Durbens and Khongirads. However, although a solemn oath to secrecy was sworn, their plans were betrayed to Temuchin by Dai Sechen, his father-in-law. Warned in time, Temuchin did not wait for Tughrul, but assembling his forces near the Onon immediately began hostilities. Before the allies could unite, he attacked and crushed the Taijiuds and Durbens on the Bur Nor and then the Khatakins, Saljiuds and Khon-

[53] The name given in most texts is Borokul, but as he was then only a boy, it is likely that his name has slipped in instead of that of Jelmei, who had joined Temuchin soon after Burgurji and was one of his most trusted officers.

[54] All the records dealing with this event imply that when Tughrul's cry for help reached Temuchin, the latter was already in home territory, but this is unlikely. Even had he been no further east than the extreme upper reaches of the Kerulen, he would have been approximately 450 miles from the site of his betrayal. Hence, the end of the forced march back to rescue Tughrul would have found the Mongol cavalry in poor shape to oppose the relatively fresh Naimans. Personally, I believe that when Temuchin sent out his four generals he was no great distance from the Sari.

girads on the Kulun Nor.[55] Discouraged by this disaster, the Khongirads decided to go over to Temuchin, but on their way were attacked by Juchi Khassar who was unaware of their intention. Therefore, surprised and enraged, they instead joined Jamukha who had withdrawn from the Wang Khan and was making plans to form a coalition of his own.

Before the end of the year the never very popular Tughrul became the object of a third attempt to dispossess him of his throne. This time it was a plot headed by Djagambo, but the conspiracy was discovered, and while the principal culprits escaped to the Naiman Bai Bukha, all their property was confiscated. Djagambo, however, seems soon to have been restored to favor.

By 1201 the indefatigable Jamukha had grouped around himself and his own clan of Jajirad, the Taijiuds, Khongirads, Ikiras, Khorolas,[56] Durbens, Khatakins and Saljiuds. Indeed, so great was his success that he also persuaded the Tatars, Mergids, Oirads and Naimans to send contingents. At the junction of the Kan and the Argun this concourse proclaimed Jamukha Gur Khan (Universal Lord). Hence, both as leader of the coalition he had formed and as bearer of this title he challenged equally his sworn brother and the Wang Khan. In actual practice the only properly accepted holder of this title was the ruler of Khara Khitai and on this occasion it is unlikely that Gur Khan indicated anything more than military command of the assembled forces. One may be sure, nevertheless, that had Jamukha been victorious in this his supreme effort he would have assumed the title in earnest. But fortune now deserted him. As had happened with the first league, the plans of the confederate chiefs for a surprise attack were betrayed to Temuchin. This time the enemy were far too numerous for him to deal with single handed and he sent to Tughrul for aid. Together they advanced down the Kerulen

---

[55] In some accounts of this campaign it would appear that Tughrul also participated, but in his famous message to the Wang Khan after their break in 1203, Temuchin speaks as if he had been alone.

[56] Several years before, Temuchin had married his sister Taimulun to Podu the chief of the Khorolas.

and suddenly appeared before Jamukha at Koyitan between
the Bur Nor and Kulun Nor.[57] Taken by surprise, the Jajirad
leader called upon two shamans with him to raise a storm in
the faces of the enemy while he prepared for battle. The
storm rose, but instead of blowing in the direction intended,
turned against the confederates—a sure sign of Heaven's dis-
pleasure—and helped Temuchin and the Wang Khan win a
complete victory.

The army of the coalition scattered, the Tatar, Naiman,
Mergid and Oirad troops returned home; and while Tughrul
went after Jamukha, Temuchin pursued the Taijiuds. After
many minor encounters along the Onon, the latter were at
length brought to battle, but fought so furiously that Temuchin
himself was severely wounded and barely escaped defeat. Dis-
union in the Taijiud ranks however undid them and, relent-
lessly pursued by Temuchin, they were eventually forced to
submit. Among those who now made peace was a twenty-one
year old warrior, Jirkhoadai of the Besut clan, who under
the name of Jebe was to become one of the greatest captains
in Mongol history. The submission of the Taijiuds was soon
followed by that of the Khongirads who were to make a similar
contribution in the shape of two other outstanding soldiers,
Tokuchar and Anchar Noyan. Had it been up to Dai Sechen,
the Khongirads would almost certainly have come over to
Temuchin earlier, but, as in many clans of that turbulent day,
the chief's power was by no means absolute and a majority
among the aristocracy had evidently forced the old man to
join the coalitions formed against his son-in-law.

Though still the vassal of the Kerait Khan, Temuchin had
become incontestably the most powerful of the rival Mongol
princes and felt that the day had come when he could deal
with the Tatars. Since their overthrow in 1198, this once
powerful people had much declined, and though still num-

---

[57] D'Ohsson, Vol. I, p. 63, says that the battle was fought at a place called Edi
Khurgan, the Yüan Ch'ao Pi Shih at Koyitan, but both names may very well apply
to the same area. For the location of Koyitan; see Grousset, Le Conquérant du
Monde, p. 123.

bering four large clans [58]—the Alukhai, Dutaut, Alchi and Chaghan—enjoyed no more than a shadow of their former power. It was this that made Temuchin so early in his career dare to move against them on his own. Assembling his forces in the spring of 1202, he marched east and at Dalan Nemurges near the mouth of the Khalkha Gol forced a decisive battle.[59] On the eve of this he gave the following order of the day to his officers. " If we are victorious, you shall not seek for booty; when all is over it will be divided into equal shares. If the soldiers are forced to fall back to the initial position, they shall advance again and fight with increased vigor. He who, having retreated, does not resume the advance, will be beheaded." [60] The battle began and the Tatars were utterly defeated, and, pursued south to the Ulkhui Shilugeljit Gol, which rises in the Khinghan, the majority were made prisoners.[61] But at the outset of the engagement, Altan, Kuchar and Daaritai, the last Temuchin's paternal uncle, flagrantly disobeyed orders and began plundering the enemy. No sooner was Temuchin informed of this than, the victory complete, he took from them all their spoil. He thereby incurred their secret hostility, but showed to all that, no matter how noble the offender, he intended to be obeyed.

After the fighting was over he took council with his relatives and on their advice ordered the massacre of every male Tatar captive higher than the hub of a wheel, but the women and young children he distributed among his subjects. Among those who fell to his particular lot were two Tatar women, Yesui and Yesugan, who became his wives and of whom we shall hear more later.

This campaign is of special interest. First, it provides our earliest example of the establishment and enforcement of that

[58] These were doubtless all Omuk or main clans to whom were subordinate various sub-clans or yasun.

[59] For the location of Dalan Nemorges; see Grousset, Le Conquérant du Monde, p. 143.

[60] See Vladimirtsov, The Life of Chingis Khan, p. 45.

[61] In some reports only the Alchi and Chaghan Tatars are mentioned in this overthrow, but in view of Temuchin's unmolested withdrawal into Tatar country the following year (1203), it seems certain that all four tribes must have been involved.

discipline in the Mongol army that played so large a part in making of it the greatest fighting force of its day. Second, it shows us that while Temuchin was prepared to destroy his enemies ruthlessly when he judged it expedient, at the same time he limited such treatment to those he considered immediately dangerous. Hence he slaughtered all the adult males of the vanquished, but spared the children who could later serve him as soldiers.

Certain writers, drawing on the " Sanang Setsen," believe that the Mongol Khan next crossed the Khinghan into the valley of the Nonni, and having offered the Solangs (Solons) the choice of war or peace, received the submission of their chief and one of his daughters in marriage. But it is unlikely that Temuchin would have had the temerity to tamper with the Manchurian vassals of the Chin while himself still no more than one of a number of rival contestants struggling beyond their northern border. In reality the expedition in question is almost certainly to be identified with the campaign undertaken by Juchi Khassar to the east of the Khinghan during the winter of 1214-15.

Notwithstanding his triumph over the Tatars, Temuchin shortly found himself the object of another attack by Tukta Biki who came down from Barkuchin, to which he had a second time fled in 1200. Perhaps the Mergid believed that the Mongol Khan's expedition to the east had exhausted his cavalry. If so he was disappointed for he was again defeated. But undaunted he returned to the attack, and joining forces with the Oirads, Khatakins, Saljiuds, Durbens and the débris of the Tatars, who together had formed a third coalition under the leadership of Buyuruk the Naiman, once more took the field.[62] This time the confederate array was very strong. Buyuruk, bent on revenge for the disasters of 1199, was certainly in considerable strength. Therefore, Tughrul and

[62] The *Yüan Sheng Wu Ch'in Cheng Lu* and Rashid ad-Din both include the Taijiuds among the confederates, but though there may have been a handful of them present, the majority were certainly following Temuchin, otherwise he would scarcely have been strong enough to have gone against the Tatars during the spring of 1202.

Temuchin, attacked while part of the Kerait troops were absent under Ilkha, thought it prudent to avoid an encounter until the prince could join them. Retreating east, they made for the Khongirad country, and there, despite the efforts of the enemy, Ilkha soon arrived. The early winter was then passed in marches and counter marches amid tempests of snow and wind which finally so weakened the confederates that they abandoned the campaign. During the enemy withdrawal, the Khatakins and Saljiuds had the ill fortune to fall in with Jamukha who, though a member of the league, had only then come up. Seeing how things stood, he fell upon the two clans, plundered them, and informing the Wang Khan of what he had done, won his way back into his good graces.

The enemy host dissolved, the victors took up their quarters for the remainder of the winter in the district of Achia Kungur, which was also in the land of the Khongirads.[63] While there Temuchin, anxious to strengthen his ties with his suzerain, sought the hand of a Kerait princess for his son Juchi, offering at the same time a daughter of his own for one of Tughrul's grandsons. But the Wang Khan rejected the proposal, and in the words of the " Yüan Ch'ao Pi Shih," " chilled the heart of Temuchin." Taking advantage of this estrangement, Jamukha, who had already turned Ilkha against Temuchin, succeeded with him in persuading the old Khan that the Mongol was plotting with the Naimans. At the same time he also came to an understanding with Altan, Kuchar and Daaritai, who were only awaiting their chance to revenge themselves on Temuchin for their humiliation of the previous year. Hence early in 1203, after the allies had returned home, they openly seceded and joined the ranks of his enemies. This defection was a serious blow, for being of the noblest

---

[63] This is the location given by Rashid ad-Din. It is worth mentioning, that while this campaign is referred to by the Persian, the *Yüan Sheng Wu Ch'in Cheng Lu* and the *Yüan Shih*, nothing specific is said about it by the *Yüan Ch'ao Pi Shih* which seems to confuse the event with Jamukha's overthrow at Koyitan in 1201. (For some interesting notices on the subject; see Grousset, " L'Empire Mongol " (1^re phase), *Histoire du Monde*, Tome VIII, pp. 110-113.

lineage among the Mongols, their following was considerable and left Temuchin much weakened.

Despite the numerical superiority of the Kerait army, now further strengthened by the deserters, Tughrul knew too well how formidable a soldier was his vassal to resort to arms if treachery would succeed instead. So he sent a message to Temuchin expressing his willingness to accede to the recently rejected marriage proposals and invited him to come in person to make the necessary arrangements. But warned in time that the Kerait ruler really intended to kill him, Temuchin excused himself. Their designs discovered, Ilkha and his father decided to make a sudden attack on the Mongol camp, but once more their would-be victim was warned and beat a hasty retreat. The rupture between the Wang Khan and his vassal was thus complete but, though the desertion of his kinsmen brought Temuchin's fortunes to a low ebb, it was to prove the turning point in his career. Henceforth he would play his own hand and go steadily forward to the unification of all the nomads of the north.

With Jelmei and a mobile rear-guard at his back to observe the advancing Keraits, Temuchin hurried to Khalakhaldjit Elet (Khaladjin Alt), a spur in the Khinghan Mountains near the sources of the Khalkha Gol,[64] and prepared to meet the enemy. A few days later a bitter engagement was fought, but despite the bravery of the Mangud and Urud chiefs Kuildar and Jurchedei on Temuchin's side, and of Ilkha on the other, darkness put an end to an indecisive battle.[65] As Tughrul's force was three times that of his own, Temuchin withdrew in the night and fortunately was not pursued. This was to prove an irreparable blunder on the part of the Keraits, but the old Khan, shaken by the battle and grieving over his son Ilkha, who had been severely wounded in the face by an arrow, could think only of returning home. Temuchin went south to the upper reaches of the Ulkhui Shilugeljit Gol and there

[64] For the location of Khalakhaldjit Elet or Khaladjin Alt; René Grousset, L'Empire des Steppes, p. 226.

[65] Both Jurchedei and Kuildar had formerly been followers of Jamukha whom they had left for Temuchin with their clans.

took refuge in the forests of the Khinghan. But soon afterward he returned north and made his way down the Khalkha
Gol. Provisioning his army by game killed in the course of
great battues, he followed the river to its entrance into the
Bur Nor.[66] There, after desertions on the retreat had reduced
his troops to 4,600 men, he was joined by the Khongirads.
He then continued north to the Kulun Nor where he pitched
camp.

Hoping for a possible reconciliation with the Wang Khan,
or at least to gain time in which to improve his prospects,
he sent the following message to Tughrul. " Today I am
camped on the Tunggé— (a small river flowing into the Kulun
Nor) —where the good grazing makes strong my horses. Oh
Khan my Lord, have you forgotten the days when, driven
from your throne, my father came to your help, overthrew
the usurper and swore to be your brother? It is not for that
that I call you father? This is the first of my claims upon
you."

" Again, Oh Khan my father, was it not at my call that
your brother returned from his flight into distant lands? Did
I not save him from the ambuscades of the Mergids and
sacrifice for you two of my most dearly beloved relatives,
Taichu the younger and Sacha Biki the elder? This is my
second claim upon you."

" Again, Oh Khan my father, you came before me as a
smouldering fire and as the sun behind the clouds; I gave
you food and clothed you with garments. If any one dis-
believes the truth of my words, tell him that at Murutchèsèul,
the Mountain covered with birches, I took from the enemy
(Mergids) their herds, their tents—even their clothing—and
all of it gave to you as a gift.[67] When I saw you exhausted,
haggard and faint, I did not allow you to suffer hunger one

[66] See Howorth, " The Kireis and Prester John," *Journal of The Royal Asiatic
Society*, 1889; also Grousset, *Le Conquérant du Monde*, p. 163.

[67] Murutchèsèul was in the valley of the Manza or Mandja, an affluent of the
Chikoi, where in 1197 Temuchin had frustrated a Mergid attack on Tughrul; see
D'Ohsson, Vol. I, p. 55, and Grousset, *Le Conquérant du Monde*, p. 117.

day. I have not left you destitute a single month. This is the third of my claims."

"When I sent my spies among the Mergids, you took the opportunity to go against them without waiting for me, you captured from their chief his children, his wives, and made prisoner a whole clan without giving me a soul. Nevertheless later when the Naimans surprised you so that you lost your people and your goods and fled, I sent to you my four heroes, Bugurji, Chilaun, Borokul and Mukhali; they restored to you your possessions without recompense. That is my fourth claim." [68]

"Again, like a gerfalcon, I crossed the Bur Nor and took for you the cranes with the azure feet, who are the Durbens and Taijiuds, from there, passing as a falcon to the Kulun Nor, I took for you the blue cranes with the blue feet, who are the Khatakins, Khongirads and Saljiuds. Among the claims I have upon you, this is the fifth."

"Also, have we not made a pact to protect ourselves against calumny? When a venemous serpent would distill envy and suspicion in us, we ought to consult together and dispel all error, to believe nothing in advance and to keep our hearts unchanged. But, when a false statement was made against me, you believed it, you allowed it to undermine your faith. Without searching after the truth, you upheld yourself on it in order to separate from your faithful son."

"Finally, Oh Khan my father, I have right on my side. What have I derived from my numerous services? What have I done to frighten you? Why are you unable to remain calm and without fear? Let your sons and daughters-in-law sleep content in the peace of their hearts. I, your son, have I complained that I have been ill treated? That my lot was hard; that I wished a better? When one of the wheels of a wagon is broken, it is unable to advance and if the ox pulls beyond its strength, it galls its neck and its efforts are in vain. If one unyokes it and leaves the cart alone in the road, brigands on

[68] As remarked earlier, I believe one should read Jelmei instead of Borokul as the latter was still very young.

the watch come and take all, and if the ox is left yoked it will die of hunger. This cart, my father, resembles us. We are the two wheels which can only turn together."

Simultaneously, he sent a message to his treacherous relatives, whom he addressed in these words. " You conspire after my death. However, from the first day, I said to the descendants of Bartan Baatur, why is it that the sacred country of our ancestors is always without a lord or master? To you Kuchar, I said: son of Taiji, be Khan. You refused. I said to you Altan, son of Kutula Khan, who was once our chief, be in your turn as your father our Khan. You were unwilling and I was greatly afflicted. At your instigation, I ascended the throne. You declared, it is you who will be Khan. I consented and said: I will not leave our country to dwindle away. I will guard intact its laws and usages. Of your own free will you elected me in order to prevent outsiders from taking the sacred mountain where the three rivers rise. As chief of a numerous people and commander of the army, I have given to all the accustomed gifts. I have captured great herds, women, youth, tents without number, and have made presents of everything. I have driven toward you the game of the mountains, I have beaten up the game of the plains. Now you follow my father the Khan; doubtless you know that he is broken and unstable. One pities me now. Wait until next winter and be not surprised if then people pity you! " [69]

The bearer of these messages was also charged with words for Ilkha and Jamukha. Left to himself, the Wang Khan would, it seems, have made peace, but Ilkha who knew well that reconciliation was impossible, declared for war. " When Temuchin," he said, " spoke of my father as Khan he called him ' old murderer ' while he did so, and when he called me his sworn friend he jeered at me touching the Mergids, and said that I had come into the world to handle ram's tails and remnants. I know the hidden sense of his speeches; I

[69] This message and that to Tughrul have been taken from Grenard's *Gengis Khan*, which seems to me to give the most coherent version of both any where available. I have, however, altered the spelling of several names of tribes and places to make them correspond with those already used in the text.

know what his plans are. Battle is my first and last answer to Temuchin. Bilkha Biki and Todoyan raise you the great standard; feed our steeds carefully."

This response made it plain to Temuchin that peace was out of the question. His position still very precarious, he therefore retired north to Lake Baljuna at the source of the River Tura or Turga, which is just east of the final reaches of the Onon before it joins the Ingoda, and there passed the summer.[70] But the tide began to turn and his following once more to increase. Many of those who now came to him were from the Kerait camp where Tughrul had again narrowly escaped assassination. Fearing that the old Khan's vacillation would undo them, Jamukha, Altan, Kuchar and Daaritai formed a plot to kill him. As previously the conspiracy was discovered, but as on the former occasion, the would-be murderers escaped, Jamukha, Altan and Kuchar to Bai Bukha, and Daaritai to Temuchin.

Despite his uncle's previous treachery, Temuchin was constrained to pardon him. During the autumn Juchi Khassar also came in. Not present at Khalakhaldjit Elet, he had been captured soon after the battle. He now arrived a fugitive, his family in the hands of Tughrul. Seeing an opportunity of putting this to advantage, Temuchin in his turn resorted to treachery. Sending to the Wang Khan a message purporting to be from Juchi Khassar, he deceived the old Kerait into despatching two men to conduct his brother to his camp. No sooner had these arrived than they were compelled to tell all that they knew. Learning that the Keraits were feasting and quite unprepared, Temuchin, who had already moved into the valley of the Kerulen, made a forced march up the river and fell upon the enemy at Jedjer Undur,[71] between its head-waters and those of the Tola. Although taken by surprise, the Keraits fought with desperate fury and not until after three days did they surrender. Even so a few escaped. Among these were

[70] According to some authorities, Lake Baljuna is located between the north bank of the Argun and the Tarei Nor into which flows the Uldja.
[71] The Che-Che Yun-tu of the *Yüan Shih*.

the Wang Khan and his son Ilkha. Both made for the Naiman border, but on the Nekun Usu Tughrul was slain by Khorisu Bechi, one of the T'ai-Yang's officers, who did not recognize him. His head was taken to Bai Bukha who is said to have bitterly regretted his death and to have had the skull made into a drinking cup and mounted in silver. Ilkha, who had been a witness of his father's death, fled south and made for the Etsin Gol in Hsi Hsia. Thither he was pursued by Yeh-lü Akhai, a Khitan in the service of the Mongol. This officer was a member of the Khitan royal house and like his brother Tukha had originally been sent by the Chin to reside at the Kerait court. There both frequently met Temuchin, and on war breaking out between him and his suzerain, they sided with the Mongol in whose service they remained,[72] early evidence of the impression that even then the personality of the future conqueror made upon outsiders.

Fleeing up the Etsin Gol, Ilkha found a temporary refuge in the Tsaidam, but later turned west and made for Khara Khitai where, near Kucha in the Uighur kingdom of the T'ien Shan, his depredations ultimately resulted in his death.[73] Had this brave but unfortunate soldier not been wounded at Khala-khaldjit Elet, it might have fared ill with Temuchin and the world might never have heard of Chingis Khan.

Djagambo either escaped from the disaster of Jedjer Undur or was absent, for it was not until later that he surrendered. Afterward he foolishly revolted only to be speedily crushed.[74] Of his two daughters, given to Temuchin at the time of his submission, Soyurghaktani was eventually married to the con-

[72] See the biographies of " Yeh-lü Akhai " and " Tukha " in the *Meng-wu-erh Shih* of Tu Chi.

[73] This is from the " Restitutions of M. Pelliot," *Journal Asiatique*, 1920. According to an account reported by D'Ohsson, Vol. I, p. 82, Ilkha reached Cuman, perhaps Guma between Khotan and Yarkand, then under Khilji Khara Sultan of the Khalaji Turks—(supposedly a Khara Khanid)—and was captured and slain at Kusatu Char Kashme. For a curious story, perhaps relating to Ilkha's brief appearance on the Etsin Gol; see Appendix B.

[74] See the *Yüan Ch'ao Pi Shih*. According to the *Yüan Sheng Wu Ch'in Cheng Lu*, Djagambo did not submit until after the Naiman defeat in 1204 in which he was involved.

queror's youngest son Tului and became the mother of the
famous Kubilai and the no less famous Kulagu, the conqueror
of Baghdad.

The Keraits were split up between the Mongol clans, the
common people being distributed among the Khan's followers,
while the aristocracy became his immediate vassals. Outstanding among these was a certain Khadak Baatur who was destined
to become one of the chief nobles of the empire. Brought before
Temuchin after the battle, the victor asked him why he had
fought so obstinately when all was lost. " It would have been
unbearable for me," replied the warrior, " to allow you to take
and kill my lawful lord; I fought for three days, to give the
Wang Khan time to escape as far as possible. Now if you bid
me die, I will die; if you grant me life, I will serve you with zeal."
Temuchin said: " One who refused to abandon his lord, and
in order that the latter might win time and space, fought
single-handed against me for three days, is a gallant man.
Be you my companion." This incident, as Vladimirtsov
remarks, characterizes the Mongol conqueror's attitude to the
vanquished. Always he upheld the aristocratic principle of
the feudal lord's authority over his subject. He invariably
encouraged loyalty and admired courage, but punished with
death those who betrayed their master.

Temuchin's victory over the Keraits made him incomparably
the most powerful figure on the steppes. Neither under Khabul
nor Kutula had the Mongols achieved such a position. With
eastern Mongolia united it was inevitable that a struggle should
ensue for the mastery of the whole country. During neither
the 11th nor the 12th century had a leader of the stature of
Temuchin arisen, but now both the man and the hour were at
hand. Inured to hardship and adversity, able diplomat and
great soldier, Temuchin united in himself that balance of the
statesman and the warrior that made of him the man of iron
who would restore the empire of the steppes and astonish the
world.

CHAPTER IV

# CHINGIS KHAN, EMPEROR OF MONGOLIA

THE OVERTHROW of the Keraits had a profound effect
on the nations of the steppes. Most disturbed of all was
the Naiman Bai Bukha. Not only as the protector of Temuchin's enemies, but as the holder of the title T'ai-yang, which
made him the premier sovereign north of the desert, he could
expect an attack from the Mongol Khan.

Determined if possible to take time by the forelock, he set
about forming a fourth coalition, and during the winter of
1203-4 appealed to all Temuchin's old enemies. So great was
his success that in addition to Jamukha and the Jajirads, he
enlisted the Durbens, Khatakins and Saljiuds, the remains of
the Tatars—for the most part those of the Dutaut clan—Arin
Taiji and a remnant of the Keraits, Kutuku Biki the Oirad
and Tukta the Mergid. Not content with this he called upon
the Onguds to attack from the south and sent the following
message to their chief Alakush Tagin (1201-11). " You know
that the sun and the moon reign in the heavens together, but
on earth there can not be two rulers; be my right wing and we
will take from Chingis Khan (Temuchin) his bow and his
arrows (power).[1] The Onguds had long had an alliance with
the Naimans for purposes of tribal intermarriage and many of
Alakush Tagin's nobles were in favor of siding with the T'ai-
yang, but the chief felt so unequal to a struggle with the
Mongol that he refused.[2] Instead he informed Temuchin of

[1] This version of the T'ai-yang's message is from the *Yüan Sheng Wu Ch'in Cheng
Lu* and it resembles closely those found in the *Yüan Ch'ao Pi Shih* and in Rashid
ad-Din. (For a comparison of all three; see Grousset, " L'Empire Mongol " (1ʳᵉ
phase), *Histoire du Monde*, Tome VIII, p. 576.)

[2] The Mongols and Turks are exogamus and always marry outside their own
clans; the Borjigins and the Khongirads had an arrangement similar to that existing
between the Naimans and the Onguds.

85

the Naiman's words and promised later to march north with help. Grateful for this friendship, the Mongol Khan sent him a present of 500 horses and 1,000 sheep.[3] The only important nomad figure to hold aloof from the impending conflict was Buyuruk, Bai Bukha's brother.

Conversant with all that was taking place, Temuchin was not idle and in the spring of 1204 held a great assembly (kuriltai) on the plain of Temeyen Keer between the Bur Nor and the mouth of the Kerulen.[4] First the army and the Guard (Keshik) were further organized and strengthened and then plans for the forthcoming campaign were discussed at length. Among those present were many who objected that the army's mounts were still too lean from their winter in the open to make an immediate advance advisable. But Belgutai and Temuge Ochigin, two of the Khan's brothers, drawing attention to the moral effect of being the first in the field, urged that they take the initiative and promised that they would supply sufficient horses to enable the army to move at once. Impressed and pleased with their argument, Temuchin gave orders for the mobilization of his troops. When all was ready, he sacrificed to the suldé or guardian spirit of the Tuk or great white standard with the nine yak tails, and sending Kubilai Noyan and Jebe ahead with an advance force, set out on the 16th day of the fourth moon, i. e., early in May, 1204. As among all nomad peoples of that time, the Mongols believed that the suldé or guardian spirit of the Altan Uruk (Golden House) or imperial family resided in the great standard that led the army to war. Vladimirtsov says that this suldé is believed by the Mongols to have led them to the conquest of the world.

Proceeding west via the Kerulen and Tola rivers, the Mongol army, despite its early start, marched the intervening seven hundred miles to the Naiman country at a leisurely pace, and reaching the border during the summer, remained there until

[3] See the biography of " Alakush Tagin " in the *Meng-wu-erh Shih.*
[4] This is the T'ieh-mai-k'ai of the *Yüan Shih.* For the location of this place; see Grousset, *Le Conquérant du Monde,* p. 183.

autumn.[5] The advance was then resumed and at Saari Keer the forward troops of the Mongols made contact with the Naiman scouts who were watching from the Khan Kharka Mountains; perhaps the present Burgut to the west of the Khodasin River.

Face to face were two powerful armies. That of the confederacy was certainly the larger, at a guess 50,000 to 55,000, unless increased by troops from Buyuruk. The army under Temuchin was approximately 45,000, exclusive of any reinforcements that the Onguds may have sent.[6] But the latter was the more united and better led, so the disparity was less than it seemed. In the great states to the south, i. e. Hsi Hsia, Chin, and Khara Khitai, bigger forces could be mustered, but even in the empire of Chin it is doubtful if a similar body of cavalry could have been found to equal either army in mobility, horsemanship or archery.

With the arrival of the main Mongol army at Saari Keer, Dodai Cherbi, one of the officers of the Guard, spoke to Temuchin as follows: " We are few in numbers and are fatigued by our long march. Let us rest here in the steppes of Saari Keer and graze our horses until they have recovered. But to mislead the enemy, let us in the daytime array a large number of dummies and order that during the night each man light five separate fires. As to the Naimans, one hears that they are very numerous, but it is said that their T'ai-yang is a man of little character and has never yet himself taken the field. Our deception will deceive him regarding our numbers; then, as

[5] Very probably the main army spent most of the summer on the Tola.
[6] Of course all such estimates are very risky and may easily be far off the mark. In this instance they have been based on the belief that when Temuchin advanced against the T'ai-yang, he had available for active service about one third of the total man-power of Outer Mongolia, which consisted of approximately 140,000 effectives. (See Chap. on The Mongol Army.) The T'ai-yang and his allies, from the enumeration of the various members of the confederacy, certainly disposed of rather better than a third, while the absence of Buyuruk and certain of the Oirads, plus the losses sustained by the Tatars in 1202 and the Keraits and the Mongols themselves in 1203, would more or less account for the remaining 35,000 to 40,000.

As for the Onguds, it is possible but not certain that they sent north some troops. The *Yüan Shih* and the *Meng-wu-erh Shih*, biog. of " Alakush Tagin," say that they did, but Rashid ad-Din implies they did not.

soon as our cavalry are refreshed, we will assail his advance-guard, and hurling it back upon the main army, take advantage of the confusion to press forward and win an overwhelming victory." Approving this advice, Temuchin gave the necessary orders and so deceived the enemy as to his real strength.

Consequently, the T'ai-yang, who was camped by the Kha-chir River in the Khangai, was informed that, contrary to previous reports, the Mongol army seemed very large. He thereupon turned to his son Kuchluk and said; " One thought that the Mongol cavalry was foundered, but they have more camp fires than there are stars in the sky. The battle will be terrible. They are warriors who throw themselves into combat without blinking an eye; even when wounded in the face so that the blood streams down, they never falter. Is it wise to seek battle with them here? Surely it is better to retire behind the Altai. Our horses are in good condition. Following us, the enemy will become exhausted and then we can fall upon them." [7]

On hearing his father's words, Kuchluk scornfully exclaimed: " The T'ai-yang trembles like a woman! What of the numbers of the Mongols! The greater part of them have passed over to us with Jamukha. But my father has never made a campaign; he has never been further from home than a pregnant woman goes to urinate or a calf to seek its pasture."

Exasperated, the T'ai-yang retorted: " Kuchluk is a young man of abounding conceit; let us hope that in the hour of battle, when death hovers over him, this dauntless courage does not vanish."

But the commanders of the Naiman army supported the prince and the general-in-chief Khorisu Bechi deplored the T'ai-yang's caution. " On the day of battle," he said, "your father Inanch Bilkha never showed the backs of his soldiers nor the cruppers of their horses to the enemy. But you, are you already afraid? If we had known you to be so fearful we would have

---

[7] According to Rashid ad-Din, the T'ai-yang's advice was the outcome of seeing the lean condition of a horse which had escaped from the Mongol lines. D'Ohsson, Vol. I, p. 86.

preferred to have given command of the army to the princess Gurbésu, although she is but a woman. What a misfortune it is that Koksu Sabrak is so old! For you, oh faint hearted T'ai-yang, it is here that you would hide yourself! "

Furious at these insults, Bai Bukha gave orders to break camp, and moving down the Tamir to the Orkhon, crossed the latter and made for Chakirmaut at the foot of the eastern slopes of Mt. Naku.[8]

When Temuchin saw the confederate army before him, he gave Juchi Khassar the center of his own, assigned the rear to Temuge Ochigin, placed Jelmei, Kubilai, Jebe and Subudei over the van, and stationed the Manguds and Uruds, who were among his best troops, on the extremity of either wing. He himself took charge of a picked body of troops, including the still small guard, which he employed as a special reserve to reinforce the attack all along the line. Curiously enough, neither Bugurji nor Mukhali are mentioned, but both were doubtless present, for it is unlikely that Temuchin would have undertaken so important a campaign without them.

The Mongols opened the battle and according to the " Yüan Ch'ao Pi Shih," their vanguard forced the Naimans back to the mountain itself. The T'ai-yang then turned to Jamukha who was beside him and said: " Who are those that pursue our men in the manner of wolves pursuing a flock of sheep to their very pens? " " They," replied Jamukha, " are the four hounds of Temuchin fed on human flesh; he keeps them leashed on an iron chain; their skulls are of brass, their teeth like chisels; their tongues are like bodkins, their hearts of iron. Instead of horse whips, they carry curved swords. They drink dew; they ride with the wind; in battle they devour human flesh. Now

---

[8] The scene of this great battle seems to have been on or very near the subsequent site of Khaidu's final defeat in 1301.

For the original account of this engagement; see the trans. of the *Yüan Ch'ao Pi Shih* by Palladius, also Grousset, *Le Conquérant du Monde*, pp. 190-199. Grousset has taken his description from the recent translation of the same work by the celebrated Sinologist and Orientalist Pelliot.

Mt. Naku is very likely the small range lying between the Burgut mountains and the Orkhon river—see *British General Staff Map*, sheet 22, " Mongolia."

they have been unleashed; their spittle runs; they are full of joy. These hounds are Jebe, Kubilai, Jelmei and Subudei."

At these words the T'ai-yang trembled and gave orders to withdraw from the flanks of the mountain; whereupon the Mongols began to envelop his army. Seeing this, Bai Bukha said: " And who are those warriors, like young horses loosened at daybreak, gorged with mares milk and gamboling about their mother, who hurl themselves forward to outflank us? " " They," rejoined the Jajirad, " are the soldiers of the Uruds and Manguds. They pursue armed men like game, they tear from them their blood stained weapons, they slay them and take from them everything."

Again the Naimans were ordered to retire, this time up the mountain and the T'ai-yang once more addressed Jamukha. " Who is that behind them like a hungry falcon impatient to advance? " " That," said Jamukha, " is my sworn brother Temuchin, clad from head to foot in iron armor; he has flown hither like a hungry vulture; do you see him? You used to say that as soon as the Mongol comes he will fare like the lamb and not even his hoofs or his hide will remain. But behold! "

A fourth time the Naimans were forced to withdraw and the T'ai-yang said; " Who is that other chief that advances against us? " " That," answered Jamukha, " is one of the sons of Oelun, fed on human flesh. He is over eighteen feet tall. At a single meal he devours a sheep of three years. He wears a triple cuirass; he is more powerful than three bulls. He can swallow a man entire with his quiver without choking or even losing his appetite. When the fury of battle comes over him and he looses his irresistable arrows, he transfixes ten and twenty men at a shot though they be on the further side of the mountain. His arrows overwhelm an enemy at more than sixteen thousand feet. It is Juchi Khassar."

Then espying Temuchin's youngest brother, the T'ai-yang again questioned the Jajirad. " That," Jamukha informed him, " is Temuge Ochigin, the youngest son of Oelun. Some call him indolent because he likes to take to his couch early and to lie there late, but in the hour of battle he is never backward."

At last the Naimans were forced to retreat still higher, even to the summit of the Naku escarpment. At that point Jamukha abandoned the field and treacherously tried to win grace for himself, for he sent to tell Temuchin that he had filled the heart of the T'ai-yang with fear and that he and all his army were hurrying for the mountain top. But his words were in vain.[9]

The day being far spent, the conqueror did no more than surround the mountain. During the night many of the trapped soldiers attempted to escape, but in the darkness great numbers fell from the rocks and were killed. Kuchluk, however, got away with some horsemen and, though nearly overtaken on the Tamir while resting, eventually reached the Altai in safety where he sought refuge with his uncle Buyuruk. There he was shortly joined by Jamukha and a remnant of his following.

The succeeding morning found the T'ai-yang wounded and dying. Unable to rouse him and seeing the whole confederate army in the confusion of defeat, Khorisu Bechi called upon the Naiman officers with him to descend the mountain slope and die, arms in hand. Thereupon with one accord they hurled themselves upon the victorious Mongols, and heedless of offers of quarter and honorable treatment from Temuchin, who admired their desperate courage, perished to the last man. After all was over, the conqueror made a point of publicly praising their loyalty and bravery.

Although some of the Naimans escaped and subsequently joined Kuchluk, the majority gave up and surrendered as did also the Khatakins, Durbens, Saljiuds and the Keraits of Arin Taiji. Among the more important prisoners taken were Gurbésu, the favorite wife of Bai Bukha, whom the conqueror took for himself, and T'a-t'a-t'ong-a the seal bearer of the T'ai-yang. When brought with the insignia of his office before Temuchin, the latter inquired its use, and on being informed

[9] According to D'Ohsson, Vol. I, p. 87, who quoted Rashid ad-Din, Jamukha, having perceived the disposition of the Mongol army, turned to his officers and remarked that the Naimans had greatly under-estimated the enemy and gave orders for his troops to withdraw before the battle began.

by the prisoner and told that he had hoped to bring it to
Kuchluk, the Mongol praised his fidelity and invited him to
enter his service in the same capacity. Having accepted, Tʻa-
tʻa-tʻong-a, who was an Uighur and like so many of that people
lettered, was charged with the task of drawing up a script for
the Mongols who, in common with most of the inhabitants
of the steppes, were illiterate.[10]

Besides Kuchluk, there also fled from the field the Mergids,
Oirads and Tatars. The first of these Temuchin immediately
pursued and at Kharadal-hudjaur came up with those under
Tukta Biki. Outnumbered, the fugitives were defeated, and
while the chief and his sons escaped to Buyuruk, many of their
people were obliged to submit. From the " Yüan Chʻao Pi
Shih " it seems that Kharadal-hudjaur must have been located
in the valley of the Sari, which is probably to be identified
with the Khodasin of today.[11] It was at this battle that Kudu,
one of Tukta's sons, lost his wife, the famous Toragana, who
was given to Ugedei.

During the same operation Dair Usun and the Uwas Mergids,
overtaken on the Tar and unable to fly further, also surrendered
and the chief gave to Temuchin his daughter the beautiful
Kulan.[12] But no sooner had he done this than he revolted,
and flying with his clan to the valley of the lower Selenga,
barricaded himself in the gorges of Kuru Khapchal. Simultaneously others of the Mergids also rebelled, and going in
the same direction took refuge at Taikhal Khorkha. In due
time all were reduced and like the Keraits, split up among
the Mongols, but the undertaking Temuchin left to his generals.

He himself went against the last of the Tatars. Isolated
from all possible help, they were utterly crushed and, like
their confrères three years before, suffered a terrible massacre.

[10] See the article on " Tha-tha-Toung-o " (Tʻa-tʻa-tʻong-a) in Nouveaux Mélanges
Asiatiques by Abel Rémusat.

[11] It is possible, however, that Kharadal-hudjaur was near the Altai, since it was
in that range that Tukta sought refuge with the Naiman Buyuruk. (For a few
words on the matter; see Grousset, " L'Empire Mongol " (1 re phase), Histoire du
Monde, Tome VIII, p. 169.

[12] Kulan became the mother of prince Kulgan to whom later 4,000 troops of the
Mongol army proper were assigned.

This time Temuchin even ordered the extermination of the women and children, but despite the strictest injunctions against any mercy, not only his two Tatar wives Yesui and Yesugan but several of his officers secretly saved some children. Juchi Khassar too, at the prayer of his wife, spared five hundred of the thousand allotted to him for slaughter. Learning of this, Temuchin is said to have been greatly angered, but apparently took no action, and later both Tatar officers and men are frequently heard of in the Mongol army.[13] Notwithstanding the day and age and the long and bitter feud existing between Mongol and Tatar, this holocaust of death was a deed of atrocious cruelty.

Like Jamukha, the princes Altan and Kuchar were still at large, but their following was negligible. From the Khinghan to the Altai the only hostile forces of consequence were those of Kutuku the Oirad, Tukta the Mergid and the two Naiman chiefs, Kuchluk and Buyuruk, but all combined were much inferior to those of the Mongol Khan. Taking refuge in the Altai and the valleys to the south, they were for the time being too disorganized to be an immediate danger and could safely be left until later. Moreover, the Mongol cavalry required rest before undertaking so distant an expedition, but the hour of final reckoning was only postponed.

In the " Yüan Ch'ao Pi Shih " no other battle has received the attention given that fought at Chakirmaut, and indeed it is the most important ever won by Chingis Khan. Later he overcame far larger armies in his wars against the Tanguts and Chin and commanded many more thousands than he did at Chakirmaut, but never was so great an issue at stake. Complete victory over the T'ai-yang and his allies meant the lordship of the steppes, defeat, the probable dissolution, perhaps forever, of his lately won power.

For the year 1205 we have little information, but in view of the great assembly held in 1206, it was doubtless spent in

[13] D'Ohsson, *Histoire des Mongols*, Vol. I, pp. 92-93. Reference to this last and final expedition against the Tatars is to be found only in Rashid ad-Din's article on the Tatars.

organizing and regrouping the newly conquered clans; it is likely that only then were the last of the insurgent Mergids compelled to surrender. But one new expedition, a small one, was undertaken.

During the previous century both the Keraits and the Naimans had raided Hsi Hsia and now Temuchin, who had become their neighbor in his turn, decided to send south a small army. His pretext for this act of hostility is unknown, but it may be supposed that he regarded the Tangut failure to apprehend his enemy Ilkha the Kerait as sufficient casus belli. Ostensibly the raid had no aim beyond plunder, but as we shall see later it had another object as well. In April the Khitan Yeh-lü Akhai and another officer [14] crossed the Hsi Hsia border, and after taking two small towns,[15] ravaged the departments of Kua Chou and Sha Chou (Tun-huang). In May they captured another place of minor importance,[16] but before the hot weather set in returned north with their loot— principally captives and camels.

The reference to Kua Chou and Sha Chou would indicate that the two commanders marched up the Etsin Gol or Hei-shui River until ready to swing west to the Shu-lo Ho. One may therefore assume that this first inroad was confined to the most westerly part of Hsi Hsia. Strangely enough no mention is made of Hei-shui Ch'eng, represented today by the ruins of Khara Khoto just east of the lower Etsin Gol, so it was probably too strong for the invaders to take. This is not hard to understand, for up to then the Mongols had had little experience with walled towns, and Hei-shui Ch'eng was well fortified. Not only was it an important station on the northern east-west trade route between China and the West, but to a limited extent it commanded the main corridor leading from Outer

---

[14] The name of the other Mongol commander as given by the *Hsi Hsia Shu Shih* is Chieh-ku-li-t'u. For this expedition, see the *Hsi Hsia Shu Shih, Hsi Hsia Chi* and the *Meng-wu-erh Shih*.

[15] These were Li-chi-li Chai and Ch'i-lin-ku-sa Ch'eng and were very likely located on the Etsin Gol or Hei-shui Ho and perhaps corresponded to the modern towns of Mao-mu and Chin-t'a.

[16] This was Lo-ssŭ Ch'eng.

Mongolia into Hsi Hsia. Hence it possessed good walls and a strong garrison. This time it escaped attack, but later the Mongols were to make a point of reducing it.

Not once throughout the incursion did the garrisons of Kua Chou and Sha Chou or the field forces of the Tangut ruler Li Ch'un-yü (1196-1206) challenge the Mongols in the open. But in June all places destroyed by them were repaired and in December an army was ordered to make a counter raid. It marched north but returned without fighting. The following year the king was deposed and succeeded by Li An-ch'üan (1206-11), a man of considerable energy.

Victorious over the T'ai-yang, the senior nomad prince of the steppes, it was necessary that Temuchin receive a title that would indicate his position as political successor to the Naiman and restorer of the ancient nomad empire. " And so," in the words of the " Yüan Ch'ao Pi Shih," " when all the generations living in felt tents became united under a single authority, in the year of the Leopard (1206), they assembled near the sources of the Onon, and raising the White Banner on Nine Legs, they conferred on Chingis (Temuchin) the title of Khaghan." [17]

The word Khaghan goes back to the days of the Juan-juan— fifth and sixth centuries—and was borrowed from them by the rulers of the first Turkish empire—sixth and seventh centuries—and after that was assumed by every nomad ruler powerful enough to unite all the peoples of the northern steppes.

In point of fact it is unlikely that Temuchin, as Vladimirtsov believed, had received the title of Chingis in the first election that made him Khan or took the additional appellation of Khaghan in this later one.[18] Possibly not until the spring of 1206 did he become known as Chingis and never, contends Pelliot, did he assume the title of Khaghan, which indeed the word Chingis made superfluous. Only with the accession of his son Ugedei were the Mongol rulers first termed Khaghan.[19]

[17] This took place during the spring of 1206.
[18] Vladimirtsov, The Life of Chingis Khan, pp. 63-64.
[19] Pelliot, " Notes sur le Turkestan," Toung Pao, 1930.

At the same time that he assumed a special title for himself, Temuchin, whom we shall now call Chingis Khan, also took one for the newly created nation, so that henceforth, Mongols, Keraits, Naimans, etc., would be known under the common name of Mongol. The " Sanang Setsen " [20] says that he added the prefix Kuku, i. e., blue, the color of the sky, to indicate that the Mongols were under the protection of Heaven. In this he was following the example of the Turkish Khaghans who gave their people the name of Kuku Turk.[21]

" Chingis Khan," says Vladimirtsov, " introduced a definite religious idea into the political conception of his own suzerainty and of that of his clan. A prominent part at the kuriltai of 1206 was played by the sorcerer and Shaman Kukchu (also known as Tab Tangri), son of Munglik, whom the Mongols viewed with superstitious reverence. Kukchu announced that the Everlasting Blue Sky favored Chingis Khan, who was its own preordained envoy on earth (jayagatu) and all his clan. Chingis himself readily accepted the view. ' The Sky has ordered me to govern all peoples,' he said. ' With the protection of the Everlasting Sky I defeated the Keraits and attained to supreme rank.' The White Banner on Nine Legs was now inhabited by the guardian genius (Suldé) of Chingis's clan (the Borjigin). The Suldé would protect his troops and lead them to victory; he would conquer all peoples for the Everlasting Blue Sky. To this day the Mongols preserve and reverence the White Banner of the Suldé, which is the same, they believe, that led the armies of Chingis Khan from victory to victory. They believe that the soul of the great emperor has itself entered this Suldé banner, and that he has himself become the guardian genius of his glorious clan.[22]

Regarding the meaning of the word Chingis, " it is only a plausible guess," writes Vladimirtsov, " that it was the name

---

[20] The *Sanang Setsen* was written by the Ordos prince of Uchin during 1662. Containing many legends strongly influenced by Lamaism, it is of relatively little historical value for the career of Chingis Khan, but is still the most popular history among the Mongols of today.

[21] See Grousset, *L'Empire des Steppes*, p. 274, n. 1.

[22] Vladimirtsov, *The Life of Chingis Khan*, pp. 64-65.

of a spirit of light worshipped at that time by the Shamanist Mongols. The supposition is confirmed by the fact that many regarded Temuchin as predestined by the Sky." [23] Not only Chingis Khan but his successors regarded themselves as the representatives of Heaven (Tengri). Consequently their order was the order of Heaven, revolt against them, revolt against the divine will.

But if the Mongol rulers accorded themselves so exalted a position, their natural reverence for Heaven and general super- stition resulted in their respecting the representatives of other religious cults, and one finds that Buddhist bonze, Moslem mullah and Christian priest were all exempt from taxation.

" Considering his religious and social views, Chingis Khan," says Vladimirtsov, " could not but found the constitution of his empire on a strictly aristocratic basis. His conception of it was the average steppe aristocrat's conception of the consti- tution of his particular clan, only on an immensely enlarged scale. In the same way as an aristocratic family or clan is the head of a tribe, so, in the system of Chingis, the ' golden clan ' (Altan Uruk), with its vassals and followers, is the head of all the Mongol tribes, of all the ' generations living in felt tents,' of all peoples, of all the world. At the head of the imperial clan is the emperor who is the head of his own clan, and of the aristocracy (Baatut, Noyat, Nokut and Darkhat) that had joined him, rather than the head of the people (Arat or Kharachu) or of the nation (Ulus)." [24] Lowest in the whole Mongol hierarchy were the slaves or *bogul*, who for the most part were prisoners taken in successful forays to the south of the steppes.

" Chingis Khan never conceived of himself as a popular leader. He was and remained the leader of an aristocratic clan that had unified all the Mongol aristocracy. His messages and speeches, decrees and statutes are never addressed to the

---

[23] Vladimirtsov, *The Life of Chingis Khan*, pp. 37-38. Pelliot, for his part, believed that it indicated the universal nature of the conqueror's authority; see Grousset, " L'Empire Mongol " (1re phase), *Histoire du Monde*, Tome VIII, p. 77.

[24] A tribe was known as an Irgen, a state as an Ulus-Irgen. (See René Grousset, *L'Empire des Steppes*, p. 248, n.)

people, but always to the princes, noyans (noyat) and bagaturs
(baatut) ." [25] Unlike the Turkish Khaghans of the eighth century, who would seem to have been nearer to the people as a
whole, he strove almost entirely for his family and the supporting nobility. On the Orkhon Inscriptions, the Turkish Khaghan
Bilkha (716-34) says that his aim has been to make conquests
for the good of his subjects; to make those people that were
few, numerous, and to make rich the poor. The only even
nearly comparable statement that has come down to us from
the Mongol ruler is the following utterance from the Bilik.
" My bowmen and warriors," he once declared, " loom like a
thick forest; their wives, sweethearts and maidens shine like
red flames. My task is to sweeten their mouths with gifts of
sweet sugar, to decorate their breasts, backs and shoulders
with garments of brocade, to seat them on good geldings, give
them to drink from pure and sweet rivers, provide their beasts
with good and abundant pastures, and to order that the great
roads and highways that serve as ways for the people be kept
clear . . ." It is very probable, however, that the warriors
who loomed like a thick forest were The Guard—10,000
strong—rather than the whole army, and that the conqueror
was addressing the most privileged among his troops.[26]

Well illustrating Chingis Khan's outlook and the aristocratic
nature of the newly created empire are the gifts and honors
he bestowed upon those who had helped him. Ninety-five of
his officers who had particularly distinguished themselves were
made commanders of 1,000, Kubilai was appointed senior
commander of the army and Jebe and Subudei were raised to
the rank of chiefs with their own following. To Jurchedei, for
his bravery at Khalakhaldjit Elet and fidelity during the subsequent retreat, he gave Ibakha, one of the daughters of the
Kerait Djagambo, and confirmed him in his rank as chief of
the Uruds. " During the retreat," he proclaimed, " you shel-
tered me like a high mountain; in the battle you were like a

---

[25] Vladimirtsov, *The Life of Chingis Khan*, pp. 65-66.

[26] For the Orkhon Inscriptions, see Lacoste, *Au Pays Sacré des Ancien Turcs
et des Mongols*, pp. 80-81; for Chingis Khan's utterance, Riasanovsky, *Fundamental
Principles of Mongol Law*, p. 89.

shield." To the descendants of the equally brave Kuildar, who had died of wounds received in the same battle, he gave other rewards. Shiki Kutuku, an adopted son, acquired as a captive in the Tatar war of 1198, he made chief judge of the empire. But to Bugurji and Mukhali went still greater honors. The former he nominated commander-in-chief of all the troops of the West or Right Wing (Baraunghar), the latter of the East or Left Wing (Junghar). These honors, which except for the members of the imperial family made them the greatest nobles in the realm, they were to hand down to their descendants. He further forgave both of them nine death offenses in advance, a favor also extended to others rewarded at this time. According to the "Yüan Ch'ao Pi Shih," Chingis Khan declared that he would also reward the women who had helped in his rise to power.

Most handsomely of all did the conqueror recompense his own family. To his mother Oelun Eke and his youngest brother Temuge Ochigin were given 10,000 families from among the conquered, to his son Juchi, 9,000 families, to Jaghatai, 8,000, to Ugedei, 5,000, to Tului, 5,000, to his brother Juchi Khassar, 4,000 to Aljigidei the son of Khachiun Ulchi, another brother, 2,000 and to Belgutai, 1,500 families.[27]

As can readily be seen from the nature of these gifts and honors, Chingis Khan had in mind more than the recognition of faithful service; he also wished to establish on a firm basis the organiaztion of the empire. To further this object, he drew up a code of laws, the famous Yasa. This was far more than a codification of the common law of the Mongols current at the time. Rather was it an imperial code intended to supplement and take precedence over the customary usages of the day, but, like the Bilik, it was not compiled all at once but was the work of the conqueror's whole life. Not unnaturally the newly-introduced alphabet was used to commit to writing both the Yasa and the Bilik.[28]

[27] This enumeration is from the *Yüan Ch'ao Pi Shih* which, however, places it in a part of the chronicle dealing with some much later events.
[28] For a study of the Yasa and Bilik of Chingis Khan; see Riasanovsky, *Funda-*

Vladimirtsov has been at considerable pains to point out the importance that Chingis Khan attached to the Yasa. Making use of his sayings on the subject in the Bilik, he quotes the conqueror as follows: " If the rulers who come after the present one (i. e. himself), and the grandees, bagaturs (baatut) and noyans (noyat) who surround them do not in all things obey the Jasak (Yasa), the work of government will be jeopardized and discontinued. Then will they be glad to find a second Chingis Khan, but they will find none." And again: " If the descendants who will be born and take my place, five hundred, or a thousand, or ten thousand years hence, preserve these laws and do not change the Jasak of Chingis Khan . . . they will be granted great prosperity by the Sky." As the Russian savant says, " The Great Jasak " was thus made obligatory on all, including Chingis Khan and his successors. He promulgated an unalterable law good for all time which, applied with pitiless severity, made of the Mongols, the Franciscan Plano Carpini tells us, " the most obedient people in the world toward their chiefs—more even," he says, " than our priests toward their superiors." With the appointment of selected nobles to command the army, the promulgation and enforcement of the Yasa was the most important step ever taken by the conqueror to weaken those tendencies in feudalism danger-

*mental Principles of Mongol Law.* This author believes that while the original draft of the Yasa was probably drawn up at the great Kuriltai of 1206, its final promulgation may have been as late as that of 1218. Furthermore, he thinks that after the conqueror's invasion of the Chin empire, Chingis Khan was not a little influenced by some of the Chinese officers that he met, and in support of his contention quotes an excerpt from the biography of " Ke Pao-yü " in the *Hsin Yüan Shih.* (See Riasanovsky, pp. 27, 29 and 32.)

Vernadsky, another authority on the subject, considers that subsequent additions were made to the Yasa by the successors of Chingis Khan, but is of the opinion that none of them ever contradicted the ordinances of the great conqueror. From the fragments of the Yasa that have come down to us from Juwayni, Bar Hebraeus, Rashid ad-Din and Makrizi, Vernadsky divides the famous code as follows: 1. International Law; 2. Public Law; (a) supreme power of the Khan, (b) the Nation, (c) The Statutes of Bound Service, (d) Immunity Privileges, (e) Military Statutes, (f) Hunting Statutes, (g) Administration and Administrative Ordnances and (h) Taxation; 3. Criminal Law; 4. Private Law; 5. Commercial Law; 6. Judicial Law and 7. The Codification and enforcement of the Yasa. (See Vernadsky, " The Scope and Contents of Chingis Khan's Yasa," *Harvard Journal of Asiatic Studies,* pp. 337-360, Cambridge, 1938.

ous to unity and to provide the new empire with the rudiments of a bureaucratic organization.

At the great kuriltai of 1206 Chingis Khan also completed the organization of the Guard (Keshik) and army, but this has been dealt with already so is here omitted.

In addition to the military and civil organization of the empire, Chingis Khan instituted the office of Biki, who was to be vested with the powers of a state priest. This title, more commonly borne by the leaders of forest clans and tribes, was held by chiefs who added to their secular authority the spiritual powers of a Shaman. This rested on their relationship with the clan's ancestor and protecting spirits. Chingis now appointed as Biki the old Baarin chief Usun. Belonging to the senior Yasun of the Borjigin clan (omuk), he could be regarded as particularly close to their legendary ancestor Budunchar, and therefore able to represent him. " Usun," Chingis Khan said to him, " you are the eldest descendant of Baarin, you must be Biki; in your capacity as Biki you shall ride a white horse, dress in white clothes, and in every company take first place; it shall be your duty to find out which year and which moon is auspicious." [29]

When granting so many rewards and making so many appointments, the conqueror did not forget the Ongud chief and created Alakush Tagin a prince of the empire, made him hereditary ruler of a thousand families and commander of 5,000 men.[30] Although at the time these honors were merely titular, and since peace still existed between Chingis Khan and the Chin, there was no legal reason why the Ongud chief should not accept them, the Chin would doubtless sooner or later have brought Alakush Tagin to account for such independence. But, as we shall learn further on, events in the south made it difficult for the Chin to interfere in the now very dangerous situation in the north. This promotion of relations with the Ongud is of special interest, as it is our first definite indication that Chingis Khan planned an early attack on the

[29] See Vladimirtsov, *The Life of Chingis Khan*, p. 77.
[30] See the biography of " Alakush " takin in the *Meng-wu-erh Shih* of T'u Chi.

Chin. By his display of gratitude toward Alakush Tagin, he
cleverly prepared the ground for the blow he ultimately
intended to strike.

His house in order, Chingis Khan resolved to go against the
Naiman and Mergid forces in the Altai, and as soon as the
kuriltai had broken up, he marched west. Evidently his move
took them by surprise, for Buyuruk was attacked and killed
while hunting in the Ulugh Tagh (Mongolian Altai).[31] But a
great part of the enemy escaped and Kuchluk and Tukta
fled to the Irtish where they assembled a considerable army.
Jamukha also got away but this time he fled almost alone,
to the Tanlu Mountains (Tannu Ula) on the Kirghiz border.

Perhaps on account of this Chingis now turned his attention
in that direction, for in 1207 he sent two envoys into the valley
of the Yenisei. This region was then divided between the
Kirghiz proper on the upper reaches of the river and the
Kem-kemjiuts on its principle tributary the Kemchik. A fertile
country, where much grain was sown and exported by Uighur
and Moslem merchants, it was also rich in sables and other
furs. Arriving there, the Mongol envoys were well received
and soon after the rulers of both peoples made submission
and presented Chingis Khan with a gift of gerfalcons, for which
the country was famed. Simultaneously, the Tumeds, who
may have been a branch of the Durben Oirads and who dwelt
between the Ija and Angara rivers, also recognized Mongol
suzerainty.

During September of the same year Chingis Khan ordered
a second inroad into Hsi Hsia. As on the previous occasion
the army's ostensible aim was plunder, its real object reconnaissance, but unlike that of 1205, it advanced into the present
Ala Shan region.[32] There the town of Wu-la-hai, known to

---

[31] The *Meng-wu-erh Shih* dates this expedition in 1205, the *Yüan Shih* in 1206.
Since I feel that the Mongol cavalry would have been in far better condition by
1206 for such a campaign, I have followed the *Yüan Shih* and assigned it to the
later date. The only Mongol expedition in 1205 was that against the Tanguts, but
it did not call for many troops.

[32] The *Hsi Hsia Chi* calls the country Ho-hsi (west of the river) which was the
general name applied by the Chinese to the region lying west of the Yellow River.
To the Mongols of that day it was known as Kaschi.

the Mongols as Urahai, was taken and the winter spent in plundering the surrounding country. The next year (1208) supplies began to run short and reports came in that the new ruler Li An-ch'üan (1206-11) was assembling troops. The numbers of these made them so formidable that the invaders decided to retire and in February or March, 1208, withdrew to the north.[33]

Before the return of this army, Chingis Khan had himself gone west on a much more important undertaking. In the autumn of 1207 he again marched toward the Altai to finish with Kuchluk and Tukta, but, overtaken by an early winter, he was obliged to call a halt until the spring of 1208. That year his troops fell in with Kutuku Biki the Oirad, who since 1204 had apparently been unable to return to his proper habitat and was in touch with the allies. Far too weak to dare risk an engagement, Kutuku submitted without fighting and supplied guides for the subsequent advance which began in the spring. Going by way of the Ulan Pass (9,200 ft.), which crosses that part of the Siberian Altai called the Tabun Ula, Chingis came out on the Bukhtarma, an affluent of the Irtish.[34] There he inflicted upon the enemy a crushing defeat, half the vanquished soldiers being drowned in the Irtish and Tukta himself slain. Wishing later to pay the brave old warrior the customary honors, his sons cut off his head and fled with the remainder of their men to seek an asylum among the Uighurs of the T'ien Shan. Kuchluk for his part was fought off the field by a body of picked troops, and made first for Arslan Khan of the Kharluks and then for his overlord the Gur Khan Chiluku (1178-1211). As for the surviving Naimans, some may have submitted to the victor but many more appear to have got away and taken refuge in the northwestern part

---

[33] Regarding this raid and its predecessor, many works say that Chingis Khan himself was with the armies. However, since it was not until early in 1208 that the last of the Naiman and Mergid forces were defeated, it is unlikely that he went south so early.

[34] For the location of the battle of Bukhtarma; see Grousset, Le Conquérant du Monde, p. 202. The Ulan Pass in question is not to be confused with the pass of the same name in the Eastern or Mongolian Altai.

of Khara Khitai where later in the year Kuchluk gathered them together.[35]

Determined to wipe out the Mergids, Chingis Khan sent a force in pursuit of them under Subudei, then aged thirty-two. The ensuing campaign, which is particularly interesting since it was the occasion of Subudei's first independent command, is most imperfectly known. According to the " Yüan Ch'ao Pi Shih " and the " Yüan Sheng Wu Ch'in Cheng Lu " the Mergids were overtaken on the Chui or Jam where they were defeated and two of Tukta's sons killed.[36] Barthold believes that the action took place on the eastern confines of the Uighur kingdom of the T'ien Shan, so perhaps the battle was fought on the present Khobuk just over the Uighur border.[37] At all events, the beaten soldiers led by Kultukhan, the sole surviving son of Tukta, tried to. enter the dominions of the Idikut Barchuk, but were forcibly driven off and finally joined Kuchluk on or near the Imil.[38]

On his way back from the Altai, or possibly during the winter of 1207 when he was waiting to cross the range, it seems that Chingis Khan's oldest and bitterest enemy was delivered to him. Ever since the defeat and death of Buyuruk in 1206, Jamukha, all but a handful of his people gone, had been reduced to living a life of brigandage in the Tanlu Mountains (Tannu Ula). Now at last his men, thinking to be rewarded, handed

[35] The *Yüan Shih* says that the overthrow of Kuchluk and Tukta occurred in the winter of 1208; D'Ohsson, Vol. I, pp. 104-105, during the autumn of the same year, while the *Yüan Ch'ao Pi Shih* speaks of the campaign as starting in the autumn and being resumed in the spring but gives no year. Since Chingis Khan marched against the Tanguts during April or May, 1209, it is unlikely that he went west to the Altai as late as either the autumn or winter of 1208. Consequently, I feel that the operation must have begun in the autumn of 1207 and finished in the spring of 1208.

[36] The *Yüan Ch'ao Pi Shih* gives no date, the *Yüan Sheng Wu Ch'in Cheng Lu* the year 1217, which shows that it has confused this battle with the later defeat of the Mergids to the north of the Aral Sea in 1216. (For the date of the final defeat of the Mergids; see Barthold, p. 270.)

[37] Léon Cahun, *Introduction à l'histoire de l'Asie, Turcs et Mongols des Origines à 1405*, p. 249, identifies the Jam with the Imil, but the location implied by Barthold seems more likely; see Barthold, *Turkestan down to the Mongol Invasion*, p. 362, n. 4.

[38] See Grousset, *Le Conquérant du Monde*, p. 203.

him over to the Mongol Khan.[39] But the latter declared, " Is
it possible to leave alive men who have betrayed their own
lord! ' Let them be put to death, with their sons and grandsons '." Chingis then turned to Jamukha, and according to
the " Yüan Ch'ao Pi Shih," proposed that they resume their
old relationship. But Jamukha replied, " In those days long
ago when we became sworn brothers we cooked our food and
ate together; we spoke words to one another that can not be
forgotten. Then there came people between us who set us
against one another. Remembering those old words, I grow red
with shame and have not the courage to face my sworn brother.
You wish me to be your comrade, but though I bore the name,
in fact I should not be so. Today you have gathered people
under your rule and there is no way in which I can be your
comrade. If you do not slay me, I shall always be like a louse
on your collar or a spine on your inner gate. Because of me
you will be uneasy by day, and at night will sleep fitfully.
Your mother has wisdom; you are a hero; your brothers have
talent; your comrades are valiant knights; you have seventy-
three geldings in your great lords. But I from childhood have
had neither parents nor brothers; my wife is a babbler; my
comrades not trusty; so my sworn brother, above whom is the
Sky, has surpassed me. Now grant that I may die quickly that
my brother's heart may be at peace, and that I may die without the shedding of blood. Then after death, I will forever
be the protector and helper of your descendants." Jamukha
was then crushed to death without bloodshed—(this was a
mercy, for the Shamanist Mongols believed that a man's soul
resided in his blood)—so that his spirit might dwell unchanged
among men, and Chingis Khan ordered that he be buried with
great honors.[40] Thus passed the Jajirad chief, a man of unques-

---

[39] It is from the *Yüan Shih* that one learns that Jamukha fled to Buyuruk, and
from the *Yüan Ch'ao Pi Shih* that he was betrayed after the defeat and death of
Tukta the Mergid. D'Ohsson, however, dates the affair on the heels of the T'ai-
yang's defeat.

[40] D'Ohsson, Vol. I, pp. 91-92, quoting Rashid ad-Din, says that Jamukha was put
to a terrible and lingering death. Since he was Chingis Khan's anda, it was
impossible for the former to order his death, so Jamukha was handed over for

tionable ability and courage. Had fate not given him Temuchin for a rival, he might easily have restored the old Mongol kingdom of Khabul and Kutula, but fortune was not kind and he went down before a greater man than himself.

Perhaps at the same time, though very possibly much earlier, there also perished Altan and Kuchar, who had proved so faithless to the vows sworn at the time of Temuchin's original elevation.

None now openly opposed Chingis in Mongolia, but there was still one more struggle in store for him and this a strange one. It will be remembered that at the great assembly of 1206 a prominent part had been played by Munglik's son the Shaman Kukchu or Tab Tangri. As Vladimirtsov says, " Chingis Khan was not only religious, but superstitious. The primitive religion of the Mongols was a favorable ground for superstition. The desire, or, we may even say, the need to know the will of the Everlasting Blue Sky and of the guardian spirits, was a constant stimulus for communing with shamans, sorcerers and divinators." Consulted frequently by Chingis Khan and belonging to the same clan (borjigin), Kukchu had no intention of being left in the background, and early began to interfere in state affairs. At length, so presumptuous did he become that after a quarrel with Juchi Khassar he came to Chingis and said: " The Spirit has revealed to me a holy command of the Everlasting Sky; first Temuchin will rule over the nations, and after him Khassar. If you do not eliminate Khassar your cause is in jeopardy." Alarmed by these words, Chingis temporarily lost his head and would, it seems, have deprived his brother of all authority, but warned of what had happened, their mother Oelun Eke intervened and the conqueror confessed that he had been afraid and gave Khassar back his liberty. Nevertheless he later reduced his subjects to 1,400 families.

Undiscouraged by his failure to sow discord in the con-

execution to Aljigidei, the son of Khachiun Ulchi, one of Temuchin's brothers. However, considering the day and age and the binding nature of andaship, it is more probable that Jamukha was put to death as reported by the *Yüan Ch'ao Pi Shih.*

queror's house, the shaman, supported by his brothers, grew more and more insolent and finally shamefully insulted Temuge Ochigin. This time Chingis Khan realized that the situation had become intolerable and, pressed by his wife Burte, mastered his superstitious awe of the shaman sufficiently to tell his brother that he might deal with Kukchu as he saw fit. A short time afterward Tab Tangri was again visiting Chingis, so availing himself of the opportunity, Temuge posted three wrestlers outside the Khan's quarters who seized and broke the shaman's back. " In order to quiet public opinion, which was excited by the murder of the famous shaman, Chingis," says Vladimirtsov, " made the following notable statement: ' Tab Tangri beat my brothers and slandered them iniquitously. That is why the Sky withdrew its love from him, and with it his life and his body.' In his statement Chingis Khan pointed out clearly that the Sky favored and continued favoring himself and his clan, and was prepared to punish anyone who attempted to rise against the Khan of the Mongols, or his kin." To Munglik, the father of Kukchu, Chingis Khan spoke very differently. " You failed to teach your own sons. He (Tab Tangri) wished to be equal to me, that is why I undid him. If I could have foreseen such qualities in you and yours, I would have undone all of you long ago. But if, after giving one's word in the morning, one were to change it by nightfall, or after giving it in the evening, withdrew it in the morning, one would be brought to shame by the judgment of men; I have promised to free you from death. So let there be an end of the matter." [41] Once again Chingis Khan had shown that he would brook neither opposition nor interference from any person, even when that person had been as useful to him as Kukchu and was the son of as old and faithful an adherent as Munglik.

While the new empire of the northern steppes had been in the process of creation, that of Khara Khitai had been in the throes of dissolution. Ever since Yeh-lü Ta-shih's conquest

[41] For a full dress account of Chingis Khan's contest with Tab Tangri, see Vladimirtsov, *The Life of Chinais Khan,* Chap. VIII.

of the Tarim and Central Asia, the Moslem element had looked for their day of deliverance, not because they were unduly oppressed but because rule by a heathen was not to be borne by the followers of the prophet. But so great had been the effect of the terrible disasters suffered by Moslem arms at Khojend in 1137 and at Khatwan near Samarkand in 1141, that for long no leader hardy enough had been found to challenge seriously the power of the Gur Khan. But at last, as the reign of the aging and easy going Chiluku (1178-1211) drew to a close, disturbances began. In the year 1205 the Khara Khanid rulers of Khotan and Kashgar rose in revolt and, joined by Arslan Khan of the Kharluks, himself a Moslem, attempted to throw off the Khara Khitan yoke. Despite his years, Chiluku vigorously repressed the rising, but, though he imprisoned the son of the Khan of Kashgar, he did not deal harshly with the rebels. This forbearance was due to a hope that leniency would appease his Moslem subjects, for, as the great Russian expert Barthold says, the Gur Khan foresaw even then that the movement would embrace all the Moslem provinces of the empire.[42] And so it happened. Two years later in 1207 a more formidable revolt broke out under the leadership of the Khara Khanid Othman of Samarkand (1200-12) and Muhammad Ala ad-Din Shah of Khwarazm (1200-20), the latter the most powerful of the Gur Khan's vassals. In the autumn Bokhara fell to the Khorezmians, but a joint invasion of Farghana by the two rebels was severely defeated at Ilamish by Chiluku in person. News of this reverse quickly spread south and both Khurasan and Mazanderan rose against Muhammad, who was kept busy until the spring of 1208 restoring his authority. For several months Othman and the Shah remained quiet and evidently once more recognized Khara Khitan suzerainty.

Meanwhile other events were transpiring. Kuchluk, whom we left a fugitive at the court of the Gur Khan, had been well received, and in addition to being given one of Chiluku's daughters in marriage had obtained permission to gather to-

---

[42] See Barthold, *Turkestan down to the Mongol Invasion*, p. 362.

gether those of the Naimans refuging in Khara Khitai. With these, and the Mergids, who joined him about the same time, his forces numbered all told some 8,000. It turned out that the Gur Khan had done an extremely rash thing, but in need of as many non-Moslem troops as possible, his decision to trust the Naiman prince is understandable.

Soon the empire was shaken by a third rebellion and in 1209 the Uighurs, exasperated by the exactions of the Gur Khan's fiscal agent, murdered him and, headed by the Idikut Barchuk, rose in open revolt. Hardly had this happened than news came that Othman of Samarkand and the Khwarazm Shah were again in arms. Knowing the Moslem insurrection to be much the more dangerous of the two, Chiluku turned west and early in 1210, 30,000 Khara Khitan troops took the field and Samarkand was besieged and captured without interference from the Shah.[43] But looking upon the city as his principal source of wealth, the Gur Khan again treated the insurgents with leniency.[44] Reports then reached the victorious army that Kuchluk and Arslan the Kharluk had plundered the imperial treasury at Uzgand. Instead of being able to prosecute the war in the west, Chiluku had to hurry north to deal with the treacherous Naiman. Hearing this, Arslan abandoned his ally, and Kuchluk, left in the lurch, was defeated on the Chinbuje, a tributary of the Chu close to Balasagun. He escaped, however, with most of his troops.

No sooner had the Khara Khitan army left Transoxiana than the Khwarazm Shah made his appearance and once more occupied Bokhara. Joined by Othman, who thus rebelled for the third time, he crossed the Syr Darya (Jaxartes) and marched north through the Arys Pass to the Talas or Taraz valley where he was encountered by a general of the Gur Khan.

[43] An army of 30,000 may be thought very meager for the reduction of Samarkand, but the largest field armies of Khara Khitai rarely exceeded 50,000. Their superiority lay not in numbers, but, as remarked in an earlier chapter, in the system of cavalry warfare that they had brought from the east. (See Wittfogel and Feng Chia-sheng, *History of Chinese Society: Liao* (907-1125), p. 668.)

[44] Beside numerous and flourishing industries and the commercial wealth that passed through the gates of Samarkand, the city also controlled the great silver mines of the upper Zarafshan.

This time the Moslems were victorious and captured the Khara Khitan commander, but instead of pursuing their success, returned south. The defeated army retired to Balasagun, where a great part of the population being Moslem and expecting the Shah shut the gates. Enraged, the beaten army stormed the city and slew 47,000 of the inhabitants.[45] Notwithstanding the ruin of his capital, Chiluku still hoped to make headway against his enemies. At this juncture it was pointed out to him that his funds were exhausted and that the only way to reimburse himself was to order his troops to give up the booty seized from Kuchluk, most of which was his own recently plundered treasure from Uzgand. Worn out, and not knowing where else to find money, the Gur Khan gave the order. The response was an immediate mutiny, and Kuchluk, who had reassembled his troops, suddenly appeared and made the old monarch prisoner. This happened in 1211, but although Chiluku lived on until 1213, his son-in-law not only treated him generously but left to him all outward marks of royalty. To complete the story it only remains to be said that Othman, having accepted the Khwarazm Shah's suzerainty, soon found himself unable to control the fury of his subjects against the exactions of his overlord's troops. In 1212, Samarkand revolted and a terrible massacre of the hated Khorezmians took place. Vengeance was swift and frightful. That same year the city was taken, over 10,000 of the populace were slain and Othman himself beheaded. The Shah then made an end of the Khara Khanid princes of both Farghana and Isfijab (present Sairam). This brought about a collision between him and Kuchluk— (there is no evidence of any previous understanding between the two for the overthrow of the Gur Khan)[46]—and from 1212 to 1214 an intermittent war was carried on in Farghana.

There had been no more interested spectator of these events than the Mongol Khan and he had early fished in the troubled waters. Learning of the Uighur revolt he despatched two

[45] See Wittfogel and Feng Chia-sheng, *History of Chinese Society: Liao* (907-1125), p. 652.
[46] Barthold, *Turkestan down to the Mongol Invasion*, p. 367.

envoys to the Idikut to offer his protection.[47] Fearful for the future, Barchuk gladly received the Mongol representatives and sent them back with two of his own to give Chingis Khan the following message: " The fame of the world conquering sovereign has come to me. I have agreed until very recently with the Gur Khan, and was just preparing to explain through an embassy a change in my position, and to yield myself with upright heart to thee, all conquering and mighty sovereign. While thinking over this, I saw thy envoys coming toward me, and then I beheld a blue Heaven through the clouds around me. I beheld a bright sun in the Sky. I saw also a blue shining river where just before the ice had hidden everything. I was filled with delight to my innermost being. I yield to thee the land of the Uighurs. I myself am the servant and son of Chingis Khan the Immovable." [48]

The conqueror was delighted with this response and promised to give to Barchuk his daughter Altun Beki in marriage, but demanded that he come in person to make his submission. Late in January or early in February, 1211, the Idikut arrived at the Mongol camp on the Kerulen and personally recognized the suzerainty of Chingis.[49] Simultaneously, or very soon afterward, there also arrived Arslan Khan of the Kharluks and Buzar or Ozar, the ruler of Almaligh (near present Kulja). The previous year (1210) Chingis Khan had despatched 10,000 men under Kubilai Noyan to the country of the Kharluks. This he had done perhaps to intimidate Arslan, perhaps to demonstrate his ability to protect any of the Gur Khan's ex-vassals who cared to seek his protection. Arslan it will be remembered had twice rebelled against Chiluku, so could look for nothing but dire retribution. Buzar was a former horse thief who had taken advantage of the disintegration of the Khara Khitan empire to carve out a small realm for himself and could likewise expect to be severely punished. Hence, both

[47] The title Idikut was originally that of the Basmil rulers who had preceded the Uighurs in the region of Bishbaligh, present Ku Ch'eng. (Barthold, " Turks," *Enc. Isl.*)

[48] D'Ohsson, *Histoire des Mongols*, Vol. I, p. 110.

[49] See *Yüan Ch'ao Pi Shih* and the *Yüan Shih*.

joined the Idikut in his submission to the Mongol Khan. To the former, Chingis gave another of his daughters, to the latter one of those of his eldest son Juchi.

Khara Kitai thus passed from the political stage. The provinces of Transoxiana, Farghana and the Syr fell to the Shah of Khwarazm; the principality of Amaligh, the Khanate of the Kharluks and the kingdom of the Uighurs to Chingis Khan, and soon after, the valleys of the Chu, Issyk Kul and upper Tarim to Kuchluk. Through the dissolution of the powerful and potentially hostile empire of the Gur Khan, the Mongol conqueror saw his authority extended beyond the desert and his far western flank made relatively safe. But even prior to the Naiman's coup d'état, he had turned his attention south.

CHAPTER V

# CHINGIS KHAN ATTACKS HSI HSIA AND CHIN

HAVING completed the unification of the nomads of the north, it was inevitable that Chingis Khan, like his Hsiungnu and Turkish predecessors, would be drawn south after booty and glory. Also, as neither the Tanguts nor the Jurchids could feel safe with the powerful and militant state that he had created at their very doorstep, he could expect both to intervene at the outbreak of any serious trouble. Aware of this, he resolved to be first in the field. There was, however, another and equally compelling motive driving the Mongol toward war.

At that period in his career territorial acquisition in China formed no part in his plans, but just as he wished to break the military strength of Hsi Hsia and Chin, he also desired to efface the political supremacy of the Chin emperor. Since the days of the Turkish empire the ruler of China had been for the people of the northern steppes the greatest monarch on earth, so that it was necessary for Chingis Khan to vindicate his own claim to supreme authority by forcing the Chin ruler, the most powerful in China, to pay tribute to him and recognize his suzerainty.[1] Added to this there was no better means of increasing his popularity and hold upon the recently united tribesmen than an expedition to China with the propect of looting its fabulous riches.

Since they were thoroughly conversant with this political outlook and knew well what was going on in the north, the failure of the Chin to obstruct Chingis Khan's rise to power requires some explanation. Before his victory over the Keraits in 1203 they may have felt that one or other of the successive

[1] See Grenard, *Gengis Khan*, pp. 111-112.

113

coalitions formed against him and the Wang Khan would stop him. But after the overwhelming defeat sustained by the T'ai-yang of the Naimans and his allies in 1204 it was apparent that a menace had arisen in the north. During 1205 the situation might still have been retrieved, since there were considerable Naiman and Mergid forces at large who would have welcomed an opportunity to co-operate against the common foe. Unfortunately, hostilities with the Sung loomed on the political horizon and the Chin, fearing to fight two wars at once, took no action. In the spring of 1206, as already seen, Chingis Khan's supremacy was acknowledged by nearly all the tribes from the Khinghan to the western Altai, while Alakush Tagin, chief of the Onguds, had entered into an alliance. North and south of the desert he thus challenged the authority of the Chin emperor. The same year war with the Sung broke out, and though hostilities ceased as early as 1207 it was not until July or August, 1208, that peace was signed. By it the Sung were obliged to increase up to 250,000 taels of silver and 250,000 bolts of silk the annual tribute agreed to in 1165, pay an indemnity of 300,000 silver taels, give up a number of places in the valley of the Huai, recognize the suzerainty of the Chin emperor and send north the head of the minister whom the Chin held responsible for the war.[2] Only then did the reigning emperor Madaku (1190-1208) turn his undivided attention to the north. That year (1208) he sent his uncle Yün-chi prince of Wei on an embassy, ostensibly to receive the tribute formerly paid by Chingis Khan, but really to investigate. Doubtless ever since 1198, when he had received the honorary title of Commander of the Frontier, Chingis had sent an annual present to the Chin court, which would be termed tribute.

Reaching the north, Yün-chi was received by the Mongol ruler but was shown scant courtesy. Concluding that this boded ill for the future, he advised the emperor to attack Chingis Khan as soon as possible. However, Madaku died,

[2] This was Han T'ou-chu.

and nothing could be undertaken until the succession of the new emperor. This turned out to be Yün-chi who, under the title of Wei Shao Wang, ascended the throne in 1209.[3]

The significance of the Chin embassy was not lost upon the Mongol Khan and he began to make plans for war. That year four Chinese officers, who had been punished by the emperor, had fled to him with their families and the next year (1209) still others arrived.[4] Desiring vengeance, all urged him to go against the Chin at once. Earlier still, in 1206, a member of the ruling house had invited him to aid a revolt in Liaotung,[5] but he refused to be persuaded and postponed the invasion until he could throw the whole weight of his army into the struggle.

Up to that time the Mongols had never faced the vast hosts that they would be called upon to meet once the invasion of China began. So Chingis wisely decided to make the first onslaught against the less powerful Tanguts. As seen, he had long intended to make his opening move in that direction and in 1205 and 1207 had sent against Hsi Hsia two small expeditions. Neither of them had been more than feelers to test enemy strength and to whet the appetite of his troops for plunder. Freed from the last of his nomad enemies by his victory in 1208 over Kuchluk and Tukta Biki, he prepared to invade Hsi Hsia in person.

The force that now took the field against the Tanguts was a powerful army. Its exact strength we do not know, but since Chingis Khan was able to meet every host the enemy sent against him, it must have been considerable. In the days of Chao Yüan-hao (1032-48) the regular troops of Hsi Hsia numbered 158,000, and there is no reason to suppose that they were fewer in 1209.[6] Drawn from a very mixed population,

---

[3] " Yüan Shih."

[4] These last were Li Ts'ao and T'ien Kuang-ming; see the *Hsi Hsia Chi Shih Pen-mo* and *Hsi Hsia Shu Shih*.

[5] The rebel was known as Ta-pien and was called the Ai Wang of Chin; see the *Yüan Shih Hsin-pien* of Wei Yüan.

[6] The forces of Chao Yüan-hao (1032-48) were distributed as follows: 7,000 troops held the northern frontier, 13,000 protected the capital and towns of the

the Hsi Hsia army consisted of both cavalry and infantry, the latter undoubtedly supplied by the Chinese, the former by the Tanguts, the T'u-fan or Tibetans, the Shara Uighurs and by other nomad tribes of Turko-Mongol stock.

From the " Hsi Hsia Shu Shih " it seems that the Mongols set out in April and, advancing from the Tola, went down the Ongin Gol and across the Gurban Saikhan Ula.[7] Once over this range they must have marched east and parallel to the Khurku Mountains until within sight of the Hei Shan (present Khara Narin Ula), then swinging south, have crossed the Hsi Hsia border into the country known to the Chinese as Ho-hsi.[8] Continuing in the same direction, they presumably passed along the eastern side of the Dabsun Nor and made for Wu-la-hai taken during the expedition of 1207.

From the Tola to Wu-la-hai the distance covered was at least 650 miles. Of this some 450 miles is gobi, which in many stretches provides a limited amount of grazing, but the last 200 miles is partly sand, which varies from semi shrub-covered hillocks to considerable dunes. Over this the Mongols would have travelled as fast as possible.

Up to the Gurban Saikhan Ula, and somewhat east, advance depots of sheep for food were probably established, but from there on the troops would have depended on what they could carry.

Once the vicinity of Wu-la-hai was reached, they were in

Ho-lan Shan (Alashan), 30,000 were posted on the Kan Chou and Yü-hsiang front to oppose the T'u-fan (Tibetans) and Hui-ho (Uighurs of the T'ien Shan), 100,000 were cantoned along the Hsi Hsia-Sung border, and 8,000, including 3,000 cuirassiers, composed the Imperial Guard. (See Cordier, *Histoire Générale de la Chine et des ses relations avec les pays étrangers*, Vol. 11, p. 97.)

[7] Certain works declare that the invasion began in the auaumn of 1210, but since Chingis Khan set out against the Chin during the spring of 1211, the date April, 1209—see the *Yüan Shih, Hsi Hsia Chi Shih Pen-mo* and the *Hsi Hsia Shu Shih*—is far more likely to be correct.

[8] The *Hsi Hsia Shu Shih* says that in the third month (April 6 to May 5) of 1209, Chingis Khan moved his army to the country north of Hei-shui i. e., to the territory of the Ongin Gol and Gurban Saikhan Ula, and from there marched southward through Ho-hsi to Wu-la-hai. In A. Herrmann's *Atlas of China*, there is a map of the dominions of the Sung, Liao, Chin and Tangut dynasties which shows a route running from the Ongin toward the Hei Shan and thence to the Ho-lan Shan or Ála Shan. Today this is still in use, so I have assumed that the Mongol inroads of both 1207 and 1209 followed it.

a region of comparative plenty and doubtless sent out raiding parties to drive in sheep from the Ho-lan Shan.

As soon as Li An-ch'üan (1206-11) learned that the Mongols were approaching Wu-la-hai, he ordered 50,000 men under his nephew Li Tsun-hsiang and the general Kao Liang-hui to hold them up.[9] Marching north, they encountered the invader somewhere beyond the town, only to be disastrously beaten, and though the prince escaped, Kao Liang-hui was captured and put to death on refusing to bow before Chingis Khan. The Mongols then pushed on to Wu-la-hai. In May they carried it by storm, and while fighting in the streets, captured the commander and imperial tutor Hsien-pei U-ta.[10]

Their next move called for an advance over the Ho-lan Shan to attack the capital Chung-hsing, the Erikhaya of the Mongols. As today, there was only one practicable road for troops across the range and this was commanded by the fortress of K'e-i Men.

From the outset of the war, Li An-ch'üan had stationed seventy thousand men to cover it but on receiving news of Li Tsun-hsiang's defeat—it is not unlikely that the vanquished army constituted the greater part of the force—he sent a further fifty thousand under Wei-ming Ling-kung, who took over supreme command. Deploying his men along the slopes adjoining the plain, the general awaited the arrival of Chingis Khan, who appeared soon after the capture of Wu-la-hai. Confident in the number of his troops, Wei-ming Ling-kung launched a furious attack and forced the Mongols to retire. But, either because his losses had been heavy or his victory was won over only a part of the invading army, he returned to his position and remained on the defensive.

[9] The " Yüan Shih " and the " Hsi Hsia Chi " say that the prince commanding the Tangut army was the heir apparent, but give no name. The " Hsi Hsia Shu Shih " calls him Li Ch'en-chen, and the general, Kao I. T'u Chi in the " Meng-wu-erh Shih " says that Li Tsun-hsiang was the nephew of Li An-ch'üan whom he succeeded in 1211. The general with him is often called Kao Ling-kung, but T'u Chi declares that it should be Kao Liang-hui. Since T'u Chi is always at special pains to correct wrongly given names, I have followed him.

[10] The " Hsi Hsia Shu Shih " calls him Hsi Pi-Shih, but I have followed T'u Chi's rendering of the name.

For two months Chingis Khan vainly waited for him to make another attack. Then early in August he decided to try to lure him into the open. Accordingly, he struck camp as if departing, and leaving a detachment to simulate a rearguard, placed the rest of his men in ambush. Wei-ming Ling-kung was completely deceived, and descending on to the plain to crush a small force, suddenly found himself face to face with the entire Mongol army. Compelled to give battle, he suffered a crushing defeat and was himself taken prisoner.

Pressing on from the battle field, the victorious Mongols arrived before K'e-i Men, which must have surrendered almost immediately, for no mention is made of any resistance. The way now lay open to the capital, and crossing the mountains without loss of time, Chingis Khan pitched his camp at Po (Pai) Wang Miao (the ancestral temple of the Tangut kings) and began the siege. Chung-hsing stood in the principal economic area of Hsi Hsia and, like the present town of Ning-hsia, depended on a system of irrigation canals. It was therefore not an easy place to take and could be expected to oppose a desperate resistance.

The enemy at his gates, Li An-ch'üan took personal command and directed the defense with such energy that by the end of October the Mongols had not gained a single foothold on the walls. But there then occurred a catastrophe that nearly brought the capital to its knees. Seeing that the autumnal rains had swollen the Yellow River, Chingis Khan ordered the construction of a great dyke to turn the river into the city, and the waters entering Chung-hsing, took a fearful toll of life and property.

Faced with this predicament, Li An-ch'üan sent in November to beg the Chin for help. Many Chin ministers and high officers urged that troops be despatched to break the siege, for they pointed out that the conquest of Hsi Hsia would certainly be followed by an attack upon the empire. But Wei Shao Wang said that both contestants were equally the enemy of Chin, and turned a deaf ear to the Tangut cry for succor. The siege dragged on until January, 1210, when the walls of the city were on the point of collapse. Then suddenly the pent up waters of the river burst the dyke built by the Mongols, and spreading over the surrounding plain, forced them to retire to higher ground.[11]

How much damage the Mongol camp sustained is not said, but, great or small, Chingis Khan was undismayed. Despite his failure to take Chung-hsing, he evidently felt that the rigors of the investment would make Li An-ch'üan come to terms, for he sent his prisoner Hsien-pei U-Ta to negotiate.

Conditions within the city were far too serious to risk revealing them to the enemy. When Li An-ch'üan was informed that the embassy was approaching, he came out on the walls, and seeing U-Ta on the water, informed him that he would not be allowed to enter.[12] Notwithstanding this, peace was made and, giving Chingis Khan one of his daughters in marriage, the Tangut ruler sent the following message: " Having heard of your glory (power), we were greatly afraid, but now we will be your right hand (vassal) and will serve you faithfully and will supply you with the products of our realm—camels, woollen cloth and falcons." He then collected so many camels that it was with difficulty they were brought to Chingis Khan.[13] Content with this, the conqueror withdrew to the north, but not until April 1210 did he set free Wei-ming Ling-kung.

Chingis Khan thus successfully concluded his first major expedition against a civilized state. Opposed to him had been a powerful army whose total forces in the field numbered well over one hundred thousand men. Doubtless some of these were levies, but a large percentage must have been regular troops.

In the first clash with the enemy to the north of Wu-la-hai,

---

[11] Hyacinth, quoting from the edition of the *Yüan Shih* used by him, says that the Tanguts broke the dyke. (D'Ohsson.) Often the month of January finds the Yellow River frozen in both this region and further to the south, but in such inland areas considerable annual variations in temperature are common.

[12] Only in the *Hsi Hsia Chi* does one learn these details concerning the manner in which negotiations were carried on.

[13] The *Yüan Ch'ao Pi Shih.*

the invaders may have been numerically superior, but in the second battle their army was probably the smaller of the two. By 1209 the entire effective force of the Mongols did not exceed one hundred and thirty-five thousand, and with an attack by the Chin always a possibility, Chingis Khan can hardly have invaded Hsi Hsia with even half his army. Yet he carried all before him, and though unable to capture Chung-hsiung, forced the Tangut ruler to become his vassal. Having dealt Hsi Hsia such a blow, Chingis Khan could safely march against the Chin with the greater part of his troops.

The Mongols had barely departed when the Tanguts, enraged with Wei Shao Wang for having left them in the lurch, made a raid over the Chin border and in September plundered Chia Chow on the Yellow River.[14] This brought to an end a peace that had lasted since 1165. Without any permanent territorial gains or losses to either side, hostilities continued until 1225 when the two joined in a belated alliance against the Mongols.

No sooner had Chingis Khan returned victorious from Hsi Hsia than he received an embassy from the Chin to make known officially the accession of Wei Shao Wang. Receiving the chief envoy, he was informed that a new Son of Heaven had ascended the throne and that the news must be acknowledged by a Kowtow. Chingis Khan asked who the new emperor was, and on being told that he was Yün-chi, turned his face south and spat. " I thought," he exclaimed, " that the ruler of the Middle Kingdom must be from Heaven, Can he be a person of such weakness as the prince of Wei! Why should I

---

[14] In 1210 or 1211 the Tanguts are reported to have clashed with a certain Pai-ssŭ-po, who is spoken of as being a powerful chief of the Hei Ta-ta. According to the narrative, Li An-ch'üan took the field against the invader, but was defeated and only obtained peace at the price of his daughter and acknowledgment of Pai-ssŭ-po's suzerainty. Usually the term Hei Ta-ta (black or uncivilized Ta-ta) was used to designate the tribes of Outer Mongolia. But Wu Kuang-ch'eng, author of the *Hsi Hsia Shu Shih*, says that here the Hsi-fan or Tibetans are intended. While one might expect the Tibetans of the Kokonor and Tsaidam to have taken advantage of Hsi Hsia's weakened condition to make such an attack, the account of it is very reminiscent of Chingis Khan's inroad of 1209-10. Therefore, either the story of Li An-ch'üan's surrender of his daughter and agreement to become Pai-ssŭ-po's vassal has been added by mistake, or the whole affair is a garbled version of the Mongol invasion.

Kowtow for him!" He then mounted his horse and rode away.[15] The "Yüan Shih" says that, enraged at the envoy's report, Wei Shao Wang resolved to slay Chingis Khan when he should come with tribute. Apparently the envoy never dared repeat Chingis Khan's exact words, or Wei Shao Wang could not have failed to perceive that his position as universal emperor had been challenged and that war was inevitable.

Even early the next year (1211), when Na-ho-mai-chu, commander of the northern frontier, reported that the Mongols were preparing for war, and insisted that since there was now peace between them and Hsi Hsia, an invasion of the empire must be immiment, Wei Shao Wang refused to take heed. Instead, he declared that Na-ho-mai-chu's conduct was responsible for Chingis Khan's hostility and had him thrown into prison.[16]

It is hard to understand the emperor's blindness, especially after his own advice three years earlier to his predecessor Madaku. Conceivably he believed that the Mongol cavalry was too exhausted by the invasion of Hsi Hsia to make an immediate attack likely. If such was his idea he was gravely mistaken. The Mongols were in no such difficulty, and Chingis Khan, having crippled the Tanguts, was resolved to invade the empire at once.

Wishing to justify his aggression in the eyes of the world, he appealed to the vendetta existing between his family and the Chin since the twelfth century. Before setting out he ascended a high mountain—probably Burkhan Khaldun, sacred to his clan and to himself since his early days—and implored Heaven's help.[17] "Oh eternal Heaven," cried he, "I am armed to avenge the blood of my uncles Okin Barkhak and Ambakai whom the Altan Khans (Golden Emperors) slew with ignominy. If you approve, lend me help from on high and permit that here on earth men, as well as spirits good and bad, assist me."[18]

[15] "Yüan Shih."

[16] *Meng-wu-erh Shih*, De Mailla, *Histoire Générale de la Chine*, Vol. IX.

[17] Burkhan Khaldun was an eastern spur in the range today known as the Kentei Khan.

[18] Rashid ad-Din; see D'Ohsson, *Histoire des Mongols*, Vol. I, p. 124. Among the

When Chingis Khan made this momentous decision he was sure of the situation south of the desert. The flight of the Chin officials who had come to him in 1208 and 1209, the revolt in Liaotung during 1206, and the friendship of Alakush Tagin, all indicated that the power of the central government was on the wane. To the east among the Khitans, he may have expected to find allies of even greater value than the Onguds, but as far as one can ascertain, he received no encouragement there until he had amply demonstrated the superiority of his army over that of the Chin. As regards affairs within the empire, he was well informed. Not only the malcontents in his camp since 1208 and 1209, but the Onguds must have told him much of value concerning political, economic and military conditions. Hardly less useful informants were the Moslem and Uighur merchants in whose hands was most of the trade between China and Central Asia. Acquainted with many highways and districts in the empire and having connections in the most varied quarters, they were admirably fitted to provide Chingis Khan with detailed reports.

The overland trade had always brought enormous profits to those dealing in it, but was also fraught with considerable risks, as goods had to be taken on credit. Hence a temporary suspension of trade due to war caused heavy losses.[19] To none was this commerce of such importance as to the Moslem capitalists, and at that time the land route was of more than usual consequence. Since the opening of the 13th century the sea trade going via the Persian Gulf had become exceedingly precarious, for war having broken out between Kish and Ormuz, each did all in its power to intercept and prevent vessels sailing from the port of the other. Moreover, Chinese competition in the easterly part of the sea route was becoming

Mongols and Turks to the north, the Chin emperor was always known as the Altan Khan (The Golden Ruler).

[19] Islamic capitalism rose on the heels of Islamic conquest and pressed east and west in the wake of the Moslem armies. Not, however, until the rise of the Uighur kingdom of the T'ien Shan in the second half of the ninth century did the overland trade to China assume large proportions, as only then were merchants afforded sufficient protection. (Hartman, " China," *Incyclopaedia of Islam*, Vol. I, p. 844.)

alarmingly strong.[20] Therefore, when the dissolution of the Khara Khitan empire made the normal overland road also unsafe, the Moslem capitalists were placed in a serious dilemma. But suddenly in 1210 the situation was relieved by the submission of the Kharluks to Chingis Khan. This provided the merchants with a northern route, and they found themselves able not only to resume trade with China but once more to penetrate Mongolia. Trade with settled peoples has always been of importance to the nomads of the north, especially for the purchase of armor, weapons (e. g., sabres) and various articles of clothing. For these they bartered hides, wool, furs and horses. The interests of Chingis Khan therefore coincided with those of the Moslem capitalists, who, saved from their predicament by the Mongol conquest and grateful for the law and order that prevailed along the new route, willingly acted as the conqueror's spies.[21]

But Chingis Khan's greatest asset was his army. Victorious over Hsi Hsia, where much valuable experience had been gained concerning the military methods of civilized states, the army and its leaders were confident of success. If numerically much inferior to the Chin, the Mongols enjoyed greater mobility and unsurpassed leadership. As in the invasion of Hsi Hsia, the conqueror relied entirely upon the Mongol army proper and apparently made no call upon his Kirghiz, Kharluk and Uighur vassals for troops. But this time, with the power of the Tanguts temporarily broken, he was able to employ a far greater force than in 1209. Yet he had before him a formidable task.

The Chin empire, even if on the decline, was, as Vladimirtsov remarks, by no means a " colossus on feet of shale." [22] Its prestige was very great and the central government still strong. How outstanding was its renown is well illustrated by the following anecdote. During the spring of 1218 a Mongol

[20] For some interesting references to Chinese maritime trade during the 12th and 13th centuries; see Goodrich, A Short History of the Chinese People, pp. 146-47.
[21] For a brief but very able account of the overland trade at this period; see Barthold, Turkestan down to the Mongol Invasion, pp. 393-396.
[22] Vladimirtsov, The Life of Chingis Khan, p. 95.

embassy arrived at the court of the Khwarazm Shah, then the greatest potentate in Islam. After the public audience the Shah called in the leader of the embassy, himself a Moslem, to question him in private about the Mongol army, and in the course of the conversation asked with incredulous wonder; " Has Chingis Khan really conquered the Chin and taken the city of Tamghach? " (Chung Tu, the capital of the empire).[23]

Unlike the Khorezmian empire, that of the Chin suffered from none of the ecclesiastical and dynastic disorders that helped Chingis Khan to overthrow Muhammad Shah, who was at odds with the Islamic clergy and the queen mother Turkan Khatun. Also, more fortunate than the Moslem ruler, whose main economic areas, Khwarazm and Sogdiana, were exposed to devastation as soon as the line of the Syr Darya was crossed, the comparable but larger areas held by the Chin in Honan and Kuan-chung (Shensi and eastern Kansu) remained protected by the Yellow River long after the subsidiary territories to the north were lost.

During the first war with the Sung, concluded in 1141, these regions had all seen a considerable exodus south of those who wished to escape Chin rule.[24] But if economically damaging from one aspect, the migration had enabled the new government to undertake considerable redistribution of land among the remaining population. So for a time at least, and despite the ever present evil of latifundia, it did not have to deal on a large scale with the problem of landless peasantry.[25] Consequently, a succession of good years and the heavy tribute

[23] Nasawi; see Barthold, *Turkestan down to the Mongol Invasion*, p. 397. Tamghach was a corruption of the word Tabghach, which was the name of a Turkish people known to the Chinese as the T'o-pa who ruled northern China during the fifth and sixth centuries. Like the Khitans and Jurchids after them, their military prestige was very great and, as in the case of the Khitans, their name was frequently applied to China whose emperors were often termed the Tamghach Khan. This title was also sometimes borne by the Khara Khanid rulers of Transoxiana.

[24] This exodus south, so common a feature during the turmoil that for two centuries upset northern China after the fall of the Han dynasty (206 B. C.-220 A. D.), contributed greatly to the spread of the Chinese into the sub-Yangtse areas.

[25] See the *Chin Shih* and Mabel Ping-Hua Lee, " The Kin," *Economic History of China*, pp. 321-322.

wrung from the Sung made possible a fair degree of prosperity throughout the country. But with the close of the century the picture began to change. In 1194 the Yellow River burst its dikes and, flooding Shantung, changed the course of its lower reaches from the north to the south of the province (where it remained until 1853, when a similar catastrophe returned it to the old channel). Then came widespread monetary disorders through the failure of the government to redeem the bills which it had issued and circulated as equivalent to cash. The chaos caused by this was such, that in the words of Yeh-lü Ch'u-ts'ai; "the people's strength was worn out and the resources of the state exhausted."[26] Finally, from 1210 on, the country was afflicted by a series of famines which further aggravated the situation. Hence, while very potent in some respects, the Chin empire had a deteriorating economy.

Turning to the Jurchids themselves, though the nobility were in the process of transformation from a military bureaucracy into a landed aristocracy, both they and the Jurchid rank and file still retained much of their energy and martial spirit. Moreover, their army was not only the largest in the world but was considered the most powerful. Originally composed entirely of cavalry, it had added large numbers of infantry during the wars with the Sung. Therefore, its organization was modified to enable the use of both arms, so necessary in China where military operations involved many sieges. On the eve of the Mongol invasion it had given ample proof of its power, and in 1206, 145,000 troops had forced their way south to the Yangtse, and, as we have seen, compelled the Sung to sue for peace the following year (1207).

The exact numerical strength of the Chin army is not known, but one can make an approximate guess at it. According to the returns for the year 1195, the population of the empire was 48,490,000. This figure, of course, covers only those taxed and does not include the very poor or such persons as evaded the revenue collector.[27] Of this total, a so-called military popu-

[26] See Rémusat, " Vie de Yeliu Thsoutsai," *Nouveaux Mélanges Asiatiques*, Vol. II.
[27] E. H. Parker, *China*, pp. 195-196. The population of the Sung empire about

lation of 6,158,636, consisting of various groups, pastoral and Chinese, provided the army and was supported by the rental collected from government lands.[28] The troops of the empire may therefore have numbered 500,000 or more, perhaps about 120,000 being mounted bowmen recruited from the Jurchids, Solangs (Solons), Mukri, Khitans and Onguds, the rest Chinese. These last, though mostly infantry, also included some cavalry from the border regions, and probably varied greatly in the matter of equipment, some being provided with body armor, some not.

Beside their army, the Chin also possessed impressive defenses. South of the Mongol plateau, in the valleys of the Sang-kan and Yang rivers, were the heavily fortified cities of Hsi Ching, Te-hsing Chou and Hsüan-te Chou, and to the northwest and southwest of the capital Chung Tu, the nearly impregnable forts of Chü-yung Kuan and Tzu-ching Kuan.

Both these strongholds were situated on the present so-called Inner Wall, but due to the control of the border regions, first by the Khitan dynasty of Liao and then by the Chin, the Great Wall system enjoyed considerable less importance than it did during several other periods of Chinese history. So, when Chingis Khan appeared upon the scene, it is likely that the famous rampart was in a state of disrepair. Nevertheless, during the twelfth century two walls covering a number of small frontier towns were built or added to far beyond the Great Wall proper. One of these extended along the crest of the Khinghan between the Khitans and Khongirads,[29] and the other along the outer fringe of the southern Mongolian

the year 1200 was approximately 45,000,000; see John King Fairbank, *The United States and China*, p. 139.

[28] The census for the " military population " was taken in the year 1183; see E. H. Parker, *China*, pp. 195-196.

As regards the system of recruitment for the Chinese troops of the empire, my information is scanty, but it very likely resembled the method employed by the Khitans who selected special groups, many doubtless living on the frontier, and trained them for military activities of various kinds. (For the system under the Khitan or Liao; see Wittfogel, *History of Chinese Society: Liao*, p. 529.)

[29] This was the old Khitan frontier wall which was repaired in 1181. (See Joseph Mullie, " Les Anciennes villes de l'empire de Grand Leao au Royaume Mongol de Barin," *T'oung Pao*, 1922.

graslands. This, running from the Khinghan to the borders
of Hsi Hsia, was known to the Chinese as the Wai-pao and to
the nomads as the Ongu. It was the charge of this rampart,
falling under the jurisdiction of the commander for the northwest, that had given to its guardians their name of Ongud.
As military works, neither can have been intended to withstand
more than raiding expeditions. Further, as Owen Lattimore
has pointed out in " Mongol Journeys," the failure of the wall
in Inner Mongolia to take full advantage of high ground
indicates that it was built by people who knew more about
maneuver than positional warfare. It must therefore have
been erected under Ongud rather than Chinese supervision.[30]

In his " Inner Asian Frontiers of China," the same author
stresses the fact that contrary to the common conception of a
once purely pastoral Manchuria and Inner Mongolia, parts of
both have also been the scene of agricultural and urban
activity.[31] Lying between the cities and agricultural lands of
China and South Manchuria on the one side, and the prairies
of western Manchuria and Outer Mongolia on the other, these
intermediate regions have been moulded by Chinese as well
as by nomad influences. Then, as now, small towns, often
built at the order of some nomad chief, sprang up in direct
contact with the steppes, and in the time of Chingis Khan a
string of such towns—Huan Chou, Feng-li, Ch'ang Chou, Fu
Chou, Ching Chou, Feng Chou and Yün-nei—stretched along
the southern edge of the Ongud prairies. The area thus formed
a social, economic and political borderland between China and
the tribes of the north.

As in the case of Kuku Khoto (Kuei-hua), built by the
famous Tumet Altan Anda Khan (1543-83), most of these
towns were established to supplement the purely pastoral

---

[30] Lattimore has a theory that the Ongu or Wai-pao, like other walls of the same
type, were built for the purpose of differentiating between Chinese subject and
nomad lord. In other words, they were erected as a form of tribute by the Chinese
of the border regions. (See Lattimore, *Mongol Journeys*, pp. 129-130.) Walls of
the same kind were erected by the Moslems north of the Chirchik in the valley of
the Syr Darya.

[31] For a discussion of this phenomenon see Lattimore, *Inner Asian Frontiers of
China*, pp. 66-72.

sources of wealth of successive nomad chiefs and their supporting aristocracy. Located on or near the end of the trade routes entering China from the north and west, they formed small but thriving centers of commerce and industry where Moslem as well as Chinese merchants flourished. Surrounding many such towns were areas of cultivation worked by Chinese colonists and captives brought in for the purpose. Therefore, in addition to their position as tribal leaders, the rulers and nobility of such regions became landed and moneyed aristocracy and the whole country less nomad than that beyond the desert.

With their mixed population and varied economy, such nomad states naturally developed a political outlook colored by Chinese as well as by nomad ideology, and were drawn now into the orbit of China, now into that of the north. Hence their political orientation tended to change from period to period. But if they acknowledged the suzerainty of the Son of Heaven or the ruler of the North as circumstances demanded, they invariably pushed forward their frontiers and extended their authority when either power became weakened by internal disorder or military disaster. Such was the beginning of the Tabghach (T'o-pa), Khitan and Jurchid empires, though the last began far to the east and not south of the gobi.

At the time with which we are dealing, there was no possibility of Ongud expansion at the expense of either Mongol or Chin. Consequently, Alakush Tagin, believing that the former were on the rise and the latter on the wane, decided to throw off his allegiance to the Chin as soon as Chingis Khan should march south. His policy was by no means endorsed by all the Onguds and one has seen that as early as 1204 certain of them opposed his alliance with the Mongol Khan against the T'ai-yang of the Naimans. Perhaps they were afraid of exciting the wrath of the Chin or perhaps, content with things as they existed, they were averse to aiding the rise of a power whose overlordship might prove heavier and more exacting than that of their present masters. But in the end the will of Alakush

Tagin prevailed and Chingis Khan was apparently promised an unhindered entry into the Ongud domain.

The map will make plain what this meant. The conqueror obtained a friend on the very threshold of Chin territory, and when the time came the Mongols could be sure of a free passage through the Wai-pao. But even had no such friendship existed, Chingis Khan would doubtless have forced his way through the Ongud realm. Elsewhere the empire was extremely difficult to penetrate. On the west it was covered by Hsi Hsia and the Yellow River, on the northeast by forests and to the east by the sea. Behind the line of the Khinghan lay the principal recruiting grounds of the imperial cavalry, a territory where much hard fighting could be expected and no loot comparable to that accumulated in the cities of China.

The details of Chingis Khan's plan of campaign have not come down to us, but from subsequent developments it is evident that he hoped to divide the Chin field forces by breaking into the empire simultaneously at two different points. The armies of the center and left wing were to strike in the neighborhood of Huan Chou and Ta-shui-luan, the army of the right wing at Ching Chou.[32]

To facilitate the advance of these forces and to overcome the difficulty of feeding a vast number of horses in one place, the western army must have concentrated on the Tola, and the eastern army along the Kerulen. Southward, in both the regions to be attacked, good grazing abounded, and should

[32] As regards the location of Ching Chou, the *Chung Kuo Ku-chin Ti-ming Ta-tzu-tien* and A. Herrmann, *Atlas of China*, both locate it in Suiyuan, but give no specific situation. However, on the Shara Muren, Suiyuan, there is a ruin, now known as Boro Baishing, which from a neighboring Nestorian inscription seems to date from the Chin period. Though very dilapidated, its strategic position and the remains of many bastions on the walls indicate that it was a place of considerable military importance. Further, it is the most extensive ruin in the northern part of the province. Joseph Mullie, *T'oung Pao*, 1922, quoting from the annals of the Chin dynasty, says that Ching Chou stood some 80 li (approx. 27 miles) south of the rampart constructed by the emperor Madaku (1190-1208). Today, 79 or 80 li north of Boro Baishing, there stretches an old wall which must be Madaku's work, i. e., the Wai-pao or Ongu. It is therefore assumed that Boro Baishing on the upper Shara Muren is the ruin of Ching Chou. (See " Preliminary Report on Nestorian remains North of Kuei-hua, Sui-yüan," by H. D. Martin, *Monumenta Serica*, 1938).

the Chin march thither and give battle, as expected, the terrain was admirably adapted to Mongol tactics.

By February, 1211, preparations for the campaign were nearly complete and Chingis Khan, who was encamped by the river Kerulen,[33] sent his son-in-law, the Khongirad Tokuchar, with 2,000 men to mount guard on the western border.[34] It is often concluded that no other troops were left in the north, but considering the proximity of Kuchluk in Khara Khitai this is unlikely. Chingis must have left behind a much greater force, perhaps as many as 20,000-25,000 troops under the over-all command of Temuge Ochigin.[35] So the army of invasion can hardly have exceeded 110,000 effectives. Of these one may suppose that about 70,000 formed the Central and Left-wing armies and some 40,000 the Right-wing.[36] Leading the former with Chingis himself were Mukhali, general-in-chief of the Left-wing army, Jebe, Subudei, Juchi Khassar and Tului.[37] In command of the other were the princes Juchi, Jaghatai and Ugedei, and though not mentioned, most certainly Bugurji.[38] Beside these famous captains there were three others who particularly distinguished themselves in the war: Chaghan, a Tangut and adopted son of Chingis Khan,[39] and the two Khitan brothers Yeh-lü Akhai and Yeh-lü Tukha. Since both were well acquainted with the country north of the Great Wall, the conqueror now attached Tukha to Jebe's staff and Akhai to that of the princes.[40]

[33] *Yüan Shih, Hsin Yüan Shih* and *Meng-wu-erh Shih*.

[34] *Yüan Sheng Wu Ch'in Cheng Lu*, commentaries by Wang Kuo-wei.

[35] When Chingis Khan marched west against the Khwarazm Shah in 1219, Temuge Ochigin was put in command of all troops left in Outer Mongolia.

[36] On a campaign of such magnitude one can reasonably assume that the Central and Left-wing armies numbered the whole of the Guard (Keshik), contingents furnished by various members of the imperial family and the greater part of the Left-wing army. The other force led by the princes Juchi, Jaghatai and Ugedei would certainly include all their own guardsmen, a considerable portion of the Right-wing army and perhaps a few troops contributed by others of the family.

[37] Gaubil, whose main source of information was the "Yüan Shih Lei Pien," alone mentions Tului and Juchi Khassar. (Gaubil, *Histoire de Gentchiscan et toute La Dynastie des Mongols ses successeurs conquérants de la Chine*, p. 16.

[38] It will be remembered that Bugurji was commander-in-chief of the Left-wing army.

[39] *Yüan Shih*, biography of "Ch'a-han" (Chaghan).

[40] *Meng-wu-erh Shih*, biographies of "Yeh-lü Akhai" and "Yeh-lü Tukha."

Chingis Khan's departure from the Kerulen is dated by the "Yüan Shih" in February or March, and by the "Hsin Yüan Shih" and "Meng-wu-erh Shih" in April. Nothing is said by any of the three about the crossing of the gobi, but the "Meng-wu-erh Shih" affirms that in May Chingis reached Ta-shui-luan. Since April and May provide better marching conditions in the gobi than February or March, and since the date of Chingis Khan's arrival at Ta-shui-luan allows all the time necessary to move from the Kerulen to the prairies south of the desert, the two latter sources are the more acceptable from the standpoint of logistics.[41] Furthermore, the "Yüan Shih" is rather confused in its relation of events for 1211.

The Mongol line of march can only be conjectured. The central and left-wing armies possibly went from the Kerulen in two bodies, one by a road approximating to the present caravan highway from the river to Dolon Nor, and the other over or parallel to the most easterly of the main routes now connecting Urga and Kalgan. Although in parts an empty waste, the region is less barren than some of the country crossed in 1209, and has been successfully traversed by several armies only less numerous than that of Chingis Khan. In the preceding centuries large Hsiungnu, Juan-juan and Turkish hosts had marched over the same deserts and plains, and equally large forces had gone north at the command of Han Wu Ti (140 B. C.-87 A. D.), T'o-pa Tao (423-452) and T'ang T'ai Tsung (627-649). Nearly two centuries later, during 1388, a Ming army 100,000 strong was to penetrate as far north as the Bur Nor, and in 1696 the Manchu emperor K'ang-hsi

---

[41] The *Yüan Shih* of Sung Lien says that Chingis Khan left the Kerulen during the second month of 1211 (Feb. 15-March 16) in which the defeat of the Chin at the Yeh-hu Ling is also dated. T'u Chi in the *Meng-wu-erh Shih* states that the conqueror started preparing for the invasion during the second month but only left the Kerulen in the third month (April 15-May 13)—in 1211 there was an intercalary month (March 17-April 14)—and did not reach Ta-shui-luan until the fourth month (May 14-June 12), which is the date given by the *Chin Shih* for the arrival of the Mongols in the empire. I am not aware of T'u Chi's authorities, but his dates fit in admirably with the climatic and grazing conditions involved. Among other things, the later start would have enabled the grass-fed Mongol horses to put on a little weight after their winter in the open.

(1669-1722) was to lead 108,000 soldiers, with many thousand non-combatants, over the same country.

Holding a course west of the two eastern columns under the conqueror, the princes probably advanced from the River Tola to the Khorio Gol, along or near the present Urga-Kalgan highway that joins the road from Uliassatai. From the Khorio Gol it is an easy march to the upper Shara Muren, and the princes very likely arrived before Ching Chou about the same time that Chingis Khan appeared on the upper Luan Ho.[42] The distance covered by the eastern armies was rather under 500 miles, that by the western approximately 530. Notwithstanding a considerable expanse of gobi, the routes indicated have a limited supply of water in the form of wells and water holes. This might have proved insufficient for so great a host of men and horses, but the Mongols seemingly timed their advance to avoid a shortage. During early spring the normal supply of water is augmented by melted snow in clay troughs and hollows along the way, and this, as well as the grazing and topography, would have been explored by scouts before the army set out.[43]

As in 1209, depots of livestock were very likely established along the initial stages of the advance, but further south the grazing, again being poor, would all be needed for the army's mounts, at least 300,000 in number and probably more. For the staff of a civilized army the provisioning of 110,000 men on such a march would constitute a major commissariat problem, but the ability of the Mongols to travel great distances on quantities of food quite inadequate for civilized troops must have enabled them to carry all they required on their remounts.[44] Doubtless each column moved tumen by tumen at regular intervals, in order not to exhaust the water on the

[42] For present day routes over the gobi; see the *British General Staff Map of Asia*, sheet 22 (Mongolia), published 1931; the *Hoku Shina Chizu* (Map of North China), published in Dairen, 1936, and A. Herrmann, *Atlas of China*, published at the Harvard University Press, 1935.

[43] Later in the summer this additional supply of water is practically all dried up.

[44] The Monogls often used camel or ox-drawn two wheeled carts for transportation, but these were employed principally for their short semiannual migrations between summer and winter pastures.

road by too great a demand on it at once. Also it is likely that each such body made use of the terrain to extend its front several miles, thus advancing as a group of minor units all in touch with one another and ready to unite if necessary. In accordance with the usual Mongol practice, a screen of scouts would have covered the front, rear and flanks of the advancing columns, and couriers would have kept touch between them and general headquarters. Although never less than 180 miles and sometimes as many as 230 miles separated Chingis Khan from the princes, one may be almost certain that communication between them never failed.

They reached the Ongud frontier in May. The Ongu or Wai-pao was crossed without opposition, and while the advance forces of the Eastern armies under Jebe and Subudei respectively took Ta-shui-luan and Huan Chou, the princes entered Ching Chou.[45] Chingis Khan then suspended operations, and camping perhaps at Ta-shui-luan, passed the summer resting his men and horses and awaiting a move on the part of the Chin[46]

While thus inactive he received a visit from Alakush Tagin who very likely came from receiving the princes at Ching Chou and now offered the service of his troops.[47] Encouraged by this fresh show of friendship, the conqueror proposed a marriage alliance and gave his daughter Alaghi Beki to the prince's eldest son.[48] He must also have made use of the respite to bring south several thousand head of sheep, for his Ongud host could not have fed the invading army indefinitely.

---

[45] The *Meng-wu-erh Shih*, biography of " Jebe," specifically states that in the fourth month (May 14-June 12) the Mongol vanguard under Jebe took Ta-shui-luan, while the biography of " Subudei " says that the latter captured Huan Chou. In the main text of the *Meng-wu-erh Shih* the fall of Huan Chou is dated for the seventh month (Aug. 10-Sept. 11). However, the subsequent and speedy reduction of the other small towns of the grassland inclines one to believe that it fell much earlier, in May or June.

Ching Chou is listed in the *Meng-wu-erh Shih* among the places occupied by the princes up to the ninth month (Oct. 9-Nov. 6), but it must have succumbed in May or June, for it belonged to the friendly Ongud chief.

[46] *Meng-wu-erh Shih.*

[47] I think it highly probable that Ching Chou was then the summer capital of the Onguds, their winter capital being Tung-sheng (Tokoto) near the Yellow River.

[48] *Meng-wu-erh Shih*, biography of " Alakush Tagin."

Meanwhile Wei Shao Wang had been apprised of what had taken place, and regretting his hasty imprisonment of Na-ho-mai-chu, set him free. Nien-ho-ho-ta, commander for the north-west, was then directed to try to negotiate peace with Chingis Khan, but his overtures failed. The Chin had therefore no alternative but to fight.[49]

Too late to prevent the Mongols establishing themselves in the Ongud country, the Chin determined to arrest any further progress south. Wan-Yen Hu-sha and Tu-chi Ch'ien-chia-nu, joint commanders of Hsüan-te Chou, were ordered to march north and begin raising fortifications at Wu-sha Pao.[50] Simultaneously, instructions were sent out for another and larger army to go and build similar works along the Yeh-hu Ling to the south of Fu Chou.

Both these locations were on the northern face of the range that separates Mongolia from China. Moreover, while the former covered Wei-ning and the roads running from it to the southwest and southeast, the latter straddled the highway between Fu Chou and Hsüan-p'ing and blocked the Huan-erh-tsui and Ts'ui-p'ing K'ou defile.[51] All direct approach to Hsi Ching (Ta-T'ung) and Hsüan-te Chou was thus barred.

Our records make no mention of any troops being despatched toward Ching Chou, yet troops could have been sent and the Chin have enjoyed a considerable margin of numerical superiority over both Mongol armies. Instead we find them massing an overwhelming force to deal with Chingis Khan alone. Evidently they believed that the best way to end the invasion was to strike a shattering blow at its leader. Consequently, they assembled the flower of their troops for an advance on the Eastern army, and resigned themselves to the possible

[49] Meng-wu-erh Shih.

[50] Li-tai T'ung-chien Chi-lan, Meng-wu-erh Shih. Wan-yen, which Pelliot believes is the Jurchid corruption of the Chinese word Wang (Prince), was always prefixed to the names of those belonging to the imperial family. Hu-sha, Na-ho-mai-chu, etc., are Chinese renderings of Jurchid names.

[51] Huan-erh-tsui, the northern entrance of the pass, is almost certainly to be identified with the Te-sheng K'ou of modern times, which is approximately seventeen miles northwest of present Kalgan (Chang-chia K'ou).

devastation of the northwest by the Western army. Victorious over Chingis Khan, they could expect the retreat of the princes.

Though the size of the army under Wan-yen Hu-sha and his colleague is unknown, the other was more than twice the strength of that under Chingis Khan, so that at least some of the Chin had formed a very high opinion of the Mongol war machine. Doubtless they had received reliable reports of the terrible reverses suffered by the Tanguts in 1209. Realizing that their cavalry was inferior to that of the invaders, they refused to split up their forces, and Chingis Khan found himself the object of an unexpectedly powerful counter offensive.

It was probably this cavalry inferiority that discouraged the Chin from launching a flank attack from the Khinghan. For although first class, the imperial cavalry in Manchuria can hardly have been numerous enough to have opposed the invading armies single handed.

Of the two Chin armies, that for the Yeh-hu Ling was certainly the bigger and intended to strike the main blow, the other to operate in a covering role. From Wu-sha Pao the smaller force could threaten Chingis Khan's right flank as soon as he moved southward to meet the larger army and at the same time protect the latter's left from an attack by the conqueror's sons if they were called from the west. Should the princes cross the mountains and advance east in an attempt to cut the communications of the Yeh-hu Ling army, it would be equally well placed to march south and intercept them in the valley of the upper Yang. If none of these things happened, it could perform the function of a reinforcement.

To meet the approaching situation, it was vitally important that Chingis Khan be able either to dispose of the Wu-sha Pao force before engaging the Yeh-hu Ling army or that he weaken the latter by diverting part of it elsewhere. To this end he might have sent troops south across the Tu-shih K'ou to make a feint at the capital. Had such a force approached Chung Tu, it is highly probable that the Chin would have detached men to oppose it. But the way over the Tu-shih K'ou lies through rough and mountainous country and might easily have held a

trap. The conqueror's other alternative was to order the princes
east deliberately to challenge the Wu-sha Pao army while he
dealt with the other. But the Chin program was ruined by the
lateness of its execution and communication difficulties.

Then, as today, there were no more than three roads leading
to the foot of the plateau on which Wei-ning and Fu Chou
stood. The most important of these began at Chung Tu, and
after winding through the Chü-yung Kuan defile, passed along
the lower reaches of the Yang River to Hui-ho Pao. The other
two started from Hsi Ching, one going via the Sang-kan River
and Te-hsing Chou to Hsüan-te Chou, while the second
followed the upper Yang to join the road from the capital.

Since the valley of the lower Yang had to be used by both
armies, the Chin decided to send the smaller force under Wan-
Yen Hu-sha and Tu-chi Ch'ien-chia-nu on ahead. Instructed
to raise defenses at Wu-sha Pao, the two commanders were
apparently told to remain encamped until the arrival of the
other force at the Yeh-hu Ling. During August they reached
their destination and began work. Apprised of this, Chingis
Khan immediately seized his chance. Jebe and Yeh-lü Tukha
were ordered to try to surprise the generals before they could
either finish their defenses or retreat to Wei-ning.[52]

The blow met with unqualified success, for the Mongols,
probably swinging north beyond Feng-li and the present Anguli
Nor to conceal their move, suddenly fell upon the Chin, who,
attacked unexpectedly before the completion of their work,
were severely defeated and forced to retire to Hsüan-p'ing.[53]
Chingis Khan's right flank was thus completely cleared. Jebe
then destroyed Wu-sha Pao and Wu-yüeh Ying[54] and moved
on to Wei-ning. Defending the town were two officers, Liu
Po-lin and Chia-ku Ch'ang-ku. Feeling that the place had
little hope of resisting, Liu Po-lin escaped over the walls by

---

[52] *Meng-wu-erh Shih*, biographies of " Jebe " and " Yeh-lü Tukha."
T'u Chi names Fu Chou, which he mistakenly identifies with Wei-ning.
[53] *Meng-wu-erh Shih*; *Chin Shih*, biography of " Wan-yen Hu-sha " and *Ssŭ Ch'ao Pieh Shih*.
[54] Wu-yüeh ying is not to be found on any map, nor is it mentioned in any
historical geography of Chinese place names that I have been able to consult.

a rope and went to offer his services to Jebe. Well received by the Mongol commander, he was told to return with Tukha and persuade the town to surrender. This he did, and retained in his rank of commander of 1,000, was ordered to help the Khitan to gain the capitulation of other towns in the region.[55] The names of these are not recorded, but Chi-ning (see map) will have been among them. After that Jebe rejoined Chingis who had arrived at Fu Chou with the rest of the army during late August or early September. Unlike Wei-ning, the town resisted and had to be carried by storm.[56] The same fate may also have overtaken its neighbors Feng-li and Ch'ang Chou, though one simply learns that they fell.

Still camped at Fu Chou in September, Chingis Khan received news that the second army had reached the Yeh-hu Ling and was raising defense works.[57] As general-in-chief the Chin had appointed the commander of Hsi Ching, Ke-shih-lieh Chih-chung.[58] This officer, though unpopular in certain quarters, enjoyed considerable influence with the emperor and had made a name in the war with the Sung (1206-7). Under him were Ting Hsüeh or Ta Shih in command of the vanguard, and Wan-yen Wu-nu as Inspector General, while the recently defeated Wan-yen Hu Sha was ordered to join with his forces and give the other commanders the benefit of his experience.[59]

According to various estimates, Chih-chung's host numbered 300,000, 400,000 or 500,000 men.[60] Doubtless the army in-

[55] *Meng-wu-erh Shih*, biographies of "Yeh-lü Tukha" and "Liu Po-lin." In the latter it is implied that Chingis Khan and not Jebe was before Wei-ning, but this must be a mistake.

[56] *Yüan Shih*, biography of "Chinkai."

[57] The *Yüan Sheng Wu Ch'in Cheng Lu* says that Chingis Khan was preparing to leave Fu Chou, the *Li-tai T'ung-chien Chi-lan* that he was on the point of making another drive south. Probably Chingis only intended to make a local move for hygienic and other reasons, as it was to his advantage to remain north and give battle where the terrain was so advantageous to his army.

[58] The commander was also known as Ke-shih-lieh Chiu-chin and Ke-shih-lieh Hu-sha-hu. (See the *Yüan Sheng Wu Ch'in Cheng Lu* and the *Chin Shih*, biography of "Ke-shih-lieh Chih-chung.")

[59] *Li-tai T'ung-chien Chi-lan; Meng-wu-erh Shih*.

[60] The *Yüan Shih* and the *Meng-wu-erh Shih* say 300,000; the *Hsin Yüan Shih*, *Li-tai T'ung-chien Chi-lan* and *Yüan Ch'ao Ming Ch'eng Shih Liao*, biography of "Mukhali," 400,000 and the *Meng Ta Pei Lu*, section on the Pai Ta-ta, commentary by Wang Kuo-wei, 500,000.

cluded large numbers of non-combatants, but even so these figures, especially the last two, are certainly vast exaggerations. A similar instance is encountered in the reports of K'ang-hsi's 1696 campaign. Then the 108,000 effectives are reputed to have been accompanied at the beginning of the expedition by four times as many non-combatants.[61] The empire's opponent was then Galdan (1676-97), so to oppose Chingis Khan, a far more formidable antagonist than the Jungar Khan, perhaps as many as 150,000 effectives may have been mobilized, and to carry supplies and labor on the fortifications at the Yeh-hu Ling, a considerable number of workmen.[62] The " Yüan Ch'ao Pi Shih " refers to the host as the main army of the Chin and declares that it was composed of Khitan and Jurchid troops.[63] With them, says the " Meng-wu-erh Shih," were numbers of Chinese infantry, but it was the former, mounted bowmen like the Mongols, that constituted the army's main strength.[64]

Even allowing for relatively small losses at Wu-sha Pao and Fu Chou, and for patrols sent out to watch the line of the Khinghan, Chingis Khan can have had little more than 65,000 troops with him. Had he been reinforced by the Onguds, one might speculate on at least another 10,000 to 15,000, but the biography of Alakush Tagin says that the prince was left by

[61] In 1696 K'ang Hsi moved across eastern Mongolia with three columns of 36,000 men each. To oppose him Galdan had no more than 30,000 all told. Prior to the revolt of his nephews Tse Wang Araptan and Serung Dondub, Galdan could have mustered 50,000 to 60,000 troops. (Courant, *L'Empire Kalmouk ou l'Empire Mantchou.*)

[62] Such workmen were regularly drawn from the Chinese militia forces of both the Jurchids and Khitans (see Wittfogel and Feng Chia-sheng, *History of Chinese Society: Liao* (907-1125), p. 521).

[63] The term Jurchid may here refer to the Mukri or Mo-ho, a related people who founded the Kingdom of Po-hai in the seventh century, as well as to the Jurchids proper, who succeeded the Khitans as the masters of Po-hai in 1116. For a brief account of Po-hai see Gibert, *Dictionnaire Historique et Géographique de la Mandchourie*, pp. 756-764.

[64] As regards the *Yüan Ch'ao Pi Shih's* statement that the host was the main army of the Chin, it is worth mentioning that Wittfogel declares that both Khitans and Chinese were excluded from the élite army of the empire. However, by the opening of the 13th century, this seems to have been changed for the Khitans, as some of them are found even in the Guard. (For Wittfogel's remarks, see " Dynasties of Conquest," *China*, Chap. VIII, p. 117.)

Chingis to hold his own country.[65] This was doubtless done to avoid possible desertions at a critical moment by those of the Onguds still hostile to the Mongol alliance.[66]

Separated by not more than twelve to fifteen miles, a clash between the two armies was only a matter of time. Despite the importance of the ensuing battle, all available accounts of it are lacking in detail.[67] The " Yüan Ch'ao Pi Shih," which is by far the earliest record, merely says that the Mongol army of the center encountered and defeated the main forces of the enemy. The " Yüan Sheng Wu Ch'in Cheng Lu," however, is fuller. According to it: " After the Chin army had reached the Yeh-hu Ling, two Khitan officers of the staff came to Chih-chung and said: ' Since the capture of Fu Chou, the Mongols have become much occupied with their booty and their horses are grazing loose near the town, so if we now attack them with our cavalry they will be unprepared and we shall win a decisive victory.' Chih-chung, however, thought otherwise. ' In their present position,' he replied, ' the enemy are not easy to overthrow, but tomorrow we will make a combined onslaught with both cavalry and infantry, which will be surer than what you suggest.'

" When Chingis Khan was informed that the Chin cavalry was advancing, he ordered his men to prepare for action and moved toward Huan-erh-tsui.[68] At this juncture Chih-chung summoned a Khitan officer called Shih-mo Ming-an. ' You,' said he, ' have often been sent to the north, you are familiar with Chingis Khan; go and enquire of him why he is warring against us; ask what grudge he bears the Chin, and, if he fails to give you a bold answer, upbraid him.' Ming-an went to the Mongol camp but, after speaking as bidden, he surrendered. Nevertheless, unmoved by his submission, Chingis Khan had

---

[65] The *Meng-wu-erh Shih*, biography of Alakush Tagin, says that among the forces left with Mukhali in 1217 were 10,000 Wang-ku or Onguds under the command of Chen Kuo, nephew of Alakush Tagin—others went west with Chingis Khan in 1219.
[66] *Meng-wu-erh Shih*, biography of Alakush Tagin.
[67] The *Yüan Shih* provides little information on the subject and has mistakenly reported a battle at the Yeh-hu Ling in 1211 and a second at Huan-erh-tsui in 1212.
[68] The *Yüan Sheng Wu Ch'in Cheng Lu* calls the place Yeh-ma-ch'ih.

him bound hand and foot and threatened to slay him after the battle.

" The two armies then met and the Chin sustained a terrible reverse, men and horses trampling each other down in the rout and the dead being without number. Chingis Khan next advanced on Wan-yen Hu-sha, whom he attacked and crushed at Hui-ho Pao, thus destroying the best forces of the Chin.

" The enemy vanquished, Chingis Khan had Ming-an brought before him and demanded an explanation of his words. ' I have long wished to come to you,' answered the captive, ' but could think of no way of meeting you. At last there came this opportunity, so I acted as ordered, for otherwise I should never have beheld the light of your countenance.' This reply flattered Chingis Khan, and Ming-an was released." [69]

Supplementing the " Yüan Sheng Wu Ch'in Cheng Lu " are several brief excerpts from other works, which fill in certain gaps and so help give a more complete picture of what took place.[70]

Evidently the army of Ke-shih-lieh Chih-chung reached the Yeh-hu-ling shortly after the fall of Fu Chou and the battle of Wu-sha Pao, and, while work was started on the construction of defense lines, scouts were sent out to observe the Mongols. These returned to say that the invaders appeared much occupied with the loot of the captured town.[71] As related, Chih-chung failed to take the advice of his Khitan staff officers, nor did he wait for the arrival of Wan-yen Hu-sha. Instead, trusting in the numbers of his army, he decided to attack on his own. The next morning he ordered his entire force into position, and to throw Chingis Khan off his guard despatched

---

[69] The *Meng-wu-erh Shih*, biography of " Shih-mo Ming-an," reports that Chingis Khan sent the commander back to the Chin.

[70] See the *Meng-wu-erh Shih*, the *Yüan Shih*, the biographies of " Mukhali " in the *Ssŭ Ch'ao Pieh Shih* and *Yüan Ch'ao Ming Ch'en Shih Liao*, the biography of " Chaghan " in the *Yüan Shih*, that of " Wan-yen Hu-sha " in the *Chin Shih* and the *Sung Yüan T'ung-chien Ch'uan-pien*. For excerpts from these works; see Appendix C.

[71] Bretschneider, *Recherches Archéologiques et Historiques sur Pékin et ses environs*, says that Fu Chou contained an imperial residence, so the booty seized may have been considerable.

Shih-mo Ming-an to parley. But this officer not only gave himself up to the Mongols but provided most exact information concerning the plans, numbers and arrangement of Chih-chung's host.[72] The invaders were therefore on the alert, and the approach of the Chin across the intervening plain was at once reported to Chingis Khan.

Learning that their advance guard was in sight, the conqueror instructed the Tangut Chaghan to go and make a reconnaisance. The officer soon returned and informed him that there was no need to fear the enemy as they seemed disorganized. Thereupon Chingis commanded his troops to move toward Huan-erh-tsui.

Apparently Chih-chung deployed his Khitan and Jurchid horsemen on the front and wings of his army and the infantry behind. The former were immediately attacked by successive waves of Mongol light troops, and evidently with too little space in which to maneuver, at length faltered under the storms of arrows poured into their ranks. Seizing the opportunity, Mukhali (see Appendix C) delivered a tremendous assault, his troops charging lance in hand. This was promptly supported by the Guard (Keshik) under Chingis Khan, and the Khitan and Jurchid cavalry were hurled back upon their own infantry. With no chance to reform, they trampled down the foot soldiers and involved the whole army in such boundless confusion that by noon the Mongols were driving a broken and flying enemy from the field.

Pursued through the Huan-erh-tsui and Ts'ui-p'ing K'ou defile to the valley of the Yang below, the defeated troops suffered tremendous losses, but at Hui-ho Pao part of them under Chih-chung rallied and, joining Wan-yen Hu-sha, turned to fight a second battle.

Hu-sha had been proceeding toward the Yeh-hu Ling when he learned that the Mongols were coming through the range. Surprised by this unexpected and terrible news, he fell into a panic and retired back to Hsüan-p'ing. There the officers of the garrison begged him to make a stand, but he could think

---

[72] See the *Li-tai T'ung-chien Chi-lan.*

only of retreat and in the night took the road for Hsüan-te
Chou. But he was not fast enough. At Hui-ho Pao, barely
ten miles on the way, he was overtaken first by Chih-chung
and then by the pursuing Mongols.

The victors must have made use of their remounts to ride
the thirty miles from Huan-erh-tsui to Hui-ho Pao without
resting, for it was the following day that they came up with
Hu-sha. The latter's men were certainly fresher than the
pursuers, but the general was in a panic and had doubtless
become still more alarmed when joined by the débris of Chih-
chung's routed army. At all events, compelled to give battle,
he suffered an annihilating reverse and escaped with difficulty
to Hsüan-te Chou.

Thither he was followed by the main forces of the Mongols,
so leaving the city to be taken and sacked, he continued his
flight to Te-hsing Chou.

Chih-chung, having seen the day lost, fought his way off
the field at the head of 7,000 picked troops, and passing Hsüan-
te Chou, fled to the Sang-kan River.[73] There, opposite the
mouth of the Hu-lai Ho, Yeh-lü Tukha and 3,000 horsemen
came up with him and he was forced to fight yet a third battle.
His biography reports that the conflict lasted an entire day,
but that with night-fall he and his staff gave up the struggle
and made for Yü Chou, while their men broke and fled.

Arrived at the town, Chih-chung seized all the horses and
municipal funds, and, making his way through the Tzu-ching
Kuan, reached Lai-shui Hsien. There he quarrelled with the
magistrate and in a fit of rage had him flogged to death. He
then took the road to Chung Tu where, despite his defeat and
these outrages, no one dared bring him to justice. Chih-chung's
seizure of horses at Yü Chou shows that the Mongols were
hot on his heels, so he may have been pursued as far as the
Tzu-ching Kuan. Another detachment, perhaps under Tukha,
seems to have gone up the Sang-kan and invested Hung Chou.

[73] The direction of Chih-chung's flight is guess work, but as he was at the head
of a considerable body of cavalry it seems probable that he may have gone past
Hsüan-te Chou and then southwest to the Sang-kan, rather than have taken the
more direct but difficult route to the river via Huai-an.

For some weeks the town resisted, but by December it had been taken.[74]

Simultaneously Chaghan rode up the Yang River and besieged T'ien Ch'eng and Pai-teng Ch'eng. History is silent as to the fall of the former, but the latter surrendered at the end of seven days. The biography of Chaghan says that after the victory at the Yeh-hu Ling he was instructed by Chingis Khan to besiege Pai-lu (Pai-teng Ch'eng), which capitulated after a week. However, it is likely that he did not receive his orders until the battle of Hui-ho Pao was over. On the way, he must have taken T'ien Ch'eng, though it is only in the biography of the Chin deserter Liu Po-lin, and apropos of Chingis Khan's subsequent withdrawal that one learns that the town was captured. As for Hsüan-p'ing and Hui-ho Pao, both doubtless succumbed soon after the battle fought at the latter.

Meanwhile the army under Chingis Khan followed Hu-sha to Te-hsing Chou. Again the general fled and before the end of October the city had fallen.[75] This time the fugitive continued his flight to the capital, but unlike Chih-chung, he was temporarily disgraced.

Master of two of the three strongest cities in the north, Chingis directed Jebe and another officer to try to surprise the Chü-yung Kuan. Again Jebe won a spectacular success. Finding the place fully prepared for him and far too strong to take by storm with the troops at his disposal, he fell back in apparent retreat. Deceived, the defenders were lured into the open, and pressing after him for thirty-five miles, were suddenly subjected to a fierce counter attack at Chi-ming Shan, a high hill towering over the final reaches of the Yang, and completely routed. Flying back in disorder, they spread panic among the men left in the fort, and the commander Wan-yen Fu Shou abandoned it to the pursuing Mongols.[76] Chingis

---

[74] The *Meng-wu-erh Shih* includes Hung Chou among the places taken by the Central and Left-wing armies, so the town may have fallen to Tukha or one of his officers.

[75] Feng Ch'eng-chün, biography of *Ch'eng-chi-ssŭ Han* (Chingis Khan).

[76] *Yüan Ch'ao Pi Shih*, and *Meng-wu-erh Shih*, biography of " Jebe." The name of

Khan was at once notified of its occupation and during the last days of October or early in November marched down the defile and pitched camp at Lung-hu T'ai, not twenty-five miles from the Chin capital. On the way detachments must have been thrown out to reduce Wei-ch'uan, Chin-shan, and Ch'ang-p'ing in order to secure possession of the pass.

The " Chin Shih " and " Meng-wu-erh Shih " date the fall of Wei-ch'uan, Chin-shan and Ch'ang-p'ing in the eleventh month of the Hsin-wei year (Dec. 7, 1211 to Jan. 5, 1212), but the investment of all three will certainly have begun earlier so as to make sure of the Chü-yung Kuan. Wei-ch'uan perhaps succumbed to Jebe along with the pass, as it is possible that the garrison joined the defenders of the great fortress in their disastrous pursuit to the Chi-ming Shan.

As soon as news reached Chung Tu that the Chü-yung Kuan was lost, the city was placed under martial law and all men capable of bearing arms prohibited from leaving. Terrified at this disaster and the catastrophic defeats suffered by his armies, Wei Shao Wang prepared to depart for K'ai-feng, and was only persuaded to stay by the Imperial Guards who pledged their loyalty to defend him to the last man.[77]

Elated with his success, Jebe led his troops to the city, but outside the walls was encountered and fiercely repulsed by 5,000 of the Guards. Greatly impressed by their courage, he enquired the total strength of the force. In reality it amounted to no more than 5,000, but the local peasantry told him it numbered 200,000.[78]

This exaggeration can hardly have deceived the Mongols, but Chingis Khan decided that the time was not yet ripe for an attack on the capital. Instead, troops were sent out to raid and plunder at large, and by January of the next year (1212), Ch'ing Chou and Ts'ang Chou in the south and Mi-yün,

[77] the Chin commander, Wan-yen Fu-Shou, is to be found in the *Li-tai T'ung-chien Chi-lan*.

[77] *Li-tai T'ung-chien Chi-lan.*

[78] *Yüan Shih Hsin Pien.* The figure in the text is 500, but this is so insignificant that I have assumed it is a slip for 5,000.

Feng-jun, Luan Chou, P'ing Chou, Fu-ning and Lin-yü to the east had been captured or intimidated into surrender.[79] The renegade Liu Po-lin now came to Chingis Khan and suggested that he take advantage of the disorder caused by his victories to launch an attack on Tung Ching.[80] From Linyü, the most easterly point so far occupied by the Mongols, to Tung Ching, it is nearly 200 miles, but convinced that the project was feasible, Chingis Khan ordered Jebe to try it. Nothing indicates more clearly than the success of this expedition, the shattered state of the Chin forces in the north. Marching via Ch'ang-p'ing, Mi-yün, Feng-jun, Luan Chou and Fu-ning to Lin-yü, Jebe advanced up the coast and, presumably passing Chin Chou without opposition, reached the Liao Ho, which was crossed on the ice.[81] From the river, he drove straight on Tung Ching in the hope of taking it unawares, but to his disappointment found the garrison on the watch. Knowing that only a regular siege would enable him to occupy the place by force, he once more made use of a ruse. Beating a precipitate retreat, he left his baggage as if in flight. Perceiving the deserted camp, the citizens threw open their gates and proceeded to loot it. Having retired six days distance— (perhaps one hundred miles, which would be about equivalent to the distance that infantry could march in the same time) — Jebe commanded his men each to take a spare mount, and, making a forced march of twenty-four hours, returned unexpectedly in the night. Finding the gates left open for the New Year celebrations, his men poured into the city which was taken and plundered without resistance.[82] After this remarkable feat of arms, Jebe returned to Chingis Khan, whom he

---

[79] *Chin Shih; Meng-wu-erh Shih*—T'u Chi says that wherever the Mongols appeared the inhabitants surrendered.

[80] *Yüan Shih Hsin Pien.*

[81] Jebe's line of march is that suggested by T'u Chi.

[82] The *Yüan Ch'ao Pi Shih*, and the *Meng-wu-erh Shih*, biography of " Jebe." Differing from these sources are the *Yüan Shih* and the *Yüan Shih Hsin Pien*, which date the capture of Tung Ching in the twelfth month of the Jen-shen year (Dec. 25, 1212 to Jan. 23, 1213). However, as Chingis Khan was never further east than Te-hsing Chou during the Jen-shen year, the *Meng-wu-erh Shih* must be correct in assigning Jebe's expedition to the twelfth month of the Hsin-wei year (Jan. 6 to Feb. 4, 1212).

rejoined at Lung-hu T'ai some time in February, 1212. This was the last of the conquests made by the Eastern armies and it is now time to turn to the three princes who had covered Chingis Khan's flank on the west.

Despite the absence of all but one absolutely sure date concerning their campaign, we know that they began operations with the occupation of Feng Chou, Tung-sheng and Yün-nei. These they must have reached by marching from Ching Chou over the Yü-yang Kuan, perhaps early in June,[83] in the expectation of drawing against them, according to plan, a portion of the enemy forces. The loss of Yün-nei was a particularly grievous blow to the Chin, for its conqueror Yeh-lü Akhai not only took the town but, appearing unexpectedly, drove off great numbers of horses from the Imperial grazing grounds.[84] However, as seen, none of these reverses diverted the Chin from massing against the Eastern army, and the princes, doubtless on orders from their father, called a halt. This lasted until September or the beginning of October, when the great victories at Huan-erh-tsui and Hui-ho Pao set them free for an advance into Shansi.

Their line of march is not given, but from the places attacked they apparently avoided the dangerous defiles to the south of the plain of Feng Chou and swung east from Tung-sheng to the Hung-ta River. There a detachment was sent south to invest Ning-pien, while the main force proceeded up the river to the Sha-hu K'ou. In possession of the pass, the princes pushed through it and reduced Shuo-p'ing and Hsüan-ning.

The " Yüan Sheng Wu Ch'in Cheng Lu " alone lists Hsüan-ning among the places reduced by the princes, but on the strength of it, I have taken it for granted that the Right-wing army advanced into Shansi via the Sha-hu K'ou and Shuo-p'ing. Also, since the country between the plain of Feng Chou

---

[83] The *Meng-wu-erh Shih* dates the fall of Tung-sheng and Yün-nei in the fourth month of 1211 (May 14 to June 12). The former, being the winter capital of the Onguds, may have surrendered almost immediately.

[84] As regards Yeh-lü Akhai's raid on Yün-nei, the *Yüan Shih* infers that it occurred in the tenth month (Nov. 7 to Dec. 6), but the *Ssŭ Ch'ao Pieh Shih* dates it prior to the advance of the princes into N. Shansi, which seems far more likely.

and the Sha-hu K'ou is very rugged, and so extremely dangerous if held by a hostile force, it would seem logical for the
Mongols to have reached the Sha-hu K'ou by way of the
longer but safer road up the Hung-ta River.

From Hsüan-ning they could have made for Hsi Ching, but,
evidently thinking it too strong, marched south to the upper
reaches of the Sang-Kan where they captured Shuo Hsien. They
then crossed the Great Wall to Wu, and sweeping southeast
into the valley of the upper Hu-t'ou, took Hsin to the south,
and ascending the river, seized Tai Chou.[85] North of the
latter lies the Yen-men Kuan, the pass in the T'ai-ho Ling
commanding the road which links Ta-T'ung (Hsi Ching) and
T'ai-yüan. Over this the princes went some time in December
or at the latest early in January 1212,[86] and regaining the Sang-
kan River, turned towards Hsi Ching.

According to the "Yüan Sheng Wu Ch'in Cheng Lu," the
foregoing devastation so terrified the Chin that the city was
abandoned. Other reports, notably the biography of Mo-jan
Chin-chung in the "Chin Shih," imply that it remained
untaken until considerably later.[87] Possibly the princes pitched
camp in the neighborhood until Chingis Khan sent instructions
for them to retire, and contented themselves with sending out
detachments to ravage the surrounding country and the valley
of the Sang-kan.

The Mongol withdrawal probably began in February after
Jebe's return from the Liao River. But, whether then or later,
it was immediately followed by the arrival at Chung Tu of
20,000 men from Manchuria. These had been despatched by
T'u Ch'an-i, the Chin commander of Hui-ning or Shang Ching,

[85] Kuo is not included among the towns taken by the princes, but being on their
line of march, may also have been attacked.

[86] The *Chin Shih*, which is the only work to provide this information, reports that
Tai Chou, located just south of the Yen-men Kuan, was taken by the Mongols
during the eleventh month of the Hsin-wei year (Dec. 7, 1211-Jan. 5, 1212), so it
is reasonable to suppose that the invaders went north soon after the fall of the town.

[87] Following Rashid ad-Din, T'u Chi is of the opinion that Hsi Ching remained
untaken until the twelfth month of the Ping-Tzu year (Jan. 9 to Feb. 7, 1217)
when it surrendered to Samukha. The *Yüan Shih* only records one siege, the
unsuccessful attempt by Chingis Khan in the autumn of 1212.

the administrative center of the Jurchid homeland, so were doubtless mostly cavalry and hence exceptionally welcome.

While there is no record on the subject, we may assume that Chingis Khan retired north via the Chü-yung Kuan and Yeh-hu Ling, and the princes from Hsi Ching. Since they were now in posssession of the Sha-hu K'ou, they perhaps marched through the pass and directly over the mountains beyond to Feng Chou, instead of following the more circuitous route of their advance.

It is clear that Chingis Khan annexed little territory in China proper, for after his departure the Chin were able to re-garrison the Chü-yung Kuan, Te-hsing Chou and Wei-ch'uan, but apparently not Hsüan-te Chou. Twenty thousand men, however, were assembled for its reoccupation. These were placed under Ke-shih-lieh Chih-chung, who, notwithstanding his reverses of the previous year, was appointed Deputy Military Commander of the Empire. But instead of being marched to the city the force was split up, 3,000 going to Wei-ch'uan with Chih-chung and the rest elsewhere—doubtless to Te-hsing Chou, Chin-shan and the Chü-yung Kuan.[88] Hence, the " Meng-wu-erh Shih " may be correct in reporting that Hsüan-te Chou remained in Mongol hands. Certainly 20,000 soldiers were quite inadequate to garrison so many places.

Besides Hsüan-te Chou, and very likely Hsüan-p'ing, Chingis Khan retained the town of T'ien Ch'eng, where he stationed Liu Po-lin. Westward, he withdrew even further north, for the " Ta-chin Kuo-tzu " implies that the Chin temporarily recovered Feng Chou.[89] So Chingis would seem to have been content with the country of the Onguds, the small towns of the grassland, i. e., Ching Chou, Fu Chou, Huan Chou, etc., and the passes and other strategic points giving access to the south.

[88] See the *Chin Shih*, main text and biography of " Ke-shih-lieh Chih-chung," also the *T'ung-chien Kang-mu*. Though it is from the *Chin Shih* that one learns that Chih-chung took charge of the 3,000 men ordered to Wei-ch'uan, his biography reports that he merely sent them there.

[89] It should be menetioned that Wang Kuo-wei does not regard the *Ta-chin Kuo-tzu* as a very trustworthy source of information.

Although surprise may be felt over the abandonment of so much territory, it should be remembered that the campaign had not been undertaken for the purpose of territorial acquisition. The Mongols had not yet sufficient experience to enable them to hold and govern large agricultural and urban areas. To them, as to their Hsiungnu and Turkish predecessors, the vast booty seized during the invasion was ample recompense for the war, while possession of the Ongud prairies, from which fresh incursions could be made, insured the possibility of further loot. As primarily intended, the campaign had resulted in breaking the prestige of the Chin and raising Chingis Khan to the first place among the rulers of East Asia.

After re-entering the Ongud domain, some of the Mongol troops may have continued north across the desert and returned later with fresh horses, but the majority will have remained behind with the conqueror. The location of his headquarters is unknown, but Yü-erh-lo,[90] Huan Chou or Ta-shui-luan would any one of them have enabled him to watch the situation in the south and were excellent points from which to resume hostilities.

During Chingis Khan's absence the land of the Onguds had been the scene of a political upheaval. After the Mongol advance moved south, the malcontents among the nobility slew Alakush Tagin and his eldest son and replaced him by one of his brothers.[91] But warned in time, the murdered prince's nephew Chen-kuo, his second son Po-yao-ho, still a child, and the Mongol princess Alaghi Beki got safely away to the Mongol troops stationed at Yün-nei. Somehow the rebels escaped the conqueror's vengeance. Perhaps they retired to the most desert

[90] Yü-erh-lo, located in the southern part of the Khongirad country, was often called Ta-li-po and is to be identified with the present Dalai Nor in Chahar. In the time of Chingis Khan there was a colony of Chinese peasants and fishermen settled by the lake; see Ch'ang-ch'un, Arthur Waley, p. 64.

[91] According to T'u Chi, who quotes the Chin Shih, Alakush Tagin was succeeded by a brother, whom the Chin murdered at a banquet soon after his accession. (See the Meng-wu-erh Shih, biography of "Alakush Tagin.")

The Yüan Shih implies that the Ongud prince was murdered prior to the Mongol invasion, but T'u Chi, who seems to have gone into the matter with his usual thoroughness, clearly shows that this did not happen until after Chingis Khan's arrival in Chin territory. Besides the Chin Shih, T'u Chi used Rashid ad-Din.

parts of the Ongud territory in the west or they may have sought refuge in the Ordos. At all events, when Feng Chou was recovered they were able to submit to the Chin. Possibly as an appeal to those of the Onguds loyal to the Mongols, the Chin executed Alakush Tagin's murderer and set up Pai-ssŭ-po, a two year old son or grandson of the old prince whom the insurgents had spared, but they vested the new commander of Feng Chou with all real power. This arrangement was very distasteful to the Onguds, and on the commander refusing to betroth his daughter to the young prince they made peace with Chingis Khan.[92] This turn of events, if due partly to poor diplomacy on the part of the Chin, also owed much to the fact that even the most recalcitrant of the Ongud nobility realized that the star of the Mongols was in the ascendant and further opposition useless.[93] But a more important event had taken place to the east.

Earlier in this chapter it was suggested that Chingis Khan must have considered the possibility of receiving support from the Khitans. Certain writers have gone so far as to say that at his instigation they joined him soon after the war began, but though an insurrection broke out, he had no hand in it. Undeniably some of the Khitan royal house were on the look-out for a chance to regain their independence. Yet nothing occurred which immediately affected the military situation, and at Huan-erh-tsui the Chin met the Mongols with an army that included great numbers of Khitan cavalry whose officers tendered the commander-in-chief loyal and sound advice.

The Khitan revolt was the result, not of Mongol machinations, but of over suspicion on the part of the Chin. No sooner had hostilities begun than the government sent Jurchid colonists to settle among the Khitans. Alarmed by this, Yeh-lü Liu-ke, a member of the ruling family and commander of 1,000

---

[92] Alliances of this sort were quite common among the Mongols and their neighbors.

[93] For the Ongud revolt; see the *Meng-wu-erh Shih*, biography of " Alakush Tagin " and the *Meng Ta Pei Lu*, section on the " Pai Ta-ta," which contains a reference by Wang Kuo-wei to the subject as recorded by the *Ta-chin Kuo-tzu*. According to the *Chin Shih*, after the execution of Alakush Tagin's murderer, the old prince's nephew was put on the throne.

on the Khinghan frontier, left his post, and flying to the country between Han Chou and Lung Chou, raised the standard of rebellion. Making raids into the surrounding districts, he successfully eluded the garrison of Han Chou, and, safe from attack by any large Chin force so long as Chingis Khan was in the field, soon found himself at the head of a considerable following. Seeing in the Khitan rebel a potential ally, the Mongol Khan decided to open negotiations. Accordingly, in March (1212) he directed Anchar Noyan and Shiki Kutuku to approach him.

In his choice of these two officers, Chingis Khan showed his usual judgment. Shiki Kutuku, as an adopted son, could be expected to promote his interests to the utmost. Anchar Noyan belonged to the Khongirad aristocracy, so as a neighbor of the Khitans had doubtless met Liu-ke before the war. Furthermore, he was the younger brother of Chingis' first wife Burte.

The rebel, aware that sooner or later he must face a full-scale punitive expedition, was anxious to obtain the Mongol Khan's protection. He had therefore set out in that same March for the conqueror's camp and on the way fell in with the two emissaries. When these learned that the Khitan prince was near, they presented themselves and asked where he was going. " This," replied Liu-ke, " is the army of Liao on the march to submit to the Mongols, but the road being long and our horses weary, we are making a temporary halt." "We," said Anchar Noyan, " have been ordered by Chingis Khan to conquer the Nu-chen (doubtless those of the Jurchids lately settled among the Khitan), so it is by the grace of Heaven that we meet here. If you really wish to serve the Mongols, what proof can you give of your sincerity? " Thereupon Liu-ke, accompanied by his men and the two Mongol commanders, ascended the Chin Shan (sacred to the Khitans), where, having slain a white horse and a white cow, he turned north, and breaking an arrow, swore allegiance to Chingis Khan.[94] " I will

[94] The location of the Chin Shan—see Map—would indicate that it is to be identified with the Mu-yeh Shan, the sacred mountain and burying place of the

return," said Anchar Noyan, " and inform Chingis Khan of everything and ask him to make you ruler of Liao." [95]

Liu-ke's secession did not entail that of all the Khitans, but not only did it give the Mongols a foothold on the upper Liao, and so a base for later military operations in Manchuria, but it could be expected to encourage other defections. For the moment no advance was made into Manchuria, but T'u Ch'an-i, lately moved from Hui-ning or Shang Ching to Chung Tu, foresaw the future and besought the emperor to put the province of Liaotung and the eastern capital (Tung Ching) into a proper state of defense.[96] But his advice fell on deaf ears, and not until April, 1213, shall we see a belated attempt to crush Liu-ke.

The campaign just concluded was in many respects Chingis Khan's greatest feat of arms. Later, after the outbreak of war with the Khwarazm Shah, he will march further and command more troops, but never will he be opposed by such powerful armies, nor will his ability as a soldier be better demonstrated. Foiled in his original plan to divide the Chin forces, he remained alert to recover the initiative, and when the armies sent against him arrived one by one instead of simultaneously, he struck like a hurricane. First at Wu-sha Pao, then at Huan-erh-tsui and Hui-ho Pao, he inflicted three defeats so crushing that the flower of the Chin army was destroyed and the key towns of Hsüan-te and Te-hsing taken after but a show of resistance. The Moslem historian Rashid ad-Din, writing over one hundred years afterward, declared that the Mongols still regarded Huan-erh-tsui as one of their greatest victories.[97] Nine years after the catastrophe the celebrated Taoist sage Ch'iu Ch'ang-ch'un was so impressed with

Khitan rulers. (See Parker, *A Thousand Years of the Tatars*, p. 239, also Bretschneider, *Medieval Researches*, Vol. 1, note 640.)

[95] The account of Yeh-lü Liu-Ke's rebellion and treaty with the Mongols is from his biography in the *Meng-wu-erh Shih*, but all dates are from the *Ken Dai Kyo Ryako Tohoko* of Yanai, an outstanding Japanese authority on Mongol history, who has specialized on the chronology of Liu-Ke's revolt and the conquest of Manchuria.

[96] *Yüan Shih Hsin Pien* and De Mailla, *Histoire Générale de la Chine*, Vol. IX.

[97] D'Ohsson, footnote on Huan-erh-tsui.

the sight of the terrrible field of carnage that on his return from Chingis Khan in 1223 he held a service at Te-hsing Chou in commemoration of the thousands who had perished.[98]

The casualties of the Chin were terrific. Wang Kuo-wei states that they lost so many trained soldiers that subsequently they were unable to oppose the invaders in the open.[99] This is certainly an extraordinary exaggeration for so reliable and learned an authority as Wang Kuo-wei, for the following years will find the Chin putting more than one powerful army into the field. But unquestionably the imperial cavalry was badly decimated and henceforth the Chin were at a serious disadvantage when opposing the Mongols.

The principal cause of Chin defeat was the mishandling of their troops. Most of the generals were men whose experience had been gained fighting the Sung in 1206 and 1207, when both Wan-yen Hu-sha and Ke-shih-lieh Chih-chung made their reputations. Though there are no figures extant on the number of Jurchid and Khitan horsemen present at Huan-erh-tsui, they were probably not much inferior to the entire army of Chingis Khan on the field. However, instead of capitalizing on their mobility and archery, Chih-chung stationed them too close to his infantry. Without sufficient room in which to maneuver— (it was probably this faulty arrangement that gave rise to Chaghan's remark that the Chin seemed disorganized) — they were forced back onto their own infantry and the army and the empire were involved in an irreparable disaster.

Making this campaign still more outstanding is the pursuit of Chih-chung by Yeh-lü Tukha and Jebe's seizure of the Chü-yung Kuan and Tung Ching. The two latter achievements speak for themselves, but the former was hardly less astonishing. Carried out over sixty miles of mountainous country after two pitched battles, it gives an amazing idea of the endurance of the Chin as well as of the Mongol cavalry. The operation of the princes in the west is also of particular interest, as it is the first example of a maneuver frequently to

[98] *Ch'ang-ch'un* by Arthur Waley, p. 63.
[99] *Meng Ta Pei Lu,* " Pai Ta-ta, commentaries by Wang Kuo-wei.

be employed by the Mongols in other such wars. Just as in 1220, during the conquest of the Khorezmian empire, the principal function of Jebe and Subudei was to obstruct and disorganize the sending of troops from western Persia, so must the southward drive of the princes in the autumn and winter of 1211 have been made to stop the despatch of soldiers from Shansi. Brilliantly begun, the first phase of the Chin war was over and the second about to start. This was to necessitate for the Mongols the adoption of a new technique, the art of taking cities, with which as yet they had had little experience.

CHAPTER VI

# THE MONGOLS BEGIN THE CONQUEST OF CHINA

WHEN CHINGIS KHAN withdrew to the north, he had every intention of returning south as soon as his cavalry should again be fit for the field. Of this none were better aware than the Chin. Despite a second though unsuccessful attack by the Tanguts on Chia Chou during April (1212), a general famine the same month and another in Shansi and Shensi during June, they made strenuous efforts to prepare for the coming storm. A large field army, powerful in numbers if not in cavalry, was assembled and placed under the command of Ao Tun-hsiang,[1] and in June 30,000 troops were sent to Chung Tu, 20,000 from Shensi, 10,000 from elsewhere.[2]

With the autumn the Mongols appeared. Though in considerable force, their army was probably inferior to that of the previous year and seems to have had a very limited objective, namely, the occupation of what is now the " intramural " area. Chingis Khan, as the Khitans before him, had apparently decided that the responsibilities of governing the region would be more than offset by the greatly increased pressure he would be able to exert from it upon his enemy. Exactly what prompted this step we do not know, but one may suppose that his Khitan officers, as well as such Chinese renegades as Liu Po-lin, had something to do with it.

Late in September or early October (1212) two forces moved south, one under the conqueror himself via Wei-ning and Pai-teng Ch'eng to Hsi Ching,[3] another through the Huan-erh-tsui

[1] See the *Chin Shih*, biography of " Ao Tun-hsiang."
[2] *Chin Shih.*
[3] This is the route incorrectly reported by the *Li-tai T'ung-chien Chi-lan*—which fails to include anything for 1212—as Chingis Khan's supposed advance on Hsi Ching in 1211. As already seen, the conqueror himself never moved against the city

155

defile to Te-hsing Chou. Leading this second army, or at
least in nominal command of it, was prince Tului to whom
were attached Chingis' adopted son, the Tangut Chaghan, and
two other officers.[4] Strange to say, such great names as
Bugurji, Mukhali, Jebe and Subudei are not once mentioned
throughout the entire campaign but all were doubtless present.
One learns, however, that Liu Po-lin [5] was with the conqueror,
who very likely called him in as a siege expert, and perhaps
in a similar capacity with one or other of the armies, another
deserter, Ke Pao-yü. This soldier had been taken at the battle
of Wu-sha pao, and going over to the Mongols, rose in their
service to hold one of the highest positions in the siege unit
recruited from among the Chinese.[6]

Chingis Khan had not been in front of Hsi Ching long when
Ao Tun-hsiang marched to the city's relief. On learning of
the general's approach, Chingis ordered part of his troops to
draw the enemy into the valley of Mi-ku K'ou and, trapping
them, again won so tremendous a victory that Ao Tun-hsiang
barely escaped with his life.[7] There is no information as to the
exact location of Mi-ku K'ou, but it must be either to the north
or east of the city, for while the west is too open for an ambush,
the presence of the other Mongol army at Te-hsing Chou
necessitated Ao Tun-hsiang advancing from the south. The
Chin general may, therefore, have gone through the Ts'ui-p'ing
defile to the southeast of Hsi Ching and thence into the valley

in that year. Moreover, the *Li-tai T'ung-chien Chi-lan* has mistakenly named
Wu-sha pao instead of Wei-ning, but since the former had been completely destroyed in 1211, the latter must have been the town involved. For further information on the subject, see Appendix C.

[4] These were Yeh-ku Noyan, the eldest son of Juchi Khassar, and Chugu, a son
of Anchar Noyan. The *Yüan Sheng Wu Ch'in Cheng Lu* names Yeh-ku and Chugu,
the *Yüan Shih* the Tangut Chaghan, and the *Meng-wu-erh Shih*, Tului and Chugu.
However there is no reason why all four should not have been present.

[5] *Meng-wu-erh Shih*, biography of " Liu Po-lin."

[6] Subsequently Ke Pao-yü went with Chingis Khan against the Khwarazm Shah
as did also his son Ke Te-hai, who in 1218 participated in the overthrow of Kuchluk.
(For information on Ke Pao-yü; see Gaubil, p. 37, for Ke Te-hai; Bretschneider
Vol. I, p. 125, n. 312.)

[7] See biography of " Ao Tun-hsiang " in the *Chin Shih*, also the *Yüan Shih* and
*Meng-wu-erh Shih*.

of the Sang-kan River. At the same time there is always the likelihood that the Yen-men pass was also used.[8]

To meet the army of relief, Chingis Khan evidently temporarily raised the siege, for we are told that after the battle he resumed the investment. Undismayed by the diaster, Mojan Chin-chung, the commander of Hsi Ching, continued to resist. At length, while directing an assault which cost his troops heavy casualties, the conqueror was struck by an arrow from the walls and severely wounded. Thereupon the siege was raised and the army retired to the north.

In the east the other army was at first hardly more successful and, repulsed in all its attempts to take Te-hsing Chou, withdrew before the end of October. But ordered to make another attempt, doubtless with reinforcements, it finally succeeded in carrying the place by storm. For all that, as in the previous invasion, after sacking the city the Mongols eventually retired and the Chin once more reoccupied it.[9] During either the first or second stage of the siege a Mongol force encountered and defeated Ke-shih-lieh Chih-chung and 3,000 men at Wei-ch'uan.[10] This time the general was demoted to the command of the Pei K'ou, which was a subordinate position placing him under the officer charged with the defense of the Chü-yung Kuan, and a little later was dismissed altogether.

Once more the Mongols had vanquished the Chin in every battle only to withdraw at the end of the campaign. But had

---

[8] To reach his destination, Ao Tun-hsiang could have made use of the roads crossing both the Tzu-ching Kuan and Tao-ma Kuan. Once over the Heng Shan, these routes join for a short distance only to split on either side of the Great Wall, one going to Tai Chou at the foot of the Yen-men Kuan, the other to the Ts'ui-p'ing K'ou.

[9] Both the *Yüan Sheng Wu Ch'in Ch'eng Lu* and *Yüan Shih* report a siege of Te-hsing Chou for 1212 and another for 1213, but the details given by the earlier source for the first investment are the same as those provided by the *Yüan Shih* for the second. Consequently T'u Chi, author of the *Meng-wu-erh Shih*, believes that it is possible there was no more than one siege, that of 1213. In referring to the leaguer of 1212, the *Yüan Shih* calls the city Feng-sheng which is another name for Te-hsing Chou. In connection with this campaign, it should be mentioned that the *Yüan Sheng Wu Ch'in Cheng Lu* also includes a siege of Hsuan-te Chou for 1212 and the *Yüan Shih* one for 1213, but T'u Chi declares that the city remained in Mongol hands after its capture in 1211.

[10] The *Chin Shih* has mistakenly assigned this action to the year 1211.

Chingis Khan not been wounded, I am convinced, in view of what occurred the next year (1213), that this would not have happened. If unable to take Hsi Ching, the Mongols were learning the art of siege-craft and had a second time reduced Te-hsing. Though the place was again abandoned, it was soon to be recovered and the Mongol conquest of China to begin in earnest.

Disheartened but undaunted, the Chin made ready for the continuation of the struggle and late that year or early the following (1213) despatched 100,000 troops under the command of Wan-yen Kang and Chu-hu Kao-ch'i to station themselves in the neighborhood of Wei-Ch'uan. Nevertheless they were becoming hard pressed for soldiers and in November issued a pardon to all criminals in Liaotung and the departments of Chung Tu and Hsi Ching [11]—presumably in the expectation of recruiting troops from among them. In addition to its military embarrassments the government was also faced with the problem of famine relief, and in December sent great quantities of food from K'ai-feng to the provinces north of the Yellow River.

Perhaps due to the famine, but probably owing to the combined effects of it and of the war, the first signs of strain began to manifest themselves within the empire and in March, 1213, an abortive insurrection broke out in Ta-ming Fu. The next month the government learned that the Khitan rebel Yeh-lü Liu-ke had declared himself Liao Wang, and in June the Tanguts invaded Kansu and Shensi where they captured Ch'ing-yang and Pao-an. Simultaneously, Shensi was swept by another famine. But to none of these disasters could the Chin pay more than passing attention.

Late in July or early in August Chingis Khan returned. Te-hsing was once more besieged and fell in less than a month and with the beginning of September the conqueror moved toward the Chü-yung Kuan. At Wei-ch'uan he made contact with the great army under Chu-hu Kao-chi and Wan-yen Kang,

[11] *Chin Shih.*

who had apparently passively watched the loss of Te-hsing Chou. The ensuing battle was another catastrophic defeat for the Chin, the beaten troops being pursued to the Pei K'ou of Chü-yung Kuan [12] and the road littered with the dead. The only work to give even the briefest account of the engagement is the " Yüan Ch'ao Pi Shih." According to it: " on arriving before the enemy, Chingis Khan perceived that the whole army of Chin was present. Therefore, taking the offensive, he forced it to retire a little and thus enabled Tului and Chugu to penetrate its flanks from the sides, and the troops of I-lieh, Hu-lang-an and Tieh-ke-lieh were so completely defeated that the bodies of the slain strewed the field of battle." [13]

The valley in which Wei-ch'uan (present Huai-lai) stands varies from twelve to sixteen miles across, which even assuming, as is probable, that neither army actually numbered 100,000, allows little room for extensive movement.[14] Hence, following the " Yüan Ch'ao Pi Shih," it would seem that Chingis Khan must have initiated a frontal attack with the center of the army, while the two wings worked along the neighboring heights until able to descend upon the rear and flanks of the Chin. This was a common maneuver with the Mongols and was almost certainly followed by a general onslaught and the crushing victory attested to by all accounts.

Notwithstanding the panic caused by this disaster, the Chü-yung Kuan refused to surrender. Naturally very strong, it had been further strengthened by trenches and other works; according to some records the gates of the Pei K'ou were sealed with iron and the surrounding country for 100 li (approximately 30 miles) strewn with caltrops.

---

[12] The *Yüan Sheng Wu Ch'in Cheng Lu, Yüan Shih* and *Meng-wu-erh Shih.*

[13] Chugu was the son of the Khongirad Anchar Noyan. I-lieh, Hu-lang-an and Tieh-ke-lieh are the three principal officers named by the *Yüan Ch'ao Pi Shih* as commanding the garrison of Chü-yung Kuan, and from their names must have been of non-Chinese stock. Evidently they and their troops were attached to the army of Wan-yen Kang and Chu-hu Kao-ch'i, neither of whom are referred to by the Mongol chronicle.

[14] At T'u-mu, about twenty miles to the west of this battle-field, the Mongols of the 15th century were to win an equally crushing victory, for in 1451 the Oirad Khan Yisun Taiji (1439-55) inflicted upon the Mind a terrible defeat in which the emperor Ying Tsung (1449-64) was taken prisoner.

Having camped before the pass for over a month, with still
no sign of the garrison giving up, Chingis Khan decided to
descend on to the plain by another road and, late in October,
he sent Jebe to see if he could seize the Tzu-ching Kuan.
Advancing up the Sang-kan River to the mouth of the Hu-lai,
the general followed the latter to its upper reaches and somewhere in the vicinity of Yü Chou turned toward the Fei-hu
Kuan. This he took by surprise, and pressing on, unexpectedly
fell upon the Tzu-ching Kuan, which was also captured.[15]
When Chingis learned of this, he left a small force under an
officer named Kita to blockade the Pei K'ou and marched
with the main army to join Jebe.[16]

In the meantime, informed that the Mongols had taken the
Tzu-ching Kuan, the Chin despatched Chu-hu Kao-ch'i to prevent them coming out onto the plain but, reaching the Wu-
hui Ling, the commander found that he was too late.[17] Seeing
the Mongols before them, his men—probably many of them
those defeated at Wei-ch'uan—broke and fled. Chingis Khan
thereupon moved on I Chou, which capitulated almost immediately. From there Jebe and Subudei led a picked force of
cavalry to the southern mouth of the Chü-yung Kuan. Advancing by forced marches over a small track, they surprised the
garrison, which was slaughtered in great numbers. Apprised
of this, the Khitan commander of the north mouth, where lack
of provisions had caused cannibalism to break out, surrendered
and Jebe marched through the defile and joined hands with
Kita.

Simultaneously Chingis Khan led the main army to Cho
Chou, before which he arrived on the 10th of November, and

[15] The route is that given by the *Meng-wu-erh Shih*, but it is from the biography
of " Mukhali " in the same work that one learns that it was Jebe who took the Tzu-
ching Kuan. In other works Chingis Khan is spoken of as its conqueror, but since
it was surprised, it is far more likely to have fallen to the general and a comparatively small force.

[16] Associated with Kita was another officer named Bukha.

[17] The *Yüan Sheng Wu Ch'in Cheng Lu* reports that the general was Ao Tun,
i. e., Ao Tun-hsiang, but since his biography says that early in 1213 he was
appointed commander of Hui-ning Fu or Shang Ching, this is unlikely. It is from
the biography of Mukhali in the *Ssŭ Ch'ao Pieh Shih* that T'u Chi and others have
learned that the commander was Kao-ch'i.

where he detached 5,000 men under Kita to watch all roads into Chung Tu.[18] Then leaving the siege of Cho Chou to Mukhali,[19] he himself went on to pitch camp at Lung-hu T'ai.[20] On the 19th of the month, presumably shortly after his arrival, he despatched A-la-ch'ien, another Tangut in his employ, to offer the Chin peace but, although a return mission was sent, nothing was achieved. The only event of note to arise from this exchange of embassies was the final desertion of Shih-mo Ming-an to the Mongols.

While these disasters were overwhelming the imperial armies, a palace revolution had shaken the government in the capital. As early as May or June the recently disgraced Ke-shih-lieh Chih-chung had been recalled to Chung Tu, and much against the advice of T'u Ch'an-i and other ministers, was pardoned and made Vice-Commander of the Empire. At the same time he was given a special body-guard of 5,000 men and ordered to remain inside the city. But ignoring these instructions, he spent the time hunting outside. At length, September brought tidings of the terrible reverse suffered by Chu-hu Kao-ch'i and Wan-yen Kang, and of the approach of the Mongols to the Chü-yung Kuan. Much alarmed, Wei Shao Wang sent to reprimand Chih-chung for his behavior, but the minister, furious at criticism, slew the messenger and prepared to seize Chung Tu. To accomplish this he first treacherously murdered the commander of the troops covering the city, and taking over his men, proclaimed that he had been summoned to the capital to suppress the governor, who was planning an insurrection. He then marched on Chung Tu, and nearing the walls, sent ahead horsemen to spread a report that the Mongols

---

[18] This figure is from the *Yüan Sheng Wu Ch'in Cheng Lu,* but de Mailla, see *Histoire Générale de la Chine,* Vol. IX, says only 4,000. Named with Kita ıs another officer called Khatai.

[19] Mukhali is named both by the biography of "Shih T'ien-ni" in the *Meng-wu-erh Shih* and in the old biography of "Mukhali" by Chang K'uang-yen—see the *Yüan Ch'ao Ming Ch'en Shih Liao.*

[20] It is from the *Hsin Yüan Shih* of K'e Shao-ming that one learns the conqueror again pitched camp at Lung-hu T'ai. T'u Chi says that the place was the She-la Tieh-K'e of the Mongols. In the *Yüan Ch'ao Pi Shih* the place is called She-la K'e-erh (Shara Keer).

were approaching. Deceived, the guards at one of the gates opened them and Chih-chung entered unopposed. Making his way to the Forbidden City, he overwhelmed the 500 palace guards, slew their officers and seized the emperor. Elated with his success, he proclaimed himself (September 13) Regent of the Empire and the same night celebrated his triumph with a great banquet, at which he commanded the attendance of the most famous courtesans in the city. The next day he ordered the execution of the recently defeated Wan-yen Kang and shortly after had the emperor murdered. He then summoned to the capital the cavalry units stationed at Chi Chou and P'ing Chou, but though supreme he dared not mount the throne, and on the advice of his late opponent T'u Ch'an-i, called Prince Utubu from Chang-te Fu to fill the position. In October the new emperor succeeded under the title of Hsüan Tsung (1213-23), but Chih-chung refused him all proper respect, remaining seated in his presence and offering never so much as a greeting in the public audience.[21]

Toward the last days of November a Mongol force, apparently detached by Chingis Khan from his camp at Lung-hu T'ai, marched on Chung Tu, but at Kao Ch'iao on the Tsao Ho, a few miles to the north of the city, was defeated by Chih-chung.[22] Too unwell to mount a horse, the minister conducted the battle from a cart. The following day the attack was resumed and again the enemy were repulsed, but owing to tardiness on the part of Chu-hu Kao-ch'i, whom Chih-chung had called to his aid, the day was far less successful than its predecessor. Enraged at this, Chih-chung wished to have him executed, but was refused permission by the emperor. Nevertheless he sent Kao-ch'i out in his place and, detaching troops to reinforce the 5,000 men already under his command, threat-

---

[21] For information on Chih-chung's usurpation; see the *Chin Shih,* biography of " Ke-shih-lieh Chih-chung," also the *Li-tai Tung-chien Chi-lan* and *De Mailla, Histoire Générale de La Chine,* Vol. IX.

[22] The Tsao Ho was a canal that once ran from Ch'ang-p'ing to Chung Tu. (*Li-tai T'ung-chien Chi-lan,* and de Mailla, *Histoire Générale de la Chine,* Vol. IX, note by Amiot.) Gaubil (*Yüan Shih Lei Pien*) makes Jebe commander of the Mongol force.

ened him with death if beaten. Despite this, and desperate efforts on the part of the general, the Mongols were victorious. Knowing that his superior would keep his word, Kao-ch'i hurried back to the city before the news of his reverse had time to arrive and surprised Chih-chung in his residence. Seeing himself trapped, the latter tried to escape by climbing over a wall but, falling and injuring himself, was seized and decapitated. Hurrying to the emperor with the dead man's head, Kao-ch'i openly confessed what he had done. In the meantime Chih-chung's men, learning of his death, fell upon those of the slayer and order was restored only after Hsüan Tsung had publicly pardoned Kao-ch'i and made him Vice-Commander of the Empire.[23]

Chih-chung, the prime actor in this bloody drama, was in many respects an able man and could have been a source of real strength to the empire. During the course of his checkered career he had displayed considerable ability in the several posts that had fallen to his lot, but always, as on this occasion, his arrogance, temper and unbridled ambition undid him.

The same day (Nov. 30) that Chih-chung was murdered, Cho Chou fell to the Mongols after a siege of twenty days.[24] While still before the town there had come to Mukhali three Chinese soldiers, Hsiao Po-tieh, Shih T'ien-ni and his cousin Shih T'ien-hsiang. All arrived with their troops and expressed a wish to join the Mongols. Therefore Mukhali ordered Hsiao Po-tieh to take up his quarters at Pa Chou, doubtless he had held the town for the Chin, and bid Shih T'ien-ni and Shih T'ien-hsiang join the besieging army with their men.[25] Dis-

[23] For these last days of Chih-chung; see his biography, the *Li-tai T'ung-chien Chi-lan* and de Mailla, Vol. IX.

[24] The *Yüan Sheng Wu Ch'in Cheng Lu* states that I Chou and Cho Chou fell the same day that they were invested, but this is probably true of I Chou alone. A note from the biography of " Mukhali " in the *Yüan Ch'ao Ming Ch'en Shih Liao* says that the old biography of " Mukhali " by Chang K'uang-yen reports Cho Chou to have fallen only after forty days of continuous assault. However, T'u Chi has preferred to follow the Moslem historian Rashid ad-Din, who declares that the town was taken after twenty days on the 16th day of the 10th month of the year (1213). It is from T'u Chi that one also learns that Chu-hu Kao-ch'i's defeat and the fall of the town occurred the same day.

[25] The *Yüan Shih* says that Shih T'ien-ni surrendered to Mukhali in 1214 at

heartened by this desertion, the undoubted precursor of others, but far more by the staggering military disasters that had over-taken the empire during the reign of his predecessor, Hsüan Tsung in December sent to Chingis Khan to try to arrange peace.[26] But either because the terms offered were inadequate or because the invasion had thus far yielded too little booty— the territory over-run up to then had already been frightfully ravaged in 1211 and 1212—the emperor's overtures were turned down. Instead plans were made for a campaign that would strike a crushing blow at Chin economy north of the Yellow River and bring the empire to its knees.

With the exception of the 5,000 men patrolling the roads to Chung Tu, Chingis Khan divided all his available forces into three armies. One under the princes Juchi, Jaghatai and Ugedei and the general Liu Po-lin was to overrun western Hopei and Shansi, a second under Juchi Khassar, Jurchedei, Anchar Noyan and Tolun Cherbi was to ravage the country between Chung Tu and the sea, and a third under Mukhali, Tului and himself to devastate the rest of Hopei and Shantung. With the first army was very likely Bugurji and with the third Jebe and Subudei. Yeh-lü Akhai and Tukha were also present, but we do not know to which force they were attached. All told the three armies may have totalled 90,000 to 100,000 effectives, including the Chinese troops of Liu Po-lin, and those of the lately joined Shih T'ien-ni and Shih T'ien-hsiang. The main forces of the Chin broken, Chingis Khan rightly guessed that the remainder would act on the defensive. Together these could probably have crushed any one of the three

Mi-Chou, the biography of " Mukhali " in the *Meng-wu-erh Shih*, the same year, but at Pa Chou. However, the biography of " Shih T'ien-ni " in the *Meng-wu-erh Shih* definitely declares that he came over at Cho Chou in 1213 and that in 1214 he was presented to Chingis Khan. The conqueror was then outside Chung Tu and bestowed upon him a golden tiger seal and made him a commander of both cavalry and infantry, a clear indication that he had proved his worth and fidelity in the foregoing campaign. As regards Shih T'ien-hsiang, his biography gives no informa-tion as to exactly when and where he deserted to the Mongols, but informs us that he participated in the operations of 1213-14, so, as he was a cousin of Shih T'ien-ni, I have assumed that he too submitted to Mukhali at Cho Chou. These soldiers were to become two of the greatest Chinese captains in the service of the Mongols.

[26] This peace attempt is recorded only by the *Chin Shih*.

columns, but the disposition of the Mongols made cooperation impossible. Before troops from Shantung and Hopei could join those in Shansi, they must first fight Chingis. Similarly a drive from Shansi for a concentration in the east against the conqueror involved a preliminary battle with the three princes. By themselves, neither the eastern nor western provincial forces were equal to such engagements. To the north the defenders of Chung Tu, numbering 36,000 regular troops,[27] dared not move against the small blockading force for fear of being taken in the rear by the army operating between the capital and the sea. Thus each of the Mongol armies protected and promoted the blows of the other. To meet this deluge the Chin had far too few regular troops to garrison every place in the threatened area. Consequently, only the cities and strategically important towns and forts received regular troops, the rest being instructed to provide their own defense.

Before the end of December the three armies were on the move. That of the princes speedily traversed the whole of western Hopei, and marching via Pao Chou, Chen-ting—untaken [28]—Hsing Chou, Ming Chou, Tz'u Chou and Chang-te Fu, reached Huai-ch'ing and Meng Chou in the southwest corner of the province. There the army turned north, and entering Shansi, looted five towns in the T'ai-hang Mountains. At one of these, Lu-an, the princes divided their forces the better to ravage the country. One body by-passed the Ling-shih defile, penetrated the valley of the Fen River, and after taking Fen Chou and T'ai-yüan Fu, continued north to the foot of the T'ai-ho Ling, while the other advanced to P'ing-yang, crossed the Fen, and sacking five places in the mountains to the west, finally reached Wu in the vicinity of the Great Wall. To the east the army under the conqueror was no less successful, and moving from Pa Chou, it began operations in three

[27] The *Yüan Shih Hsin Pien* by Wei Yüan.

[28] Another town which successfully resisted the princes was Wo or Chao Chou.

The places enumerated above were by no means the only ones taken during this drive, but those interested will find all marked on the end map dealing with this campaign. I have adopted the same procedure in covering the activities of the eastern army and have only burdened the text with the names of towns and cities of major importance.

columns. The two on the west under the Khan and Tului
first took the small towns on the shores of the Hsi-ting Hu
and then dealt with the larger places in their path, e. g. Ho-
chien, Shen Chou, Te Chou, En Chou and Po Chou, while that
on the east under Mukhali, to mention only a few of the more
important points attacked, made for Ch'ing Chou, which successfully resisted, Ts'ang Chou, Ti Chou, I-tu Fu, and Teng
Chou, the last giving the Mongols their first sight of the sea.
Mukhali then apparently turned west, and advancing toward
Chi-nan, T'ai-an and Tung-p'ing Fu, besieged and captured
the first two, but thinking the city of Tung-p'ing too strong,
ignored it. Meanwhile the rest of the army had continued
south, but, as the eastern force had done with Tung-p'ing,
left Ta-ming Fu unmolested. Perhaps at Chi-ning to the south
of Tung-p'ing the three columns united, and after reducing the
former, together marched east and took I Chou. At the latter,
however, they again seem to have split, and while Mukhali
and his troops made for Mi Chou, the rest went against Hai
Chou in the east and P'ei Chou and Hsü Chou in the south,
the last like Meng Chou in the west bringing the Mongols to
the banks of the Yellow River. All four put up a desperate
resistance, Hai Chou, P'ei Chou and Hsü Chou successfully
defying every effort and Mi Chou, where all the inhabitants
were massacred, falling only after Chingis Khan and the main
army had started back for the north. The achievements of
the northern force, which was certainly smaller than the other
two, were far less spectacular but must have been of more
immediate concern to the Chin capital, for Shun Chou, T'ung
Chou, Chi Chou, Luan Chou and P'ing Chou were all attacked.
The two first remained untaken but the other three fell.[29]   In
the words of a Chinese historian: " Everywhere north of the
Yellow River there could be seen dust and smoke and the
sound of drums rose to Heaven." [30]  Far to the west also the

[29] The names of all places enumerated have been taken from the *Yüan Sheng Wu
Ch'in Cheng Lu*, the *Yüan Shih* and the *Meng-wu-erh Shih*, the last plus its
biographies of " Mukhali," " Shih T'ien-hsiang " and " Liu Po-lin."

[30] Biography of " Mukhali " in the *Yüan Ch'ao Ming Ch'en Shih Liao*.

empire was beset and the Tanguts made an abortive attack on a small town.[31]

By early February, 1214, the Eastern armies had returned to the north and concentrated at Ta K'ou i. e., in the open country immediately to the west and northwest of Chung Tu. The greater part of the troops of the princes remained at large, and while a small force was left before Lan Hsien in western Shansi, the rest were ordered south to ravage still further the territory devastated during their advance.[32]

In approximately two months the Mongols had over-run Shansi and the great plain. If many of the places taken were small, others were considerable, T'ai-yüan Fu, P'ing-yang, Pao Chou, Ho-chien, Te Chou, Chi-nan and I-tu Fu all being towns of over 100,000 inhabitants.[33] Had these been as well defended or as strongly situated as their counterparts Chen-ting, Ta-ming Fu, Tung-p'ing and Hsü Chou, they might have been able to hold out long enough to wear down the invaders. But it is well to bear in mind the ruthless use the Mongols made of the thousands of captives they rounded up in the surrounding districts. These were regimented into groups and were driven forward both to erect siege works and to head assaults. Often, we are told, the besieged recognized their relatives in the van of the storming parties and refused to fight and so gave the Mongols an easy victory.[34] But Chingis Khan relinquished the greater part of this vast area and the Chin reoccupied most of the towns and cities lost. Only in the eastern part of the so-called " intra-mural area " did he set up a regular adminis-tration—the western portion still being in Chin hands. In addition he also retained the Chü-yung and Tzu-ching passes and while blockading Chung Tu, the towns of I Chou, Cho Chou, Pa Chou and Chi Chou. Compared with the Chin in their day of conquest, the Mongols were still slow to assume

---

[31] Hsi-ning or Hui Chou; see the *Chin Shih*.

[32] See the *Chin Shih* and *Meng-wu-erh Shih*.

[33] See A. Herrmann, *Atlas of China*, pp. 43 and 52.

[34] See the *Meng Ta Pei Lu* and the *Yüan Shih Hsin Pien*. The Khitans during the 10th century also resorted to this barbarous practice.

the responsibilities of permanent occupation. But the Chin had arisen as a border power in touch with both China and Korea and so were more conversant with administrative matters. Already the Mongols had made themselves masters of more of China than had ever fallen to their Hsiungnu or Turkish predecessors and were set upon the path that was to make them lords of the whole country.

Late in February, or early in March, Chingis Khan, who was again camped at Lung-hu T'ai,[35] received news that the Right-wing army, i. e., the forces of the princes, had retaken Huai-ch'ing and Chang-te Fu, and had defeated and killed the Commander of Chin-nan (S. E. Shansi).[36] Meanwhile his own troops had made two unsuccessful attempts to storm Chung Tu.

Even in China, a land of great cities, the Chin capital was considered very large and its defenses exceptional. The walls, which were constructed of stamped clay and crowned with crenellated brick battlements, measured 54 li (approximately 18 miles) in circumference and attained a height of 40 feet. Their width is unrecorded, but judging from existing remains it must have been considerable. Those of present Peking, which are undoubtedly rather bigger, are 40 feet across the top and at least 50 feet at the base. Piercing the walls of the city were twelve gates, some say thirteen, and in addition to the fortifications protecting them, 900 towers and a triple line of moats.[37] Besides these formidable defenses, there were four small towns or forts constructed outside the main city but connected to it by subterranean tunnels. Each of these was about one mile square, had two gates, was fortified with towers and moats and contained granaries, arsenals and treas-

[35] The *Yüan Sheng Wu Ch'in Cheng Lu* says at Jen Tien. Wang Kuo-wei identifies Jen Tien with the She-la K'e-erh (Shara Keer) of the *Yüan Ch'ao Pi Shih*. This T'u Chi implies was one and the same with She-la Tieh-K'e which he says was the Mongol name for Lung-hu T'ai.

[36] This is from the *Chin Shih*, which also includes I-tu in Shantung among the places retaken, but the great distance of this town from the others makes it unlikely that it fell to the Right-wing army, so perhaps another place is intended.

[37] See Siren, *The Walls and Gates of Peking*, and Bretschneider, *Recherches Archéologiques et Historiques sur Pékin et ses environs*.

uries of its own. At the time of their building during the previous century the inhabitants of Chung Tu had laughed in derision, but Nien Han, the Chung-hsien Wang of Chin, who then commanded the city and had ordered their construction, declared with prophetic foresight, " Within one hundred years from now my work will be vindicated." And so it proved, for when the Mongols camped at Ta K'ou, the government issued instructions for the wealthy to move into the eastern of the four posts, the families of all officials into the southern, the imperial house into the western and their relatives into the northern. To each were detailed 4,000 soldiers and to the main city, 20,000. Also, supposedly before the Mongols began the leaguer, all tiles and stones, and stores of hay and food were collected from the surrounding country and brought in. Shortly afterward, snow began to fall and still further increased the difficulties of the invaders. Nevertheless they made an assault on the Nan-hsün Men, which was forced or purposely relinquished, for the Mongols penetrated half a li into the city, but having got so far, found their retreat cut off and the street by which they had entered set on fire, and only regained the open country after heavy losses in men and horses. For all that they soon afterward made a general attempt to storm the main city, but attacked from Nien Han's four towns, were beaten off and forced to retire.[38]

Despite this second failure, the Mongol generals wished to try a third attack but Chingis Khan, learning that peace was being discussed in the city, refused and late in March or early in April sent A-la-ch'ien to the capital with peace proposals. For one reason or another these were rejected, but, undiscouraged, he sent the Tangut back with the following message: " The whole of Shantung and Hopei are now in my possession while you retain only Yen Tu (Chung Tu); God has made you so weak, that should I further molest you, I know not what Heaven would say; I am willing to withdraw my army, but

[38] For the siege of Chung Tu, as well as the description of Nien Han's four towns; see the *Yüan Shih Hsin Pien* and the *Hsin Yüan Shih*.

what provision will you make to still the demands of my
officers? " [39]

When the Chin emperor had heard these words, he turned
to his ministers and asked their opinion. Thereupon Chu-hu
Kao-ch'i spoke up and said: " I have heard that both the men
and horses of the Mongols are greatly fatigued and suffering
from sickness; should we therefore not take this opportunity to
fight a decisive battle? " But Wan-yen Fu-hsing, an officer
of Jurchid stock and commander of the troops in Chung Tu,
opposed him. " Our troops," he declared, " have been collected
from every direction— (many were from Shensi) —and at the
last moment. Though they are in the capital, their families
are scattered far and wide in the various lu (districts) from
which they have come. Hence their loyalty is uncertain. If
defeated, they will fly like birds and animals; if victorious, they
will at once want to return home and who then will guard the
capital? For the sake of the dynasty, should we take such a
risk? Rather ought we to consider the situation. In my
opinion the best policy is to send an envoy to seek peace. Then,
after the enemy has withdrawn, we can take measures for the
future." [40]

Having listened to both men, the emperor was convinced
of the soundness of Fu-hsing's advice— (Hsüan Tsung had
already tried to bolster the loyalty of his troops and in January
had made special presents to them) [41]—and sent the general out
to Chingis Khan to inform him that they would discuss terms.
Consequently, A-la-ch'ien returned to Chung Tu and probably
early in May peace was concluded. By it the Chin emperor
gave to the conqueror a daughter of his predecessor, 500 boys

[39] The *Yüan Shih* and *Meng-wu-erh Shih*.

[40] These speeches have come from the *Yüan Sheng Wu Ch'in Cheng Lu*, which
has been followed by T'u Chi. In the *Yüan Ch'ao Pi Shih* there is a somewhat
different version of the affair. There we learn that when the Mongols invested the
caiptal, the Chin minister Wang Chin said to the emperor: " The Mongols have
destroyed our best troops and have taken our strongest fortress the Chü-yung
Kuan; if we again fight, our men will certainly be defeated and fly; let us therefore
enter into negotiations with Chingis Khan, who I think will be willing to retire,
as disease has broken out among his men."

[41] See the *Chin Shih*.

and girls for her retinue, 3,000 horses, 10,000 liang of gold and 10,000 bolts of silk.[42]  Though there must also have been other conditions, the only one recorded is the release of the relatives of Yeh-lü Akhai and Tukha, held prisoners ever since the defection of the two brothers to Chingis Khan.[43]  Notwithstanding the gift of a royal princess, no reference is made to any recognition of Mongol suzerainty, but as in the case of the Tangut King Li An-ch'uan, the forced bestowal of a princess was a sign of subserviency and a definite humiliation.  Besides thus honoring Chingis Khan, the emperor ordered Wan-yen Fu-hsing to accompany him on his withdrawal as far north as Huan-erh-Tsui.  Not until then did all hostilities cease, for one learns that even while negotiations were being carried on, the town of Lan Hsien in Shansi was taken by the army of the princes.

According to some accounts, Fu-hsing went no further than the Chü-yung pass where the conqueror is related to have ordered the massacre of all the surviving captives with the army.  While the Chin general may very well have ended his journey at the famous pass, from now on to remain in Mongol hands, it is unlikely that the invaders perpetrated such an outrageous piece of barbarity after the conclusion of peace.[44]

No sooner had Chingis Khan retired than Hsüan Tsung, seeing Hopei, Shansi and even the districts near Chung Tu desolate, and feeling unsafe so near the Mongols, resolved to transfer his capital south.  When he heard of the emperor's intention, T'u Ch'an-i came to him and begged him to move

[42] These are the terms recorded by the *Yüan Shih,* but it is only from Chang K'uang-yen's biography of " Mukhali " that we learn the exact quantity of gold and silk.  Even allowing for the scarcity of precious metals in China and the much greater purchasing power of gold and silver in those days—at least five times what it is today and probably more—10,000 liang sounds like a small sum for the Mongol conqueror to have received from Hsüan Tsung, and the figure of 10,000 might have been a slip for 100,000.  A bolt of silk under the Sung, doubtless the same under the Chin, measured 30 English yards.

[43] See the biography of " Yeh-lü Aqai " in the *Meng-wu-erh Shih.*

[44] It is from the *Yüan Ch'ao Pi Shih* and the *Yüan Sheng Wu Ch'in Cheng Lu* that one learns of Fu-hsing's journey to Huan-erh-tsui; from the *Yüan Shih,* the *Li-tai T'ung-chien Chi-lan,* Gaubil and de Mailla, that he went no further north than the Chü-yung Kuan, and that there Chingis Khan massacred his prisoners.

rather to Liaotung which he contended was easier to defend
than Honan. But thinking of the greatly superior economic
resources of the country south of the Yellow River as well as of
the natural barrier formed by the river, Hsüan Tsung persisted
in his resolution, and though temporarily delayed by heavy
rains, set out in June for K'ai-feng. In charge of the capital
he left the Prince Imperial Shou Chung, and to assist him
Wan-yen Fu-hsing and the brave defender of Hsi Ching, Mo-jan
Chin-chung. The latter, having come to the city after the
departure of the Mongols, was kept there by the emperor who
bestowed upon him many honors and ordered him to act in
concert with Fu-hsing.

Hsüan Tsung's departure for the south was more than the
transfer of a capital. It was the end of the Chin as a border
power. With the abandonment of Chung Tu as the seat of
the imperial government, the Chin openly resigned themselves
to the loss of Inner Mongolia and ultimately to that of Manchuria. Henceforth the Chin would fight the war as a purely
Chinese state. While much stronger, their position resembled
that of the short lived Sino-Turkish dynasties of Later Tsin
(936-46) and Later Han (947-50) after the Khitans had extended their authority inside the Great Wall. Although Hsüan
Tsung's decision was due largely to military and economic
exigencies, his preference for the south as opposed to Manchuria was also symptomatic of a metamorphosis that had been
taking place among the Jurchids since the latter part of the
12th century. Then the emperor Ulu or Shih Tsung (1161-89),
perceiving that the Jurchid nobility were becoming affected by
contact with the Confucian scholar bureaucracy, and realizing
the dangers of assimilation, officially deprecated the abandonment of Jurchid speech, customs and dress for those of the
Chinese. Nevertheless, by the opening of the 13th century a
majority among the Jurchid aristocracy, including many of the
imperial family, were well along the road to assimilation and
were more Chinese than Jurchid. Consequently, their Chinese
possessions held a greater attraction for them than Manchuria,
and the appeals of T'u Ch'an-i, and those like him who tended

to remain Jurchid, went unheeded and the dynasty moved south instead of north. Shortly after the rejection of his advice, T'u Ch'an-i died and the empire lost one of its bravest and most faithful adherents.

Hsüan Tsung was no more than thirty miles on his fateful journey when he began to suspect the loyalty of the 2,000 Khitan troops in his guard.[45] This was under the supreme command of Chu-hu Kao-ch'i who now received orders to take from the Khitans their horses and to send them back to Chung Tu. As soon as word of this came to the ears of the 2,000 men, they promptly mutinied, and slaying their commanding officer,[46] chose K'an-ta in his place and set off for the capital on their own.[47] Getting timely warning of their approach, Wan-yen Fu-hsing hurried men to the Yung-ting River and at the Lu-Kou bridge barred their road. Unable to force a passage, K'an-ta resorted to a strategem. Pretending to desist in his attempts, he secretly sent half his force—1,000 men—to cross the river higher up. This was successfully accomplished, and the detachment, falling suddenly on the rear of Fu-hsing's troops, took them unawares while their horses were grazing loose about the bridge. Thrown into utter confusion, the surprised soldiers fled from the field with the loss of arms, armor and mounts. The whole Khitan force then pressed on to Chung Tu, outside which they seized still more horses, but being too weak to dare remain in the neighborhood, they departed and sent an offer of friendship to Yeh-lü Liu-ke and another of submission to Chingis Khan.

By the time that the conqueror learned of these events it was already July and he was camped at Yü-erh-lo. Informed that Hsüan Tsung had left Chung Tu, he became greatly angered: " The Chin Emperor," he exclaimed, " made a peace agreement

[45] The *Yüan Shih Hsin Pien* of Wei Yüan is the only work in which the number of the Khitan insurgents is given—we are further told that they all belonged to the Ch'i clan.

[46] Pen-chu-hsiang is the name of the murdered officer given by T'u Chi, but in the *Yüan Sheng Wu Ch'in Cheng Lu*, from which the whole incident has been taken, Su-wen is the name accepted by Wang Kuo-wei.

[47] Three other officers were associated with him, namely T'a-t'a-erh, Cha-la-erh (Jalaar) and Pi-she-erh.

with me, but now he has moved his capital to the south; evidently he mistrusts my word and has used the peace to deceive me! " [48]   Thereupon he sent his former envoy A-la-ch'ien to Chung Tu to obtain further information, and on being informed of all that had taken place, began making preparations to send south an army to capture the city.  In this decision he was encouraged by Shih-mo Ming-an, who gave it as his opinion that unless hostilities were soon resumed the Chin might recover sufficiently to reconquer everything that they had lost.[49] While Chingis can hardly have feared that this would happen, he must have been very disappointed at the transfer of the central government to K'ai-feng, where it would be much bolder in dealing with his demands than if it had remained in the north.  Nevertheless, with the emperor gone, he knew that he had a far better chance of taking the great metropolis.  In the matter of a casus belli he was lucky.  A little time before, the Chin had refused to let pass an embassy that he had despatched to the Sung,[50] so, using this and Hsüan Tsung's departure for the south as an excuse for again beginning the war, he assembled an army for the siege.  At the head of this he placed the Saljiud Samukha, and to help him sent Shih-mo Ming-an, the brothers Yeh-lü Akhai and Tukha, Liu Po-lin, Kita, a certain Shen-sa and the recently submitted Khitan rebel K'an-ta.  This mixed force of Mongols, Khitans and Chinese marched south via the Chü-yung Kuan and probably reached Chung Tu in the early part of September.  But before it arrived, the Prince Imperial had left for the south on orders from the emperor who had learned of the impending siege. Though this had a disheartening effect on the city, the invaders found it ready to oppose an obstinate resistance.

Despite the absence of any figures concerning the size of Samukha's army, it must have been considerable, for in addi-

---

[48] This outburst on the part of Chingis Khan is recorded in the *Ch'eng-chi-ssŭ Han* of Feng Ch'eng-chün.

[49] *Meng-wu-erh-Shih*, biography of " Shih-mo Ming-an."

[50] The report of this embassy and the conqueror's resolve to use its failure to reach the Sung as an excuse for recommencing the war is from the *Yüan Ch'ao Pi Shih*.

tion to investing Chung Tu, it also surrounded Shun Chou to the northeast and Tʻung Chou to the east. Perhaps the general's troops, exclusive of work battalions, numbered about 50,000.[51] There is every indication that the entire operation was a stupendous blockade rather than a regular siege, for one hears nothing of attempts to carry any of the three places by storm. This is not strange, for even with the large numbers of captives and subject peasants at their disposal for labor and assaults, the experience of the Mongols earlier in the year had taught them that the capital anyway could only be taken by force at the price of heavy casualties. Moreover, since there seemed no likelihood of an army of relief being sent to oppose them, time was on their side, so instead of decimating their forces in costly assaults, they resolved to rely upon starvation and disease to do their work.

Nothwithstanding the desperate nature of the situation, Chung Tu remained undaunted. Autumn dragged into winter and when in January the next year (1215) Chingis Khan himself returned south and again pitched camp at Lung-hu Tʻai,[52] the great city was still far from submission. But sure of the end, the conqueror patiently waited, and to occupy the time made gifts to his officers, naming Samukha governor of Hsüan-pʻing, which was created the administrative center of the surrounding country, and dividing Eastern Hopei into districts. The following month (February), Tʻung Chou capitulated and

[51] This guess is based not only on the fact that Samukha was a commander of 10,000, and that the seven associate commanders, except Shen-sa and Kʻan-ta, were very senior, so certainly commanded a few thousand men each, but that it is hard to see how Samukha could even have blockaded Chung Tu, an immense city of eighteen miles in circumference, and two towns besides, without at least 50,000 effectives. In 1221 the Mongols employed 50,000-60,000 men for the conquest of Khwarazm, and while in some respects the operation was more difficult than that under consideration, the capital city Gurganj did not compare either in size or strength with Chung Tu. (For the Mongol attack on Khwarazm; see Barthold, *Turkestan down to the Mongol Invasion*, pp. 433-437).

As for the troops of the garrison, the departure, first of the emperor, then of the heir-apparent, will have left them not a little reduced in numbers from the 36,000 present at the beginning of the year.

[52] In the *Meng-wu-erh Shih* the place is called Tieh-miao Kʻe-erh, which would seem to be a variation of She-la Tieh-Kʻe, which, as already mentioned, Tʻu Chi affirms was the Mongol name for Lung-hu Tʻai.

its commander was requited for his treachery by being reappointed commander of the town. This was a heavy blow to the morale of the troops in the metropolis, where famine was at last making its presence felt, but there was no talk of surrender.

In March Chingis Khan sent A-la-ch'ien to K'ai-feng to offer peace, but about the same time there arrived representatives from Chung Tu who had managed to slip through the investing lines and came to beg for food and reinforcements. The efforts of the Mongol envoy came to naught and the emperor decided to make a desperate if belated effort to save his late capital. Early in April, Li Ying, the Commander of southeastern Hopei, was ordered to collect men and supplies from the districts of Ho-chien, Ts'ang Chou and Ch'ing Chou and to march to the relief of the city. Concurrently the commander of Chen-ting was to go with his forces and those of Chung-shan, and joining Wu-ku-lun Ching-shou and the army of Ta-ming Fu—this numbered 39,000—to march north through the western part of the province with a second convoy. Further, each man was to carry a load of 3 tou (approximately 70 lbs.) and Li Ying and Ching-shou were to set an example. In the rear of these forces the governor of Ta-ming Fu was to organize still another to follow as soon as possible.

When Chingis Khan learned of the approach of these armies, he despatched two small forces to meet them, one under Shih-mo Ming-an, the other under Shen-sa.[53] The first surprised Ch'ing-shou at Hsüan-feng Chai near the Yung-ting River and completely routed his greatly superior force, while Shen-sa fell upon the other between Pa Chou and Yung-ch'ing. There Li Ying, who was a heavy drinker and no disciplinarian, was attacked while drunk and sustained a crushing defeat, his great convoy of 1,000 cartloads of food being lost and he himself taken prisoner.[54] Notwithstanding this disaster, the Chin gov-

---

[53] The *Meng-wu-erh Shih* says that Shen-sa's force numbered no more than 400 men, Ming-an's 500, but the biography of Shih-mo Ming-an declares that the general had 3,000 troops, which is far more likely.

[54] These details for the attempted relief of Chung Tu are from the biography of

ernment immediately began making plans for a second attempt at relief, but was finally persuaded to leave the city to its fate by Chu-hu Kao-ch'i, who we are told hated Wan-yen Fu-hsing.[55]

During May Shun Chou fell and Ming-an captured the small towns of Ku-an, Feng-i Kuan and Fu Ch'ang. Simultaneously two mixed detachments of Mongols and Chinese took Ho-chien, Ch'ing Chou and Ts'ang Chou, the first of which surrendered and 1,000 of whose defenders entered the invading army.[56] Thus, less than a month after Li Ying's defeat, the whole of his strategically important command slipped from the hands of the Chin.

At last the Mongols were able to concentrate their entire army outside Chung Tu. Inside conditions were so desperate that cannibalism had broken out. Seeing that the place must succumb, Wan-yen Fu-hsing suggested to Mo-jan Chin-chung that they throw open the gates, and sallying forth with the garrison, die arms in hand.[57] But his colleague, who up to then had been largely responsible for the defense, was for flying south. Thereupon a violent quarrel broke out, and Fu-hsing having drawn up and despatched a memorial containing the measures that he considered necessary for the preservation of the empire and accusing Chu-hu Kao-ch'i of treason, took leave of his ancestors and committed suicide. When he learned of this, the hitherto brave Chin-chung became panic stricken and prepared to fly. Hearing of his intention, the imperial princesses left in the city begged him to take them with him, but though he promised to do so, he secretly departed with none but his own relatives. Making his way through the Mongol lines, probably under cover of darkness, he eventually reached K'ai-feng, where he was at first appointed to a post

"Wan-yen Fu-hsing" in the *Chin Shih*, the *Yüan Sheng Wu Ch'in Cheng Lu* and the *Meng-wu-erh Shih*, main text and biography of "Shih-mo Ming-an." The *Yüan Shih* is very brief but says that Li Ying was killed.

[55] This is reported by the *Yüan Shih Hsin Pien*.

[56] See De Mailla, Vol. IX and the *Meng-wu-erh Shih*. The former, who provides most of our information, declares that one detachment numbered 3,000 Mongols and Chinese, but says nothing about the strength of the other.

[57] *Chin Shih*, biography of "Wan-yen Fu-hsing."

in the government, but later degraded and executed.[58] Abandoned by their commander, the officers of Mo-jan Chin-chung opened the gates of the city and in June surrendered to Shih-mo Ming-an, who had succeeded Samukha in command of the besieging army.[59] Apparently the Mongol general went north with Chingis Khan who left between April and the fall of the metropolis. Kita and the brothers Akhai and Tukha, all still present, were far older adherents of Chingis than Ming-an, but evidently convinced of the latter's superior aptitude for siege warfare, and knowing that he was well acquainted with the city, the conqueror put him in charge.

Despite the city's submission, the besieging soldiers got out of hand, and unable to resist the lure of so gigantic a prize, sacked a great part of the capital and slew many thousands of the inhabitants. A Khorezmian embassy to the Mongol Khan, which passed by Chung Tu a few months later reports that the bones of the slaughtered formed whole mountains, that the soil was greasy with human fat and that the rotting bodies brought on an illness from which many of the embassy died.[60] In the ensuing uproar one of the Imperial palaces was set on fire, and one learns that the part of the city in which the conflagration broke out burned a whole month.[61] Nevertheless a vast booty fell into the hands of Ming-an who sent to inform Chingis Khan that Chung Tu was his. Delighted, the conqueror, who was then camped at Liang-ching outside the Tushih K'ou, sent a message of praise to the general and instructions to forward the loot and with it the principal Chin notables. At the same time he sent south his adopted son Shiki Kutuku and two officers of the Guard, Onggur and Arkhai Khassar, to take an inventory of the imperial treasure. On

---

[58] See the *Chin Shih,* biographies of " Wan-yen Fu-hsing " and " Mo-jan Chin-chung."

[59] See the *Meng-wu-erh Shih,* biography of " Shih-mo Ming-an."

[60] Juzjani, Barthold, *Turkestan down to the Mongol Invasion,* pp. 393-394.

[61] See Gaubil ("Yüan Shih Lei Pien "), the *Li-tai T'ung-Chien Chi-lan* and de Mailla, Vol. IX. The *Ssŭ Ch'ao Pieh Shih* declares that Ming-an burned Chung Tu, but this is unlikely, the *Yüan Shih* that he forced his way into the city, while his own biography in the *Meng-wu-erh Shih* makes a point of declaring that no sooner was he master of Chung Tu than he set about relieving the famine raging within.

their arrival the Chin treasurer offered all three bribes. These were accepted by Onggur and Arkhai Khassar, but Shiki Kutuku could not be induced to take anything. Informed of this, the conqueror asked Kutuku on his return why he had refused. " Formerly," replied Shiki Kutuku, " all in the city belonged to the Emperor of Chin, but with its fall, everything became yours; how could I take your property? " Greatly pleased with this answer, Chingis Khan praised Shiki Kutuku and reprimanded his colleagues.[62] Generous to a degree, the conqueror was at the same time extremely jealous of all that he regarded as belonging to him and could be speedily roused to wrath by liberties of the kind just described.

With the treasures of Chung Tu, there also arrived many Chin officials. Among these was a young man of great stature and outstanding appearance. Inquiring his identity, the conqueror was told that he was a member of the Khitan royal house named Yeh-lü Ch'u-ts'ai. Addressing him, Chingis said: " The house of Liao and the house of Chin were ever enemies; I have avenged you." " My grandfather, my father and myself," replied the Khitan, " were all subjects and servants of the Chin; I should be a despicable liar if I were to tell you that I had hostile feelings for my lord and father." [63] Such an answer could not fail to impress Chingis Khan, who immediately took him into his service. Twenty-five years of age when this happened, Yeh-lü Ch'u-ts'ai first became the Mongol conqueror's chief astrologer, then his principal minister, and lived to become not only the greatest statesman of the empire but one of the noblest figures in history.

Chung Tu in his possession, Chingis Khan rewarded Shih-mo Ming-an by making him military commander of the city and placed under his authority a mixed force of Mongols and Chinese, the former led by Kita.[64] Simultaneously, nearly all the

[62] This incident is recorded by both the *Yüan Ch'ao Pi Shih* and *Yüan Sheng Wu Ch'in Cheng Lu.*
[63] See " Vie de Yeliu Thsutsai," *Nouveaux Mélanges Asiatiques,* Vol. 11, par Rémusat. This author took his information from the biography of the Khitan in the *Yüan Shih Lei Pien.* Yeh-lü Ch'u-ts'ai was born in 1190 and died in 1244.
[64] This is from the biography of " Shih-mo Ming-an " but that of " Yeh-lü Akhai "

important places still untaken in northern Hopei surrendered. Only at Hsin-an to the west of the Hsi-ting Lake did the Chin retain a foothold. All possible land communication between K'ai-feng and the northeast was thus ended. A great event in the world of that day, the capture of Chung Tu was the real beginning of Mongol dominion in China. It was also the last occasion for nearly three years on which Chingis Khan himself appeared in the Middle Kingdom. In July (1215) he moved from Liang-ching to Yü-erh-lo and then in the autumn of the same year back to the Kerulen River which he had not seen since the spring of 1211.

Some authorities, notably the *Yüan Shih*, date Chingis Khan's return north of the desert during the first month of 1216 (Jan. 21-Feb. 18), but T'u Chi, who assigns it to the autumn of 1215, points out that not only is the grazing in Mongolia very poor for marching in February but that the Khitan Yeh-lü Liu-ke visited the conqueror on the Kerulen during the eleventh month of 1215 (Nov. 23-Dec. 21).

Everywhere north and east of the Yellow River, Chin power was shaken to its foundations and, even in those parts free of the Mongols, the authority of the central government was challenged. Despite the many disasters suffered at the hands of Chingis Khan and his generals, nothing struck so heavy a blow to Chin prestige as the emperor's flight from Chung Tu. No sooner did report of it reach Manchuria than P'u-hsien Wan-nu, Commander-in-Chief east of the Liao River, made plans to revolt and the following year, in February 1215, declared his independence.[65] Two months later an unsuccessful insurrection broke out in Hsi Ching, so that both far and near the Chin were hampered by rebellion; [66] but this was only the

says that the latter received the appointment and that his younger brother Tukha was second in command and Shih-mo Ming-an only third. Since Akhai did not go west with the conqueror until 1219 and Tukha south with Mukhali until 1217, it is possible that Ming-an became commander of Chung Tu only after 1217. However, when the celebrated Taoist sage Ch'iu Ch'ang-ch'un passed through Hsüan-te Chou in 1220, Tukha was commander of the town, so it is probable that it was to Hsüan-te, and not Chung Tu that he was appointed. (See the *Meng-wu-erh Shih*.)

[65] *Chin Shih*, biography of " P'u-hsien Wan-nu."
[66] *Chin Shih*.

beginning. In April famine swept the province of Honan where desperate efforts were being made to provide for some 1,000,000 members of soldier's families who had come south. At first the government tried to establish the immigrants on the waste lands of the province, but these proved so inadequate that other means became necessary.

One of the principal measures adopted was the recall and redistribution of those lands in Shantung directly under the government. A dangerous expedient at the best of times, a worse moment could not have been chosen for so risky an undertaking, and though later it was stopped, the damage was done. Carried out by corrupt and dishonest officials, who were themselves in many cases wealthy or would-be-wealthy land owners, and who took advantage of the situation to increase their own holdings, the measure not only completely failed to relieve the immigrants but left the Shantung peasantry beggared.[67]

These unhappy people, already suffering from the terrible Mongol devastation of the previous year, and burdened by ever increasing taxation, now became desperate. A revolt broke out and the province of Shantung was overrun by a fierce jacquerie known as the Red Coats. In March, 1215, the government sent troops to try to restore order, and though 30,000 of the insurgents are reported to have been slain and 10,000 the succeeding month, the rebellion continued with unabated fury. So formidable did it become that in October a large band of peasants was able to march north into western Hopei and loot five small towns in the department of Chenting.[68] The previous month (September) this city had capitulated to the Mongols and the renegade commander, only just settling down under his new masters, found himself again called upon to take the field. Leading out his forces, he vigorously attacked the Red Coats who sustained a crushing defeat and the loss of their leader.[69] But in Shantung the rebels continued.

[67] Mabel Ping-Hua-Lee, *The Economic History of China*, The Kin, pp. 325-326.
[68] These towns were Shen Chou, Ch'i Chou, Shu-lu (Ku Ch'eng), An-p'ing and Wu-chi.
[69] See the *Chin Shih.*

unchecked, and during February, 1216, plundered three important districts, though they failed to take the towns.[70] Further south, however, they were more successful and in April and May under another leader sacked five places.[71] At length the Chin called from Manchuria one of their best captains. This was Ke-shih-lieh Huan-tuan, who during the foregoing year had greatly distinguished himself against the rebel P'u-hsien Wan-nu. Arriving, presumably by sea, he took command of the imperial forces and in July decisively defeated the insurgents, whose leader was captured and sent to K'ai-feng for execution. Nothwithstanding this reverse, the revolt went on, and in 1217 the emperor was compelled to call in yet another outstanding soldier, Wan-yen Chung-yüan. The struggle continued until 1217 when the Chin lost the province to the Sung, but the Red Coat rebellion was still unsuppressed in 1223.[72]

Only less formidable because further away were the continued attacks of the Tanguts. Undaunted by their failure in 1214, the following year (1215) found them once more on the offensive, and though beaten off at certain points in Shensi,[73] they were successful in southeast Kansu. Attacking the city of Lin-t'ao, they took it and defeated and made prisoner the commander of Kuan-chung (Shensi and eastern Kansu). This was a serious reverse, for with the loss of the Ongud country and cut off, except by sea, even from eastern Manchuria, the Lin-t'ao area and the adjoining region to the west was the last sure source of supply upon which the Chin cavalry could rely for mounts. A major effort of reconquest was called for and in December a powerful army moved on Lin-t'ao. Outside the walls a great battle was fought, a Tangut force 80,000 strong was defeated and the city recovered. The new commander for Kuan-chung was then heavily reinforced, and the next Tangut

---

[70] T'ai-an, Te Chou and Po Chou.

[71] Lai-wu, Hsin-t'ai, Yen Chou, I Chou and T'eng Chou.

[72] For the Red Coat rebellion; see the *Chin Shih,* main text, and the biographies of " Ke-shih-lieh Huan-tuan," " Wan-yen Chung-yüan," and " Meng Ku-kang."

[73] From Feb. to March 1215 the Tanguts were before Huan Chou in East Kansu and in November the same year besieged both Pao-an and Yen-an in Shensi—see the *Chin Shih.*

inroad, during June or July, 1216, was easily repulsed though the town attacked was a far westerly point.[74] Against Hsi Hsia, as in the war soon to break out with the Sung, the Chin were still able to win field battles. Only in their struggle with the Mongols did their efforts in the open continue to meet with but occasional success. The reason for this is not hard to seek. The Tanguts even then were little superior to them in cavalry and the Sung definitely inferior. The Mongols on the other hand, with their inexhaustible supply of horses, were able to make unlimited use of cavalry and so enjoyed an immense advantage in pitched battles.[75]

To meet their many enemies, Mongol, Tangut and Red Coat, the Chin were obliged to resort to extreme measures. As early as October, 1214, after Hsüan Tsung's arrival in K'ai-feng, a levy en masse was ordered, and in April, 1215, the authorities in the province of Shansi received special instructions to conscript all able-bodied men. During September the same year (1215) the emperor also called upon all retired military officers to come to the capital to help organize the new army, and proclaimed that henceforth ability and not precedence of rank would be the only road to promotion. Further, 20,000 infantry were recruited in Shensi and despatched to Honan for the express purpose of covering K'ai-feng to the west, 40,000 from elsewhere to guard it on the east and 2,000 cavalry sent into the city. To add still more to the defense of the metropolis, in size now the greatest in the empire, special garrisons were stationed in Yüan-wu, Yen-chin, Feng-ch'iu, Ch'en-liu, Ch'i Hsien and T'ung-hsü. A look at the map will show that these places formed a circle about the capital, the first four on the north side of the Yellow River, the other three on the south side, while far to the west all approach down the river was barred by the mighty fortress of T'ung Kuan. As an additional precaution, the families of the garrisons in the seven small towns north and south of the river were ordered to go and live in

---

[74] This was the town of Ho Chou on the Ta-hsia River.

[75] Before the loss of Manchuria and Inner Mongolia to the Mongols, the Chin cavalry was of course greatly superior to that of either the Sung or the Tanguts.

them. Simultaneously, a system of connected block houses was begun in the vicinity of K'ai-feng, and at Chün Chou, Hua Chou and Ts'ao Chou, north of the Yellow River.[76] From this recital it might be thought that the Chin had gone over entirely to the defensive, but as will be subsequently seen this was not so. Even at the time of taking these steps for the defense of the capital, the emperor made the following promises to his officers: The reoccupation of Chung Tu would be rewarded by promotion to the rank of a first-class commander; the recovery of a district by the government of that district and a victory over the Mongols by command of a city. Later in the month (October) the third condition was broadened, and rewards of one kind or another were promised for the defeat of 3,000, 2,000 or 1,000 troops, whether Mongol or Tangut.[77]

How effective the new army might have become it is hard to say. Its principal weakness was shortage of cavalry, but also many of the infantry were never fully trained. By September (1215) the Mongols were again as far south as Tung-p'ing and Ta-ming Fu and the next year (1216) appeared in Shensi and Honan. Consequently many troops, their training but half finished, were obliged to take the field to meet them. It was precisely this handicap that the Commander of Shansi, Ao Tun Ch'e Ho-sheng, declared two years later was largely responsible for their frequent reverses.[78]

After the fall of Chung Tu, the Mongols suspended all major operations in China until the end of summer. But if hostilities on a grand scale were arrested, it was not because Chingis Khan was satisfied with what had been accomplished, but because he merely wished to rest and refresh his cavalry. As in 1211, he was still resolved to wring from the Chin emperor recognition of his suzerainty. To this end, in July 1215, while camped at Yü-erh-lo, he ordered the mobilization of four armies to undertake another southward offensive. One composed of

---

[76] These measures are from the *Chin Shih.*
[77] *Chin Shih.*
[78] *Chin Shih,* biography of " Ao Tun Ch'e Ho-sheng."

Mongols, Khitans and Chinese and led by the Khongkhotat Tolun Cherbi was to invade western Hopei, a second, all Chinese and commanded by Shih T'ien-ni, was to march into the most easterly part of the province to recover P'ing Chou, a third, of which the composition and leader are unnamed, was to penetrate Shansi and a fourth, consisting of 10,000 Mongols under Samukha, was to advance through the Ordos for an attack on Ching-chao (Hsi-an) in southern Shensi.[79] At first sight Samukha's force would seem very inadequate for such an undertaking, but it was to receive a powerful reinforcement from the Tanguts. Since the Ordos belonged to Hsi Hsia, Chingis Khan called upon Li Tsun-hsiang (1211-23), Li An-ch'üan's nephew and successor, to honor his uncle's oath of fealty and give the army right of way. At the same time he demanded that 30,000 troops be sent to join the expedition. Afraid to incur the conqueror's wrath, Li Tsun-hsiang complied with both requests,[80] but time being necessary to equip and organize such a force, Samukha's departure was considerably delayed.

While none of these forces were large, they indicate that Chingis Khan was prepared to make another general onslaught in the near future. Samukha's objective in particular would signify that he wished first to ascertain how much resistance he might expect when the time came. Nevertheless, during August he despatched A-la-ch'ien to offer the Chin terms. Arrived in K'ai-feng, the envoy promised Hsüan Tsung peace if he would order the submission of all places still resisting the Mongols in Hopei and Shantung, and would give up the title of emperor and content himself with that of King of Honan.[81]

---

[79] The *Yüan Sheng Wu Ch'in Cheng Lu* says that Samukha was directed to march on Ching-chao (Hsi-an), the *Yüan Shih* that he invaded Kuan-chung (Shensi), but neither make any mention of T'ung Kuan in his original instructions. Perhaps therefore Samukha's subsequent attack on the great fortress was in excess of his orders, or possibly Chingis Khan left it to the general to undertake any additional operations he considered feasible.

[80] It is the *Hsi Hsia Shu Shih* that reports Chingis Khan's demand for right of way, also his call for 30,000 Tangut troops. The *Yüan Shih* also mentions the participation of the Tanguts.

[81] The demand that the emperor give up Hopei doubtless included not only the

Although refugees were already pouring over the Yellow River before the Mongols to escape the unspeakable horrors that the invasion of 1213-14 had taught them to expect, the Chin government still felt too strong to have to accept such humiliating conditions and A-la-ch'ien was dismissed with a refusal.[82]

Consequently the war went on. In September the town of P'ing Chou surrendered and Shih T'ien-ni marched across Hopei and joined Tolun Cherbi at Chen-ting. There the commander at first seemed prepared to put up an obstinate resistance, but eventually capitulated and entered the service of the Mongols. The two generals then moved south and laid siege to Ta-ming Fu. For a time all attempts to storm it failed but at length Shih T'ien-ni put himself at the head of an assault and the city was carried. Turning southeast, the victors moved on Tung-p'ing. This place, naturally very strong— (it stands on the eastern shores of the Tung-p'ing Lake and has a small river to the north of it) —was defended by Meng Ku-kang, one of the bravest commanders in the empire. Unable to reach the city across the lake or to force the river, the Mongols could only assault one section of the walls. This was a great advantage to the garrison who, skilfully directed by Meng Ku-kang, repulsed every attack and at length, worn out, the invaders raised the siege and retired. But if baffled by the city, part of the army remained in the province, for in November the new governor for Shantung was so terrified by the report of its ravages that he dared not leave Hsü Chou. The rest of the force went west and attacked Chang-te Fu, which fell sometime in December. In January, 1216, Ta-ming was again sacked, but must have been without a garrison. Also plundered were En Chou and Hsing Chou, both of which doubtless succumbed to the generals on their return north, whither they seem to have gone during January or early February (1216).[83]

present province of that name, but also Shansi, which like the other was north and east of the Yellow River and often called Ho-tung.

[82] Doubtless the ravages of the Red Coats added to the emigration southward.

[83] For this expedition; see the *Yüan Sheng Wu Ch'in Cheng Lu*, the *Meng-wu-erh Shih*, main text, and biography of Shih T'ien-ni and the *Chin Shih*, main text and biography of " Meng Ku-kang." K'e Shao-ming, author of the *Hsin Yüan Shih*,

In Shansi the third force was equally active, Shen Hsien, Tai Chou and P'ing-ting fell in 1215, while Hsi Ching to the north was apparently blockaded; and if during February and March the following year, T'ai-yüan was unsuccessfully besieged, Huo Chou and the Ling-shih defile were taken.[84] Between the Mongols on the one hand and the Red Coats on the other, life north of the Yellow River was nothing short of a nightmare.

No sooner had Tolun Cherbi and Shih T'ien-ni retired than the Chin launched a limited counter offensive. Late in February, or at the latest in March, the commander of Ching Chou in southern Hopei, moved north and successively recaptured Hsien Chou, Ho-chien and Ts'ang Chou,[85] the two latter, as already noted, towns of considerable strategic value. Emboldened by his success, he marched on Ch'ing Chou and by May was master of it too. Westward, during July and August, three small towns were retaken by another general, while to the south the Chin re-entered all places occupied by the Mongols.[86]

While these events were taking place, Samukha had been waiting for the Tanguts, and at last word came that 30,000 cavalry were marching east. So crossing the Yellow River, supposedly at Tung-sheng, he entered the Ordos and by September was before Yen-an. There he was joined by his allies who on the way had captured An-sai. His line of march is largely guess work, but perhaps after crossing the Yellow River, he advanced to Yin Chou, and then, like Mukhali in 1221, went by way of Sui-te and K'e-jung Chai to Yen-an. Whether the town was taken is not stated, but in October he and the Tanguts made an unsuccessful attempt on Fang Chou. Then marching via Yao Chou and T'ung Chou, they crossed the Wei River in November— (possibly to the north of Hua Chou)—and de-

includes Ts'ao Chou among the places taken, but his account of this campaign seems very inaccurate.

[84] See the *Chin Shih.*

[85] See the *Chin Shih* and the *Meng-wu-erh Shih,* biography of " Shih T'ien-ni."

[86] In the west the towns retaken were Shen Chou, Huo-lu and Wei Chou, in the south, Chang-te Fu, Ta-ming Fu, En Chou and Hsing Chou.

feated and slew the commander of Ching-chao (Hsi-an), who tried to bar the road east to T'ung Kuan.[87]

After an initial failure to seize the famous fortress, Samukha made a detour and surprised it from the mountains to the south.[88] He then hurried down the Yellow River to Yao Kuan, where he learned that four Chin armies were converging upon him to prevent his proceeding further. One, 10,000 strong, had been ordered from Lung-an in the south, a second, numbering 5,000, from Meng Chou in the north, a third had been commanded to block his road eastward and a fourth to go from Lu-shih to try to come up with him at Ling Pao, while still a fifth, also from Lu-shih, had been despatched to Shang Chou which commands the alternate route east from Shensi. Not waiting to be trapped, he turned into the mountains, and perhaps crossing the Lo River some 35 miles to the southwest of Lo-yang (Ho-nan Fu), made a forced march over the range covering Ju Chou.[89] Hot on his heels pressed the army from Lu Shih, but despite mountain tracks so rough that they had to be reinforced by the spears of his soldiers before they became passable, he reached Ju Chou and captured it before the pursuers could come up. From Ju Chou, he advanced northeast to Hsing-hua-ying, a small town no more than six miles west of K'ai-feng and though the capital was far too strong to attack—(since the fall of T'ung Kuan it had been further strengthened by the construction of trenches outside and the

[87] This was Ni-p'ang-ku-p'u-lu-hu and from his biography in the *Chin Shih*, we learn that he belonged to the Meng-an tribe, i. e., to the Meng-an-mo-k'e, also known as the Mo-ho, or Mukri, who had founded the state of Po Hai in eastern Manchuria during the 7th century and who had been conquered by the Khitan in 926. In the biography of another Chin soldier, Hsü Ting, it is said that previous to marching on the T'ung Kuan, the Mongols occupied T'ung Chou and Yao Chou. They must therefore have crossed the Wei River at the ford fifteen miles south of T'ung Chou and have engaged Ni-p'ang-ku-p'u-lu-hu near Hua Chou, which is approximately half way on the road between Ching-chao (Hsi-an) and T'ung Kuan.

[88] The *Meng-wu-erh Shih* reports that on the way Samukha passed through Chin-k'eng. This the *Chung Kuo Ku-chin Ti-ming Ta-tzu-tien* says was south of T'ung Kuan, but I have been unable to locate it on a map.

[89] The *Yüan Sheng Wu Ch'in Cheng Lu* and other works, notably the biography of "Wan-yen Chung-yüan" in the *Chin Shih*, name the range crossed the Sung Shan; but the mountains actually traversed must have been those imemdiately north of the Ju Ho.

erection of engines of war on the battlements)—his troops
ravaged the surrounding country.[90]

This can have gone on but a few days when, toward the end
of December, Samukha, fiercely attacked by the army from
Lu-shih and simultaneously threatened by other forces, was
compelled to retire. Very likely he retreated by the easier
route along the south bank of the Yellow River and the valley
of the Lo—a direct northward crossing was out of the question
because of the arc of fortified towns protecting K'ai-feng on the
other side of the river. At first he met with no opposition, but
at Mien Chou was forced to give battle to the army originally
despatched to obstruct his path east. As the troops from
Lung-an and Meng Chou had but recently reoccupied T'ung
Kuan, they were not present. The engagement was a victory
for Samukha, who also took the town. So making the most of
his success, he pressed on, and going via Shen Chou to the
San-men-chi ford, crossed the Yellow River on the ice early in
January, 1217.[91] Once over the river, he moved north and
arrived at P'ing-yang. But Hsü Ting, the commander for
south Shansi, expecting a Mongol attack on the city, had
instructed the commanders of Chiang Chou, Chieh Chou, Hsi
Chou, Chi Chou and Meng Chou to hold themselves in readiness for an emergency. Therefore, when news arrived that
Samukha was making for P'ing-yang, he at once gave orders
for them to advance to its relief. At the same time he proclaimed that all persons forcibly impressed into the Mongol
army would be pardoned and rewarded on their return to the
service of the Chin. Forthwith, some 13,000 deserted the
besieging army, which is reported to have numbered 60,000
Mongols, Tanguts and unwilling Chinese. Caught between the
garrison and the relieving troops, Samukha suffered consider-

[90] The speed with which K'ai-feng learned of the fall of T'ung Kuan is doubtless
to be explained by the government's use of carrier pigeons.

[91] This is the date given in the *Meng-wu-erh Shih*. The *Hsi Hsia Shu Shih* says
that the month was February. However, since the *Yüan Shih* and *Yüan Sheng Wu
Ch'in Cheng Lu* both imply that the crossing was effected in the 12th month of the
Ping-tzu year, i. e., January 9, 1217-February 7, 1217, I have accepted the earlier
month.

able losses and after ten days gave up the siege and retired. The Tanguts went west to Hsi Hsia, and perhaps crossing the Yellow River by the Ho-ching ford, finally reached home. On the way, however, they were attacked at Ning Chou in the valley of the Huan by the commander of Ch'ing-yang. Samukha too might have experienced trouble, but not only were Huo Chou and the Ling-shih defile still in the hands of the Mongols, but evidently to divert the Chin in Shansi, Mongol detachments stationed at Tai-Chou, Shen-hsien and P'ing-ting were ordered to converge on T'ai-yüan.[92] Again Hsü Ting acted with energy, and the commanders of Chiang Chou, Ho-chung, Lu-an, P'ing-yang and Meng Chou were ordered north, but though T'ai-yüan was relieved, Samukha made an unmolested retreat. Reaching Hsi Ching in February, he received the surrender of this long embattled city,[93] which was the last place held for the Chin in the valley of the Sang-kan. Too strong to take by assault except at great loss, the Mongols had patiently blockaded it into surrender.

Thus closed one of the most remarkable campaigns in the annals of Mongol warfare. The only others that resemble it for boldness are the overthrow of Kuchluk by Jebe in 1218, and the joint expedition of that general and Subudei against the Alans and Kipchaks during the summer of 1221. In both operations the mountains crossed, the T'ien Shan and the Caucasus, are higher than any traversed by Samukha and the distances covered greater, but in neither was the enemy attacked so powerful, nor the armies commanded as large. Under Jebe were 20,000 men to whom were later added a few Moslem auxiliaries, while in 1221 the Mongol force can hardly have exceeded 25,000. Samukha on the other hand began operations with 40,000 men, and not only penetrated into the

---

[92] Ch'eng t'ien-chen and Heng Ch'eng are also mentioned as points from which the Mongols converged, but I can locate neither of them. For this remarkable expedition by Samukha; see the *Yüan Shih, Hsin Yüan Shih, Meng-wu-erh Shih, Hsi Hsia Shu Shih, Li-tai T'ung-chien Chi-lan* and the *Chin Shih,* main text, and biographies of " Hsü Ting " and " Wan-yen Chung-yüan," also the *Yüan Sheng Wu Ch'in Cheng Lu.*

[93] See the *Meng-wu-erh Shih.* Although the final blockade of Hsi Ching may have begun simultaneously with that of Chung Tu, it is possible that it did not start until late the following year.

heart of the still powerful Chin state, but from start to finish maneuvered in a country bristling with fortified towns and strongholds, and where the surrounding forces, if less mobile, were numerically vastly superior to his own. Plotted on the map, his line of march from Hua Chou to Hsing-hua-ying and then west to the San-men-chi ford is approximately 600 miles. Supposing that Samukha defeated the Chin commander of Ching-chao (Hsi-an) near Hua Chou about the middle of November, 1216, and crossed the Yellow River as late as the third week of January, 1217, he had some sixty days in which to cover the distance. Even with spare mounts this is an amazing feat, but there is more to be taken into account. With time off for surprise attacks on T'ung Kuan and Ju Chou, a brief halt in the vicinity of K'ai-feng, and a day of battle at Mien Chou, Samukha's marching time was probably nearer fifty days, and considering much of the terrain crossed, the distance covered more like 700 miles than 600 miles.

From the " Li-tai T'ung-chien Chi-lan " it is apparent that this expedition greatly alarmed the Chin—doubtless they feared a repetition of Samukha's thrust with a simultaneous drive from Hopei [94]—for they sent north to inquire what peace terms Chingis Khan would give. According to the source just named, " after the conqueror had listened to the Chin envoy, he turned to those about him and said: ' The present situation may be compared to a hunt, we have taken all the deer and other beasts, only a rabbit is left, why not let it go! ' Thereupon Samukha, ashamed of having rendered no great service, exclaimed, ' The Chin emperor ought to have peace only when all places still resisting the Mongols in Hopei and Shantung are relinquished and he himself has dropped the title of Emperor for that of King, which he must hold as the vassal of Chingis Khan.' Such terms were impossible of acceptance and hostilities continued." While there is every likelihood that the Chin sought peace from Chingis Khan in 1217, Samukha's retort is so like the demand made on the conqueror's behalf at K'ai-feng

[94] The Mongols finally destroyed the Chin with a variation of this maneuver in a campaign that lasted from 1230-32.

by A-la-ch'ien in August, 1215, that it would seem that the
two occasions have been confused. In my own opinion, A-la-
ch'ien's embassy in August, 1215, must have been preceded by
one from the Chin, and Chingis Khan, to try the mettle of his
officers, spoke the words recorded above. As hoped, some of
them led by Samukha advocated the continuation of the war
and A-la-ch'ien went south in 1215 with the conditions outlined.
What became of the brilliant Samukha we do not know.
Perhaps he died prematurely, but at all events nothing more
is heard of him after the beginning of 1217.[95]

The operations of Samukha, Tolun Cherbi and Shih T'ien-ni,
plus those in Shansi, had demonstrated that a major onslaught
could destroy the Chin. At the same time, before this could
be effected, it was clear that Chin authority north of the Yellow
River must be eliminated before an attack could be made on
Honan, the main stay of Chin power. The two incursions
north of the river had also indicated that this initial phase
would be largely a matter of sieges. Resolved to open a final
offensive, Chingis Khan decided to delegate the first stage to
Mukhali and early in 1217 called him to his camp on the Tola.
There he discussed the campaign with him, and in September,
1217, sent him south. No better choice could have been made.
From November 1214, to September, 1216, Mukhali had successfully reduced the towns and cities of southern Manchuria,
and left all firmly in Mongol hands.[96]

Before he reached Hopei preliminaries had already started.
These had been opened by the Chin who were expecting the
coming blow. In April the city of Chen-ting was retaken by
its new commander Wu Hsien [97] and during the summer, Pa
Chou by another officer. But this second success was short

---

[95] The present writer has been unable to locate a biography of Samukha, but
all works dealing with him call him Samukha Baatur, a sure indication that
Chingis Khan regarded him as an exceptional commander.

[96] During the summer of 1217 a revolt broke out and Pei Ching was lost, but
Shih T'ien-hsiang crushed the rebellion and recovered the city. (See the *Meng-wu-
erh Shih*, biography of " Shih T'ien-hsiang.")

[97] *Li-tai T'ung-chien Chi-lan* and *Chin Shih*, biography of " Wu Hsien."

lived and the Tangut Chaghan defeated the general, recovered Pa Chou and also Hsin Ch'eng.[98]

By October Mukhali had begun operations and November found him as far south as Ta-ming Fu, but Chingis, evidently bent on accelerating the progress of the war by a thrust through Shensi, again called upon Li Tsun-hsiang for troops. The campaign of the previous year had been a heavy drain on Hsi Hsia, which was still engaged with the Chin on its own and we are told that the king's subjects made him return a refusal. This at once aroused the conqueror to fresh activity. Putting himself at the head of an army, he advanced south, and marching through the Ordos, crossed the Yellow River in January or February, 1218—presumably on the ice—and laid siege to Chung-hsing.

There is no specific reference to the Mongol line of march, but the " Hsi Hsia Shu Shih " says that Chingis went over the Yellow River and invested the Tangut capital. Since the city lay on the western side of the river and the only Tangut territory east of Chung-hsing was the Ordos, the invading army must have passed through it. T'u Chi believes that Chingis Khan was not with the army, but though the " Yüan Shih " is very vague on the subject, both the " Ssŭ Ch'ao Pieh Shih " and " Hsi Hsia Shu Shih " are quite emphatic concerning his presence.[99]

Memories of the last investment still vivid, Li Tsun-hsiang left the city in time, and entrusting it to his son Li Te Wang, fled to Hsi-liang, the Erijeu of the Mongols. From there he negotiated with Chingis Khan, and agreeing to resume his allegiance, secured the conqueror's withdrawal—the month is unrecorded. Doubtless the principal peace condition was a promise to provide the troops so recently refused to help in

---

[98] *Yüan Shih* and *Meng-wu-erh Shih*. The *Chin Shih* declares that as early as January, 1217, the city of Ta-ming was again taken and looted by the Mongols and in February the town of Kuan Chou. For February it also reports the sack of Tai Chou and Hsin Chou in Shansi, but all were isolated operations of little real importance.

[99] Formerly I was in accord with T'u Chi, but have since changed my opinion— see *The Mongol Wars with Hsi Hsia* (1205-27), J.R.A.S., parts 3-4, 1942, p. 205, n. 1.

the drive through Shensi. This would almost certainly have commenced later in the year, but events far to the west upset Chingis Khan's calculations. War broke out with the Khwarazm Shah, and the Mongol conqueror had not only to forego the invasion of Shensi, but demanded that the Tanguts help against the Moslems instead of the Chin. But Li Tsun-hsiang again refused.[100]  Though very angry, the conqueror was unable to punish the Tanguts then, but eventually they were to pay dearly for their temerity. This, however, as well as Mukhali's activities, will be dealt with later.

[100] The *Meng-wu-erh Shih,* like the *Hsin Yüan Shih,* declares that the expedition was made because Hsi Hsia refused to contribute troops for the war against the Khwarazm Shah. The *Yüan Shih Hsin Pien,* for its part, affirms that the siege of Chung-hsing was raised on the promise that men would be sent, but says that when they were called for, A-sha Kan-po (Asha Ganbo) persuaded the Tangut ruler not to provide any.

From Barthold's *Turkestan down to the Mongol Invasion,* one learns that the Mongol embassy to the Khwarazm Shah Muhammad did not reach the west until the spring of 1218. It was only after it had begun its eastward journey home that the caravan sent out at the same time arrived at Utrar (Otrar) where it was destroyed. Though no month is named for the withdrawal of the Mongols from before Chung-hsing, one gathers that this took place early in 1218. It is therefore likely that they had retired before the catastrophe of Utrar occurred. Certainly the expedition had begun prior to it. Without doubt the renewal of Li Tsun-hsiang's oath of allegiance included a promise of military aid, but it must have been for war against the Chin, not against the Khwarazm Shah.

# Chapter VII

# THE CONQUEST OF MANCHURIA

THE FIRST ACT in the Mongol conquest of Manchuria has already been covered and it will be remembered that in March, 1212, Chingis Khan made an alliance with the Khitan rebel Yeh-lü Liu-ke, who agreed to recognize his suzerainty. Owing to the tremendous losses suffered in 1211 by the Chin cavalry, the majority of which came from Manchuria, the conqueror had little to fear from an offensive across the Khinghan. Consequently he was able to devote the greater part of his forces to the far more alluring and profitable task of ravaging and plundering northern China. Due to the same cause Liu-ke had for several months been safe from any Chin punitive expedition strong enough to necessitate the despatch of even a small Mongol force to help him. But having established a foothold in Manchuria, Chingis had no intention of either neglecting or losing it, and when ready to move planned to use his position on the upper Liao as a spring board from which to launch a general conquest.[1]

Besides the strategic importance of securing his eastern flank, the acquisition of the whole country promised to be fairly easy. Although in the region of the Lao-ha and Luan Rivers the small towns and immediately surrounding rural districts were inhabited largely by Chinese, in close proximity to these centers lived a considerable semi-pastoral population descended from the Ghei and earlier pastoral tribes.[2] The territory was therefore influenced by nomad as well as by Chinese ideology

---

[1] This part of the Liao River is known to the Mongols as the Shara Muren.

[2] The Ghei, confederates of the Khitan, seem to have lived in much the same part of the country today inhabited by the Kharchin Mongols, and even if by the 13th century in the process of evolution toward agriculture, would constitute a definite pastoral element in southern Jehol. (For the presence of the Ghei in this region; see Parker, *A Thousand Years of the Tartars*, pp. 249-250.)

and so was likely to prove less hostile to the Mongols than the great provinces of China proper. On the lower Liao and in the Liaotung peninsula was an isolated though almost purely Chinese population. Ever since the 3rd century, B. C., this portion of Manchuria had been for long periods at a time intermittently a part of China, and notwithstanding its limited means of communication with the Middle Kingdom, by sea from Shantung and by land via the narrow coastal corridor that runs through present Shan-hai Kuan, its ties with China were much closer than those with the adjacent regions to the north. But after the destruction of Chin power in Hopei, and with the vast military requirements of the dynasty elsewhere, this outpost could expect no adequate assistance and must inevitably fall before the first determined onslaught.[3] The principal towns in this country were Liao-yang (Tung Ching), Hsien-p'ing and Chin Chou, which, with Ta-ting or Pei Ching on the Lao-ha River, were the largest places in Manchuria.[4] In a somewhat similar predicament were the valleys of the Hurka or Mutan and upper and middle Sungari. This territory, falling under the jurisdiction of the governor of Hui-ning or Shang Ching, possessed a very mixed economy of agriculture, pastoralism and hunting, and was the natal ground of the Mukri and Jurchids who supplied the most reliable soldiers in the Imperial army. But with the ever increasing demands of the war, it had been continuously drawn upon for troops so was in little condition to oppose a strenuous resistance. Northward the Tungus tribes hunting and fishing along the Ussuri and lower Sungari were a negligible military quantity, while the Solangs or Solons of the Nonni were not nearly powerful enough to risk exciting Mongol hostility by supporting the waning power of their one time overlords in the south.[5] Hence,

[3] For the relations of the Chinese in this part of Manchuria with the rest of the country and with China proper; see Lattimore, *Inner Asian Frontiers of China*, chap. V.

[4] Prior to the transfer of the Chin capital to Chung Tu in 1153, the town of Hui-ning or Shang Ching in the valley of the Sungari was probably larger than Ta-ting or Pei Ching, which attained its greatest extent during the second half of the century.

[5] Today the Solons practice both hunting and herding, some clans being reindeer

from Chingis Khan's point of view the conquest of Manchuria was both possible and most desirable. Had Hsüan Tsung (1213-23) followed the course urged by T'u Ch'an-i prior to his abandonment of Chung Tu, and retired to Liaotung instead of Honan, the invasion of Manchuria might have been a difficult undertaking, but that of northern China would have been correspondingly easier. After the destruction of their best armies on the battle-fields of Huan-erh-tsui and Hui-ho Pao, and with the rebellion of Liu-ke, the Chin were irrevocably doomed to lose part of their empire. But they refused to resign themselves to this fate without a struggle, and before Chingis Khan marched south in 1213, took measures to try to put down the Khitan insurrection.

Early that year (1213) the central government sent orders to the commander of Hsien-p'ing to march west against Yeh-lü Liu-ke. The leader of this expedition was none other than Wan-yen Hu-sha,[6] so badly defeated by the Mongols in 1211. After his desertion of Te-hsing Chou, we have seen him disgraced, but like Ke-shih-lieh Chih-chung, he was subsequently pardoned, and after a brief appointment as commander of the province of Shensi, was sent to take over Hsien-p'ing.[7] He now set out and proclaimed to his men that for every ounce of Liu-ke's flesh and bone he would pay an ounce of gold and silver, and promised that the rebel's slayer would be made the head of 300 families.

Alarmed by the reports that reached him concerning the strength of Hu-sha's army, Liu-ke sent post haste to Chingis Khan for help and soon received 3,000 horsemen under Anchar Noyan and two other officers.[8] With this meager addition to his own forces, he advanced to meet the enemy and some time

riding hunters of the forest, others horse riding herdsmen of the steppes. This divided economy also probably prevailed during the 12th and 13th centuries. For a reference to the Solons of today; see Lattimore, *Inner Asian Frontiers of China*, p. 113.

[6] This general was also known as Wan-yen Ho-shih and Wan-yen Ch'eng-yü. (*Chin Shih*, biography of " Wan-yen Hu-sha.")

[7] See the *Chin Shih*, biography of " Wan-yen Hu-sha."

[8] These were Pu-tu and A-lu-tu-han.

in April came up with him at Ti-chi Na-wu-erh (Nor).[9] There, largely owing to the courage of his step-son,[10] who made a fierce charge early in the battle, Hu-sha's troops were thrown into confusion, and unable to recover, were finally driven from the field in utter rout. According to one report the beaten army numbered 60,000,[11] but considering the small reinforcement despatched by Chingis Khan and the fact that Hu-sha can hardly have employed any but local forces—those of the department of Hsien-p'ing, plus some from the province of Liaotung—this is highly improbable. In reality both armies were probably quite small.

Despite this being his first important victory, Liu-ke wisely forwarded all the beaten army's baggage and supplies to his benefactor the Mongol Khan, who greatly pleased with this gesture allowed him to assume the title of Liao Wang. The Khitan then began the organization of his government, made his wife Yao-li-shih queen, appointed Yeh-lü Ssŭ-pu head of the civil administration, Yeh-lü Ti commander-in-chief of the army and T'ung-ku-yü chief of staff.[11a] Nevertheless, he was obliged to receive a Mongol officer as adviser[12] to replace Anchar, whom the conqueror recalled.

The Chin now changed their tactics and sent the ex-magistrate of Kuang-ning to try to win back Yeh-lü Liu-ke by diplomacy, but the attempt failed and they once more resorted to arms. No sooner had Hsüan Tsung ascended the throne in October, 1213, than despite the presence of the Mongols at

[9] I have been unable to identify Ti-chi Na-wu-erh (Nor), but it was probably a small lake located somewhere between the lower Liao and the northern reaches of the Lao-ha River.

[10] Yeh-lü An-nu.

[11] De Mailla, *Histoire Générale de la Chine*, Vol. IX.

[11a] The biography of " Yeh-lü Liu-ke "—see the *Meng-wu-erh Shih*—affirms that the victorious Khitan prince occupied Kuang-ning, which he made his capital. There were once two towns of this name, one eighty to ninety miles southwest of Hsien-p'ing, and another of Liao times located east of the Liao and some twenty-five miles north of Liao-yang. It is undoubtedly the place west of the river that is here intended, but as Yanai, author of the *Ken Dai Kyo Ryako Tohoko*, declares, there is no indication that Liu-ke was ever so far south in 1213. Perhaps, he says, Kuang-ning made nominal submission to him.

[12] This was a man named K'e-t'e-ke.

the very gates of the capital, he sent north orders for P'u-hsien Wan-nu, an officer of Jurchid stock, to take command of all forces in Liaotung and to replace Wan-yen Hu-sha as commander of Hsien-p'ing. Simultaneously the latter was relegated to the comparatively unimportant command of Hai Ch'eng or Ch'eng Chou, where he died soon afterwards.

The next, year (1214) [13] Wan-nu received instructions to assemble as large an army as possible and to reopen the attack on Liu-ke. If the Khitan again applied to Chingis Khan for help, we are ignorant of the fact, but it is more than likely that the Mongol representative joined with some troops. Resolved to gain any advantage that might be derived from being first in the field, Liu-ke marched to meet his adversary and encountered Wan-nu on the Pei-hsi, a small stream a few miles northeast of the town of K'ai-yüan near Hsien-p'ing. Again the Chin were defeated, but though Wan-nu was obliged to relinquish Hsien-p'ing and had suffered a reverse nearly comparable to that sustained by his predecessor, he reassembled his troops and retreated to Liao-yang (Tung Ching), where he awaited his chance to strike back.

As in relating the Chin defeat at Ti-chi Na-wu-erh (Nor), certain chroniclers have greatly exaggerated and report that P'u-hsien Wan-nu was at the head of 400,000 troops,[14] This fantastic figure nevertheless indicates that his effort, backed as it was by most of the military resources of Liaotung, was on a far greater scale than that of Wan-yen Husha. The repercussions of the disaster were considerable and several places in the province, among them An-tung at the mouth of the Yalu, made nominal submission to Liu-ke, who now made Hsien-p'ing his capital and renamed it Chung Ching.

Great as was this set back, the Chin undertook one more campaign and before the close of the year (1214) the commander-in-chief of the Left-wing army was sent against Liu-ke, but the Khitan, now stronger than ever, once more emerged

---

[13] There is no reliable evidence upon which we can name any specific month for the reopening of hostilities in 1214.

[14] De Mailla, *L'Histoire Générale de la Chine*, Vol. IX.

victorious. Little is known about the vanquished general or his reverse; perhaps he commanded the remaining forces left in the Department of Hui-ning or Shang Ching, but at all events his was the last attempt made to overthrow Liu-ke. From that time on the Chin remained almost entirely on the defensive.

Though forced to this role, they might have been able to make the conquest of Manchuria slower than it proved, but at this juncture they found themselves seriously hampered by a rebellion.

P'u-hsien Wan-nu, learning that a brutal murder committed by him had been reported to the emperor, and apprehensive that he might be punished for his defeat at the hands of Liu-ke, had some time prior to the end of 1214 begun to make plans to revolt. Shortly afterward he was informed of Hsüan Tsung's departure for K'ai-feng and, hardened in his determination, rebelled during February 1215. Unlike Liu-ke, he refused to see the writing on the wall for Manchuria and resolved to carve out a separate kingdom. Suddenly declaring his independence, he rushed a force north which fell upon Liu-ke's camp outside Hsien-p'ing. Though the town remained untaken, the Khitan prince was forced to withdraw and Wan-nu, having revenged himself, officially declared his realm Tung Chen.[15] He next turned south where in April (1215), not only the towns of Shen-yang and Ch'eng Chou surrendered, but the Mukri recognized his authority.[16]

Meanwhile K'ai-feng, ignorant of Wan-nu's rebellion, sent him fresh instructions. These arrived by sea during April, so, sizing up the situation, Wan-nu resolved to eliminate the remains of Chin power in Liaotung before the central govern-

---

[15] In most works, including the biography of " P'u-hsien Wan-nu " in the *Chin Shih*, the rebel's kingdom is called Ta Chen, but Yanai—see the *Ken Dai Kyo Ryako Tohoko*—says that this is a mistake for Tung Chen. The same author also affirms that, contrary to certain statements, e. g., reports in the biographies of " Yeh-lü Liu-ke " and " P'u-hsien Wan-nu," the town of Hsien-p'ing remained untaken by the latter.

[16] The Mukri, formerly the founders of the kingdom of Po Hai (712-926), had been successively the subjects of the Khitans and Jurchids.

ment could learn the truth and interfere. He thereupon despatched 9,000 men to P'o-ssŭ Lu, a town just north of An-tung which Ke-shih-lieh Huan-tuan, Vice-Commander of Liaotung, still held for the Chin. The expedition was a failure and the force obliged to retire. During May, however, he was more successful and pillaged a number of districts,[17] so in June he made still a third foray and attacked Ta-ning-chen (K'ai Chou) in the Liaotung peninsula, but was repulsed with such losses that he did not again take the field until October. He was then called forth to stem the advance of Huan-tuan, who had gone over to the offensive. Somewhere to the south of Liao-yang he gave battle but suffered a sanguinary defeat.[18] Following up his victory, Huan-tuan called the Mukri back to their old allegiance and set about the methodical reduction of all places continuing to hold out for the rebel. Hard pressed, Wan-nu was obliged to withdraw most of his troops from Liao-yang and, forced further and further east, finally retreated beyond the River Yalu early in 1216, i. e. into the part of Korea subject to the Chin.[19] Having, for a time anyway, broken the power of Wan-nu, Ke-shih-lieh Huan-tuan sent a report of his doings to K'ai-feng, which as we have seen, summoned him south to deal with the Red Coats. It is always tempting to speculate, and while Huan-tuan too would have ultimately gone down before the Mongol armies had he remained in Liaotung, the conquest of the province would certainly have taken longer than it did.

Yeh-lu Liu-ke no sooner learned that most of Wan-nu's men had left Liao-yang than he made a descent upon it. Arriving unexpectedly, he quickly took the place and by the end of October (1215) was master of the whole department.[20] Elated

---

[17] These were Shang-ku Ch'eng, Wang-yun-i and San-ch'a-li, but I have been unable to identify any of them.

[18] The biography of "P'u-hsien Wan-nu" says that he marched to I-feng and I-ch'ih, where he was defeated. The *Chung-Kuo Ti-ming Ta-tzu-tien* says that I-feng is South of Liao-yang.

[19] For P'u-hsien Wan-nu's revolt; see the biographies of "P'u-hsien Wan-nu" in the *Chin Shih*, the biography of "Ke-shih-lieh Huan-tuan" in the *Meng-wu-erh Shih* and the *Ken Dai Kyo Ryako Tohoko* of Yanai.

[20] See the biography of "Yeh-lü Liu-ke" in the *Meng-wu-erh Shih*.

by this success, several of his subordinates, notably Yeh-lü Ssŭ-pu, urged him to declare his independence and to take the title of emperor, but Liu-ke refused. " I have sworn an oath," said he, " to be the vassal of Chingis Khan; I cannot violate that oath. To make myself emperor in the East, is to oppose Heaven, and to oppose the will of Heaven is a great crime." [21]

Sententious though these sentiments may appear, they show that Liu-ke was a far-sighted statesman and had no illusions about his power. Realizing that the words of his officers had most certainly reached the ears of Chingis Khan, he decided to dispel all doubts concerning his loyalty by a personal appearance at the camp of the conqueror, and in December (1215) set out for the Kerulen accompanied by his eldest son Hsieh-she.

Reaching the north about the end of the month, he arrived to find a great assembly (kuriltai) in progress and was enthusiastically welcomed and named senior vassal of the empire. With him, Liu-ke brought ninety cart-loads of gifts, which included five hundred bolts of silk and a great quantity of gold and silver, and presenting them to Chingis, he requested that his son Hsieh-she be taken into his service. Much pleased with such homage, the Mongol Khan enrolled Hsieh-she among his companions and bestowed upon Liu-ke a golden tiger seal, but at the same time he asked for a census of the Khitan's subjects. These he learned numbered 600,000 families, i. e., about 3,000,000 persons, the majority of which were Chinese.

Confident of his position, Liu-ke now told Chingis that on the capture of Liao-yang, the Mongol representative had seized the wife of P'u-hsien Wan-nu and kept her for himself. Furious at this breach of discipline—(the conqueror would expect her to be sent north) —the Mongol Khan immediately commanded that the delinquent be sent to him bound hand and foot. Warned in time of his master's wrath, the offender went to Yeh-lü Ssŭ-pu for advice. Already disappointed by Liu-ke's refusal to establish an independent Khitan kingdom, Ssŭ-pu declared for rebellion, and joined by T'ung-ku-yü, spread

[21] For Yeh-lü Liu-Ke's declaration to his officers; see Gaubil, p. 26.

abroad a false report that Liu-ke was dead. To thoroughly commit all involved, he next ordered the murder of 300 Mongols who had been charged with the escort of some 3,000 Khitans to the camp of Chingis Khan. Three, however, escaped and informed the conqueror of all that had taken place. Close on the heels of these tidings, which must have reached the Kerulen during January, 1216, came others informing both Liu-ke and the conqueror that the insurgents had marched south, captured Ch'eng Chou, taken Liu-ke's wife and proclaimed Yeh-lü Ssŭ-pu Ta Liao Wang. Seeing that Liu-ke was greatly cast down by this news, Chingis turned to him and said: " Be not discouraged, for if the grazing is good and our horses in condition, I will give you an army for an attack on the Ao-lu-ssŭ." [22]

T'u Chi [23] tells us that the Ao-lu-ssŭ are to be identified with the Manchus, doubtless the ancestors of that people, so Chingis had in mind an expedition to the far eastern part of Manchuria. Being much more of a steppe nomad than Liu-ke, in his eyes the territorial loss suffered by the Khitan prince could easily be compensated for by acquisitions in another direction. Further, by the time this insurrection broke out, the conquest of western Manchuria was far advanced, so he had little doubt about the eventual suppression of Yeh-lü Ssŭ-pu and his followers.

Shortly after the departure of the troops sent to besiege Chung Tu in September, 1214, he had begun the organization of an army for the long contemplated thrust over the Khinghan. This force was to operate in two bodies, one under his brother Juchi Khassar in the valleys of the Sungari, Nonni and T'ao-erh, the other under Mukhali in the departments of Pei Ching and Liaohsi, i. e., in the country watered by the Lao-ha, Luan and Ta-ling rivers. As always, Chingis Khan had chosen his time with unerring insight. The Chin emperor gone to the south, Chung Tu besieged and Yeh-lü Liu-ke twice victorious over the

---

[22] The account of Yeh-lü Ssŭ-pu's revolt is from the biography of " Yeh-lü Liu-ke " in the *Meng-wu-erh Shih*.

[23] See the biography of " Yeh-lü Liu-ke " in the *Meng-wu-erh Shih*.

forces of Liaotung, he could count on considerable demoraliza-
tion among the troops defending Manchuria. At the same time,
a thrust over the Khinghan would still further isolate Chung Tu
and make impossible the despatch of relief from that direction. The attack on the capital and advance into Manchuria
were thus the southern and northern prongs of the same offensive. Widely separated though the armies might be, they
mutually assisted each other and completely restricted the Chin
to a defensive role.

Before the end of October Juchi Khassar and Mukhali were
ready to start, and marching from Chingis Khan's camp at
Yü-erh-lo, probably advanced together as far as the head
waters of the upper Liao, but there the prince continued east,
while Mukhali went south into the basin of the Lao-ha. For
the sake of clarity, the expedition of Khassar, of which there
is all too little recorded, will be dealt with first.

Proceeding along the valley of the upper Liao for perhaps
one hundred or more miles, Juchi Khassar turned north and
reached Lin-huang on the most northerly feeder of the river.[24]
This had formerly been the northern capital of the Khitans,
but after their overthrow by the Jurchids, it had steadily declined in size and importance. From it the Mongol prince took
possession of Pien Chou which is located between the Liao and
T'ao-erh rivers. On his departure, Chingis Khan had said to
him: " If the Jurchids submit, march from Pien Chou along
the Sungari and Nonni and make for their head-quarters on
the T'ao-erh; otherwise take and plunder their towns." [25] From

[24] It is from the biography of " Shih-mo Yeh-hsien "—see the *Meng-wu-erh Shih*—
that one learns the army passed through Lin-huang, but the report has mistakenly
said that the general in command was Mukhali. This is not strange, since the
Chinese historians have little or nothing to say about Khassar's part in the conquest of Manchuria. The *Yüan Ch'ao Pi Shih* (Secret History of the Mongols) on
the other hand completely ignores Mukhali and implies that not he but Khassar
took Pei Ching or Ta-ting.

[25] This is T'u Chi's version of the conqueror's words to his brother, and like that
given by Palladius, which is a little different, has come from the *Yüan Ch'ao Pi Shih*.
However The Mongol Chronicle confuses the expedition with that of 1213-14. The
correction of this error is due to T'u Chi.

T'u Chi identifies the Wu-la Ho of the original text with the Sungari, the Na-wu
Ho with the Nonni and the Wu-erh Mu-lien (Muren) with the T'ao-erh.

these meager instructions it is not easy to be sure just what Khassar was called upon to do. However we know that he successfully accomplished his mission and returned to the main Mongol camp, presumably that on the Kerulen, by way of the T'ao-erh. Fortunately the "Sanang Setsen," though incorrectly pre-dating the expedition by twelve years and making Chingis Khan its leader, throws some light on the subject. Apparently after the occupation of Pien Chou, the army marched to the Sungari, swam it on horse-back with little opposition and took Ning-chiang on the eastern bank.[26] Concerning its capture, the Mongol chronicle has a colorful but improbable story. According to it, the Mongol leader sent to the commander of the place saying; " If you will make me a present of 10,000 swallows and 1,000 cats, I will cease attacking the town," upon which the swallows and cats were sent. As soon as they arrived, lighted wool was fastened to their tails and they were let loose. The swallows then returned to their nests and the cats to their homes, and setting the town afire, enabled the Mongols to enter. In reality, Ning-chiang, where the majority of the buildings were doubtless largely of wood, must have been taken by means of inflammable projectiles.

From the Sungari, Juchi Khassar moved into the valley of the Nonni and then in to that of the T'ao-erh where the Solangs (Solons) were summoned to submit. " Bring tribute," he said to their chief, " or prepare for war." Terrified, the Solang ruler sent him one of his daughters, two clans for her escort and a tent of panther skins as a dowry. Satisfied, Khassar marched up the T'ao-erh and over the Khinghan to the upper reaches of the Khalkha Gol and so to the Kerulen. Less known than perhaps any other expedition undertaken during the reign of Chingis Khan, it was no mean achievement, and in addition to making the conqueror definitely master of both sides of the Khinghan, covered nearly one thousand miles.[27] The date of

---

[26] For the location of Ning-chiang; see Gibert, *Dictionnaire Historique et Géographique de la Mandchourie*, pp. 668-669.

[27] Mention of this expedition is to be found in Gibert's *Dictionnaire Historique et Géographique de la Mandchourie*, p. 481.

its termination is unrecorded, but it may very well have ended as early as January, 1215.

With Juchi Khassar there must have been several outstanding officers, but unlike the report of his expedition to the sea during the winter of 1213-14, none are mentioned. Quite otherwise is it with Mukhali, whose chief subordinates are all named. Among these, the greatest were the Mongols Uyer and Mongkha Bukha, the Turk Shih-mo Yeh-hsien and the two Chinese soldiers Shih T'ien-ni and Shih T'ien-hsiang, the last destined to make a great name for himself in the forthcoming campaign and for many a year to come.

After separating from Khassar, Mukhali directed his troops towards Pei Ching or Ta-ting where Ao Tun-hsiang, defeated at Hsi Ching in 1212, was commander-in-chief.[28] In accordance with Mongol practice, Mukhali decided to begin with the capture of the small surrounding places. To this end, after first receiving the surrender of Kao Chou in November, he divided his army into two main forces, one led by himself to strike east toward the lower Liao for the reduction of Ch'eng Chou,[29] I Chou and Shun Chou, and a second under the direction of Shih T'ien-hsiang to overrun the country to the south, east and west of Pei Ching. Before the end of January, 1215, both appear to have accomplished their respective tasks. The operations of the second force are briefly related in the biography of Shih T'ien-hsiang. From the list of captured places, it would seem that while some of his troops operated in the valley of the upper Lao-ha and took Chin-yüan, Fu-shu and Hui-ho, others moved east, and having taken Ho-chung, penetrated to the upper Ta-ling River and reduced Li Chou, Chien Chou and Lung Shan. None of these places were large, some in fact can have been no more than large walled villages of a few thousand inhabitants, but their fall left Pei Ching completely uncovered.

[28] After his appointment to the command of Shang Ching or Hui-ning Fu in 1213, Ao Tun-hsiang was moved to Pei Ching. (*Chin Shih*, biography of "Ao Tun-hsiang.")

[29] The *Chung Kuo Ku-chin Ti-ming Ta-tzu-tien* identifies this Ch'eng Chou with the present town of T'ung-ch'ang Hsien to the north of I Chou, but I have been unable to locate it on a map.

Evidently soon afterwards, Mukhali himself appeared on the upper Ta-ling, perhaps at Li Chou, for having reunited his army, February found him approaching Pei Ching from the south. Learning this, Ao Tun-hsiang [30] marched forth, but at Ho-t'e, about forty-five miles south of the city, was defeated with heavy losses.[31]

As in the reports of Liu-ke's victories over Wan-yen Hu-sha and P'u-hsien Wan-nu, the strength of the Chin army is vastly exaggerated and we are told that Ao Tun-hsiang's troops numbered 200,000 of which 80,000 were slain. It is probable that the defeated host was much nearer 20,000 strong and its losses more like 8,000.

Retiring with the remains of his army, Ao Tun-hsiang shut himself up in Pei Ching and remained strictly on the defensive, but his supplies of food being inadequate, the Khitan troops of the garrison mutinied, and killing the guards at one of the gates, deserted to the Mongols. Thinking that the city must be losing heart, Mukhali ordered a series of assaults. During one of these the father of Shih T'ien-hsiang lost his life, and his son, mad with rage, made a furious effort to storm the place, but to no avail. However, a second mutiny broke out and Ao Tun-hsiang was murdered by one of his officers. But the assassin was himself killed almost immediately afterward by a certain Wu-ku-lun Yin-ta-hu,[32] who took over the defense of Pei Ching.

Disappointed at his failure to take the place by force, Mukhali decided to turn the siege into a blockade and in March withdrew from before the walls. By a stroke of great good fortune for the Mongols, the Chin had decided to send a

[30] In the old biography of " Mukhali " by Chang K'uang-yen, the commander of Pei Ching is called I Mu-ch'ing. (See the biography of " Mukhali " in the *Yüan Ch'ao Ming Ch'en Shih Liao.*)

[31] The biography of Mukhali in the *Meng-wu-erh Shih* calls the place of battle Hua-tao, but a note in the *Li-tai T'ung-chien Chi-lan* specifically states that though the old accounts give Hua-tao as the site of the action, the real location was Ho-t'e (present P'ing-ch'uan to the north of Ch'eng-te). It is strange that T'u Chi was ignorant of this.

[32] Wu-ku-lun Yin-ta-hu was also known as Yeh-ta.

new commander to replace Ao Tun-hsiang.[33] Since the siege
of Chung Tu was still in progress, this officer must have landed
on the coastal corridor near the mouth of the Hsiao-ling Ho
with the intention of reaching the city by way of the river.
But on arriving, perhaps at Chin Chou, he would have learned
of the presence of the Mongols in the valleys of the Ta-ling
and Lao-ha and have struck out over-land by another route.

Among those detailed by Mukhali to observe Pei Ching was
the Turk Shih-mo Yeh-hsien.[34] Informed of the approach of
the intrepid Chin official, he rode to meet him with a few horsemen and surprised and slew him. Taking his credentials, he
went to the city and persuaded the officer charged with the
protection of one of the gates that he was a minister from the
imperial government.[35] Once inside the walls, he went to the
residence of Wu-ku-lun Yin-ta-hu and informed him that he
was the new commander sent by the Chin to take over Pei
Ching. Deceived, Yin-ta-hu accepted his credentials and further persuaded by the masquerader that since the Mongols
had withdrawn it was unnecessary to keep the garrison on the
walls, ordered them off. The same night Yeh-hsien sent to
inform Mukhali of what had happened and while waiting for
his appearance made some reappointments among the officers
of the garrison. Consequently, when Mukhali arrived, the city
was entered with little difficulty. Yin-ta-hu, however, was
warned in time, and shutting himself up in a strong place, probably the Forbidden City, for Pei Ching was one of the imperial
seats, defied the Mongols. At length, promised his life by
Uyer and Shih T'ien-hsiang, he gave up and surrendered with
forty-six of his officers. Despite his submission, Mukhali wished

---

[33] T'u Chi says that the Chin had sent an officer to succeed the murdered Ao
Tun-hsiang, but as they could not possibly have heard of the commander's death
or had time to send a replacement, they must simply have been sending a successor
for other reasons.

[34] T'u Chi informs us that, though Shih-mo Yeh-hsien, or Hsiao Yeh-hsien, was a
subject of the Khitans, he was by race a T'u-chüeh (Turk).

[35] The biography of " Shih-mo Yeh-hsien "; see the *Meng-wu-erh Shih*, says the
expected commander, so perhaps the Chin had long intended Ao Tun-hsiang's
removal.

to bury him alive,[36] but persuaded by Shih-mo Yeh-hsien that such behavior would simply result in every town and fort west of the Liao fighting to the bitter end, he not only relented, but reappointed Yin-ta-hu commander of the city. Nevertheless, he left Uyer and Shih T'ien-hsiang in charge of all cavalry and infantry detailed for the protection of the department and ordered them to begin the conquest of the Luan River.

With the capture of Pei Ching or Ta-ting, the victors became the masters of a veritable mountain of arms and equipment, 100,000 troops— (more likely 10,000) —108,000 families and thirty-two towns.[37]

From the failure of the Mongols to storm Pei Ching, it is apparent that it had grown since the days of the Liao dynasty (916-1123). Then, a Chinese traveller of the 11th century informs us that " The city walls of Ta-ting were low and mean, forming an oblong of about a mile and a quarter round; the gates were surmounted merely by an extra storey, there were no elevated watch-towers or citadels. Houses and hotels seem to have been of the caravanserai description, but there was a bazaar with storeyed houses near the south gate." [38] After the advent of the Chin, with their great possessions in China and consequently increased facilities for trade and immigration between Manchuria and the south, the town undoubtedly gained considerably in wealth and population, and at the time of the Mongol invasion must have been a center of no little importance.

The occupation of the place probably occurred about the end of March (1215) and Mukhali's somewhat unwilling clemency soon bore fruit. Not later than April, a rebel named Chang Ching, who had collected a considerable force, murdered the

---

[36] This is from the biography of " Mukhali," but in that of " Shih-mo Yeh-hsien," one learns that the Mongol general was considering burying the entire population of Pei Ching alive. However, the former report seems far more likely. (For both biographies; see the *Meng-wu-erh Shih.*)

[37] These statistics are from the biography of " Shih-mo Yeh-hsien." The 108,000 families—i. e., perhaps 550,000 persons—were certainly not all from Pei Ching, but many from the 32 towns or villages under its jurisdiction.

[38] See Parker, *A Thousand Years of the Tartars,* pp. 249-250.

commander of Chin Chou, which was the principal place on the coastal corridor, and declaring himself Lin-hai Wang, made submission. Forwarding this news to Chingis Khan, Mukhali received word to appoint the rebel a commander of 10,000.[39] Mongol authority was thus pushed to the sea without the appearance of a single soldier.

Meanwhile Uyer and Shih T'ien-hsiang had begun operations. These had been opened by a preliminary mopping up campaign in the neighborhood of Pei Ching, and after obtaining the surrender of an important fortress in the immediate vicinity of the city, they received that of more than twenty surrounding strongholds.[40] With them one is told went the submission of 8,000 troops. The generals then turned to deal with two local soldiers, who had assembled a considerable force and were preparing to recover Pei Ching. Already their troops had occupied the town of Hui Ho, but as they were resolved upon a program of guerilla warfare, it was only after more than one hundred minor actions that they were brought to a field battle. In it one was slain and the other, Ta Lu, driven a fugitive from the field and 12,000 men forced to surrender.

Following up their advantage, Uyer and his colleagues entered the valley of the Luan and in May advanced on Hsing Chou at the mouth of the Chu or Ch'e River. There they were encountered by a second local army under another leader. Again they were victorious, the commander made prisoner and the town taken.[41]

Masters for the time being at least of the Middle Luan, Uyer and Shih T'ien-hsiang were called east to deal again with Ta Lu,

[39] Chang Ching's rebellion has been taken from the biography of "Mukhali" in the *Meng-wu-erh Shih*. There it is said that he assembled 100,000 men, but as will later be seen this was easily double his real strength.

[40] None of these places can now be identified on the map, but that near the town was named Mo-yün Shan.

[41] The *Yüan Shih*, followed by the *Meng-wu-erh Shih*, dates the defeat of this leader, Chao Shou-yü, and the fall of Hsing Chou in Dec. 1215. In view, however, of Shih T'ien-hsiang's subsequent activities and the fact that both the same sources give the month of May as the date of Chang Chih's insurrection—(see below)—which Shih T'ien-hsiang helped suppress, I believe that May and not Dec. saw the overthrow of Chao Shou-yü and the fall of Hsing Chou.

who, despite his recent defeat, had reassembled his vanquished forces, and moving east, had taken Lung Shan in the valley of the Ta-ling. There, unable to escape, he was forced to an engagement and fought with such fury that the Mongols nearly lost the battle. According to the biography of Shih T'ien-hsiang, Ta Lu charged into the thick of the melée, and despite the strength and bravery of Uyer, unhorsed the Mongol and would have slain him but for the intervention of Shih T'ien-hsiang, who saved his superior's life and won the battle, which ended in the death of the brave Ta Lu and the surrender of 8,000 of his soldiers.[42]

While these events had been in progress, Mukhali had demanded the surrender of Hsing-chung, on the Ta-ling River, but when his representatives reached the town, one was slain by the magistrate and the other barely escaped with his life. The populace, however, fearful of Mongol vengeance, killed the murderer and raised up Shih T'ien-ying in his place. Being at Lung Shan, no more than ten miles to the north, Shih T'ien-hsiang soon learned that the new official wished to give up the town, and receiving its capitulation, obtained permission from Mukhali to reappoint him commander.

By the end of May it looked as if all the country to the west of the Liao had submitted, and Chingis Khan sent instructions to Mukhali to order Chang Ching of Chin Chou to march south and join Tolun Cherbi for an offensive into northeast Hopei. Mukhali obeyed, but as a precaution detailed Shih-mo Yeh-hsien as Inspector General of the force. Consequently, when Chang Ching neared P'ing Chou and refused to proceed further on the plea of sickness, Yeh-hsien arrested him and sent him to Mukhali. Arrived at the Mongol generalissimo's headquarters, he was charged with treason, and on denying it, was bidden to call his brother Chang Chih as a hostage. Unable to refuse, he complied, but at dawn the next day tried to escape. Told in time, Shih-mo Yeh-hsien overtook and summarily executed him. Learning this, his brother Chang Chih imme-

---

[42] The campaign on the Luan River and eventual death of Ta Lu are from the biographies of " Uyer " and " Shih T'ien-hsiang " in the *Meng-wu-erh Shih.*

diately rebelled, and making himself master of Chin Chou, P'ing Chou, Luan Chou, Jui Chou, Li Chou, Kuang-ning and both the towns of I Chou, one to the north of Shun Chou, the other on the Ta-ling, declared himself Liao-hsi Wang.[43] Further, he slew the messenger sent to demand his appearance at the Mongol court.

As seen in the previous chapter, Chingis Khan's hope of subduing northeastern Hopei was not realized until September, 1215, when Shih T'ien-ni took P'ing Chou. But in addition to his disappointment of an early conquest in that direction, he was now to find that Mukhali had before him the hardest struggle of all in Manchuria.

Apprised of Chang Chih's revolt, the Mongol general, who may have been camped somewhere in the neighborhood of Hsing-chung, at once prepared to resume operations. Report of this spreading abroad, three of the places coerced into submission by Chang Chih became terrified and threw off his yoke, but P'ing Chou, Chin Chou, Li Chou, Kuang-ning, and I Chou to the north of it, remained adamant in their hostility.

Again the Mongol offensive was opened by an attack on the perimeter of enemy territory. During June or early in July, Kuang-ning was occupied by one force and Shih T'ien-hsiang with another advanced up the Ta-ling River and retook Li Chou. He then turned east, and marching over the mountains toward the sea, received the surrender of T'a Shan, Hung-lo Shan, and five other strongholds.[44] According to the *Yüan Shih*, the fort of Hung-lo Shan capitulated in August, so Shih T'ien-hsiang had probably completed operations by the end of that month. In addition to the acquisition of these places, he also seized some ten thousand head of livestock, which he drove to Mukhali, then perhaps at Kuang-ning. Elated with this

[43] For Chang Ching's arrest, attempted escape and execution; see the biography of " Shih-mo Yeh-hsien " in the *Meng-wu-erh Shih*. The date (May, 1215) for these events is recorded by the *Yüan Shih*, which has been followed by the *Meng-wu-erh Shih*.

[44] With the exception of Hung-lo Shan, the places named in this expedition only appear in the biography of Shih T'ien-hsiang. Further, apart from Li Chou, Hung-lo Shan and T'a Shan, I have failed to identify any of them.

beginning, the Mongol sent Shih T'ien-hsiang to Yü-erh-lo to make a report to Chingis Khan. There the Chinese general must have arrived during September shortly before the conqueror left for the north, and was not only officially made a senior commander, but was presented with a golden tiger seal.

Feeling the need to offset his losses by some gain, Chang Chih made a sudden attack on Hsing-chung, which he took and plundered during the spring of 1216. Despite this, Mukhali made no immediate move to recover the place, but assembling all his troops, waited until July or August before taking the field. Then, sending a detachment to reoccupy Hsing-chung, he prepared to move from Kuang-ning against Chin-chou.[45] Knowing that Chang Chih would be an extremely formidable opponent behind walls, he decided to try to draw him into the open. He therefore sent Uyer to attack Liu-shih Shan, a fort to the west of Chin Chou. " If," said he, " you make a determined assault on Liu-shih Shan, Chang Chih must send reinforcements.[46] In the meantime, I will cut the roads behind him, which will make possible a concerted onslaught in front and rear." Simultaneously Mongkha Bukha was ordered to station himself ten li (about 3½ miles) to the east of Yung-te on the upper Hsiao-ling River to watch Chang Chih's movements.

No sooner did Chang Chih learn of the attack on Liu-shih Shan, than he did much as Mukhali had predicted and despatched his nephew Chang Tung-p'ing with 8,000 cavalry and 30,000 infantry to relieve it—he was evidently anticipating a battle so sent a large force in case of a major action. Observing the enemy advance, Mongkha Bukha immediately informed Mukhali and led his men in pursuit so as to intercept Chang Tung-p'ing's retreat. Expecting such news, Mukhali was able

---

[45] It is only from Gaubil (" Yuan Shih Lei Pien ") that one gathers Mukhali had his head-quarters at Kuang-ning.

It is strange that Mukhali waited until the summer of 1216 before marching against Chang Chih, but though unmentioned, it is possible that the horses of his cavalry were smitten by some disease and so necessitated his waiting for remounts.

[46] I have been unable to identify Liu-shih Shan, but it must have been located on the Hsiao-ling River and have been of vital importance to Chin Chou.

to move at once, and making a forced march in the night came up at dawn with the enemy near Shen-shui to the east of Yung-te.[47]  Threatened on two sides, Chang Tung-p'ing had no alternative but to fight, and prepared for action.  Noticing that his opponent's infantry were without body armor, Mukhali ordered a part of his troops to dismount and instructed them to discharge their arrows upon the foot soldiers.  He then commanded the rest of his men to deliver a charge and so great was the carnage that Chang Tung-p'ing and 12,600 men remained dead on the field of battle.[48]

The way now lay open to Chin Chou, and after taking K'ai-i to the north, the victorious army pushed on and laid siege to the town.  The Mongols had not been in front of it long when Chang Chih ordered a sortie, but the venture ended in disaster, 3,000 men being slain and countless others drowned in the Hsiao-ling River.  After that Chang Chih confined himself to the defensive, but at the end of a month, feeling that many of his commanders were failing to do their utmost, he put to death twenty of those recently defeated by the Mongols.  Thereupon a certain officer, fearing that his own turn might soon follow, suddenly seized Chang Chih, and sending word to Mukhali that he would give up the town, handed the captive over to the Mongol general, who ordered his execution.  Chin Chou then opened its gates, probably about the end of September (1216), and the Mongols rode in.

A large number of the troops surrendered, 12,000 of whom were a crack force of soldiers especially recruited and trained by Chang Chih, and known as the Black Army on account of their black uniforms.  These men took the fancy of Shih-mo Yeh-hsien, who selected them from among all of Chang Chih's troops.  Impressed with his choice, Mukhali obtained permission to make him their commender.  At the same time Chingis Khan also authorized his appointment as military governor

---

[47] If this was from Kuang-ning, the distance would be 35 miles at least.

[48] For this battle; see the biography of " Mukhali " in the *Yüan Ch'ao Ming Ch'en Shih Liao, Ssŭ Ch'ao Pieh Shih* and the *Meng-wu-erh Shih*.  The first says that Chang Tung-p'ing's losses were 13,000 killed and captured.

of the country between the Luan and Liao Rivers.[49] Thus the Turk Shih-mo Yeh-hsien and the Chinese Shih T'ien-hsiang, having distinguished themselves above all of Mukhali's subordinates, were rewarded beyond all others.

There now remained for Mukhali but one more task in western Manchuria, the punishment of I Chou and Kuang-ning. The former had been in rebellion ever since the rising of Chang Chih, but the latter, taken in July the previous year (1215), had no sooner seen Mukhali march on Chin Chou than it followed suit. Consequently, although the two towns once more offered to surrender, he refused to heed their protestations of good faith, and ordered that every living soul in them, except carpenters, masons and actors, be put to the sword, and devoted both places to a terrible massacre.[50]

Master of the western side of the Liao, Mukhali lost no time in launching an invasion of the Liaotung peninsula, and in October instructed Shih T'ien-hsiang, just returned from Yü-erh-lo, and another general to cross the river. On the other side they were joined by Yeh-lü Liu-ke, who came from driving the Khitan insurgents out of Ch'eng Chou. Having heard that they had suffered a reverse at the hands of the Chin commander of Ta-ning-chen (K'ai Chou), the Khitan prince had marched on Ch'eng Chou and recaptured it. But though he recovered his wife Yao-li-shih, he was unable to prevent the escape of the rebel leader with most of his followers.[51]

Advancing down the peninsula, Liu-ke and Shih T'ien-hsiang defeated the lately victorious commander of Ta-ning-chen and took the town as well as those of Fu Chou and Su Chou. After that Shih T'ien-hsiang was recalled and made commander of Li Chou and several other places—probably in the valley of the Ta-ling—but Liu-ke was ordered to pursue and destroy the rebels. Again he failed to crush them, but so hard were the insurgents pressed that they crossed the Yalu into Korea. Con-

---

[49] See the *Meng-wu-erh Shih,* biography of "Shih-mo Yeh-hsien."

[50] *Meng-wu-erh Shih,* biography of "Mukhali."

[51] A month after the elevation of Yeh-lü Ssŭ-pu as Ta Liao Wang, one of his officers deserted to the Chin and in June (1216) he was himself murdered and replaced by Ch'i-nu-ya-erh. (*Meng-wu-erh Shih,* biography of "Yeh-lü Liu-ke.")

tent with this, Liu-ke returned westward over the Liao, and entering the recently devastated towns of I Chou and Kuang-ning, took them under his authority.

With the exception of P'o-ssŭ Lu, where the Chin still retained a foothold, all western and southern Manchuria had been conquered by the Mongols. Much alarmed, P'u-hsien Wan-nu hastened to make submission and in November sent his son with tribute to Chingis Khan. His presence no longer necessary, Mukhali then withdrew from Manchuria and repaired to the conqueror's headquarters.

Despite his departure, the Chin made no attempt to restore their power in any of the country conquered by him. Indeed their resources for such an undertaking were far too limited, but they did make one more effort to overthrow P'u-hsien Wan-nu. In May the next year (1217) an army was sent against him from P'o-ssŭ Lu but was beaten.[52] Wan-nu, however, evidently fearing an attack by a combined Chin and Korean army, marched north into the department of Shang Ching where, despite determined resistance, he seized the capital Hui-ning and changed its name to K'ai-yüan. This virtually ended Chin authority in Manchuria, and after a fruitless embassy to Korea for help, a report was sent by sea to K'ai-feng to make known the situation. A return mission was sent from the capital, but apart from further solicitations for Korean help, could promise nothing. Therefore the local authorities gathered all their remaining forces for one more attack on Wan-nu, but were too weak to accomplish anything.[53]

At this juncture Yeh-lü Liu-ke, who had been ordered by Chingis to definitely make an end of the Khitan rebels, reappeared and in January, 1218, crossed the Yalu. At what point the passage of the river was effected we are not told, but as one subsequently learns that Wi Ju was in the hands of the

---

[52] The place was called Ta-fu Ying and was somewhere east of the Yalu, but I have been unable to locate it.

[53] For these last days of Chin authority in Manchuria; see the *Chin Shih*, biography of " P'u-hsien Wan-nu."

invaders, it may have been from An-tung on the opposite side. In this connection, it is likely that the campaign was preceded by the capture of P'o-ssŭ-Lu, though nothing specific is said to that effect. Reinforced by 10,000 Mongols and 20,000 men from P'u-hsien Wan-nu, Liu-ke pressed south and made for Kang-dong to the north of the Ta-t'ung River where the insurgents were encamped. The quarry trapped in a hostile country, the outcome of the operation was never in doubt. The only serious obstacle came from a terrible snow storm which held up the army and caused a shortage of provisions but the situation was quickly relieved by a supporting Korean force.

Unable to oppose Liu-ke's now great host in the open, the rebel leader retired into the town, but soon, realizing that he was doomed, hanged himself and in February his troops threw open the gates and surrendered. The mutineers are said to have numbered 50,000—even allowing for additions to their original strength, an exaggeration—and after the decapitation of one hundred of their leaders, they were moved to the country immediately west of Lin-huang.[54]

On the conclusion of the expedition, the King of Korea recognized Mongol suzerainty, but was most offended by the boorish familiarity of the Mongol envoy sent to him. Appearing at court, the Mongol not only carried sword and bow into the audience, but seizing the king's hand, thrust Chingis Khan's greetings before him. Nevertheless, he agreed to pay tribute, but it was not until 1221 that this was fixed. Then 10,000 lbs. of cotton, 3,000 bolts of silk, 2,000 pieces of gauze and 100,000 of the largest sheets of paper were demanded, and all was paid. In 1223, however, the tribute was changed to sea-otter skins. One other matter is perhaps worth recording; on leaving Korea, the leader of the Mongol division left forty men at Wi Ju, which had been returned to Korea, to learn the lan-

[54] This Kitan revolt and its eventual suppression are dealt with in the *Meng-wu-erh Shih*, biography of " Yeh-lü Liu-ke," the *Ken Dai Kyo Ryako Tohoko* of Yanai, and in Nakaba Yamada's *Ghenko*, chap. II.

T'u Chi says that it was in February, 1219, that Kang-dong fell, but Yanai is at pains to show that it really took place in February, 1218.

For a more detailed account of the Khitan rebellion; see Appendix D.

guage of the country.[55]    Two years later, i. e. in 1220, Liu-ke
died at the age of fifty-six and left the government of Liao to be
carried on by his widow Yao-li-shih.

The great territory of Manchuria, natal ground of both the
Khitans and Jurchids, thus passed under Mongol rule. Unlike
the provinces of northern China, it did not become the scene
of successive campaigns of reconquest, and with the exception
of two isolated rebellions, accepted the new regime. This is
partly to be explained by the friendship of Liu-ke, whose forces
acted as an army of occupation for the Mongols, but also, as
previously stated, by the very considerable nomad and semi-
nomad elements in the country which made it generally less
hostile than China. While a considerable body of Khitans had
mutinied and found a temporary refuge in Korea, others had
deserted to the Mongols at Pei Ching. It was from the Chinese that the bitterest resistance had come, and despite the
butcheries of Kuang-ning and I Chou, an insurrection broke
out in the basin of the Luan River during the summer of 1217,
when the commander of Wu-p'ing seized the northern capital.
Simultaneously the Inspector General for Hsing Chou also rose,
but Uyer and Shih T'ien-hsiang fell upon the rebels before they
could unite, one being defeated and slain near Pei Ching, which
was recovered, the other on the Chu or Ch'e River, where
nearly 10,000 of his men fell.[56]   But with the suppression of
this rising, resistance of any importance ceased throughout the
country. Only to the northeast, where as yet no Mongol army
had been, was there one more struggle in store.

Learning in 1223 that the great Mukhali had died, and knowing that Chingis Khan was still far away in the west, P'u-hsien
Wan-nu decided to make a bid for freedom. Accordingly he
murdered the Mongol representative attached to his headquarters and declared his independence. Shortly afterward he
took Ning-chiang,[57] and in March the following year (1224)

[55] See Nakaba Yamada, *Ghenko*, chap. II, pp. 45-46.
[56] *Meng-wu-erh Shih*, biographies of " Uyer " and " Shih T'ien-hsiang."
[57] There is no documentary evidence to support my contention that 1223 was
the year that P'u-hsien Wan-nu took Ning-chiang, but from a military standpoint
it would be the most logical move on his part after rebelling.

sent an embassy to try to persuade Korea to join him. But he met with a rebuff, so to revenge himself made several raids over their border. During 1226 he attempted to capture Wi Ju, but a counter inroad forced him to retire.

The Mongols were occupied with the invasion of Hsi Hsia from the end of 1225 to the autumn of 1227, and with continuous though minor hostilities with the Chin from the death of Mukhali to the summer of 1228, so that it was not until 1230, after the accession of the new emperor Ugedei (1229-41), that they were able to turn their attention to Wan-nu. Wishing to make the campaign as brief as possible, they asked the Koreans to co-operate, but, like the rebel in 1224, received a refusal. This greatly enraged the Mongols, who postponed operations against Wan-nu and ravaged Korea instead. This took place in 1231 and it was not until 1233 that they finally brought the rebellion to an end. In the autumn of that year Ning-chiang was taken by storm and P'u-hsien Wan-nu slain, after which his head was shown at Hui-ning and other places, all of which surrendered.[58] With Wan-nu went the last man to resist Mongol rule in Manchuria.[59]

[58] Perhaps it was in this campaign that the Jurchid settlements on the lower Sungari, Ussuri and Amur were destroyed by the Mongols. (See Shirokogoroff, S. M., Social Organization of the Northern Tungus, p. 158.

[59] For the end of P'u-hsien Wan-nu; see the Chin Shih, biography of " P'u-hsien Wan-nu."

# Chapter VIII

## REBELLION IN THE NORTH AND FIRST CAMPAIGNS IN THE WEST

IN CHAPTER IV we left the Mergid Kultukhan, the sole surviving son of Tukta Biki, refuging in the northern part of Khara Khitai, whither he had fled after being repulsed by the Uighurs, in 1208. There he participated with Kuchluk in his rebellion and eventual capture of the Gur Khan Chiluku (1178-1211). The exact nature of Kultukhan's relationship with the Naiman chief is unknown, but probably some form of alliance existed with the Mergids ranging along Kuchluk's northern border. At all events, after Chingis Khan's departure for China, Kultukhan began making raids over the western boundary of the Mongol empire. Ever since the spring of 1211 this had been under the charge of the Khongirad Tokuchar, who though unable to stop these forays, prevented them from penetrating far. Nevertheless, such razzias, plus the presence of Kuchluk in the heart of the old Khara Khitan realm, had a disturbing effect on the tribes of the Yenisei (Kem) and to the west of Lake Baikal.

The first manifestation of this occurred in January or early February, 1216, when the Tumeds seized and imprisoned one of Chingis' officers, who with the Khan's permission, had gone among them to help himself to thirty of their women.[1] Evidently the victim's behavior was largely responsible for his arrest, for the conqueror, instead of immediately declaring war, sent the Oirad Kutuku Biki to negotiate his release. But the Tumeds foolishly interpreted this as weakness and likewise detained Kutuku. As already related, in 1207 the Tumeds had joined the Kirghiz in making submission to the Mongols.

[1] See both the *Yüan Ch'ao Pi Shih* and the *Meng-wu-erh Shih*.

Then it seems they were ruled by a chief called Taidutul,[2] but since his death, his widow, Botokui Tarkun,[3] had become regent and it was under her that the Tumeds decided to revolt. Enraged at their audacity, Chingis Khan wasted no more effort on embassies. A senior commander of the army was ordered to crush them, but being ill at the time, he could not go so the expedition had to be entrusted to Borokul, an adopted son of the conqueror.[4] Marching north, Borokul soon neared his destination, but trying to lure the Tumeds into an ambush, was himself trapped and killed, and the whole campaign was brought to an untimely end.

When he learned this, Chingis Khan began to fear that a general insurrection might break out in the north and hastily called a conference of his chief officers and told them that he proposed to go himself to deal with the Tumeds. He was vigorously opposed by his old friend Bugurji, who pointed out that under the circumstances his place was not on a distant expedition of so minor a nature, but at imperial headquarters. Realizing the truth of his words, the conqueror gave up the idea and instead sent Durbei Dokhsin the Durbet.[5] He also commanded the Kirghiz to help—this was probably done to test their loyalty—but word came back that they too had revolted and with them the neighboring forest tribes.[6] There-

---

[2] This is the name of the chief as given by Palladius in his translation of the Yüan Ch'ao Pi Shih, but the edition of the Yüan Sheng Wu Ch'in Cheng Lu, edited by Wang Kuo-wei, calls him Tai-tu-la Sha-erh-ho.

[3] For this name; see Grousset, Le Conquérant du Monde, p. 222.

[4] Borokul was of Jurkin extraction and as a child had been presented to the conqueror on the destruction of that tribe in 1198. D'Ohsson, Vol. I, pp. 156-157, quoting Rashid ad-Din, says that Chingis Khan was much attached to him.

[5] This soldier is almost certainly the Durbei Noyan of the Persian historians, who report his expedition across the Indus with Bala Noyan during the spring and early summer of 1222.

[6] See the Meng-wu-erh Shih. D'Ohsson, Vol. I, p. 157, citing Rashid ad-Din, says that the Kirghiz revolt occurred prior to Borokul's expedition, but since his defeat and death would be just the thing to encourage an insurrection, I have followed the Meng-wu-erh Shih.

The Yüan Ch'ao Pi Shih makes no reference to a Kirghiz revolt, and only mentions their submission in 1207 in which year it also dates the supression of the Tumeds. Although the oldest source extant, chronological accuracy is not one of its strong points, so I have followed the Meng-wu-erh Shih and Rashid ad-Din, both of whom speak of a rebellion on the part of the Tumeds and Kirghiz several

upon prince Juchi received orders to prepare for an invasion of the Yenisei country.

Perhaps sometime in the autumn, Durbei Dokhsin set out. Apparently he followed the route taken by Borokul, for approaching the place of his death, he made a feint as if intending to go there, but instead directed his main force in another direction. This entailed marching over tracks so narrow and difficult that his men only got through them after cutting away the undergrowth and felling numberless trees.

The "Yüan Ch'ao Pi Shih" says that the paths followed were those used by wild animals and that the general, feeling that his men might be fearful of such roads, ordered all to carry rods to beat any one refusing to go forward. Not unnaturally the steppe dwelling Mongols would hold the great forests of Siberia in superstitious awe.

His daring was fully justified. Falling unexpectedly upon the Tumeds during a celebration, possibly in the basin of the upper Oka, he completely defeated them. The two prisoners who had occasioned the war were set free and the princess Botokui Tarkun sent to Chingis Khan. Durbei Dokhsin seems to have spent the winter in the north, doubtless for the purpose of aiding Juchi if necessary, as it is implied that he did not return to the conqueror until the spring of the following year (1217).[7]

Toward the end of 1216, Juchi, who had been joined by the lately released Kutuku Biki, was ready to move. We have no information about the route that he took, but it is not unreasonable to suppose that he marched north from the basin of the Ubsa Nor and went over the Tannu Ula by one or more of the passes crossing these mountains into the valley of the upper Yenisei (Kem).[8] On the other side the insurgents gave

years after 1207. But whereas in the work of the Persian 1217 is the year given for the whole event, the *Meng-wu-erh Shih* regards 1216 as that of the outbreak and 1217 as that of its suppression. Neither the *Yüan Sheng Wu Ch'in Cheng Lu* nor the *Yuan Shih* refer to a Kirghiz insurrection, but both mention the defeat of the Tumeds during 1217.

[7] See the *Yüan Sheng Wu Ch'in Cheng Lu* and the *Meng-wu-erh Shih*.

[8] See Carruthers, *Unknown Mongolia*, Vol. I, pp. 114-115.

battle only to be decisively beaten and pursued to the river. On reaching this, the victorious army, or part of it, turned northeast, and marching along the ice, probably up the Bei Kem, reached the Sayansk range. This was crossed and the valley of the Tuba invaded, for the " Yüan Ch'ao Pi Shih " reports that a people of that name, as well as other clans, were conquered. In the words of the same work, " Juchi overthrew all the peoples of the forest from the Shibir clan southward." [9]

Despite the failure of our sources to recount any other operations for this campaign, certain local traditions indicate that the Mongol invasion went as far north as the Abakan steppes between the river of that name and the Yenisei. So it is more than likely that while one part of Juchi's force concentrated on the forest tribes, another moved down the Yenisei and subdued the Abakan and Chulim countries, both of which were certainly subject to the Kirghiz.[10]

Much of this territory, as already noted, contained agricultural settlements where grain was grown, so was a valuable economic asset to the Mongols. To make sure that no further revolts broke out, Juchi took as hostages all the Kirghiz commanders of 10,000 and 1,000 and the petty chiefs of the forest. With these he returned in 1217 to his father, who, greatly pleased with the manner in which the campaign had been conducted, praised Juchi for not having unduly fatigued his troops and made him govenor of the conquered country. At the same time he rewarded the Oirad Kutuku Biki and gave to him the Tumed princess Botokui Tarkun, to one of Kutuku's sons, one of his own daughters, and to another son, a daughter of Juchi.

[9] The *Meng-wu-erh-erh Shih* says that the rebels were defeated and pursued to the Yeh-mi-li River, where the victor turned northeast, and following the Ch'ien River (the Kem or Yenisei) on the ice, forced to submission the Wu-erh-ssŭ-t'i, Ho-po-na-ssŭ, T'ieh-liang-wu, K'e-shih-t'i-mi and Wa-i-la-i-K'e, all doubtless forest clans of the Sayansk range and Tuba valley. The Yeh-mi-li River, I have been unable to identify, but it must be a small southern tributary of the upper Yenisei, near which Juchi's victory was won.

[10] D'Ohsson, Vol. I, p. 157, quoting Rashid ad-Din, says that Juchi crossed the Kem-kemjiut (Kemchik) River and put an end to the revolt, so probably the Mongols first ravaged the Kemchik valley and then went north down the Yenisei to the Abakan steppes. For the extent of Kirghiz territory; see Kai Donner, *La Sibérie*, p. 132.

Nor was the family of Borokul forgotten, and one hundred Tumed families were given to his descendents, while the rest of the tribe was split up among the imperial family.

Hardly less satisfactory to the conqueror than the suppression of the Tumeds and Kirghiz had been the final liquidation, some months earlier, of his old and bitter enemies the Mergids. Concurrently with the despatch of Borokul against the Tumeds, or probably rather earlier, he had sent Juchi, Subudei and the Khitan prince Yeh-lü Hsieh-she with 20,000 men to join Tokuchar for an attack on Kultukhan. This was a large force for the destruction of the remnants of the Mergids, but Chingis probably expected Kuchluk to intervene. Unfortunately for Kultukhan, he had recently quarrelled with the Naiman chief, so instead of being able to withdraw south, had to fly west to the country of the Khanghlis. For a time he was able to avoid an engagement, but at length—perhaps in the last days of April (1216)—was brought to battle between the Khayli and Kimach rivers.[11] These are located north of the Irghiz in the present provinces of Turgai. There, greatly outnumbered, Kultukhan suffered an irreparable defeat, and although some of his men escaped and took refuge with the Kipchaks beyond the Volga, many others were slain and he himself made prisoner. Brought before Juchi, he was asked to give proof of his fabulous skill as an archer.[12] This he did to the admiration of the prince who sent to beg his father for the Mergid's life, but Chingis Khan refused to spare him and the great archer went the way of the rest of his family.

As seen, it was subsequent to this campaign that Juchi undertook the reduction of the Kirghiz. Assuming that his drive against the Mergids started from the Altai, the round trip made by his troops cannot have been less than 2,600 miles, a truly remarkable feat of marching. Notwithstanding this, it is likely that Juchi was back before the middle of summer and

[11] Juwayni; see Barthold, *Turkestan down to the Mongol Invasion*, p. 270.
[12] To indicate his prowess with the bow, the prince was known as Kultukhan Mergen, i. e. Kultukhan the archer.

so had plenty of time in which to refresh his men before going against the rebels.[13]

It was on the Mergid expedition that the Mongols first clashed with the Khwarazm Shah Muhammad. Having taken the field against a recalcitrant Khanghli chief, Muhammad learned that the Mergids and a Mongol force were in the same region. Being at the head of 60,000 troops, he had little to fear and advanced to deal with both, but arriving at the Irghiz, found the ice on the river too weak to bear cavalry, so waited for it to clear. When this was complete, he crossed and reached the field of battle between the Khayli and Kimach on the very day of the Mergid defeat. Going in pursuit of the Mongols, he overtook them at dawn the next day. Juchi and his colleagues had no wish to fight and declared that Chingis Khan had sent them out solely for the purpose of destroying the Mergids, but the Shah replied that he regarded all unbelievers as enemies and forced an engagement. To quote Barthold; " In both armies the right-wing overpowered the enemy's left-wing. The Moslem right-wing was commanded by the eldest son of the Khwarazm Shah, Jalal ad-Din, whose bravery saved the Moslems from defeat. It was intended to renew the battle on the following day, but the Mongols retired under cover of night, and by setting fire to piles of wood deceived the Moslems, who learned only at the break of day that the Mongols had abandoned their camp." [14] The Shah was greatly impressed with the bravery of the enemy and according to Nasawi; " A fear of these infidels was planted in the heart of the Sultan, and an estimation of their courage; if any one spoke of them before

---

[13] The late start for the suppression of both the Tumeds and the Kirghiz can be attributed to the preference of the Mongols for crossing large rivers when frozen.
[14] Barthold, *Turkestan down to the Mongol Invasion*, p. 372.
Barthold has drawn principally on Nasawi and Juwayni for the account of this battle. It is strange that the *Yüan Sheng Wu Ch'in Cheng Lu* makes no mention of it, also, that while reporting the destruction of the Mergids by Subudei and Tokuchar, it completely ignores the presence of Juchi with the army. However, it is certain that the prince was in command. Not only Juwayni, Nasawi and Juzjani make him general-in-chief of the expedition, but later we shall find Chingis Khan referring to him when he praises Yeh-lü Liu-ke's son, Hsieh-she, for having saved Juchi's life during the battle.

him, he said that he had never seen men as daring nor as steadfast in the throes of battle, or as skilled in giving blows with
the point and edge of the sword." [15]

Chingis Khan's reaction to this collision with the Shah is
unknown. Barthold thinks that he must have regarded the
whole affair as due to a regrettable misunderstanding. Certainly diplomatic relations, just opened with Muhammad, were
not interrupted. Perhaps, contrary to the information of
Nasawi, the Shah was not present and Jalal ad-Din alone was
in command. If so, the Mongol conqueror's attitude is more
understandable. At all events, as regards prestige, the Moslem
potentate rather than the Mongol Khan stood to lose, for it
must soon have become noised abroad that little more than
20,000 Mongols had held their own for an entire day against
three times their number of Khorezmians. Later when war
became inevitable, Chingis Khan would have every reason to
feel confident in the superiority of his army, but for the time
being he wished to remain at peace with his powerful neighbor
and was anxious to establish commercial intercourse between
the two empires.

The first tentative move in this direction had been made by
the Moslems. In 1215 the Khwarazm Shah had despatched an
embassy under a certain Baha ad-Din Razi and with it a trade
caravan to the Mongol conqueror. Juzjani, to whom we are
indebted for our knowledge of this embassy, says that its
primary object was to obtain accurate information on the
strength of the Mongol forces and the extent of their conquests
in China. Though this historian says that the envoys reached
Chingis Khan while he was still in China, this must be a mistake for Chin, for he further tells us that Chung Tu had already
fallen and we know that when this happened the conqueror
was at Liang-ching outside the Tu-shih K'ou. So, though for
some reason or other the embassy entered China and passed

---

[15] Fernand Grenard, *Gengis Khan*, p. 140.

This passage from Nasawi makes it quite certain that the memory of this battle
played a large part in Muhammad's decision four years later not to meet the
Mongols in the open. For the other reasons that influenced the Shah; see
Appendix A.

by Chung Tu, it must have been received by the Mongol Khan either at Liang-ching or at Yü-erh-lo, whither he went in July (1215).[16] Graciously treated by the conqueror, Baha ad-Din was instructed to inform the Khwarazm Shah that he considered him the ruler of the West, as he himself was the ruler of the East and desired that there should be peace and friendship between them, and that merchants should be free to travel from one country to another. Not even an ill-timed attempt by a member of the accompanying caravan to cheat Chingis Khan marred this good beginning, and as seen, the Mongol even ignored the subsequent clash between his troops and those of the Shah.[17]

At the beginning of 1218 Chingis sent a return embassy, which was received at Bokhara in the spring.[18] Simultaneously, a large trade caravan also set out, but travelling much more slowly, was still on the road when the envoys arrived at Muhammad's court. At the head of the Mongol diplomatic mission was Mahmud Ali Khwajah, a native of Bokhara and often called Mahmud Yalavach (the envoy). After presenting the Shah with the gifts brought for him, among which was a nugget of gold the size of a camel's hump from the mountains of China, he delivered his message. " Chingis Khan," he said, "having heard of his victories and his power, offered to make a treaty of peace with him, and to place him on a level with the dearest of his sons; he was sure that the Khwarazm Shah also had heard of the Mongol victories, especially of the conquest of China, and of the riches of the provinces subject to him; therefore the establishment of peace and of safe trade relations between both kingdoms would be advantageous for both sides." [19]

We are ignorant of Muhammad's answer in the public audience, but the following night he called in Mahmud Yalavach,

---

[16] The report of this embassy on the carnage that followed the fall of Chung Tu has already been mentioned in a previous chapter.

[17] For this embassy; see Barthold, *Turkestan down to the Mongol Invasion*, pp. 393-96.

[18] It is from Juwayni that we learn that the Shah was at Bokhara.

[19] Barthold, *Turkestan down to the Mongol Invasion*, p. 396.

and pointing out that since he was a fellow Moslem he must
tell him all he knew about Chingis Khan and remain at the
Mongol court as a spy, presented him with a considerable bribe.
Out of fear, Mahmud pretended to agree. Thereupon Muhammad asked if Chingis Khan had really overthrown the Chin
and taken the city of Tamghach (Chung Tu). The envoy
replied that it was true. The Shah observed that even that
did not give an infidel the right to call him, the ruler of a
mighty empire, his son, i. e. vassal. Alarmed, the envoy
hastened to add that the armies of the Mongol conqueror could
not compare in numbers with those of the Shah. Mollified,
Muhammad consented to make a treaty with Chingis Khan
and the envoy returned to the Mongol court.[20]

Outrageous as may seem Chingis Khan's veiled demand that
the Khwarazm Shah recognize his suzerainty, it exactly fitted
his conception, and that of his people, of himself as the unique
and omnipotent representative of Heaven on earth. Further,
as ruler of all the Mongol and Turkish peoples of the East, and
therefore restorer of the ancient Turkish empire of the 6th and
7th centuries, he was demanding that the Shah, himself a Turk,
recognize Mongol suzerainty in those western lands once conquered by the Turkish Khaghans. Also, from Muhammad's
response, he would learn what was to be expected of the Moslem
potentate in the future. Without a doubt the Shah simply
ignored Chingis Khan's feeler and in the normal course of
events it would have been some time before an issue had arisen.
But there now occurred an event which precipitated the whole
matter.

Scarcely had Mahmud Yalavach and his embassy recrossed
the Khorezmian frontier than there arrived at Utrar (Otrar)
the caravan that had set out from Mongolia at the same time.
This was exceptionally large. Juwayni says that it included
four hundred and fifty persons, all Moslems, while Juzjani relates that the merchandise—silk, targhu stuffs,[21] furs, gold and
silver—were carried by as many as five hundred camels. There

[20] Nasawi, Barthold, p. 397.
[21] A greatly valued cloth made from the wool of white camels.

were also one hundred Mongols under a certain Ukuna, who was Chingis Khan's special agent.[22] The details of what happened are by no means clear, but for one reason or another the caravan was first detained by Inalchik or Khadir Khan, governor of the town, and then wiped out and all the goods seized. According to Nasawi, the governor informed the Shah that the merchants were acting like spies and received orders to detain them, but after that, and solely from greed, he ordered their massacre and stole the merchandise. Juwayni, Juzjani and Ibn al Athir say that the Shah ordered the deed, but whether he did or not, it seems certain that he and the governor divided the spoils.

According to Juzjani, only one man, a camel puller, escaped and carried the terrible news to Chingis Khan. Whatever may have been his real feelings, the conqueror kept his head and sent off another Moslem, Ibn Kafraj Bughra, formerly in the service of the Khwarazm Shah Takash (1172-1200), to demand that Inalchik be given up to him for punishment. Even had the Shah been willing to comply, he could not have done so, for the governor was a relative of his mother, Turkhan Khatun, who enjoyed a predominating influence over the numerous Khanghli troops in the army. But quite apart from any fear of mutiny, it was unthinkable that the Shah would give up one of his subjects to be put to death by the Mongol. Furious at the insult, he ordered the execution of Ibn Kafraj Bughra and had the heads of his two Mongol companions shaved and sent them back to their master.[23] War thus became unavoidable.

It is quite evident that in 1218 the Mongol Khan was not seeking hostilities with the Moslem world but was forced into them against his will. Admittedly later on there would have

---

[22] This piece of information is only found in the Yüan Ch'ao Pi Shih.

[23] For the Utrar affair and death of Ibn Kafraj Bughra; see Barthold, pp. 397-99. Concerning the supposed embassy of the Caliph Nasir (1180-1225) to Chingis Khan urging an invasion of the Khorezmian empire, Barthold says that in the 13th century reports of this existed only in the shape of vague rumors. Earlier, however, the same Caliph had tried to promote an attack on the Shah by the Ghurid Sultan Shihab ad-Din (1203-6).

been a collision, but not until after the destruction of the Chin. With no alternative but to revise his plans, Chingis resigned himself to a limited offensive in China and made ready for war in the west. This was to be no razzia such as might have satisfied him under the circumstances, but a full scale invasion bent on conquest. Some may feel that the Mongol conqueror made a very questionable decision when he decided to leave the still strong and hostile Chin so far in his rear. But recent developments justified his resolution. Not only were the Chin still at war with the Tanguts, but since the middle of 1217 they had also become embroiled with the Sung. Hence, he had every reason to assume that Mukhali could safely carry on with the original project assigned to him.

It is not my intention to cover the Khorezmian war, since it has been very ably dealt with in numerous works. In touching upon the subject to the extent that I have, my purpose has been to make clear the reason for the Mongol conqueror's postponement of his final reckoning with the Chin. But before returning to the Chinese theatre we shall briefly relate the end of Kuchluk and the conqueror's departure from Mongolia.

The overthrow of Kuchluk was undertaken for three separate but related reasons. First it was necessary to eliminate an implacable enemy who, as successor to the Gur Khan, could be expected to challenge Chingis Khan's position as leader of the Turko-Mongol world; second the country north of the desert must be safe-guarded from invasion while denuded of most of its troops, and third a call for help had come from Almaligh. This town had been attacked by Kuchluk, who had suddenly appeared in the vicinity and taken prisoner the local ruler Buzar, since 1211 a vassal of the Mongol Khan. Despite his father's capture, the son, Sugnak Tagin, refused to give up Almaligh and sent a messenger to Chingis asking for help.

Immediately 20,000 men set out under Jebe, supposedly early in the summer (1218),[24] and approaching the town, caused the Naiman chief to raise the siege. Withdrawing west-

[24] The elevated nature of much of the country invaded would make the summer the best season for the operations carried out by Jebe.

ward, Kuchluk put to death his captive and left Almaligh to be entered by the Mongols. Jebe's line of march is uncertain, but from the biography of Ke Te-hai, a Chinese officer with him, it seems that the Altai was crossed by either the Terekti and Urumukhti Passes (9,710 ft. and 10,500 ft. respectively), or by the Ulan Pass (approx. 9,000 ft.), as it is said that the army proceeded by Kizil Bash (Ulungur Nor).[25] Afterward the advance must have gone along the foot of the Urkashar, Jair, Barlik and Ala Tau ranges to the basin of the Ebi Nor and from there by the Sairam Nor and Talki Pass (7,500 ft.) into the valley of the Ili (see Map).

Almaligh relieved, the Mongols lost no time in pursuing Kuchluk whom they overtook and defeated in a brief encounter near Balasagun.[26] The town offered no resistance, and while one part of the victorious army under Jebe pursued the Naiman prince over the T'ien Shan, the other penetrated into northern Farghana, where Ismail, the governor of Kasan and Akhsikath, made submission.[27]

Again the route taken by Jebe is guess-work, but it very probably went south from Issyk Kul over the Bedel Pass (12,600 ft.) to Uch-turfan and Akhsu. This was the road followed by Jahangir, the son of the great Timur (1370-1405), when he pursued Kamar ad-Din over the T'ien Shan during the summer of 1375 and was also that taken by the Turkish conqueror himself four years later on a similar expedition.[28]

Arrived south of the range, Jebe forbade his troops to loot and proclaimed complete religious toleration to the people of the Tarim basin. This was a master move, for Kuchluk, formerly a Nestorian Christian but converted to Buddhism by his Khara Khitan wife, had shown himself extremely hostile

[25] *Yüan Shih,* biography of " Ke Te-hai "; see Bretschneider, *Mediaeval Researches,* Vol. I, p. 125, n. 312.

[26] Our authority for this battle is Abu'l Gazi, Vol. I, pp. 94-95. Rashid ad-Din says that the two armies met but that Kuchluk's men fled before the Mongols had time to begin the action. The Chinese for their part mention no engagement at all.

[27] This part of Farghana had been in Kuchluk's hands since the end of 1214, when it was abandoned to his ravages by the Shah of Khwarazm. (Barthold, p. 369.)

[28] See Bretschneider, *Mediaeval Researches,* Vol. 11, pp. 227-228, n. 1013.

to Islam. Encountering opposition to his authority in 1211, he had subjected the country of Kashgar, Yarkand and Khotan to a pitiless devastation, and meeting with further resistance two years later, repeated the performance during 1213 and 1214. The country now rose against him, and hailing the

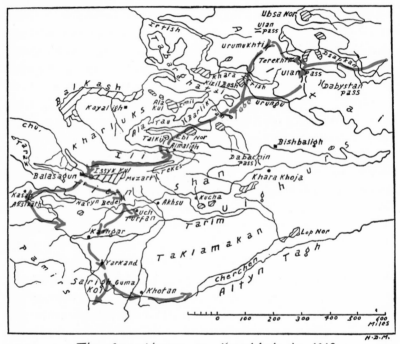

*The Overthrow of Kuchluk in 1218*

Mongols as deliverers, fell upon the remnants of the Naiman army. Finding it impossible to organize sufficient troops with which to carry on the struggle, Kuchluk fled to the eastern edge of the Pamirs and took refuge in the mountains and valleys of Sarigh Kol.[29] There he was at length hunted down and slain by Ismail, who had recently come to pay his respects to Jebe. The Mongol general then ordered the Moslem to take

[29] Sary Kul or Sarigh Kol is favored by Rashid ad-Din and the *Yüan Ch'ao Pi Shih*, but Jawayni affirms that Kuchluk was killed in the valley of Wazari in Badakhshan. However, the former location seems more probable. For location; see Herrmann, *Atlas of China*, p. 60, long. 75° lat. 37°.

the Naiman's head through his former dominions and the whole country acknowledged the authority of Chingis Khan. So ended the last of Temuchin's old enemies. Despite his faults, Kuchluk was a man of considerable ability and energy, and in the absence of as strong a personality as the Mongol conqueror, might have maintained himself in Khara Khitai and have founded a permanent state. Many of the Naiman troops must have submitted to Jebe, but others fled west, some to seek service with the Khwarazm Shah, others to the Kipchaks, where with the remnants of the Mergids, they were picked up by Subudei in 1222.[30]

Probably even before the death of Kuchluk, Chingis Khan had called an assembly to discuss the coming invasion of the Khorezmian Empire. At this, as usual, everything pertaining to the war was carefully gone over. Since the reports of the Moslem merchants had given him a very high opinion of the power of Muhammad Shah, he resolved to attack with as large an army as possible. Consequently, he called upon all his vassals to contribute troops. With the exception of Hsi Hsia, the most powerful of all, there was perfect obedience. But when his representative arrived in Chung-hsing it was otherwise. Reaching the Tangut capital, perhaps late in 1218, his envoy made known the Mongol Khan's wishes in these words. " You have promised to be my right hand. Now the Moslems have murdered my ambassador and I go to demand satisfaction of them. You shall be my right hand." Li Tsun-hsiang was about to answer, but before he could utter a word, Asha Ganbo, one of the leading Tangut nobles, retorted: " If your forces are insufficient you need not be Khaghan." The Tangut king, impressed by his reply, refused to contribute any troops. Informed of this insolence, Chingis Khan was greatly enraged and exclaimed: " How dared Asha Ganbo speak such words! It would be easy for me to send my army against them at once instead of Khwarazm; but I will not now alter my plans,

[30] *Yüan Shih*, biography of "Subudei"; see Bretschneider, *Mediaeval Researches*, Vol. I, p. 292.

but if Heaven helps and preserves me, I will march against them on my return."[31]

The Tanguts knew that Chingis Khan, commited to hostilities in the west, could not attack them for some time at least. Also they probably thought that war with so distant and powerful an opponent as the Shah of Khwarazm would prove the Mongol's undoing. If so, the reports that were to reach them during the next two years can not have failed to alarm them.

Although furious at Li Tsun-hsiang's rebuff, Chingis Khan felt that the presence of Mukhali in China would discourage the Tanguts from any drastic act of hostility and continued with his preparations for the forthcoming struggle. So absorbed did he become that, according to the *Yüan Ch'ao Pi Shih*, he for once forgot to make arrangements for the more distant future. Therefore his Tatar wife Yesui came to him and asked whom, in the event of his death, he wished to succeed him. On her pressing for an answer, he confessed that neither he nor anyone else except her had thought of this matter. Therefore he turned to Juchi and asked him what he had to say, but before he could reply, Jaghatai spoke up and demanded if Chingis really was considering leaving the throne to Juchi, for as he was probably of Mergid blood they would never recognize him.[32] Hearing this, Juchi rose, and seizing his brother by the collar, demanded how he dared speak such words, even before their father had nominated him his successor. Moreover, he upbraided him for his ungovernable temper and challenged him

[31] This speech is from the *Yüan Ch'ao Pi Shih*, but in the less reliable *Altan Tobchi* the event is related as follows: "Thereafter the Holy Ruler (Chingis Khan) sent to Siduryu (the Tangut ruler), saying, 'I am going against Sartagol (Khwarazm); keep thy promise and come with me.' But Siduryu replied: 'He (Chingis Khan) calls himself Hayan (Khaghan), while not yet master of all; why should a Hayan need a companion?' With these words he refused to help. When the Holy Ruler received this answer he became very wrath and vowed: 'Even should I lose my life, I will not leave Siduryu unpunished.'"
(See Haenisch, "Die Letzen Feldzüge Cingis Han's und Sein Tod nach der Ostasiatischen Uberlieferung," *Asia Major*, Vol. IX.)

[32] This quarrel between Juchi and Jaghatai was prophetic of the struggle that later broke out between their descendants with such dire results for the unity of the empire.

to a wrestling and archery match, vowing that should he lose
the latter he would cut off his big finger and that should
Jaghatai throw him, he would remain lying face downward on
the ground.

Thereupon the princes took hold of each other and began
wrestling, and despite the efforts of Bugurji, refused to be
separated.[33]  Only when Kököchös reminded Jaghatai that his
aspersions on Juchi's birth injured his own mother, and Chingis
Khan himself had risen and said that no one should speak
such words of Juchi, did the two princes let go of each other.
Jaghatai then admitted the great talents of Juchi, but suggested that Ugedei be the chosen one.  Chingis thereupon
turned to Juchi, who agreed that Ugedei had wisdom, but
added that he and Jaghatai might easily fight again in the
future.  So the conqueror said that he would see to it that the
two princes had their dominions apart, but bid them be warned
by the fate of Altan and Kuchar, whose sons and grandsons
he now gave them as a reminder.  He then addressed Ugedei,
who replied that he would do his best to fill the position but
feared that his offspring might prove of little worth.  Chingis
Khan finally spoke to Tului, who answered that he had already
been bidden to remind Ugedei of his duty when he forgot it
and to serve him faithfully.  The conqueror then decreed that
one of the descendants of each of his brothers should succeed
to their father, and concluding said: " Even if all the descendants of Ugedei prove unfit, surely some of those sprung from
me will be found capable of wielding authority! "

While the accuracy of this story is naturally open to criticism, it would indicate that Chingis Khan named his successor
long before the final Tangut war, which by some authorities is
believed to be the first occasion on which he definitely fixed the
succession on Ugedei.

By May, 1219, the conqueror had completed all preliminary
arrangements for the invasion of the west, and leaving Temuge
Ochigin in charge of the country north of the desert,[34] his

---

[33] Mukhali is also named, but as we know, he was then in China.
[34] No mention is made of Juchi Khassar, but as one does not once hear of him

daughter Alaghi Beki in the land of the Onguds, Yeh-lü Liu-ke
in Manchuria and Mukhali commander of all troops in China,
he moved from the Tola to the Eder where he arrived in June.[35]
Before the end of the month, he resumed the march, and probably using both the Jagisstai Pass (approx. 10,000 ft.) and
Bombutu Pass (8,700 ft) for the crossing of the Khangai,
reached the Altai about the middle of July. The route followed by the army over this great range is uncertain. However,
the " Yüan Sheng Wu Ch'in Cheng Lu," " Yüan Shih," and
Rashid ad-Din say that Chingis Khan pitched camp on the
Irtish, i. e., the Khara Irtish, and there spent the summer of
1219. This being so, he perhaps came over the Terekti and
Urumukhti Passes and down the Khran, a tributary of the
Khara Irtish and, like the larger river, flowing through splendid
grazing country. The two passes, though difficult, are open from
May until September, and as mentioned, had perhaps been used
by Jebe in 1218 when going against Kuchluk. Further to the
east are the Ulan and Dabystan passes, both approximately
9,000 ft. high and the former opening south into the Bulugun
Gol, an affluent of the Urungu and also excellent grazing country. These are passable all the year round and are easier
than the Terekhti and Urumukhti. Bretschneider tends to
favor the Dabystan Pass because of its greater road facilities.[36]
Since the conqueror was at the head of a very large army,
I personally believe that he employed all three routes and
distributed his troops on the Khran, Khara Irtish, Bulugun,
Urungu and Khobuk (Jam) to make certain of sufficient grazing before continuing the advance.

As Chingis was obliged to leave behind enough men both
to carry on the war against the Chin and to take care of possible raids from Hsi Hsia, the troops from the Mongol army

in the Khorezmian war, he must have been left behind to assist Temuge Ochigin,
who seems to have held his camp just east of the Bur Nor. See Bretschneider,
*Mediaeval Researches*, Vol. I, p. 50.

[35] It was from his camp on the Eder that Chingis Khan sent Liu Wen to bring
the celebrated Taoist sage Ch'iu Ch'ang-ch'un to him.

(See; Waley, *Ch'ang-ch'un*, p. 49, n. 41.)

[36] Bretschneider, *Mediaeval Researches*, Vol. I, p. 14. n. 5.

proper, including the 20,000 under Jebe still in the west, can hardly have exceeded 90,000. The rest of the force came from subject peoples. Only some of these are specifically mentioned; 10,000 Uighurs,[37] 6,000 Kharluks, and a contingent from Almaligh.[38] But there were undoubtedly men from the Onguds, Khitans, Solangs (Solons), Kirghiz and Kem-kemjiuts, as well as others assembled by Jebe, who probably awaited the arrival of the conqueror on the Chu, from where he could cover the main advance. Besides this great host of cavalry, there were several companies of siege and engineering troops recruited and organized in China.[39] Hence the conqueror must have crossed the Altai with 100,000 to 110,000 effectives.[40]

Accompanying Chingis Khan was his favorite wife, the beautiful Mergid Kulan, his sons Juchi, Jaghatai, Ugedei and Tului, his nephew Aljigidei, son of Khachiun Ulchi, the Ongud prince Po-yao-ho, still a child, his adopted sons Shiki Kutuku and Chaghan; Hsieh-she the son of Liu-ke, Yeh-lü Akhai, Yeh-lü Ch'u-ts'ai, Mahmud Yalavach, the Idikut Barchuk, Arslan Khan of the Kharluks, Sugnak Tagin, who had succeeded his father Buzar at Almaligh, and many of his best generals. The most outstanding of these were Bugurji, Jebe, Subudei, Tokuchar, Tolun Cherbi, Durbei Dokhsin, Bala and Taynal. There were also the Chinese soldiers Chang Jung, an engineer attached to Jaghatai, and the father and son Ke Pao-yü and Ke Te-hai. From the list of vassals, of whom

---

[37] Barthold, article on " Bishaligh," *Encyclopaedia of Islam*, Vol. I, pp. 728-730.

[38] Barthold, *Turkestan down to the Mongol Invasion*, p. 404.

[39] Gaubil, p. 34 (" Yüan Shih Lei Pien ").

[40] On such an undertaking as the invasion of the Khorezmian empire, it stands to reason that Chingis Khan took with him the largest possible number of troops available. These would include his own guard, those of Juchi, Jaghatai and Ugedei; troops belonging to other members of the Imperial family; by far the greater part of the Right-wing army and a portion of the Left-wing army. In connection with this last, we shall find only a small number of troops from it with Mukhali in China. Though 20,000 of the effectives mobilised from these various sources were already in the west under Jebe, their absence was more than made up for by the great number of auxiliaries certainly with the conqueror. The Kirghiz in particular were doubtless drawn upon heavily to keep them out of mischief. Therefore, I feel that 100,000 to 110,000 may not be far off the mark for the strength of the army that crossed the Altai with Chingis.

none except Yeh-lü Hsieh-she distinguished himself, it is apparent that the conqueror was taking with him hostages rather than army commanders.

In October Chingis Khan broke camp, and while one part of the army marched south with Jaghatai to the basin of the Ebi Nor and over the Talki defile into the upper Ili,[41] the other and larger part under Chingis himself made for the plain of Khayaligh to the south of Lake Balkash.[42] Like the crossing of the Altai, the route followed by the latter force is largely a matter of conjecture. But again I think that the advance must have been in several columns, one via the Bai Musa (4,300 ft.) between the Saur and Tarbaghatai, another via the Kergen Tash (6,300 ft.), which separates the Saur from the Urkashar and a third by way of the Jair (5,938 ft.), which lies between the Urkashar and Jair ranges. All three passes lead into the Imil valley which was on Chingis Khan's line of march when he returned in 1224, so was probably on that of the advance. A fourth column may have gone through the Kaptaghai (5,945 ft.) or Iron Gates of Jungaria.[43] From Khayaligh [44] and the Ili both forces converged on the valley of the Chu and in November crossed the Khorezmian frontier.[45] There we must leave them and return to Mukhali in China.

---

[41] See Waley, Ch'ang-ch'un, pp. 85 and 120.
[42] Vladimirtsov, The Life of Chingis Khan, p. 120.
[43] For these passes, see Carruthers, Unknown Mongolia, Vol. II, p. 406.
[44] Khayaligh was the Kharluk capital.
[45] This date is from the Meng-wu-erh Shih.

CHAPTER IX

## MUKHALI

WE HAVE already touched upon Mukhali's appointment to command of the armies mobilized for the continuation of the war in China. The campaign on which he was sent, as was explained, was not expected to put an end to the Chin, but to pave the way for a culminating blow under the conqueror himself. Due to the Khorezmian war the blow was postponed until after Chingis Khan's death, but when it fell it was largely owing to Mukhali that the Mongols had so little to conquer north of the Yellow River and were able to push the war forward to a successful conclusion as fast as they did.

Mukhali may have arrived north of the desert from Manchuria as early as December, 1216, but it was not until February, 1217, that he repaired to Chingis Khan's camp on the Tola. There he received the greatest reception ever given a commander by the conqueror. Not only was he overwhelmed with gifts, but Chingis made a point of publicly praising his great qualities as a soldier. Further, he bestowed upon him the title of Kuo Wang, which was to become hereditary. This he did because he had heard that the Chinese were in the habit of referring to Mukhali by that title and considered it a good omen.

Having resolved to send the general south, Chingis Khan evidently discussed the forthcoming campaign with him at some length, for it was not until September (1217) that Mukhali took his leave.[1] On his departure Chingis Khan gave him a golden tiger seal of authority, a nine white-tailed banner, a unique honor, and proclaimed that all under him were to

[1] The lateness of his departure is doubtless partly to be explained by the necessity of giving the army's mounts time to recuperate from the previous year's exertions.

239

obey his orders as his own. He then said to Mukhali: " I have reduced to submission all the country to the north of the Tʻai-hang mountains,[2] it is for you to subdue the country to the south."

To carry on the war Mukhali was given a considerable force, only 10,000 of which came from north of the desert, but these formed a corps d'elite and are enumerated by the " Yüan Sheng Wu Chʻin Cheng Lu " clan by clan.[3] The same work adds 3,000 Khongirads led by Anchar Noyan and 10,000 Onguds under Chen Kuo, the nephew of Alakush Tagin. Mukhali also received perhaps as many as 20,000 troops from Manchuria under the command of Uyer, Shih Tʻien-hsiang and Shih-mo Yeh-hsien,[4] a mixed force of Mongols, Khitans and Chinese led by Mongkha Bukha, Yeh-lü Tukha and Liu Po-lin [5]—these may have numbered about 15,000—and 10,000 or so Chinese soldiers from Hopei commanded by Shih Tʻien-ni; at a guess 65,000 to 70,000 effectives; [6] all cavalry.[7] It is probable that even the troops from Mongolia proper had fought under Mukhali in Manchuria so were already in the south, for his biography reports that he called his men from Liaohsi when he arrived in China. Not mentioned among the commanders listed as join-

---

[2] Tʻai-hang Mountains is the name today applied to the range that borders the eastern frontier of Shansi, but here it must stand for the system lying north of Chung Tu and south of Hsi Ching, which was also known as the Tʻai-ho Ling.

[3] These were 1,000 Khosikuls under Hsüeh Chʻih-wu-erh, 4,000 Uruds under Kita, 1,000 Manguds under Mongkha Kharaja 2,000 Ikiras under Pu-tʻu-ku-lieh-chien and 2,000 Jalairs led by Taisun the brother of Mukhali.

[4] The biographies of all three soldiers mention their participation in the war and that of Shih Tʻien-hsiang tells us that many of the men under him were from the Black Army, which it will be remembered numbered 12,000.

[5] A certain Jalaar is also named but is not again mentioned, so has here been omitted.

[6] The strength of the units from China and Manchuria are of course largely guess-work, but Liu Po-lin, Shih Tʻien-ni, Shih Tʻien-hsiang, Shih-mo Yeh-hsien and Uyer were all Commanders of 10,000.

[7] In addition to the nomad horsemen of their army, the Liao dynasty (916-1125) employed as many as 18,000 Chinese mounted troops, so the Mongols must have had as many or more.

(For the Khitan army; see Parker, " A Thousand Years of the Tartars," p. 245). Also Wittfogel and Feng Chia-sheng, " *History of Chinese Society: Liao* " (907-1125), Section XV on Army and Warfare, which is the most extensive study on the subject written in English.

ing Mukhali in 1217, but referred to the next year (1218), so doubtless included, was Shih-mo Hsien-te-pu, who in 1216 had succeeded his father Ming-an as commander of Chung Tu. In the above enumeration it is interesting to mark the large number of Chinese. This was already noticeable in the conquest of southern Manchuria and in the expedition of Tolun Cherbi and Shih T'ien-ni to Ta-ming and Tung-p'ing, but on this occasion nearly half the army must have been Chinese. This is partly to be explained by the ever increasing size of the empire which made it impossible to assign so many Mongol troops to the Chinese theater, but also to the greater ability of the Chinese in the art of taking cities. Both Chingis Khan and Mukhali realized that the reduction of some of the places to be attacked would call for very considerable skill and experience in siege craft, so purposely made use of as many Chinese soldiers as possible.

Returned to China, Mukhali first reorganized the departments of Chung Tu and Hsi Ching with an eye to facilitating the forthcoming campaign and then divided his troops into three forces, one to penetrate western and southern Hopei, a second to recover eastern Hopei and invade Shantung and a third to ravage the northern half of Shansi. Early in October the three armies commenced operations. Commanding that in the center, which was the largest, was Mukhali, who marched from Chung Tu and attacked the small towns of Sui Ch'eng and Li Ch'eng to the west and south of the Hsi-ting Hu. Neither was able to resist long, but at the latter the Mongols suffered a grievous loss. While directing an assault on the north wall, Shih-mo Yeh-hsien was struck by a stone and killed.[8] Furious at the death of so talented an officer, Mukhali swore to put every living soul in the place to death when he took it. Hearing of the fearful fate in store for the town, a Chinese officer in the army and a native of Li Ch'eng, came to Mukhali and begged that he might at least die in the place of his old mother and elder brother, who were among the beseiged.

[8] His biography tells us that he was no more than forty-one years of age.

Though of a relentless and often blood-thirsty nature, Mukhali was unable to withhold his admiration, and not only gave the man the lives of his mother and brother, but those of all in the town.

Li-Ch'eng captured, the invaders advanced into the department of Chen-ting. If an attack was made on the city itself, we are ignorant of the fact, for the only places reported occupied are the towns of Chung-shan and Hsin-lo. But even with Chen-ting untaken in his rear, Mukhali had little to fear from an attack by the garrison and in November was already pressing south to Ta-ming Fu. On the way he apparently threw out detachments to observe and blockade Wo (Chao Chou), Hsing Chou, Wei Chou, Ming Chou and Tz'u Chou. Some time in December, Ta-ming fell, whereupon the five blockaded places surrendered. Po Chou was next attacked and taken, after which Mukhali detached some of his troops to assist the Eastern army which was carrying on several simultaneous sieges in north and south Shantung.

Leading this eastern force were Shih T'ien-ni and Liu Po-lin. Since P'ing Chow, taken by Shih T'ien-ni in September, 1215, had revolted and joined the Chin commander of Ch'ing Chou and Ts'ang Chou,[9] the opening move of the two generals was eastward. Consequently October found them on the Luan Ho, but the rebellious town was so speedily recovered that Ch'ing Chou and Ts'ang Chou were captured the same month. Unable to oppose them single handed, the enemy commander called to I-tu Fu for help and fell back to Ti Chou or Lo-an. There, with the reinforcements asked for, he gave battle only to be badly beaten and driven from the field. The victors then laid siege to the town as well as to that of Pin Chou, but as neither showed signs of capitulating, they turned the investment into a blockade and in November drew off the bulk of their forces. These they directed against Ch'ang-shan, Tsou-p'ing, Tzu Chou and I-tu Fu. The first three fell, but I-tu, like Ti Chou and Pin Chou, put up an obstinate resistance and had also to be

---

[9] These two towns had been recovered for the Chin during the spring of 1216 by the commander of Ching Chou to whom they had been made over.

blockaded. Though temporarily baffled by these three places, Shih T'ien-ni and Liu Po-lin had no need to be discouraged. Not once since the battle of Lo-an had a second attempt been made to meet them in the open, so evidently arguing that there could be no force in Shantung strong enough to do so, they divided their army into two bodies, one to march east into the peninsula for the reduction of Wei Chou, Lai Chou and Teng Chou, and the other to go south against Lu Chou, I Chou and Mi Chou. Again they found all places prepared to defend themselves, and while I Chou was taken in December and news came that Ti Chou and Pin Chou had fallen, it was not until January, 1218, and after considerable reinforcements arrived from Mukhali, that I-tu and the other places were occupied.

It will be marked that neither Chi-nan or Tung-p'ing were attacked. Both were large cities and the latter, as mentioned in a previous chapter, was naturally very strong. But the army under Shih T'ien-ni and Liu Po-lin can not have been large—at a guess 20,000 effectives—so the wonder is that so much was achieved. On this initial drive they and Mukhali had each taken one large city, Ta-ming Fu and I-tu Fu respectively, but the turn of Chen-ting, Chi-nan and Tung-p'ing would come. In accordance with Mongol practice, the way for the final phase had been paved by the reduction of numerous smaller places and the general devastation of the two provinces.

Synchronized with these two thrusts was that of the third force into Shansi. From the size of the towns attacked and the very half-hearted attempt on T'ai-yüan Fu, it is apparent that this army was the smallest of the three and its offensive much in the nature of a diversion. In October the towns of Hsi Chou and Fen-hsi to the west of the Fen River and Chin Chou to the east were taken, supposedly from the mountains on either side of the valley, for the Mongols had abandoned the Ling-shih defile after Samukha's retreat. During November two small towns [10] to the South of T'ai-yüan were also cap-

---

[10] These two towns were Chiao Ch'eng and Ch'ing-yang.

tured and in December a brief attack was made on the great city, but it was not pressed and by January, 1218, the invaders seem once more to have been north of the T'ai-ho Ling.

The date of the return of the two Eastern armies is not known, but it can hardly have been later than February, 1218, for about March all the conquests of Shih T'ien-ni and Liu Po-lin in Shantung and most of those made by Mukhali in the neighboring province were lost to a sudden counter invasion by the still vigorous Chin. At the same time a smaller force was sent into western Hopei to reinforce the garrisons holding out there. This was a bitter blow to the Mongol generalissimo, who saw that much of his work would have to be done again. But making the best of the situation, he resolved to postpone the reconquest of Shantung and the extension of Mongol authority in Hopei until he could devote all his forces to the task. Instead he decided to secure what he still had in Hopei and to undertake the complete reduction of Shansi. We have no recorded reason for this decision, but it is not hard to seek. The conquest of the mountainous and difficult province of Shansi would deprive the Chin of two very real assets. In the first place it would take from them a region where the nature of the country could be expected to encourage a protracted defensive war that would be the harder to end the longer the province remained unattacked, and secondly it would deny to the Chin garrisons in western Hopei their readiest source of reinforcement and their surest haven of refuge in defeat. The latter factor had a direct bearing on the reduction of Shantung, for so long as resistance continued in Hopei, trouble and insurrection could be looked for in the eastern province. It may be thought strange that Mukhali took so many months to realize the importance of first disposing of Shansi, but he had undoubtedly gambled on being able to reduce all three provinces simultaneously without much interference from K'ai-fêng. Evidently, counting on the war raging between Chin and Sung since the summer of 1217, he did not expect the former to be strong enough to recover territory lost north of the Yellow

River. When he perceived his error he immediately revised his plans.

After his return from the south, he spent a short time at Chung Tu and then went west to Hsi Ching, where preparations were set on foot for the offensive over the T'ai-ho Ling.[11] Plans were also made for a force to move eastward over the Heng Shan to attack Wu Hsien, the commander of Chen-ting, who had recently retaken Chung-shan. This expedition was entrusted to Shih-mo Hsien-te-pu. Setting out in July, the general made for the Fei-hu Kuan, and concentrating his troops there late in August or early in September, pressed through both it and the Tao-ma Kuan. At Lang-ya Ling, about ten miles to the south of the latter, he was attacked by Chang Jo and part of the army recently sent to reinforce the garrisons in Hopei. In the ensuing battle Chang Jo was not only defeated, but, being thrown from his horse, was made prisoner. Brought before Hsien-tê-pu,[12] he was bidden to kneel, but refused. " If you are a general," he said, " so also am I; a man of spirit can die, but he will not humiliate himself." [13]

Impressed with Chang Jo's courage, Hsien-te-pu urged him to enter the service of the Mongols. At first the captive resolutely declined, but learning that his parents were in the enemy's hands, filial piety overcame his loyalty to the dynasty and he accepted to save their lives. He was then permitted to reassemble his scattered troops. These followed his example, whereupon the rank that he had held under the Chin was restored to him.

The submission of Chang Jo was a decided gain to the Mongols, who instead of having to send Shih-mo Hsien-te-pu and the forces of Chung Tu against Wu Hsien, were now able to dele-

---

[11] See the *Yüan Ch'ao Ming Ch'en Shih Liao*, biography of " Mukhali."

[12] In the *Hsin Yüan Shih* and the " Biography of Ch'eng-chi-ssŭ Han " by Feng, Ch'eng-chün, the Mongol Commander is called Shih-mo Ming-an, but Ming-an had died and been succeeded by his son Hsien-te-pu in 1216. (See *Ch'ang-ch'un* by Waley, p. 53, n. 1.)

The Chinese sources say that the Mongol force moved out through the Tzu-ching Kuan, but the battle at Lang-ya-ling would indicate that the Tao-mo Kuan was the pass used.

[13] *Meng-wu-erh Shih*, biography of " Chang Jo."

gate the task to Chang Jo. Up to his defeat Chang Jo had been closely associated with the commander of the Chin reinforcements sent into Hopei. Bitterly hated by a certain subordinate, the commander was one day cut down by the former's men. Determined to avenge him, Chang Jo led forth his troops and was on the way to make an attack when he learned of Hsien-te-pu's advance through the Tao-ma Kuan and turned aside to oppose him. He now obtained permission to repeat his attempted revenge and on the way captured Pao Chou and three other places[14] (all probably recently recovered by the Chin) — and ran his victim to earth at a fortress in the Heng Shan.[15] This was dependent for its water on one or more mountain streams outside the walls. Cutting off the supply, Chang Jo speedily obliged his enemy to capitulate. The murderer in his hands, he tore out his heart and sacrificed it to the spirit of his late superior. The dead man's soldiers were then enrolled in his army and an advance made on Man Ch'eng.

Like the seizure of Pao Chou, the ensuing capture of this town was a threat to Chen-ting, so hastily assembling as large a force as possible, Wu Hsien made a sudden descent on Man Ch'eng while most of Chang Jo's men were away on a foraging expedition. Undaunted, Chang Jo ordered the old and infirm to man the walls, and sallying forth with the few hundred troops at his disposal, destroyed Wu Hsien's siege train. This he followed by an attack on the whole army, but though it caused considerable confusion and loss, he found himself unable to regain the shelter of the town. Therefore the next day he instructed his men to raise standards on the nearby hills and spread abroad a false report that his troops were returning from their foray. Confident that this would have a disheartening affect on Wu Hsien's men, he ordered his own to beat their drums, and making a furious charge, drove the besieging army from before the town. Though elated with his success, he

---

[14] The other places were the small towns of I Chou, Hsiüng and An-su.
[15] The name of the fort was K'ung-shan T'ai, but it can no longer be identified.

wasted no time in celebration, but pushed westward and took still another dependency of Chen-ting.[16]

Although Chang Jo's biography relates his actions at comparative length, they were on a small scale and far less important than those being carried on in Shansi by Mukhali. These had begun in September when the Mongol army must have crossed the T'ai-ho Ling by way of the Yen-men Kuan. On the other side Tai Chou, Kuo, Hsin Chou, Ting-hsiang and T'ai Chou were quickly occupied and siege laid to T'ai-yüan. Taken during the first days of 1214, but recovered the same year, this city had successfully resisted the Mongols in 1216 and 1217, and now put up a desperate defense. The invaders, however, were well supplied with siege artillery, and despite the greatest efforts on the part of the garrison and their commander Wu-ku-lun Te-shun, October saw the northwest bastion brought down in ruins. Hoping still to save the city, the commander blocked the gap with wagons and behind them repulsed three heavy assaults. The Mongols then directed such a rain of stones and arrows on the place that it became impossible for any one to remain there, and launching a fourth assault, carried the place by storm. Seeing everything lost and refusing to outlive the capture of T'ai-yüan, Te-shun retired to his own quarters and committed suicide. The victors next moved on Fen Chou, which bravely resisted until November, when it too was taken by assault and where the commander died arms in hand.

To the south of this town lay the strongly held Ling-shih defile. Since it would have been a costly matter to have forced it, Mukhali must have done what the Japanese did under similar circumstances on their advance to P'ing-yang in February, 1938, i. e., made a detour through the mountains to the west and gone by way of Hsi Chou. But instead of making straight for P'ing-yang, the Mongol first attacked and took

---

[16] This was Hsiu Hsien to the west of Pao Chou. For these operations; see the *Meng-wu-erh Shih*, biography of "Chang Jo."

As regards dates, the *Hsin Yüan Shih* gives 1219 as the year for Chang Jo's first clash with Wu Hsien, but the *Yüan Shih Hsin Pien*, like the *Meng-wu-erh Shih*, names 1218, which fits the picture much better.

Huo Chou, and also probably Fen-hsi, which thus blocked the southern end of the defile. P'ing-yang was then invested, and notwithstanding the smallness of the garrison, put up a courageous defense, but like T'ai-yüan and Fen Chou was carried by storm and the commander driven to take his life.[17] Simultaneously, part of the army marched east from the Fen River and reduced Lu-an, where the commander also perished fighting to the last, Kao-p'ing and Tse Chou. The only other place that may have fallen this year was Ch'ü-wo to the east of Chiang Chou (Chin-an).

As soon as he was master of P'ing-yang, Mukhali gave command of it to Anchar Noyan and another officer, but entrusted its civil administration and that of south Shansi to a Chinese official.[18] Troops must also have been stationed at T'ai-yüan, Fen Chou and Huo Chou, since from that time on all but the final reaches of the Fen River remained permanently in Mongol hands. But there was still much to do. Not only did the mountains on either side of the river harbor considerable guerilla forces, but west Shansi was unconquered. Leaving the former to be held in check by the detachments posted along the Fen, Mukhali returned north to Hsi Ching to organize the invasion of the western part of the province.

Early in 1219 an army under the two Chinese soldiers Liu Po-lin and Shih T'ien-hsiang moved from Hsi Ching and crossed the T'ai-ho Ling to the south of Shuo Hsien.[19] The first places on their line of march were Wu and K'e-lan, both of which were quickly occupied. At the latter, warned of the army's approach, the inhabitants fled in terror and left the town to be pillaged. After this easy victory the invaders spent the summer reducing successively Lan Hsien, Shih Chou, Hsi Chou and Chi Chou. Meanwhile, Mukhali and Shih T'ien-ni proceeded down the Fen, along which they doubtless carried out

---

[17] The *Li-tai T'ung-chien Chi-lan* calls the Commander Li Ke, but in the *Chin Shih*, Ao Tun Ch'e Ho-sheng is the name given.

[18] The official in question was Li Shou-chung.

[19] With them was a Mongol officer named Ku-li-cha-ta and a Khitan called Shih-mo Po-tieh-erh. In the biog. of "Mukhali"; see the *Meng-wu-erh Shih*, both are made the leading figures in the campaign, but neither reappears again.

mopping up operations. Eventually both armies arrived before Chiang Chou (Chin-an), where they encountered a most determined defense, but in December, a tower in the walls having been undermined and brought down by Shih T'ien-ni's engineers, the city was taken by storm and all the inhabitants put to the sword.[20] This so intimidated the surrounding country that over eighty forts and hamlets were either abandoned or submitted to the Mongols. In addition Wen-hsi was captured by Liu Po-lin and Ho-chung Fu by Shih T'ien-hsiang, but the latter, like Chiang Chou, was subsequently recovered by the Chin.

With the exception of the most southerly part of the province, Shansi had been conquered. Even allowing for the presence of many recalcitrant bands in the hills, the Mongols were to all intents and purposes masters of the country. As seen, its subjugation fell roughly into two phases, the reduction of the basin of the Fen River, which was the principal food producing area, and that of the highlands between it and the Yellow River.[21] A striking feature of the whole campaign is the comcomplete absence of field battles, which clearly indicates that the Chin, short of forces for engagements in the open, were relying on the difficult terrain to help them carry on the struggle. Notwithstanding the advantage that Mukhali enjoyed from having a highly mobile force, the nature of the country and the obstinate resistance encountered at many places made the conquest of Shansi a notable achievement.

To the east on a much smaller scale Chang Jo had also been successful. Attacked a second time at Man Ch'eng by Wu Hsien, this time in the spring of 1219, he had inflicted upon his adversary another defeat and as on the former occasion retaliated by a counter raid. This resulted in the submission

[20] The *Yüan Ch'ao Ming Ch'en Shih Liao*, biography of "Mukhali," says that the siege lasted only twenty days.
December is the only definite date recorded for this entire campaign.
[21] During the conquest of the valley of the Fen the Mongols also made themselves masters of several small towns, namely Chin-yang, Ch'ing-yüan, Chiao Ch'eng and Chao Ch'eng. These are not mentioned with the more important places, but are referred to later as being in their possession.

of two small places [22] and an advance on Chung-shan, which
was eventually taken. Wu Hsien was then again beaten
outside Man Ch'eng and still a fourth time to the south,[23] after
which Chang Jo over-ran all the southern and eastern parts
of the department of Chen-ting.[24] Nevertheless, he was too
weak for an attempt on the city, which shows that his forces
were not large.

The first half of his program concluded, Mukhali embarked
upon the second (the completion of the conquest of Hopei
and the recovery of Shantung) and during August, 1220,
arrived at Chung Tu where he assembled his troops. As before
he took with him his most outstanding lieutenants, namely
Mongka Bukha, Uyer, Shih T'ien-hsiang and Shih T'ien-ni.
By September he was on the move, and after a brief halt at
Man Ch'eng, advanced on Chen-ting. Expecting this, Wu
Hsien had done what he could to prepare for the blow and,
to draw off at least part of the invading force, despatched his
best officer, Ke T'ieh-ch'iang, to make a diversion into Shansi
and lay siege to T'ai Chou at the foot of the Wu-t'ai Shan. So,
on reaching Man Ch'eng, Mukhali instructed Monkha Bukha to
lead 3,000 horsemen through the Tao-ma Kuan, and to go to
the relief of the town. Not a word is said to indicate the route
followed, but considering the very difficult terrain immediately
to the south and east of the Wu-ta'i massif, it is possible that
Mongka Bukha skirted its northern perimeter and, crossing
its western flank, suddenly descended on the besieging force
which was severely beaten and forced to retire. The general
then returned to the main army, perhaps by way of the mountains to the south of the Hut'ou River and through the Ching-
hsing Pass, over which today the railway linking Peking and
Tai-yüan runs.

---

[22] These were Ch'i-yang and Ch'u-yang.

[23] At Ch'i-yang.

[24] Ku Ch'eng, Shen-tse, Ning-chin and An-p'ing were taken by Chang Jo himself, P'ing-chih, Kao Ch'eng, Wu Chi and Luan Ch'eng by his officers. Report of
this spreading to the T'ai-hang Shan, the forts of Lu-erh, Yeh-li and Lang-shan
made voluntary submission. With the exception of the last three, all are to be
found on the accompanying map of the area.

Meanwhile Mukhali had received the surrender of Chen-ting. Although Wu Hsien still controlled several important towns besides the city itself and could have put up an obstinate and costly defense, his ultimate overthrow was inevitable.[25] Aware of this, and perhaps hoping to save life on both sides, Shih T'ien-hsiang had begged Mukhali to let him try to talk Wu Hsien into surrender before a regular siege was begun. Entering the city, he obtained an audience with Wu Hsien, whom he convinced of the futility of resistance and brought about the submission of the city. Uyer then suggested to Mukhali that, since Shih T'ien-hsiang had obtained the capitulation of Chen-ting, he be made commander of it. Mukhali, however, doubtless because T'ien-hsiang was the foremost of his Chinese captians, insisted on keeping him with him and made over the position to Shih T'ien-ni, who was also appointed Commander of West Ho-pei and given Wu Hsien as second in command. It was then that T'ien-ni, who three years before had executed a number of his own men for pillage and murder, prevailed upon Mukhali to order that such behavior also cease in the rest of the army.[26] Pointing out that, if the conquered country was to settle down, looting and indiscriminate killing must cease, he further contended that such behavior hardly befitted an imperial army. Impressed by his arguments, Mukhali gave orders that these evils stop and commanded his troops to free all the prisoners then in their hands.

Well might Shih T'ien-ni urge a change, for the preceding decade of war had made the general disorder truly terrible. Even in June that year the celebrated Taoist sage Ch'iu Ch'ang-ch'ung and his escort had encountered bandits in the Chü-yung Kuan.[27] That had happened in country under Mongol rule since November, 1213. Further south things were naturally much worse, and in March of the same year Ch'ang-ch'un's

[25] Despite his losses to Chang Jo, Wu Hsien still held Shen Chou, Chi Chou, Wo (Chao Chou), Wei Chou, Pao-t'ou Chai and Nan-kung.

(See *Chin Shih*, biography of " Wu Hsien " and the *Meng-wu-erh Shih*, biography of " Chang Jo.")

[26] See the *Meng-wu-erh Shih*, biography of " Shih T'ien-ni."

[27] See Waley, *Ch'ang-ch'un*, p. 56.

journey through eastern Hopei had been delayed several days
by the necessity of his escort and troops from Chung Tu having
to deal with a band of Chin soldiers, who since the summer of
1215, had been holding out at Hsin-an in the swamp and lake
country of the Hsi-ting Hu.[28] Not until Mukhali's advance in
September were their activities curtailed. Then the Mongol
general detailed 500 picked troops to co-operate with the men
from Chung Tu, but even so the freebooters were only partially
blockaded and were not wiped out for a number of years.[29]

Needless to say, Shih T'ien-ni's advice produced no miracu-
lous change and considerable slaughter and misery continued
on all sides. But his words to Mukhali and their acceptance
marked the dawn of a new era, an era in which Chinese influence
steadily, if slowly, softened the Mongols and mitigated the
horrors of their conquest.

After the beginning of October the invaders resumed the
advance, and while a small force, perhaps under Shih T'ien-ni,
effected the reduction of Ho-chien and Central Hopei,[30] Mukhali
marched along the foot of the T'ai-hang Shan to Tz'u Chou.
Simultaneously Shih T'ien-hsiang penetrated the Yao-shui Shan,
an outlying spur of the greater range. There the brother of
Wu Hsien and commander of the mountains and adjoining
strip of plain, had retreated. Having posted troops along the
heights, he must have planned to harry the Mongols by raids,
but being suddenly surprised in his head-quarters by an officer
of Shih T'ien-hsiang, he was forced to surrender. News of
this quickly spread and in November Hsing Chou, Ming Chou
and T'zu Chou, all three on the plain and blockaded, made

[28] See Waley, Ch'ang-ch'un, p. 53.
[29] See the Yüan Ch'ao Ming Ch'en Shih Liao, biography of "Mukhali." This
work speaks of the despatch of the 500 men from Mukhali's army but wrongly
assigns the event to 1218. The Chin Shih, biography of "Wan-yen Chung-chia-nu,"
reports these men and their leader Chang Fu to have still been at Hsian-an in 1223,
but fails to give the date of their ultimate destruction.
[30] Earlier in 1220 Ho-chien, Hsien Chou, Shen Chou, Hsu-ning, Wu-ch'ang and
No-yang had been made over by the Chin to Wan-yen Chung-chia-nu, the former
commander of Ta-ning Chen in the Liaotung peninsula. By the end of 1221
every place had been lost so he took refuge with Chang Fu at Hsin-an.
(See Chin Shih, biography of "Wan-yen Chung-chia- nu.")

submission. Soon afterward Ta-ming Fu and the towns under it followed suit, but Chang-te to the south and Lin Chou in the mountains to the west succumbed only to force. Master of Hopei, Mukhali lost no time in turning his attention to Shantung and moved swiftly on the great city of Chi-nan. This gave no trouble and surrendered. Its easy submission, as well as that of Ta-ming, make this year a turning piont in the Mongol conquest of China. Both contained considerable populations and the surrender of Ta-ming Fu involved that of eight other places. Unquestionably the capitulation of all was largely the result of the generous treatment accorded Chang Jo and Wu Hsien, but the significant thing is that in the heart of China the Mongols for the first time had received the voluntary submission of an extensive area. From now on, ever greater and greater numbers of the population north of the Yellow River began to regard the invaders as the destined masters of the country. However, to comprehend the situation properly, it is necessary to digress a little.

After the beginning of the Mongol assult on the Chin empire, the Sung, learning of the catastrophic reverses suffered by their enemy, discontinued the payment of tribute. For five years the Chin ignored this affront, but in 1217 Chu-hu Kao-ch'i, who had become chief minister, urged the emperor to make war. Left to follow his own inclinations, Hsüan Tsung (1213-23) would have sought an alliance instead but, told that Ning Tsung (1194-1224) would interpret this as a sign of extreme weakness, he gave in and in June (1217) sent south two armies. Since this happened in the lull that preceded Mukhali's arrival in China, Kao-ch'i doubtless hoped to strike a lightning blow that would net the Chin some territory to help compensate for their losses in the north.

Nevertheless there was one powerful minister who deplored the war. This was Hsü Ting, famous for his resistance against the Mongol Samukha, who bitterly criticised the project because of the tremendous losses already suffered in the contest with the Mongols and the heavy taxation under which the whole country groaned. Further, he contended that, as most of the troops to be employed were from Hopei and Shansi, they would not have their hearts in a southern offensive.[31] As it happened, they fought very well, if with uncalled for savagery, and it may be that one of Chu-hu Kao-ch'i's principal reasons for hostilities was to acquire land on which to settle them, an understandable ambition when one recalls the fiasco of 1215 that evoked the Red Coat rebellion.

At first it looked as if all would go well. The most easterly of the two armies invested Tsao-yang,[32] a key position on the Sung side of the border, while the western force moved from Feng-hsiang over the Ts'in-ling Shan mountains and laid waste the country to the south. But the frontier forces of the Sung lacked neither equipment nor leadership, and if at first caught off balance, speedily recovered and forced a general retreat. Furious but undaunted, the Chin repeated the inroad the following spring (1218) but were again obliged to retire. However, informed that his troops had wrought much havoc, Hsüan Tsung felt that the Sung would be glad to come to an accommodation and opened negotiations, but without success. Therefore, in February, 1219, the strongest forces yet mobilized for the war went south. One army besieged Tsao-yang for ninety days, while another penetrated as far as Hsing-yüan on the Han River. Both were ultimately repulsed with heavy losses, the eastern army losing 30,000 men and the western 3,000. But the latter, if severely mauled, managed to retain a small part of its conquests and added Hsi-ho Chou, Ching Chou and Feng Chou, south of the Ts'in-ling Mountains, to the empire.

Though having fought on the defensive, the Sung thoroughly appreciated the vast decline of their opponent, and having gathered a large army for a counter offensive, carried the war into Chin territory. By the summer of 1219 the generals P'eng I-pin and Li Ch'uan had crossed the final reaches of the Yellow River and were pressing north. Seeing no hope of resisting the invasion, Yen Shih, the Chin commander of South Hopei,

[31] See the *Chin Shih*, biography of " Hsü Ting."

[32] Tsao-yang is just south of the present Honan-Hupei border and thirty-five miles northeast of Hsiang-yang.

and what is today the most westerly part of Shantung, decided
to submit and in September surrendered Ta-ming Fu and the
whole of his command.[33]  Soon afterward Chi-nan was captured
by Li Ch'uan, so Chang Lin, who only the previous year (1218)
had recovered eastern Shantung from the Mongols, also went
over to the Sung.  Informing Ning Tsung of these huge acquisitions, the Sung general obtained permission to confirm
both renegades in command of the territories they had betrayed
and to Chang Lin's added the city of Chi-nan.  For a moment it
looked as if the Sung and not the Mongols were to become the
masters of Shantung.

His policy completely discredited, Chu-hu Kao-ch'i did not
long outlive these losses.  In January, 1220, the emperor ordered his execution, ostensibly for the brutal murder of his wife,
but really for having advocated the unfortunate war which
had diverted south so many of the empire's best troops.  Had
these been available for Shansi in 1219 there is little doubt
that Mukhali would have experienced considerably more
difficulty in conquering the province.

Committed to hostilities, the Chin had no alternative but
to go on with them, and in April, they sent a force across the
Yellow River, which retook three places in the southeast corner
of Hopei.[34]  This brought back Ta-ming and K'ai Chou to their
allegiance, but more important than any such trifling successes
was the unshaken loyalty of Meng Ku-kang at Tung-p'ing.
Isolated though he was by the treachery of Yen Shih and Chang
Lin, he refused to follow their example, and commanding a
strong garrison that included both Jurchid and Khitan cavalry,
prepared to hold out to the last.  But no less determined was
Li Ch'üan to make himself master of the place.  In July he
called upon Chang Lin to join him and advanced on the city
with a large army.  At the same time another force operated

---

[33] In the *Meng-wu-erh Shih*, biography of " Yen Shih," the date of the general's
surrender is 1220, but this is certainly a mistake for 1219.  The places given up
with Ta-ming Fu were Chang-te Fu, Hsiang, Chün Chou, Wei-hui, Hua Chou,
K'ai Chou, Huai-ch'ing, P'u Chou, Po Chou, En Chou and Te Chou.

[34] These were Huai-ch'ing, Wei-hui and Chang-te.

to the west of the Tung-p'ing Hu and restored Sung authority in K'ai Chou and the oft taken and retaken city of Ta-ming.[35]

Tung-p'ing could almost certainly have held out several months but, before the investment had gone on too long, Meng Ku-kang ordered one of his officers to leave the city in order to draw Li Ch'üan into an ambush. This was completely successful and Li Ch'üan, attacked simultaneously from without and from the city, barely escaped with his life, while the losses sustained by his own troops and those of Chang Lin were so severe that the siege had to be raised. This was a heavy blow to Sung prestige, and despite the subsequent capture of Hai Chou by Li Ch'üan, made all aware of the very tenuous nature of Sung power north of the Yellow River.[36] Consequently, when Mukhali arrived south in November, Chi-nan surrendered and Yen Shih, who must previously have made known his willingness to change his colors again, appeared before the Mongol general and submitted a census of the 300,000 families (approximately 1,500,000 people) under his jurisdiction.[37] For this, as on the occasion of his submission to the Sung, he was retained in his post. Such behaviour might have been expected to cause trouble with the southerners, but at the time Ning Tsung wanted peace with the Mongols, not war, so the matter was overlooked.

[35] No definite date is given for Li Ch'üan's attack on Tung-p'ing, but July is the month given for the recovery of Ta-ming and K'ai Chou by the other force. So as this was probably operating in concert with Li Ch'uan, the two armies may very well have set out at the same time. See De Mailla, *Historie Générale de la Chine*, Vol. IX.)

[36] For the war between the Chin and Sung, for the invasion of Shantung and the siege of Tung-p'ing; see De Mailla, the *Li-tai T"ung-chien Chi-lan*, the *Chin Shih*, biographies of "Hsü Ting" and "Meng Ku-kang," and the biography of "Yen Shih" in the *Meng-wu-erh Shih*.

[37] The biography of "Yen Shih" definitely states that it was the weakness of the Sung that caused him to transfer his allegiance to the Mongols. From his biography one also learns that he had under him 360,000 families. From the biography of Mukhali in the *Meng-wu-erh Shih*, one learns that Yen Shih had no more than 300,000 families. This discrepancy may be due to the fact that when he submitted to Mukhali, the towns of Chang-te, Hsiang, Wei-hui and Huai-ch'ing were no longer in his possession. In either case the census refers only to the taxable population and omits those who were too poor or who were able to escape the revenue collector.

Chang Lin for his part remained outwardly loyal to the Sung, but as early as January, 1220, he had been in contact with the Mongols and had done all he could to facilitate the progress of the Taoist sage Ch'iu Ch'ang-ch'un on his journey into Hopei.[38] Since there was friendship between Sung and Mongol, this was not extraordinary, but the day was soon to come when he too would transfer his allegiance to the northern power.

Meanwhile Hsü Ting had succeeded Chu-hu Kao-ch'i as the Chin premier,[39] and having mobilized 200,000 men for the recovery of Shantung, placed them under the command of Wu-ku-lun Shih-hu, who was ordered to go and station himself at Huang-ling-kang on the north bank of the Yellow River. According to the biography of Mukhali, this great force—probably much exaggerated—was simply intended to hold the fords of the river, while De Mailla says that its objective was the expulsion of Mukhali from Shantung. Since it was most certainly assembled and despatched to the river before the Mongols arrived at Chi-nan, I am sure that its original intention was the reconquest of the province from the Sung. However, learning that Mukhali had moved from Chi-nan to Tung-p'ing,[40] Wu-ku-lun Shih-hu thought first to settle with the Mongols, and 20,000 infantry were sent north in a vain attempt to make a surprise attack. Receiving timely warning, Mukhali is reported to have taken the field with no more than 500 cavalry and to have utterly defeated them. The smallness of the victorious force is quite incredible and it was probably at least ten times the size recorded in the Mongol general's biography.

[38] Ch'iu Ch'ang-ch'un set out from Lai Chou, then under Chang Lin; see Waley, *Ch'ang-ch'un*, pp. 49-52.

[39] Hsü Ting, being an old man and worn out with continuous labor in the service of the empire, was permitted to retire soon afterwards.
(See *Chin Shih*, biography of "Hsü Ting.")

[40] It is from the *Li-tai T'ung-chien Chi-lan* that one learns of this initial appearance of Mukhali before Tung-p'ing and of the Chin general's attempt to surprise him there. Mukhali's own biographies have omitted to mention his first stop before the place and report that Wu-ku-lun Shih-hu hoped to surprise him at Chi-nan. But as it would have been impossible for an army to have used any route that would have made likely a surprise at or near the northern city, I have accepted the account in the *Li-tai T'ung-chien Chi-lan*.

Following up his success, Mukhali concentrated all his troops
and advanced to Huang-ling-kang. The majority of the enemy
must have been infantry, for evidently having no fear of their
cavalry, he dismounted his own to give their shooting greater
effect and poured a storm of arrows into the opposing ranks.
These were thrown into terrible confusion, and charged by
the Mongols, sabre in hand, were hurled into the river where
thousands were drowned. Notwithstanding this, numbers were
able to fall back over the ford at Huang-ling-kang, and using
the river to protect their front, which was further strengthened
by various works, made impossible all hope of crossing to the
other side. But Huang-ling-kang itself was lost, and with this
crushing defeat ended the last serious attempt on the part of
the Chin to recover either Hopei or Shantung.

There are considerable discrepancies in the various accounts
that have come down to us of this battle. The " Li-Tai T'ung-
chien Chi-lan " and the biography of Mukhali in the " Meng-wu
erh Shih" affirm that the Chin took their stand on the south
bank of the river, but while the former says that Mukhali dismounted his men and charged the enemy on foot, the latter
states that he dismounted his men and defeated them by the
storms of arrows that he poured over the river, which, however he was unable to cross. On the other hand, both Gaubil
(" Yüan Shih Lei Pien ") and the biography of Mukhali in the
" Yüan Ch'ao Ming Ch'en Shih Liao " report the engagement
to have taken place on the north bank, which is almost certainly correct, but help no further. There can be little doubt
that the Mongols resorted to their usual practice under such
circumstances; the arrow storm, followed by a heavy charge.
Had the Chin been on the south bank, neither Mongol arrows
nor charge could have reached them.

By the beginning of December Mukhali had turned North,
and sending Mongka Bukha west to take Wei-hui, Huai-ch'ing
and Meng Chou, another force east to seize Tan Chou, Chi-
ning, Yen chou and T'eng Chou, himself marched against
Ch'u-ch'iu and T'ien-p'ing Chai. All except T'ien-p'ing Chai
fell before the end of the month and the investment of none

except that of T'ien-p'ing Chai and Ch'u-ch'iu call for any particular notice.[41] The former, which was very strong, repulsed a major attempt to take it and was left, while Ch'u-ch'iu, a small town entirely surrounded by water, nearly escaped. Confident of its ability to resist, it obstinately refused every summons to surrender. Mukhali therefore ordered his men to collect bundles of grass and wood, and having filled the moat with a vast quantity of these, commanded Yen Shih to deliver an assault which succeeded in carrying the place by storm. The whole army then returned to Tung-p'ing where Meng Ku-kang awaited them. Despite the failure of Li Ch'üan earlier the same year and that of Tolun Cherbi in November, 1215, Mukhali decided to try to take the place by assault. As before, every effort failed and Mukhali, furious with Uyer who had apparently been detailed to direct the storming parties, flew into an ungovernable rage and would have taken the officer's life but for the intercession of Shih T'ien-hsiang.[42] This general, between whom and Uyer there was a close friendship, begged to take over his post, and notwithstanding the greatest efforts was also beaten back by the inability of his troops to cross the small river protecting the city's northern front. At last, convinced that Tung-p'ing could not be taken by force, Mukhali ordered all assaults to cease and turned the siege into a blockade. To carry this on he left 3,000 Mongols under a son of Anchar Noyan[43] and a force of Chinese led by Yen Shih whom he appointed commander of western Shan-tung. Calling both before him, he said: "When food runs short, Meng Ku-kang will have to force his way out; as soon as this happens, enter the city, but treat the inhabitants with clemency for in that way the place may be pacified." [44] After these instructions, he departed for Ming Chou, which had revolted and whither he had already despatched his brother Taisun. Apparently he spent little or no

[41] The *Meng-wu-erh Shih* dates the attack on T'ien-p'ing Chai prior to the occupation of Chi-nan, but this is most unlikely.
[42] *Meng-wu-erh Shih*, biography of " Shih T'ien-hsiang."
[43] This was Chih-la-wa-tai.
[44] *Meng-wu-erh Shih*, biography of " Mukhali."

time in front of the town, but detaching a reinforcement under Shih T'ien-ying, continued northward.

May 1221, found Tung-p'ing so straitened for provisions that cannibalism started, and Meng Ku-kang, seeing that he must at last lose the place, decided to force his way through the enemy blockade. In June he left the city with 7,000 troops,[45] but making for P'ei Chou, one hundred and thirty miles to the southeast, was so fiercely harassed by Yen Shih and his colleague that he reached his destination with no more than 700. After that Tung-p'ing surrendered and the two victorious commanders rode in to the city. About the same time Ming Chou succumbed to the combined efforts of Taisun and Shih T'ien-ying, thus almost completing the conquest of western Shantung and Hopei.

By the time this happened Mukhali had reached the Yeh-hu Ling, where he halted for several weeks, but in August he moved west to Ch'ing-chung,[46] twenty to twenty-five miles southwest of Feng Chou, and was there welcomed by the Mongol princess Alaghi Beki. At this place he began making preparations for a great drive that would cut the western flank of the Chin in two and ultimately enable him to take K'ai-feng by a thrust from the valley of the Wei.

Knowing that the fall of Tung-p'ing and Ming Chou was only a matter of time, Mukhali had early in 1221 begun to contemplate an invasion of Kuan-chung (Shensi and eastern Kansu). As already related, had it not been for the Khorezmian war, this would most certainly have taken place earlier while Mukhali was conquering the country east and north of the Yellow River. Now that this region, with the exception of eastern Shantung, under the Sung, was in his possession, he could afford to think of turning west. He had evidently spoken of the project before reaching the Yeh-hu Ling, for when on the 23rd of May (1221)

---

[45] The *Chin Shih*, biography of "Meng Ku-kang," says that the general was ordered by the Chin to leave the city, by then completely isolated, and to go to P'ei Chou. There in 1223 he was eventually murdered by two of his subordinates because of the severity with which he maintained discipline.

[46] The *Yüan Ch'ao Ming Ch'en Shih Liao* says that the place was T'ien-te, which is the same as Tung-sheng.

a total eclipse was observed, the soothsayers in his train warned him that for the time being it would be dangerous to undertake further military operations. " I have received orders from Chingis Khan," he declared, " to complete the conquest of Chin. Honan and Kuan-hsi (Kuan-chung) are still in their possession; if I postpone all troop movements because of astronomical phenomena, when shall we accomplish this task? " [47] Nevertheless he sent west a representative to Chingis Khan to make a report on what he had done and to ask approval for the new expedition. In due time the officer returned and informed him that the Khan commanded the war to go on. Having received this order, Mukhali asked if the conqueror had said anything further. " Chingis Khan," replied the messenger, " raised his right thumb to indicate that he considers you the greatest of his generals." When he heard these words, Mukhali was overcome with gratification and said: " The Khan is very gracious and I will wage war for him until the end of my life." [48]

We are not told when Mukhali's representative reached the conqueror, but it can have been little later than the end of June (1221).[49] In the meantime a Sung envoy, Kou Meng-yii, had been received at the Mongol generalissimo's head-quarters. We do not know the nature of Mukhali's official reply, but learn that he gave the envoy a warm welcome. An amusing anecdote about his treatment has come down to us from the Chinese general Meng Hung, who was a member of the mission.[50] " On

[47] In the *Meng-wu-erh Shih* this eclipse is dated in the 8th month of the Yin-shu year, i. e., during September, 1222, but there was no total eclipse then.

[48] This is from the *Meng-wu-erh Shih*, biography of " Mukhali." In the fragments that have come down to us from the Bilik, there is a variation of Chingis Khan's message of praise to Mukhali in which a number of other officers are equally lauded. (See Riasanovsky, *Fundamental Principles of Mongol Law*, p. 89).

[49] A Chin embassy, sent to seek peace with Chingis Khan—see below—had passed through his camp during the autumn of 1220, so wishing to forestall them, Mukhali seems to have seen to it that a representative of his own arrived at imperial quarters first.

[50] In a number of works Chingis Khan is named the recipient of the Sung embassy, but more recent and careful investigations have proved that it was Mukhali who received Kou Meng-yü. (See Pelliot, " Notes sur Le Turkestan," *T'oung Pao*, Vol. XXVII, pp. 13-14.) In the same notice Pelliot reports that the celebrated Chinese Mongolist, Wang Kuo-wei, believes that we should read Chao Hung, instead of Meng Hung, for the chronicler of the embassy.

one occasion Mukhali sent for Kou Meng-yü, and when the
latter came said to him: 'We had a game of ball today, why
did you not come?' The other answered that he had not been
invited and dared not come. Mukhali retorted: 'From the
moment of your arrival you have become a member of my
household; you must come each time we make merry or have a
feast, a game of ball (polo) or a chase; why wait for an in-
vitation?! He broke into laughter, imposed on the ambassador
a penalty of six glasses of wine, and let him go only towards
nightfall when the latter had become quite drunk."[51] Though
Mukhali knew that, with the Sung masters of eastern Shantung, eventual hostilities were highly probable, for the time
being he hoped for peace and did his best to encourage friendly
relations. Quite otherwise was the tenor of his master's response to the Chin ambassador Wu-ku-sun Chung-tuan.

Attacked by the Mongols in the north, the Sung in the
south and the Tanguts in the west, the summer of 1220 saw
the Chin in a desperate plight. Determined to try to negotiate
peace with Chingis Khan, they resolved to send west an envoy
to discuss terms again. In August (1220) Wu-ku-sun Chung-
tuan left K'ai-feng and visiting Mukhali on the way, eventually
reached the conqueror's quarters, by then in the valley of the
Inderab, during July (1221).[52] Appearing before Chingis,
Chung-tuan informed him that Hsüan Tsung was prepared to
acknowledge himself the conqueror's younger brother (vassal)
but stipulated that he retain the title of emperor. When Chingis
Khan heard this proposal he said: " Formerly I asked your sovereign to cede the land north of the Yellow River and to reign
over the country south of it with the title of Wang (King). On
these conditions I would have stopped the war. But now Muk-

[51] This excerpt is quoted by Grousset from the *Meng Ta Pei Lu*; see René
Grousset, *Le Conquérant du Monde*, p. 348.
[52] For the date of Wu-ku-sun Chung-tuan's departure, crossing of the frontier
and return to K'ai-feng; see Bretschneider, *Mediaeval Researches*, Vol. 1, pp. 26-27.
The *Yüan Shih* states that the Chin envoy overtook Chingis Khan at the Iron
Gates, i. e. the Kolugha or Dar-i-Ahan between Shari-zabz and Tirmidh, but it is
well known that in the summer of 1221 the conqueror was South of the Amu
(Oxus) in Tukharistan.
(See Barthold, *Turkestan down to the Mongol Invasion*, p. 444.)

hali has already conquered all these countries, and you are compelled to sue for peace." At this Chung-tuan implored the Khan
to have pity. " It is only in consideration of the great distance
you have come," said he, " that I will offer conditions. The
land north of the Yellow River is in my possession, but there
are still some cities in Kuan-hsi (Shensi and eastern Kansu)
which are not yet mine. Tell your ruler to surrender these, and
then he may reign south of the river with the title of King." [53]
With these conditions, which the Chin rejected, Wu-ku-sun
Chung-tuan had to return to K'ai-feng, where he arrived in
January, 1222.

To what extent Chingis Khan's attitude was influenced by
Mukhali we do not know, but since the general most certainly
learned before the conqueror what the Chin were offering, he
undoubtedly saw to it that his own envoy reached Chingis
ahead of Wu-ku-sun Chung-tuan. This would be easy for him,
as he had at his disposal the imperial postal service (*yam*)
which enabled those using it to transmit information over vast
distances in an incredibly short time. Consequently, I believe
that before Chung-tuan's arrival, Mukhali had informed
Chingis that not only could Kuan-hsi be conquered, but the
whole empire. Hence the conqueror's demand that the Chin
ruler abandon the title of emperor for that of king. But as the
sequel will show, Mukhali had again underestimated his enemy.

Permission granted for the new invasion, Mukhali at once
started preliminaries, and having decided to enter Shensi
through the Ordos, demanded that the Tanguts give him right
of way. By this time Li Tsun-hsiang had heard of the tremendous Mongol victories in the west, and hoping to restore relations
with them, immediately granted Mukhali's request. In October
the Mongol army crossed the Yellow River at Tung-sheng.
With it as usual went Shih T'ien-hsiang, Uyer and Mongkha
Bukha, but not Liu Po-lin, who had died earlier in the year

---

[53] These words are from the *Yüan Shih* and have been translated by both
Bretschneider, *Mediaeval Researches*, Vol. I, pp. 33-34, and Haenisch, " Die
Letzen Feldzüge Cingis Han's und sein Tod nach der Ostasiastischen Uberlieferung,"
*Asia Major*, Vol. IX.

at the age of seventy.  However, his absence was fully compensated for by Shih T'ien-ying, who in his brief career was to
prove one of Mukhali's most talented officers.  Also mentioned
are Taisun and Boru, Mukhali's brother and son.  Again we
have no figures for the strength of the invading army, but it
may have numbered 20,000-25,000 Mongols, including Onguds,
and 25,000-30-000 Chinese and Khitans.[54]

In the Ordos, Mukhali was met by an envoy from Li Tsun-
hsiang and shortly after was joined by T'a-hai Kan-po (Taga
Ganbo)[55] at the head of 50,000 troops.[55]  Nothing is said about
a demand for this reinforcement, but Mukhali must have made
one and Li-Tsun-hsiang, to win his way back still further into
the good graces of the Mongols, despatched this large force.

Simultaneously good news arrived from the east.  In September, for what reason we do not know, Shih Kuei, the Sung
commander of Lien-shui, went over to the Mongols.  Apparently he had been ordered to open negotiations with them and
during these had abandoned the Sung, who were unable to
bring him back to his allegiance even by the threat of reprisals
to his family.  But far more important was the desertion to the
Mongols of the renegade Chang Lin in October.  Having
quarreled with Li Ch'uan's brother, who threatened his execution, Chang Lin got in touch with the Mongols and made submission.  Report of this was brought to Mukhali while on the
other side of the Yellow River, and in November, after entering
Shensi, he put him in charge of the province he had surrendered
and added Ts'ang Chou in east Hopei.  At the same time he

[54] It is worth remembering that besides this operational army, Mukhali also controlled the forces of Shih-mo Hsien-te-pu, Shih T'ien-ni, Chang Jo, Yen Shih and
Anchar Noyan, i. e., at least another 50,000 men.

My figure for the army with Mukhali is based partly on that given by the
" Yüan Sheng Wu Ch'in Cheng Lu " for the Mongol troops assigned the general in
1217, partly on the rank of the commanders under him.  As for that suggested
for the force left in the east, 50,000 is a conservative estimate, as the appointments
of all five officers named were very important.  Chang Lin, who held a command
comparable to that of Yen Shih, is reported to have had 10,000 men at his headquarters in I-tu alone.  (See Waley; Ch'ang-ch'un, p. 50).

[55] This is Cordier's restoration of the name; Histoire Générale de la China, Vol. II,
p. 225.

[56] Meng-wu-erh Shih, biography of "Mukhali"; Hsi Hsia Shu Shih and Hsi
Hsia Chi.

created Shih Kuei commander of Chi-ning, Yen Chou, Tan
Chou and probably T'eng Chou. Tung-p'ing Fu was also included, but command of it was to be shared with Yen Shih. In
this manner Shantung and nearly all Hopei acknowledged Mongol authority, but the administration was now wisely delegated
to Chinese officers who had the experience that the Mongols
lacked. So to Chang Jo was given eastern Hopei, to Shih T'ien-
ni western Hopei, to Yen Shih southern Hopei and western
Shantung, to Shih Kuei [57] southern Shantung and to Chang Lin
eastern Shantung and the town of Ts'ang Chou.[58] Moreover in
these provinces, except at Chung Tu, the garrisons were ex-
clusively Chinese.

Secure in the east and with a powerful army at his back,
Mukhali could push forward to the conquest of Shensi with an
easy mind and struck his opening blow at Chia Chou. Being
situated on the Yellow River, this town should not have been
an easy place to take, but the commander, learning of the
Mongol approach, fled and early in November the invaders
entered without opposition. Appreciating its strategic importance, Mukhali left Shih T'ien-ying there with 5,000 men
and appointed him Commander of eastern Shensi. Whereupon, despite the protests of his officers, who considered the
current too swift at Chia Chou, Shih T'ien-ying constructed a
floating bridge to connect both sides of the river, and began the
reduction of the small places in the vicinity.

To the south Mukhali took Sui-te and the forts of Ma-t'i
Chai and K'e-jung Chai. At his headquarters near the town
he received an official visit from Taga Ganbo,[59] but the Tangut,

[57] A few weeks after his appointment Shih Kuei laid siege to Ts'ao Chou to the
north of the Yellow River, but was defeated and slain by a relieving force under
Wang Ting-yü, who had reoccupied Huang-ling-kang for the Chin.
[58] The *Meng-wu-erh Shih* also adds Ching Chou some sixty miles to the southwest, but this is unlikely.
[59] The *Meng-wu-erh Shih*, biography of " Mukhali," calls the Tangut general Shu-
p'u, the *Hsi Hsia Shu Shih*, Mi-p'u, also the latter says that he was at the head of a
second Tangut army which Mukhali had demanded despite the first reinforcement
under Taga Ganbo. Since there was hardly time for this second army to have
arrived, and as Taga Ganbo is a title and not a name, I am convinced that Sh'u-p'u
or Mi-p'u and Taga Ganbo are the same person.

learning that he would be required to pay Mukhali the same
homage that he did his own sovereign, refused and withdrew
upon a separate expedition to An-sai.

The outcome of this was disastrous. Informed of his intention, Wan-yen Ho-ta and Na-ho-mai-chu, the Chin commanders
at Yen-an, despatched an army to relieve the place. Making
a forced march through the night, this suddenly fell upon the
Tanguts, who were badly beaten and driven off in confusion.
Their way lying over the mountains, many were killed falling
from precipices, but the survivors finally reached the Mongol
camp. Taga Ganbo then did homage to Mukhali by holding-
the bridle of his horse and marched with him against Yen-an.

Advancing south, presumably via K'e-jung Chai, Mukhali
arrived within ten miles of the town, which is the key to
northern Shensi, and learned that Wan-yen Ho-ta had taken up
position a little to the northeast of it with 30,000 men.[60] Outside the town is a high hill, which both now and in the past
has been fortified and it was very likely on this that Ho-ta
posted his men, as from there he could observe and command
the northern and eastern approaches to Yen-an. Being in the
van of the Mongol army with 3,000 men, Mongkha Bukha
made a careful reconnaissance, and having estimated the position and numbers of the Chin, returned to Mukhali with the
following report: " The enemy," he said, " perceiving the smallness of my force are confident of success. It is possible therefore that a sham attack followed by a pretended flight may
succeed in drawing them into an ambush."

Feeling that the plan held great possibilities, Mukhali
adopted it. The same night the main army silently took the
road, and seven to eight miles from camp, concealed itself in
two valleys to the east of the town. The next morning Mongkha Bukha advanced toward the enemy with a small body of
troops and made a demonstration. Deceived by the weakness
of this force, the Chin immediately charged to the attack.

---

[60] The biography of " Mukhali " in the *Meng-wu-erh Shih* says to the east of the
town, but the main road from the north runs northeast to southwest, not east
and west.

Whereupon, at a pre-arranged signal, the Mongols threw away their drums and banners as if in panic, and with the foe in hot pursuit fled towards the ambush. There, "with a sound of drums that shook heaven and earth and a storm of 10,000 arrows," the hidden troops fell upon the pursuers, who sustained a disastrous reverse, 7,000 men being left dead upon the field and Wan-yen Ho-ta driven a fugitive to the town.

Anxious to complete this victory by the capture of Yen-an, Mukhali surrounded it and ordered an assault, but despite this and other efforts, he could make no impression on the town. Not then wishing to become involved in a long siege, he broke camp at the end of ten days, and about the middle of December began the easier task of conquering the Lo River. Sending one force northwest to deal with Pao-an, he led the rest of his troops south and with Uyer and Shih T'ien-hsiang reduced Fu Chou, Tan Chou, Lo-ch'uan and Fang Chou. Of these, Pao-an, Tan Chou and Lo-ch'uan appear to have fallen as early as January 1222, but Fu Chou and Fang Chou only succumbed in February when both were taken by storm.[61] At the former, which was evidently besieged by Uyer, a notable Chin warrier, Chang T'ieh-ch'iang (Chang of the Iron Spear), was made prisoner and sent to Mukhali.[62] Seeing the famous champion before him, Mukhali asked him why it was that he had resisted the Mongols so long and fiercely. "For twenty years and more," replied Chang, "I have served the Chin; in all that time I have been the recipient of their gratitude and favors, and now I expect nothing but death." Such an answer could hardly fail to impress Mukhali, who intended to spare him, but his officers angered by the captive's bold words, slew him. Supposedly Mukhali had not made known his final decision, for the murder of the brave Chin warrior was an act of insubordination, something remarkably rare among the Mongols of that day.

Although Yen-an remained untaken, the army of north Shensi

[61] These dates are from the *Meng-wu-erh Shih*, but it is from De Mailla that we learn that Fu Chou and Fang Chou were taken by assault.

[62] The biography of "Mukhali" makes Shih T'ien-ying the Chin warrior's captor, but in T'ien-ying's own biography nothing is said about it, while that of Uyer specifically mentions Chang T'ieh-ch'iang's capture by one of Uyer's subordinates.

had suffered a severe defeat and had been unable to interfere
with the conquest of the Lo. So Mukhali, with every reason
to be pleased, held a great banquet for his troops at Fang Chou.
It was during this that the last smouldering remains of opposition in Shansi burst into flame. Reports arrived that Hsi
Chou had been lost to forces in the hills and that the town of
Tai Chou had revolted. Wasting no time, Mukhali marched
through Tan Chou, and crossing the Yellow River, presumably
during the beginning of March, so perhaps on the ice, attacked
and recaptured Hsi Chou in two days. This done, he stationed
Anchar Noyan between it and Shih Chou, and crossed the hills
to the upper reaches of the Hu-t'ou River and retook Tai Chou.
While these operations had been underway, or perhaps earlier,
both Chiang Chou (Chin-an) and Ho-chung had been reoccupied by the Chin and the valley of the Fen continuously
raided from the neighboring mountains. Mukhali therefore
decided to put an end to this and to recover the two cities.
Before starting he went to Hsi Ching and there summoned
Shih T'ien-ying for a conference. At this it was decided that
the Chinese soldier should move from Chia Chou on Ho-chung
Fu while he himself directed his advance down the Fen for an
eventual attack on Chiang Chou (Chinan).[63]

In August Mukhali despatched Mongka Bukha back to Shensi to keep an eye on the situation there, and then marched
slowly down the Fen reducing the untaken forts on either side.[64]
By November the work was finished, and assembling his troops
just below T'ai-yüan,[65] he began his drive against Chiang Chou.
Simultaneously Shih T'ien-ying, who had set out the month
before, i. e., in October, moved on Ho-chung Fu. On the way

[63] In the *Meng-wu-erh Shih*, biography of " Shih T'ien-ying," it is said that the
capture of Ho chung Fu was to be a preliminary to the capture of T'ung Kuan,
but in actual fact no move was made on the great fortress.

[64] These were Ssŭ-t'i Chai, I-ho Chai, San-ch'ing-yen and Ch'ing-lung Pao. The
identity of none of these places is very certain, but Ssŭ-t'i Chai was near Yü Chou
to the northwest of T'ai-yüan Fu, I-ho Chai and San-ch'ing yen in the vicinity of
Chao Ch'eng and Ch'ing-lung Pao, which put up a desperate defense, to the southeast of Chi Chou. All four forts are mentioned in the biography of " Mukhali," who
is reported to have moved the defenders into the neighboring towns.

[65] At the small town of Chin-yang.

Niu-hsin Chai, Hu-pi Pao and Jung Chou were taken,[66] and while Chiang Chou seems to have fallen to Mukhali shortly after it was summoned, Ho-chung was entered the very day Shih T'ien-ying arrived. Appearing unexpectedly while the gates were open to receive a visiting official, his men rushed the city and occupied it, but the commander, Hou Hsiao-shu, made good his escape south to the Chung-t'iao hills. Impressed with T'ien-ying's ability, and realizing that Ho-chung was of even greater strategic value than Chia Chou, Mukhali added it to his command. At the same time, he made him the senior military commander of the entire province below the T'ai-ho Ling.[67] Shih T'ien-ying then received orders to build a second bridge over the Yellow River, probably at Ta-ch'ing Kuan, and although obliged to beat off an attempt by Hou Hsiao-shu to recover Ho-chung, completed the work early in December.

This was all that Mukhali had waited for, and repassing the river, he quickly seized T'ung Chou and P'u Ch'eng, and so opened the road to Ching-chao (Hsi-an,) formerly capital of the T'ang (618-907) and still one of the mightiest cities in China. Driving on, probably via Ching Chou, which he must have blockaded, he detached Mongka Bukha to attack Feng-hsiang and himself crossed the Wei. On the other side, he found Ching-chao defended by Wan-Yen Ho-ta, who had been transferred from Yen-an, and a host reputed to have numbered 200,000. While there can be little doubt that this figure is a vast exaggeration and 100,000 or less would be nearer the truth, Wan-yen Ho-ta's troops must have exceeded those of Mukhali. His failure to give battle indicates that many of his men cannot have been fully trained, and above all that he suffered from a shortage of cavalry. Though at a disadvantage in the open, these troops were formidable behind walls, and Mukhali, evidently surprised at their number and realizing that he could not hope to take the city by force, resolved upon a blockade.

---

[66] All three places were small, but of strategic value as they covered the approaches immediately south of the lower Fen.

[67] The report of this great appointment is from the biography of " Mukhali " in the *Meng-wu-erh Shih*, but the main text names only the northwest route. However, Shih T'ien-ying could not then have controlled Ho-chung Fu.

Hence he stationed 6,000 men outside to keep the defenders occupied and sent 3,000 others to cut off communication between it and the T'ung Kuan.[68]   Then at the head of his remaining troops he recrossed the Wei, and going northwest into the valley of the Ching River, set about its reduction.  By the end of January, 1223, every place attacked including Ching Chou, had fallen, thus completely cutting off Ching-chao from outside help, so in the first days of February he marched to join Mongkha Bukha at Feng-hsiang.[69]

There a pitched battle had taken place with some troops of the garrison whom Wan-yen Chung-yüan, lately appointed to the command of Feng-hsiang, had ordered to devastate the surrounding country.  Learning of this, Monka Bukha had rushed forward and two miles from the walls had overtaken them.  Unable to escape, the Chin turned and fought, but notwithstanding the greatest bravery and the splendid leadership of Mar Sargis, a Nestorian Ongud, nearly all perished with their commander.[70]   The city, however, remained undaunted and refused to surrender.

Earlier, perhaps before he even recrossed the Yellow River, Mukhali  had again called upon Hsi Hsia for help as he now invested Feng-hsiang with a combined Mongol-Tangut army. The Tangut troops alone, says the "Hsi Hsia Shu Shih," counted 100,000 cavalry and infantry.  Commanding them was Kung-chu Hu-ch'uang, who is spoken of as being a man of great

---

[68] The biography of " Mukhali " says that the commander of the 3,000 was Anchar Noyan, but subsequent events make this unlikely.

The places taken in this operation were Ch'ien Chou, Pin Chou, Ching hsien and Yüan Chou; for Mukhali's probable line of march; see end map dealing with his campaigns.

[69] The *Meng-wu-erh Shih* implies that Mukhali was before Feng-hsiang in January, 1223, the *Hsi Hsia Shu Shih,* the *Li-tai T'ung-chien Chi-lan* and the *T'ung-chien Kang-mu,* February, while the *Hsi Hsia Chi* gives March.  However, since the biography of " Mukhali " in the *Meng-wu-erh Shih* reports that the general besieged the city for a month and then retired, it is probably that the month of March was the date of his withdrawal.

[70] Mar Sargis was also known as Ma Ch'ing-hsiang and at the time was vice-commander of Feng-hsiang; see Saeki, *The Nestorian Documents and Relics in China,* pp. 480-88.  This work includes an interesting reference to the Ongud's visit to Chingis Khan with the prince of Wei, later emperor, Wei Shao Wang (1209-13) in the year 1208.

arrogance. Under his personal direction many furious assaults were delivered on the city, but the garrison, ably led by Wan-yen Chung-yüan, repulsed them all.

After a month of fruitless attacks, the Tangut general was one day surveying the situation when he was severely wounded in the arm-pit by an arrow from the walls and died. Depressed by this mishap and wearied by their losses, the other Tangut commanders resolved to retire and suddenly withdrew. Abandoned by his allies, Mukhali's forces became too weak to continue the investment. " I have been entrusted by Chingis Khan," he lamented, " to carry out many campaigns. I have conquered Liaotung, Liaohsi, Shantung, Hopei and Shansi,[71] and the towns of all I have taken without much difficulty, but T'ien-p'ing Chai [72] and Yen-an have both resisted my arms, and now after more than a month's leaguer, I have failed to reduce Feng-hsiang. Does this mean that I have come to my end? " The siege was raised, as must also have been the blockade of Ching-chao, and early in March, Mukhali turned back towards Shansi. To cover his retreat down the Wei River, or rather to act as a diversion, Mongkha Bukha was sent over the Niu-ling Kuan (T'ien-sha Kuan) to attack Feng Chou which the Chin had wrested from the Sung in 1219.

As for the Tanguts, their desertion was not so unpremeditated as it appeared. The " Hsi Hsia Shu Shih " states that, on news arriving that the Chin had suddenly attacked and recaptured Ho-chung Fu, Hsi Hsia withdrew its support.[73] Probably this reverse in the east, together with the failure of the hitherto invincible Mongols to take either Ching-chao or Feng-hsiang, made the Tanguts feel that the hand of the oppressor was weakening.

On the departure of Mukhali westward, Hou Hsiao-shu had

---

[71] By some slip Hopei and Shansi were omitted in the list; See the biography of " Mukhali " in the *Meng-wu-erh Shih*.

[72] T'ien-p'ing Chün or T'ien-p'ing Chai to the west of the Tung-p'ing Lake was briefly and unsuccessfully besieged by Mukhali during November, 1220, and was not taken until after his death.

[73] This, with its reference to the subsequent reestablishment of relations with the Mongols, the *Hsi Hsia Shu Shih* has incorrectly dated under the year 1222, instead of 1223.

begun to plan the recovery of Ho-chung, and in January (1223) swore an oath to his officers to retake it. This he intended to do by a night attack and on February 2nd set out by forced marches from the Chung-t'iao hills. But, despite much secrecy, wind of his venture reached Shih T'ien-ying. Hoping to turn the tables on Hou Hsiao-shu, T'ien-ying made arrangements to take him in an ambush. One of his subordinates was instructed to go with 500 men and hide in two valleys to the east of Ho-chung. There he was to remain until half the enemy had passed when he was to make an onslaught on their rear. Simultaneously Shih T'ien-ying would launch an attack in front and so take Hou Hsiao-shu from two sides. Unfortunately on the fateful night the subordinate became drunk and the Chin were allowed to pass without interference. Arrived at the city, Hou Hsiao-shu surprised an unguarded section of the walls, carried the place by escalade and set the towers on the battlements ablaze. It was the flames from these that first warned Shih T'ien-ying of what had happened. Rushing into the streets with no more than forty men, he vainly attempted to expel the enemy, but his officers, seeing that it was hopeless, begged him to fly. Shih T'ien-ying, however, refused, and having drunk his own blood, fought furiously until overwhelmed and killed the following day. Master of the place, Hou Hsiao-shu sent troops to burn the bridge at Ta-ch'ing Kuan, while the rest of his men plundered Ho-chung. Tidings of the disaster were immediately brought to P'ing-yang from which Anchar Noyan made so speedy a counter attack that Hou Hsiao-shu was almost taken unawares. Knowing his troops too few to hold the place, he wasted no time in resistance, but retreated back to the Chung-t'iao hills which he only regained after considerable losses.

The news of Shih T'ien-ying's death was brought to Mukhali by the former's nephew who had managed to escape. Its only immediate effect was an order to Shih Wa-k'e, the dead commander's son, to go and rebuild the destroyed bridge and to assume command of his father's troops.[74] Afterward, as seen,

[74] For the death of Shih T'ien-ying and the loss and recovery of Ho-chung Fu;

Hsi Hsia also learned of the catastrophe, and withdrawing, obliged Mukhali to raise the investment of Feng-hsiang.

Before the end of March, Mukhali reached Ta-ch'ing Kuan but found that Shih Wa-k'e had not yet finished his work, so to fill in the time he besieged and took several forts in the vicinity. While thus occupied he was rejoined by Mongkha Bukha, who had successfully accomplished his mission south of the Ts'in-ling Mountains and taken and plundered Feng Chou.

Soon after the beginning of April (1223) the bridge was restored and Mukhali crossed the Yellow River and marched to Wen-hsi, about twenty miles to the south of Chiang Chou (Chin-an.) Neither his biography nor any other source offers an explanation for this move, but in view of the subsequent Chin invasion of southern Shansi, he had probably learned that his failure at Ching-chao (Hsi-an) and Feng-hsiang had emboldened the Chin to plan a limited counter offensive over the Yellow River. Further, reports must long since have reached him that in Oct., 1222, the Sung had willfully begun hostilities and overrun east Shantung. But he was not destined to deal with either threat. That same April he became seriously ill, and realizing that his end was at hand, called before him his brother Taisun—his son Boru was absent in the west making a report to Chingis Khan—and spoke as follows: " For nearly forty years I have waged war for the Khan, and east and west I have vanquished his enemies that he might bring to completion his great work. But Pien Ching (K'ai-feng) still remains untaken. This I greatly regret, so see to it that you do your best to take it." Having uttered these words, he died at the age of fifty-four, and so expired the greatest of the Mongol conqueror's captains.[75]

An adherant of Chingis Khan since 1190, or even earlier, Mukhali outshone any other general in the Mongol army. Not only had he participated earlier in Chingis's rise to power than such famous commanders as Jebe and Subudei, but he had been

see the *Meng-wu-erh Shih*, main text and biographies of " Mukhali " and " Shih T'ien-ying."

[75] *Meng-wu-erh Shih*, biography of " Mukhali."

entrusted with greater responsibilities. Jebe had distinguished himself against the Chin in 1211, 1212 and 1213 and had overthrown Kuchluk during 1218, while Subudei had later participated with him in that amazing expedition from 1220-1222, which took 25,000 cavalry through Iran, Georgia, southeast Russia, Greater Bulgaria and back to Turkistan, but none of these feats of arms equalled those of Mukhali. In opposing the Chin, first in Manchuria and then in the provinces of northern China, ravaged though these were, the Jalair general was up against far greater and better organized resistance than was ever pitted against Jebe or Subudei. True the last days of Mukhali were marred by his unsuccessful attempt to reduce Ching-chao and Feng-hsiang, but by that time, not only were his own forces becoming spread thin—hence the demand for Tangut aid—but the Chin, with their much shortened lines of communication, were able to strengthen greatly their hold on the towns and cities remaining to them. Had Jebe—(dead since the end of 1222) [76]—lived he might have surpassed any Mongol general of which we have a record, including the brilliant Samukha, but he died at the early age of forty-two or forty-three. Although Subudei (1176-1248), celebrated for victories from the Yellow River to the Danube, usually shares with Chingis the reputation of having been the foremost soldier produced by the Mongols, it should be remembered, that when he marched with Ugedei (1229-41) to make an end of the Chin, the troops and material at his disposal exceeded those of Mukhali, while in Europe his victories were won over armies decidedly inferior to his own in discipline, equipment, tactics and leadership. Hence, though Subudei did eventually surpass the Jalair, during the lifetime of Chingis Khan it was Mukhali who held first place among the Mongol generals.

As might have been predicted, the death of the great soldier had immediate repercussions. In May the Chin crossed the

[76] The Moslem historian Ibn al Athir reports that when Jebe and Subudei attacked the Bulghars of the Kama toward the end of 1222 they suffered heavily in an ambuscade. It seems that in this Jebe may have been slain or at least suffered wounds that soon after caused his death. See " Bulghar," *Encyclopaedia of Islam*, Vol. I, p. 790.

Yellow River and invaded southern Shansi where Ho-chung
and four other places were retaken.[77] Later in the year all were
recovered, and Shih T'ien-hsiang was put in command of Ho-
chung. But in September, 1224, the Chin, encouraged by the
Mongol struggle with the Sung, again raided over the river,[78]
and two years later, also during September, they made still
another appearance and re-entered Ch'ü-wo, Chiang Chou and
Ho-chung. This time their conquest was more enduring, but
though it lasted until 1231, extended no further north than
the final reaches of the Fen River. Even so it served to take
the first impact of the final Mongol onslaught.

Seven months after Mukhali's death, i. e., during November,
1223, Utubu or Hsüan Tsung (1213-23), who had come to the
Chin throne in the stormy days of 1213, also died and was
succeeded by Nikasa or Ai Tsung (1224-34). The first act of
the new monarch was to call a halt to the conflict with the Sung,
and in April, 1224 he sent south a peace embassy.

One of the least known wars of the Mongols is their first
contest with the southern empire. As seen, relations between
the two were at first friendly and even the establishment of
Sung authority in Shantung and southern Hopei during 1219
caused no outward hostility. Both regions had been invaded
and half conquered by Mukhali during 1217, but due to miscal-
culation on his part had early in 1218 again fallen to the Chin,
from whom the southerners had wrested them. In the eyes
of the Sung the recovery of any territory from the Chin was a
perfectly legitimate restoration of their authority in country
once belonging to them. Irritated though Mukhali must have
been at this turn of events, he seemingly accepted it. One reason
for this was that his forces were sufficient for no more than
one war at a time, another that he was well aware that Sung
success was largely due to the treachery of Yen Shih and Chang
Lin. Since these men had betrayed the Chin, they could also
be expected to betray the Sung, and so it proved. First Yen

---

[77] These were Jung Chou taken in May, and Huo Chou, Hung-T'ung and Fen-hsi
in June.
[78] On this occasion they temporarily reoccupied Tse Chou and Lu-an.

Shih and then Chang Lin went over to Mukhali. A bitter disappointment to the Sung, there was little that they could do at the time for already they had sent Kou Meng-yü on an embassy to the Mongols for the purpose of seeking an alliance. But reports of Chingis Khan's vast commitments in the west evidently made them decide to risk hostilities. Even so, they waited until Mukhali was involved both in the conquest of Shensi and the suppression of a revolt in Shansi.

In October, 1222, they struck, probably from Huai-an, and by the end of the year the general P'eng I-pin had driven Chang Lin from nearly every town and city in eastern Shantung. Early in January the next year (1223), I-tu fell to Li Ch'üan and the Chin renegade found his authority confined to Ti Chou and Pin Chou in Shantung and Ts'ang Chou in Ho-pei.[79] The Sung now turned west and during April P'eng I-pin made a sudden descent on Tung-p'ing which he compelled to capitulate through lack of supplies. With the town there surrendered Yen Shih who once more changed his colors and went back to the Sung. This time, however, it would seem that he had every intention of returning to the Mongols when an opportunity should arise.[80] Encouraged by his easy triumph at Tung-p'ing, P'eng I-pin next turned on Chi-nan and Ta-ming Fu, both of which fell and so added western Shantung and part of Hopei to the conquests of the previous year.[81] The Sung emperor, deceived by these victories, threw all caution to the winds and during the summer of 1224 ordered P'eng I-pin to march north for the conquest of the whole of Hopei.[82] The only explanation for such folly is that those directing the central government were very ill informed concerning the terrifying military power of the Mongols.

[79] *Meng-wu-erh Shih*, main text and biography of " Yen Shih."
[80] Biography of " Yen Shih." The date of the fall of Tung P'ing to P'eng I-pin is very uncertain.
[81] *Meng-wu-erh Shih*, main text and biography of " Shih T'ien-ni," also *Yüan Shih Hsin Pien*.
[82] T'u Chi, author of the *Meng-wu-erh Shih*, says that toward the end of 1223 the Sung sent Kou Meng-yü on a second embassy to the Mongols, but beyond this bare statement nothing is said.

Soon after receiving his new instructions, P'eng I-pin began operations, but on reaching En Chou was defeated by Shih T'ien-ni. His reverse cannot have been severe, for if he retired to Ta-ming, so did Shih T'ien-ni to Chen-ting. For nearly a year he made no further move. In the meantime the victor was murdered.

Early in 1225, learning that two garrisons of Wu Hsien's troops had mutinied, Shih T'ien-ni wiped them out. Enraged at this, Wu Hsien resolved to kill his superior and during March invited him to a banquet at which he had him done to death. He then headed a revolt in which he was joined by the commander of Chung-shan.

Our sources differ as to the real cause behind the rebellion. The biography of Boru says that it was his absence in the north to greet Chingis Khan that encouraged Wu-Hsien.[83] The latter's own biography says that the Chin had urged him to the step, and in this connection it is well to remember the Chin raid into Shansi the year before. Also Shih T'ien-ni and Yen Shih had early in 1223 been repulsed in an attempt to take a certain town in the southwest corner of Hopei, which, like other places immediately north of the Yellow River, was still held by the Chin.[84] But whatever the reason, several towns threw in their lot with Wu Hsien and for a moment it looked as if western Hopei might shake off the Mongol yoke. Fortunately for their cause, T'ien-tse, a younger brother of T'ien-ni, was away at Chung Tu and so escaped the hand of the assassin.

T'ien-tse is one of the outstanding figures of Mongol military history. Then twenty years of age and only captain of T'ien-ni's body-guard, he was one day to share with the great Bayan supreme command of all the Mongol armies in China. As remarkable for physique as for ability, he is said to have stood six feet six inches in height and to have possessed a voice like a great bell,[85] while so prodigious was his strength that no man in

[83] In July, 1224, Boru returned from visiting Chingis Khan and took over his father's command. He then made an expedition against the Tanguts and paid a second visit to the conqueror on the Tola during the spring of 1225.

[84] The town attacked was Ho-wei near the foot of the T'ai-hang Mountains.

[85] The *Meng-wu-erh Shih*, biography of "Shih Tien-tse," says that he was eight

the army equalled him, and his skill as an archer and horseman were proverbial. Hearing of his brother's death, he immediately obtained help from the Mongols and with 3,000 of their cavalry,[86] 700 troops of his own and 1,000 from Chang Jo, advanced on Chung-shan. There he defeated Ke T'ieh-ch'iang, took the town, and after vanquishing Wu Hsien himself, re-entered Chen-ting either in the last days of April or the first days of May.

By this time the Sung Emperor Ning Tsung (1194-1225) had died and had been succeeded by Li Tsung (1224-65), but there was no change in the empire's policy. Consequently, P'eng I-pin, observing Wu Hsien's predicament, got in touch with him and entered into an alliance for the recovery of Chen-ting. He then advanced from Ta-ming Fu, not only it seems to help Wu Hsien but also to make another attempt to conquer Hopei. Hence Yen Shih was called upon to assist, and reinforced by some of P'eng I-pin's own troops, moved north by another route. But he had not proceeded far when he again declared for the Mongols and marched to join them.[87] Undaunted, the Sung general continued towards Chen-ting and in July at Tsan-huang near the Wu-ma hills, some thirty-five miles to the south of the city, he and Wu Hsien gave battle to Shih T'ien-tse. Though almost certainly superior in numbers to the enemy, P'eng I-pin had fewer cavalry so, to prevent being taken by a sudden attack in the rear, he set fire to the slopes of the Wu-ma hills. Despite this, a body of archers got on to the burning mountain, and taken in the front and rear, Wu Hsien and the Sung general sustained a crushing defeat, the former escaping from the field with difficulty and P'eng I-pin being taken and slain on his refusal to prostrate himself before T'ien-tse.[88]

feet in height, which, assuming the Chinese foot of that day to have been approximately ten inches, is about six feet, six inches.

[86] The biography of " T'ien-tse " says that he applied to Boru for assistance, but as the Mongol was away on the Tola, it must have been from the commander of Chung Tu—Shih-mo Hsien-te-pu—that he sought and obtained help.

[87] " Meng-wu-erh Shih," biography of " Yen Shih."

[88] The " *Meng-wu-erh Shih*," biography of " Yen Shih," and the " *Li-tai T'ung-chien Chi-lan*," both speak of the execution of P'eng I-pin, but the " *Sung Shih* " says that he committed suicide.

The field army of the Sung destroyed, the Mongols went over to the offensive and Taisun, Anchar Noyan, Liu Ho-ma, the son of Liu Po-lin and Chang Jo, dividing their forces, recovered all of Hopei and western Shantung.[89] Even the peninsula seems to have been invaded and I-tu Fu was perhaps reoccupied by Chang Lin, but the Sung still had many troops in eastern Shantung and during April the following year (1226) Li Ch'uan retook I-tu.

In the meantime Shih T'ien-tse, perhaps organizing for an attack on Wu Hsien and the places still adhering to him, suddenly lost Chen-ting to his enemy, who took the city by surprise during a dark November night. With barely time to save themselves, T'ien-tse and his staff managed to escape over the walls and fly to Kao Ch'eng. Smarting under this disgrace, T'ien-tse collected a few hundred men, and joined by the same Mongol commander who had helped him retake Chen-ting earlier in the year, quickly reappeared beneath its walls. Seeing the smallness of his force, Wu Hsien sallied forth but as on the former occasion was defeated and, unable to re-enter the city, fled to Pao-t'ou Chai in the mountains to the west. The city at the mercy of the victors, the Mongol general [90] drove 10,000 of the inhabitants outside and wished to put them to the sword, but T'ien-tse, insisting that the unfortunate people were innocent of any crime, saved their lives. He now made no further delay and attacked Pao T'ou Chai, from which Wu Hsien fled to K'ai-feng, and reduced every other place still resisting the Mongols in western Hopei.[91]

Master of all Hopei and nearly every place in western Shantung, Taisun, still deputizing for Boru, began the reconquest of the eastern part of the province and marched with Chang Jo to besiege I-tu Fu. As reiterated in these pages, the Mongols

[89] The *Meng-wu-erh Shih,* biographies of " Chang Jo," " Yen Shih " and " Liu Ho-ma," mention the towns of Po Chou, P'u Chou, Ta-ming, Chang-te, Chi-nan, T'ai-an and Tung-p'ing.

[90] The biography of " Boru " calls the Mongol soldier K'e-lieh-yi-sa-han, that of Shih, T'ien-tse, Hsiao-na-t'ai.

[91] The only places that I have been able to identify are Wei-hui on the Wei River, Wei to the north of it, and Hsiang to the south of Chang-te.

usually started a campaign by the reduction of the smaller places in the invaded country. This time they adopted the opposite course. In I-tu was Li Ch'üan, and knowing that with his overthrow remaining Sung authority in Shantung would collapse, Taisun staked all on forcing his early submission. Hence in October, 1226, he approached the city and began the siege. Whether or not Li Ch'üan expected to be relieved, we do not know, but he put up an historic defense and in January, 1227, when Boru and Uyer arrived with additional troops, he was still bravely resisting. Taking command of the whole investing force, Boru first entered into negotiations with Li Ch'üan and tried to persuade him to capitulate. Had it been left to the Sung general, the city would have surrendered, but his officers refused, and to clinch the matter slew the Mongol envoy. By April the supplies of the beleaguered were becoming extremely low and Li Ch'üan resolved to try to raise the siege. Throwing open the gates, he charged the enemy and forced them to retire to the Tzu River, fifteen to seventeen miles to the northwest, where Boru turned and gave battle—more than likely he had purposely retired so as to deprive Li Ch'üan of the shelter of I-tu—and inflicted a heavy defeat upon the Sung army, 7,000 men falling on the field and many others being drowned in the river. Li Ch'üan, however, escaped back to the city where the siege was resumed. In May the people were starving and cannibalism broke out, so Li Ch'üan, having no alternative, sent to inform Boru that he would surrender and give up I-tu.

Seeing the famous Sung general in their hands, the Mongol officers wished to put him to death as he had cost them many lives. But Boru, knowing that Li Ch'üan, besides being an able soldier, had also proved a skillful administrator and was very popular in Shantung, refused on the score that his death would prolong resistance in the province. However, importuned by his officers, he sent to Chingis Khan, then in eastern Kansu, to learn his opinion. Answer came back that he might do whatever he thought fit, so notwithstanding the prognostications of his associates, who prophesied that Li

Ch'üan would one day revolt, he appointed him commander of both Shantung and Huai-nan—the latter not yet conquered—and soon received the submission of nearly every place still untaken in Shantung.[92]

One town only still held out, namely, T'eng Chou to the east of the Wei-san Hu. The summer already being far advanced, and so the weather very hot, several of Boru's officers wished to postpone its capture. Learning of this, he called them before him: " I have never heard," he expostulated, " that while in the west Chingis Khan deferred an expedition because of the heat; how can we his subjects remain inactive? " Shamed by these words, they immediately took the field, and after repulsing a sortie by the commander of T'eng Chou, who lost 3,000 men, received the surrender of the town.[93] In August, perhaps about the same time, Chang Lin crossed the Yellow River and attacked Huai-an. Being at the northern end of the Grand Canal as it then existed,[94] the place had been the base of Sung operations and there Li Ch'üan's brother was slain. During December the same year, however, Chang Lin was murdered by one of his own subordinates and his head sent to Li Ch'üan.[95]

Thus closed the last act in the conquest of Hopei and Shantung. Since the opening scene, many had passed from the stage; Shih-mo Ming-an, Mukhali, Meng Ku-kang, Shih T'ien-ni, P'eng I-pin, and Chang Lin. But Yen Shih remained—restored to his old position—and also Chang Jo, while Li Ch'üan had succeeded to Chang Lin, and Shih T'ien-tse to T'ien-ni. One other figure was soon to go; namely Boru. His work completed,

[92] Later after the death of both Boru and Chingis Khan, Li Ch'üan did rebel, but he was deefeated and driven to Yang Chou, where he died. For the overthrow of Li Ch'üan at I-tu; see the *Meng-wu-erh Shih*, biography of " Boru."
[93] Biography of " Boru "; see the *Meng-wu-erh Shih*.
[94] During Sui (581-618) and T'ang (618-907) times the grand canal had extended north of the Yellow River all the way to the Yung-ting Ho, though its course was west of that later taken by the Yüan (1260-1368) canal. With the loss of the northern provinces, however, the Sung (960-1279) deliberately destroyed the reaches lying beyond the Huang Ho so as to deny them to the Chin. For information on the subject, as well as to the great importance of Huai-an; see Chi Ch'ao-ting, *Key Economic Areas in Chinese History*, p. 140 and pp. 106-107.
[95] *Li-tai T'ung-chien Chi-lan*.

he went north in November to pay his respects to the remains of Chingis Khan, who had expired in August. The following year (1228) he returned to China but died somewhere in the vicinity of the Yen-men Kuan at the early age of thirty-two. A very able soldier, much more humane than most of his Mongol colleagues, a talented linguist and with considerable leanings toward Chinese culture, he was as much a loss to the Chinese as to the Mongols.[96]

With the desertion of Li Ch'üan, the Sung made no further efforts to re-establish themselves north of the Yellow River. Despite the foregoing conflict, both powers let the matter rest. Incredible as this may seem, it is partly to be explained by the fact that for the time being the Mongols were too busy in other directions, while the Sung temporarily regretted their ambitious policy. Nevertheless, the war had been the first round in a contest that was to break out anew and in earnest during 1234 and was to end in the ultimate destruction of the Sung.

The subjugation of southern Hopei and Shantung falls into two periods; the expulsion of the Chin by Mukhali and that of the Sung by Taisun and Boru. Since it was the latter that finally established Mongol authority in the country, one might be inclined to give them the credit for the conquest, but in reality it must be shared with Mukhali. If Taisun and Boru won the last battle, it was an easier battle than that fought by Mukhali. Notwithstanding the epic defense of I-tu by Li Chüan, the Sung soldier was not the equal of Meng Ku-kang, the defender of Tung-p'ing. Throughout the whole of Mukhali's conquest the standard of resistance was greater than that encountered by his son and brother, and the army vanquished at Huang-ling-kang more powerful than any force that the Sung ever sent over the Yellow River. Also, only when Mukhali was engaged in the west did the Sung dare make their second appearance. To the people of the two provinces, torn by nearly thirteen years of war, the permanent establishment of even Mongol authority must have seemed almost a blessing and not until 1260 was there a serious insurrection.

[96] For Boru's attainments; see the *Meng-wu-erh Shih,* biography of " Boru."

# Chapter X

# THE DESTRUCTION OF HSI HSIA AND THE DEATH OF CHINGIS KHAN

WHEN WE LAST left Chingis Khan the year was 1219 and he was in full march for the Khorezmian empire. Since then he had utterly crushed the Khwarazm Shah, the sword arm of eastern Islam, and overrun his vast dominions from east to west and north to south. Of these he permanently occupied Transoxiana, Khwarazm and a large part of Khurasan, but left the final subjugation of the others for a later day. In 1223, he began his return homeward, and spending the summer on the Kulan Bashi steppes—i. e. the plains to the north of the Alexander Mountains—the spring of 1224 along the Imil,[1] and the summer of the same year on the Khara Irtish, he reached the Tola during February, 1225. There he was greeted by Boru, the son of Mukhali and Yao-li Shih, the widow of the Khitan Yeh-lü Liu-ke. After the death of her husband in 1220 this remarkable woman had been appointed by Temuge Ochigin to carry on the Khitan government and, having acquited herself to the admiration of all, now came to beg that Hsieh-she be allowed to return home and succeed to Liu-ke. With her she brought her sons Shan-ke, T'ieh-ke and Yung-an, her stepson, T'a-t'a-erh, and her grandson Shou-kuo-nu.[2]

---

[1] While on the Imil the conqueror is reported to have been met by his grandsons Kubilai and Kulagu, the children of Tului.
(Howorth, *History of the Mongols*, part 1, p. 92.)

[2] In an article written for the Royal Asiatic Society—See *J. R. A. S.*, parts 3 and 4, 1942—I dated this visit early in 1226, when Chingis Khan was in the Nan Shan supervising the sieges of Su Chou and Kan Chou. Then I was following Feng Ch'eng-chun, author of *Ch'eng-chi-ssŭ Han*. De Mailla, *Histoire Générale de la Chine*, probably drawing on the *T'ung-chien Kang-mu*, dated the visit during December, 1226, when the conqueror was at Yen-ch'uan Chow. However, since there was no reason why the Khitan princess should not have greeted Chingis on

On seeing her before him, Chingis Khan expressed his astonishment; "Not even the swift flying sparrow hawk has yet arrived but you a woman have come!"[3] "Liu-ke is dead, replied Yao-li Shih, " and there is no ruler in the land. Hsieh-she, his eldest son, has been with you for many years—[1216-25]—but I hope now that Shan-ke, the second son, may take his place and that Hsieh-she may return home and assume his father's throne." "Hsieh-she," said Chingis Khan, "has been a Mongol for a long time. When he followed me to the west the Moslems one day surrounded my first born (Prince Juchi) at Kimach, but Hsieh-she took 1,000 men and brought him out in safety, though he himself was wounded by a lance.[4] Again at Bokhara and Samarkand, when my men were engaged in hand-to-hand fighting, he was struck by an arrow. Because he has repeatedly rendered such services, he has been made a baatur (a brave), so I cannot part with him, but must let Shan-ke succeed in his stead."

When Yao-li Shih heard these words, she wept. "Hsieh-she," she lamented, "was born of Liu-ke's first wife, so it is he who should be ruler. Shan-ke is my son. If you command that he take the throne it will seem to favor me and will be in contempt of family precedent. Therefore it will be wrong." Struck with admiration at her generosity, Chingis Khan bestowed upon her many presents, and requesting her to accompany him on the impending war with the Tanguts, promised that Hsieh-she should succeed to Liu-ke. However, Yao-li Shih obtained permission to depart, and going home with Yung-an, left her other sons in the Mongol camp.

the Tola in 1225, and as either of the other rendezvous would have entailed an unnecessarily arduous journey, I have since accepted the version of Gaubil, who relied on the *Yüan Shih Lei Pien*, and dated the visit during the spring of 1225.

[3] Feng Ch'eng-chün, who locates the meeting in the mountains of the Nan Shan, makes Chingis Khan say: "A strong eagle cannot fly hither, but you a woman have come!" It is from De Mailla that the parallel to the swift flying sparrow hawk is drawn. Gaubil quotes no dialogue, but simply records the meeting on the Tola.

[4] This incident really occurred in 1216, during the expedition of Juchi, Subudei and Tokuchar against the Mergids, when the Mongols were attacked by the Khwarazm Shah.

Before proceeding to the conqueror's final war with Hsi Hsia it is necessary to turn back two or three years.

After the withdrawal of the Tangut army from before Feng-hsiang in 1223, the Mongols were for several months too much occupied with the Chin to be able to revenge themselves on their faithless ally, but by November order was restored in Shansi and a punitive expedition was undertaken by Shih T'ien-hsiang. Marching west, perhaps from Ho-chung Fu, and presumably through eastern Shansi and the Southern Odos, he reached the Yellow River unopposed. There siege was laid to Chi-shih Chou, but the army had been in front of the town no more than ten days when it was learned that the Chin were threatening its rear. This forced a retreat, and although the invaders regained Mongol territory in safety, Shih T'ien-hsiang was severely wounded in the head by an arrow during a night attack.[5]

Despite this second Mongol failure, Li-Tsun-hsiang (1211-23) abdicated and was succeeded by his son Li Te Wang (1223-26). Supposedly to gain time the new king pretended to repent his predecessor's break with the Mongols and in January, 1224, sent an army to attack the Chin at Lan Chou. But at Chih-ku Pao, a fort covering the town, it was defeated.

Li Te Wang soon revealed his true colors, and in March stirred up the Shara Uighurs and other vassal tribes of western Hsi Hsia to make an attack on the Mongols.[6] With Chingis

---

[5] Regarding this expedition, the *Meng-wu-erh Shih* simply says that in the 10th month of the K'uei-wei year (26th Oct.-23rd Nov., 1223), Shih T'ien-hsiang attacked Hsi Hsia, but the general's biography in the same work specifies the region as the Ho-lan Shan (Ala Shan). Since this range is on the western side of the Yellow River, it is not likely that he got there. Further, since the *Hsi Hsia Shu Shih* declares that the Mongols attacked Chi-shih during November, 1223, it seems reasonable to identify the expedition with that led by Shih T'ien-hsiang.

[6] The "Hsi Hsia Shu Shih" states that Li Te Wang applied to "the tribes north of the sands" for help against Chingis Khan, who was then still in Hsiyü (the West). From the Chinese text this could mean either that the tribes in question actually dwelt north of the sands—presumably the Taklamakan and adjoining desert to the east—or were known by that name because of having come thence in days gone by. At this time all the country in question was in the hands of the Mongols, so the reference must be to the Sa-li Wei-wu-erh (Shara Uighurs), who still dwelt in west Kansu, and also it would seem along the Hei-shui River (Etsingol). Living in the same region with them were two tribes

Khan still on the way back from the west and other forces tied down in China, the troops remaining in Mongolia can not have been numerous. Therefore Li Te Wang probably instructed these tribes to make a raid northward from the Etsin Gol. How far this was successful is unknown, but in May or June the raiders were driven back, for a Mongol army made a counter inroad and invested Sha Chou.[7] At the end of a month so little damage had been done to the walls that the Mongol commander ordered a mine to be dug under them. The defenders, however, countermined and burned out the attackers. Chingis Khan, who was by then camped on the Khara Irtish, was informed of the progress of the siege and told that the reduction of the place promised to take a considerable time. Evidently feeling that the Tanguts might be encouraged to make a second incursion elsewhere, he directed Boru to undertake a diversionary attack on Yin Chou, a town in the most easterly part of Hsi Hsia. So in September the young general— he was not more than twenty-eight—marched forth accompanied by Monka Bukha, Uyer and Liu Ho-ma, and approaching the town, encountered a powerful army under Taga Ganbo, his father's old ally. The ensuing action was disastrous for the Tanguts; Taga Ganbo was captured, great numbers of his men slain and many thousand head of livestock swept off. The advance was then continued to Yin Chou, which was taken. Boru himself remained there only a few days, but Monka Bukha was left to hold all strategically important points in the region.

Alarmed by this reverse, Li Te Wang sued for an armistice. Since he was not yet ready to settle accounts with Hsi Hsia,

whom the Chinese called the T'e-lo and Ch'ih-min. Both were perhaps once vassals of the Uighurs and like them were incorporated into the Tangut realm by Chao Yüan-hao (1032-48) prior to his accession. The name, "tribes north of the sands," was probably used to differentiate the Uighurs, T'e-lo and Ch'ih-min, all originally from the north, from the Tangut and Tibetan tribes of the mountains to the south (Nan Shan).

The T'e-lo are almost certainly to be identified with a branch of the T'ieh-lo, a powerful tribe dwelling north of the T'ien Shan in T'ang times; See Bingham, The Fall of The Sui and The Rise of The T'ang, p. 28, n. 39.

[7] The Hsi Hsia Shu Shih has mistakenly made Chingis Khan the leader of the expedition.

Chingis Khan agreed to make peace on condition that one of the king's sons be sent to him as a hostage. The siege of Sha Chou, where supplies were almost exhausted, was then raised and in December the Mongols returned to the north.

It is unlikely that Li Te Wang intended to keep his promise, for as early as November (1224) he had been secretly negotiting with the Chin for an alliance against the Mongols.[8]

As related, Chingis Khan reached the Tola in February, 1225, and there he pitched camp for the summer and awaited Li Te Wang's son. By April no hostage had appeared, so an envoy was sent to Chung-hsiang to demand an explanation. On his arrival Li Te Wang took counsel with his ministers as to what he should do. Feeling that Hsi Hsia could not risk war with a people who had vanquished the Chin, many were for peace, but others were for war and it was they who carried the day. The Mongol envoy was sent back to inform Chingis Khan that no hostage would be given.

The Tanguts at once began preparations. Conscription was declared, fortifications were strengthened, and the troops scattered in 1224 reassembled. Further, Li Te Wang was urged to do all he could to obtain the active assistance of the Chin. Co-operation on their mutual border was to be facilitated by a system of fire signals. So negotiations were pressed forward and in October (1225) a secret treaty was signed and was made public in November. Without doubt it was this, and the Mongol-Sung clash in Shantung, that emboldened the Tanguts to persist in their hostile attitude.

The king's refusal to send his son did not surprise the conqueror and as soon as his envoy returned from Chunghsing, he knew that the time had come to finish with Hsi Hsia. Then, or very shortly afterward, he also learned of the negotiations in progress between Li Te Wang and the Chin emperor. This meant that he would have the latter to deal with in the west as well as in the east, and though the Chin were now much reduced their aid, if they were allowed time to organize on a

[8] See the *Chin Shih*.

large scale, would greatly add to the difficulties of the conquest. It was therefore imperative to strike hard and fast. This time his plan of campaign would be to attack the center of Tangut power only when the supporting regions to the west had succumbed.

A great army was mobilized, according to the " Hsi Hsia Shu Shih " 100,000 men, and by autumn was ready for the field.[9] War was then formally declared on the grounds that Li Te Wang had failed to send his son as a hostage and because his predecessor had refused to help in the invasion of the Khorezmian empire.

Before the beginning of November the army was on the march. With Chingis went his two sons Ugedei and Tului, one of his wives, Yesui, his old and faithful friend Bugurji, Subudei the most brilliant of his surviving generals, and the great Khitan minister Yeh-lü Ch'u-ts'ai. At home to govern in his absence, he left his son Jaghatai, while in the far west Juchi remained north of the Aral Sea, where he died during February, 1227.[10]

In many respects the ensuing war was the most dramatic in Mongol history. Not only did it end in the destruction of the Tangut Kingdom but it saw the death of the great conqueror. Little known to Moslem or European historians, the conquest

[9] One hundred thousand is doubtless a round figure, and 70,000 or 80,000 would be nearer the truth. The *Yüan Sheng Wu Ch'in Cheng Lu* says that Chingis Khan took his whole army, which is of course an exaggeration. Pétis de La Croix, quoting Rashid ad-Din,—See *Histoire du Grand Genghiz-can Premier Empereur des Anciens Mogols*, p. 370—states that the invading force numbered one hundred and seventy thousand. This he divides as follows; forty thousand men under Jaghatai, thirty thousand under Jebe and Subudei, twenty thousand Khorezmians under Ilenku (Aljigidei), twenty thousand Indians under Bala, thirty thousand Jetes and Kipchaks under Badr ad-Din and thirty thousand more Khorezmians under the command of Danishmand, while twenty thousand men were left behind with Ugedei to guard Mongolia. How unreliable is the above information can be gauged by two facts alone. Jebe had been dead since 1222 and it was Jaghatai, not Ugedei, who was left in Mongolia.

[10] See Barthold, *Turkestan Down to the Mongol Invasion*, p. 458. Earlier this same year (1225) Chingis gave his daughter Alaghi Beki to the Ongud prince Po-yao-ho, now aged seventeen and recently back from the west, and sent them to take over the government of the Onguds. (See Grousset, *L'Empire Mongol* (1ʳᵉ phase), *Histoire du Monde*, Tome VIII, p. 212.)

of Hsi Hsia is better known to the Mongols than any other of
Chingis Khan's exploits. Around it the " Sanang Setsen " has
woven an atmosphere of sombre grandeur. The Mongols still
call many of the cities of Kansu and Ninghsia by the names
under which their ancestors knew them, and speak of the Yellow River as the Khatun Gol (River of the Queen), in memory
of the suicide of the Tangut queen Gurbeljin Goa, whom they
believe to have murdered Chingis Khan.

Moving from the Tola, Chingis advanced to the Ongin Gol,
and in November stopped to stage a hunt in the neighbourhood
of Aburkha close to the upper reaches of the river.[11] During
this a wild ass frightened his mount and he was thrown heavily
to the ground. So badly did the fall injure him that camp
had to be made on the spot at Cho'orkhat.[12] The next day
Yesui informed the princes and chief officers that the Khan
was still in great pain. Thereupon Tolun Cherbi, always a
favorite with the conqueror, advocated that the army retire
and return later when Chingis was well. " The Tanguts," he
declared, " are a sedentary people and cannot trek away. We
will now return home, and when the Khaghan is better we will
come again." All agreed except Chingis Khan. " If we go,"
said he " the Tanguts will certainly think I was afraid of them.
I will be cured here. Let us send a message and see what
answer they give us." So an envoy was sent to Li Te Wang
and spoke to him as follows: " You began by promising to be
my right hand, but when I went against the Moslems, you
refused to go with me and added insult to disobedience. Now
after having conquered the Moslems, I demand satisfaction of
you."

On hearing these words, Li Te Wang denied that he had

[11] Grenard—See his *Gengis Khan*—believes that Aburkha was located between
the sources of the Tui and Ongin rivers. This is quite likely, for Chingis Khan's
most logical line of march would take him from the Tola to the Ongin. Then, as
now, there was a well used route between these two rivers, and on reaching the
latter, he probably held a hunt on its upper reaches. (See the *British General Staff
Map of Asia*, sheet 22 on Mongolia, published 1931; also A. Herrmann, *Atlas of
China*, published at the Harvard University Press in 1936.)

[12] The *Yüan Ch'ao Pi Shih* is the source for this incident, as well as for the subsequent embassy to the Tangut King.

used offensive language, but before he could say more Asha
Ganbo interposed and claimed full responsibility for all that had
gone before. " Tell your master," he said to the messenger,
" that at Ho-lan Shan (Ala Shan) we have felt tents and
camels and that there he will find us ready to give battle.
Moreover, if he desires gold, silver and silks, let him seek them
at Hsi-liang and Chung-hsing." When this reply was brought
to Chingis Khan, he exclaimed: " Is it possible to go back
now? I may die, but I will bring him to account; this I swear
by the Everlasting Sky! "

Most of the winter (1225-26) the army remained in camp,
but along the Tangut frontier a screen of scouts was stationed
to keep an eye on the enemy. The season being one of unusual
severity the men were provided with special sheep-skin coats,
and even their horses were wrapped in felt.[13]

In march, 1226, the storm broke. Resuming the advance,
the Mongols marched southward over the Gurban Saikhan Ula
and crossed the Hsi Hsia border into the present Etsin Gol
country.[14] Apprised of their approach, Li Te Wang ordered
the commander at Ch'in-ch'uan to destroy the bridge over the
Sha-chi River. Despite this, when Subudei and the advance
forces of the Mongols reached the place, the damage was repaired in a single night. Crossing the river the general made
for Hei-shui Ch'eng, the Etzina of Marco Polo, and near it
defeated a combined army of Shara Uighur, T'e-lo and Ch'ih-
min. The town was invested, and although it contained a
strong garrison of T'u-fan (Tibetan) soldiers, was taken with
great slaughter.[15]

Apparently Subudei crossed the eastern branch of the
Edsin Gol, but a large part of the army must have marched
south between the Gashun Nor (Chü-yen Hai) and Sokho
Nor to the main channel below.

[13] Rashid ad-Din; See Pétis de La Croix, *Histoire du Grand Genghiz-can Premier
Empereur des Anciens Mogols*, p. 370.
[14] In view of the rather poor grazing available in western Kansu, it is quite
likely that a portion of the army did not continue south until September when
Chingis Khan was ready to cross the Yellow River.
[15] *Meng-wu-erh Shih*, biography of " Subudei," also the *Hsi Hsia Shu Shih*.

About a month seems to have been spent resting along the river, and also one may suppose reducing any small towns in the neighborhood,[16] for it was not until May that the invaders appeared in the vicinity of Su Chou and Kan Chou. The

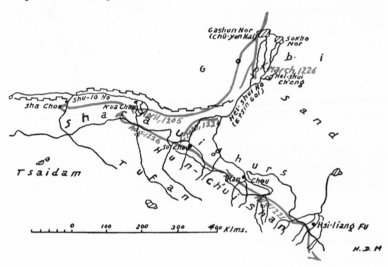

Mongol Campaigns in Western Hsi Hsia, 1205 and 1226

conqueror himself camped in the Hun-ch'ui Mountains, part of the Nan Shan close by, from where he could direct both operations and yet escape the heat of summer.[17] But his troops de-

[16] No reference is made to the recapture of the small places taken during the raid of 1205.

[17] The Hun-ch'ui Mountains are the range mentioned by the *Yüan Shih* as the site of Chingis Khan's summer camp in 1226. T'u Chi, author of the *Meng-wu-erh Shih*, says that the name is equivalent to Hsüeh Shan (Snowy Mountains), and locates the range south of Hsi-liang (Liang Chou). Wu Kuang-ch'eng, writer of the *Hsi Hsia Shu Shih*, says that the mountains were north of Su Chou, but this is a slip, as the only range to the north of the town is a barren elevation in the gobi known as the Hung-sha Ling. In the *Yüan Ch'ao Pi Shih* the range is called the Ch'a-shu-t'u, which T'u Chi says also means Snowy Mountains. Finally, the *Chung Kuo Ku-chin Ti-ming Ta-tzu-tien* informs us that the name Hsüeh Shan (Snowy Mountains) is sometimes applied to the present Ch'i-lien Mountains to the south of Su Chou. This is in agreement with A. Herrmann (*Atlas of China*, p. 52), who locates the Ch'i-lien Mountains to the south of both Su Chou and Kan Chou. Camped there, Chingis Khan could easily have supervized the siege of the two towns, so it is highly probable that the Hun-ch'ui Shan is to be identified with the Ch'i-lien Mountains of today.

vastated the surrounding country, which was also ravaged by drought and famine, and prepared for the siege of the two towns.

By June they were before Su Chou. Learning that it was well defended and determined to resist, Chingis Khan instructed [18] a Tangut in his service, who was younger brother to the city commander, to try to negotiate its capitulation. The attempt failed, and the Mongols were so enraged that when they captured the place in late June or early July, they slew nearly every living soul in it. Only 106 families, whose lives were begged by the Tangut officer, were spared. The Mongols now concentrated outside Kan Chou, where a somewhat similar incident occurred.

Many years before, so the story goes, the commander of Kan Chou, having no male heir, took a concubine. In due time she was on the point of giving birth to a child, when his wife, fearing for her position, secretly sent the woman away and married her to the chief herdsman. Soon afterwards the banished concubine bore a son who grew into a handsome youth of great strength. One day, while out herding, he fell in with Chingis Khan, who had taken the field to hunt. Impressed by the boy's speech and bearing, the conqueror adopted him and placed him in his wife's care. In reality he was made prisoner on the raid of 1205 and then presented to the conqueror.[19] Subsequently he came to command the picked thousand of the Guard (Keshik) and served with distinction in both east and west. By that time he had been given the Mongol name of Chaghan, under which we have seen him serve during the attack against the Chin in 1211.

It happened that in 1226 Chaghan's father was still in authority at Kan Chou, so Chingis called upon the young Tangut

[18] This was Hsi-li-chin-p'u or Hsi-li-chien. (See the *Hsi Hsia Chi.*) In the reign of Ugedei (1229-41) he accompanied the Mongol army sent to conquer Central Russia, and during 1239-40 led the troops that took the Alan capital in the Caucasus.

[19] The story of Chaghan's birth, capture and subsequent exploits is to be found in the *Hsi Hsia Chi* and in his biography in the *Yüan Shih.* It is from De Mailla, Vol. IX, that one learns he was taken on the raid of 1205.

to persuade him to surrender. Accordingly Chaghan shot an arrow over the walls with a message urging submission. This was brought to the commander who secretly communicated his willingness to negotiate. A Mongol representative was despatched to discuss terms, and all seemed on the point of being settled when the vice-commander learned what was afoot. Taking thirty-five officers with him, he surprised and slew his superior together with his younger son and the Mongol envoy. This done he declared that there would be no submission.

Furious at this second failure, Chingis Khan ordered that the siege be pressed, and a month later Kan Chou was carried by assault. The town at his mercy, he wished to put all the inhabitants to the sword, but Chaghan interceded and in the end only the vice-commander and his accomplices were slain.[20]

Master of the Kansu corridor, Chingis Khan detached one force to march west and reduce the valley of the Shu-lo River [21] and ordered another to move on Hsi-liang. The latter force arrived at the city during August and received its surrender from the elders.[22] Hsi-liang was probably the second city in Hsi Hsia and its failure to resist must have been a grievous blow to Li Te Wang. Not only was it the largest place on the east-west trade route running through Kansu, but it commanded the easiest access across the mountains into Tibet. After that, word came that several places in the Shu-lo valley had fallen, possibly Kua Chou was among them, but Sha Chou remained untaken until the next year. On arriving before the latter, the Mongol commander and a Tangut colleague were informed that it was willing to surrender, but on entering to receive its capitulation, fell into an ambuscade from which both escaped with difficulty.[23] But this was a minor success,

---

[20] The *Hsi Hsia Chi Shih Pen-mo* and the biography of " Cha-han " (Chaghan) say that Chingis Khan intended to bury the whole population alive.

[21] Some Chinese texts contain the two words, Shu-lo and Ho-lo, but instead of two places the words would seem to stand for the valley of the present Shu (Shuo)-lo (lai) Ho in far western Kansu.

[22] The Mongol commander was Nien-ho-chung-shan, an officer of the Guard (Keshik); See the *Hsi Hsia Shu Shih*.

[23] The Mongol commander was called Kudu Timur, the Tangut was Hsi-li-chin-p'u who had interceded at Su Chou.

and in the words of the "Hsi Hsia Shu Shih"; " Overcome by so
many disasters, Li Te Wang died and was succeeded by his
younger brother Li Hsien " (1226-27).[24]

Li Te Wang must have believed that Su Chou, Kan Chou
and Hsi-liang would hold up the Mongols for a considerable
time and weaken them sufficiently to make possible a future
victory in the east, for after the defeat of his army at Hei-shui
Ch'eng, there is no mention of any plans being made to send
a force west. As in the opening phase of the Khorezmian war,
the Mongols found the enemy putting his faith in strong walls
instead of offensive action. So, from one end of Kansu to the
other, they were able to concentrate at every point in greater
numbers than the Tanguts. Having a very powerful siege train,
they experienced no great difficulty in taking all places in their
path. Su Chou fell in four or five weeks and Kan Chou in
about two months, with the result that Hsi-liang surrendered
almost without a blow. Whatever losses the Mongols suffered
in these sieges the next months were to show that they were
far from crippling.

By September the hot weather had abated. Chingis Khan
therefore left the Hun-ch'ui Mountains and rejoined the army.
Marching from Hsi-liang along the foot of the Nan Shan, he
crossed the Sha T'ou—a belt of sand some ten miles wide—and
made for the Nine Fords of the Yellow River. Covering this
stood the town of Ying-li,[25] which made so obstinate a resistance that it was not until December that he was before Ling
Chou on the other side of the river.

Not a word is said about the route followed, but considering
the terrain, it is conceivable that after crossing the Nine Fords,
the invaders went up the Hsi River and over the mountains to
the Shan-shui River. Pursuing this river down to the plain,
they evidently circumvented Chi-shih Chou and advanced on
Ling Chou, known to the Mongols as Durmegei. The former,
though the first on their line of march, was surrounded by

[24] The *Hsin Yüan Shih* says that Li Hsien was the stepson of Li Te Wang.
[25] In the *Hsin Yüan Shih* the town of Ying-li is called Ying-ch'ang.

irrigation canals, so that it was dangerous to attack until the river was frozen.

Chingis Khan had penetrated to the political and economic heart of Hsi Hsia, and Li Hsien knew that a supreme effort must be made to stop him.

The Mongols had not besieged Ling Chou long when they heard that 100,000 men under Wei-ming Ling-kung were marching to its relief.[26] Chingis Khan did not wait for the enemy to arrive, but crossing the Yellow River won an overwhelming victory on the western side. "After such a reverse," he declared, "Li Hsien cannot recover." The army then returned to the city which soon succumbed.

It is here that one first learns of Yeh-lü Ch'u-ts'ai's presence with the army. Instead of participating in the sack, he was content with salvaging books and gathering medicinal herbs.

Ling Chou fell late in December, and while the conqueror himself moved east and captured Yen-ch'uan Chou, which was taken with great slaughter,[27] part of his troops took K'e-i Men where Wei-ming Ling Kung fell into their hands. Pressing through the pass, this time from the east, they made themselves masters of Wu-la-hai Ch'eng and took prisoner Li Te Jen, brother of the late Li Te Wang. Offered his life if he would do homage, he proudly refused and was executed.[28]

[26] One hundred thousand is the figure given for the army by the *Hsi Hsia Shu Shih*, the *Hsi Hsia Chi*, the *Hsi Hsia Chi Shih Pen-mo*, and by the biography of "Chaghan" in the *Yüan Shih*. Rashid ad-Din—See D'Ohsson, Vol. I, p. 373—says fifty tumens, i. e., 500,000 men, and that the host was under the personal command of the Tangut ruler. He further asserts that the battle was fought on the frozen flood plain of the Yellow River and cost the Tanguts 300,000 lives.

Doubtless 100,000 is no more than a round figure for a large army, but it is far more likely than Rashid ad-Din's estimate, which, like that for the Tangut casualties, is fantastic. As for the action having been fought on the frozen flood plain of the river, it was possible, but the Moslem historian is the only one to mention it.

[27] The *Hsi Hsia Shu Shih* dates Chingis Khan's march on Yen-ch'uan Chou for the twelfth month of the P'ing-wu year (December 21st, 1226, to January 18th, 1227), instead of for the eleventh month (November 21, 1226 to December 20th, 1226). However, during the earlier month, five constellations appeared together in the southwest, and the *Meng-wu-erh Shih* and other works say that this phenomenon was seen by the conqueror when at Yen-ch'uan Chou. Therefore it would seem that the eleventh month is correct.

[28] The *Hsi Hsia Shu Shih* implies that after the fall of Ling Chou, Chingis Khan

On capturing Yen-Ch'uan Chou, near which he pitched camp. Chingis Khan commanded his soldiers to exterminate the Tangut race.[29] Barely had he proclaimed this murderous edict than five constellations were seen together in the southwest and, warned that this was a bad omen, he immediately rescinded the order. Henceforth his troops, when assaulting towns, were to slay none but those in the front ranks (bearing arms) and were to abstain from indiscriminate looting.

The conqueror's order of extermination may also have extended to the Chinese subjects of the Tanguts. For certain of his officers, complaining of the dearth of grazing suffered by their cavalry during the summer, proposed that as the Chinese were unsuited to soldiering, all, subjects of Chin and Tangut alike, be wiped out and the country allowed to revert to prairie. We are ignorant of Chingis Khan's response to this proposition, but learn that as soon as Yeh-lü Ch'u-ts'ai was informed of the matter, he hurried to Chingis and vigorously opposed the terrible suggestion. "When your Majesty will conquer the south," he said " your armies will need supplies. If we establish a fair and equitable administration throughout the country, from land and commercial taxes, salt, wine, iron and the produce of mountain and marsh, we can annually obtain 500,000 ounces of silver, 80,000 bolts of silk, and more than 400,000 bushels of grain for the commissariat. How can it be said that the people are useless?"[30] Impressed with the

himself marched on Wu-la-hai Ch'eng, here mistakenly called Wu-na-la Ch'eng. But since the conqueror reached Yen-ch'uan Chou the same month—see above n. 27—the force must have been sent under one of his generals, perhaps A-lu-chu, who subsequently received orders to invest Chung-hsing.

The capture of K'e-i Men and of the commander Wei-ming Ling-kung is intimated by one work alone. From the *Yüan Ch'ao Pi Shih* one learns that Chingis Khan defeated Asha Ganbo at the Ho-lan Shan and that subsequently the general was made prisoner in a fortress of the range. The principal stronghold in the Ho-lan Shan was K'e-i Men, so after the defeat of his army on the western side of the river, Wei-ming Lung-kung, whom I believe to be the same as Asha Ganbo, might well have fled there.

[29] Only the *Yüan Ch'ao Pi Shih* and the *Hsia Hsia Shu Shih* report Chingis Khan's order for the extermination of the Tanguts.

[30] The report of the proposed extermination of the Chinese and Yeh-lü Ch'u-ts'ai's intercession are from the great Khitan's biography; See Rémusat, *Nouveaux Mélanges Asiatiques*, Vol. XI, " Vie de Yeliu Thsoutsai."

force of the Khitan's argument, the Khan not only spared the population but commanded that the general carnage of the campaign lessen.

As noticed, the conqueror's counter order was issued after certain constellations had been observed in the southwest, so Ch'u-ts'ai, who had originally entered the Mongol's service as an astrologer, doubtless made use of the phenomenon and its interpretation to further his efforts. But if the inhabitants of Hsi Hsia escaped universal massacre, the war continued with much bloodshed, and later we shall find Chingis Khan having to upbraid his officers for having failed to obey his commands.

It is to this period that an excerpt quoted by De Mailla refers. " People hide in vain among mountains and caves to escape the Mongol sword. Hardly one or two in a hundred save themselves while the fields are strewn with the bones of human beings. Since the beginning of time no barbarians have been so powerful as the Mongols are today. They destroy kingdoms as one tears up grass. Why does Heaven permit it! "

In January, 1227, Chingis Khan directed the Mongol forces at Wu-la-hai to recross the Ho-lan Mountains (Ala Shan) and to lay siege to Chung-hsing. Noise of this immediately came to Li Hsien and, resolving to make one more desperate bid in the open, he moved from the capital and marched over the mountains toward Wu-la-hai. The Mongols apparently felt that if the Tanguts were beaten on the western side of the range, their losses would be heavier than if they were able to seek the shelter of Chung-hsing. At all events, Li Hsien's passage over the Ho-lan Mountains was undisputed. On the other side, however, he suffered a sanguinary defeat and fled back to Chung-hsing where the Mongols shortly arrived.[31]

[31] *The Hsi Hsia Shu Shih* says that the battle was fought at Ho-la-ho-ch'a-erh, which is probably the Chinese transliteration of Halachar. In A. Herrmann's *Atlas of China*—pp. 42, 44 and 47—one finds Halachar located west of the Ho-lan Shan (Ala Shan) in the neighborhood assigned by the *Meng-wu-erh Shih* to Wu-la-hai. The two names may therefore stand for the same place, or perhaps one is that of the region, and the other, supposedly Wu-la-hai, the name of the town. Only in the *Hsi Hsia Shu Shih* and the *Hsi Hsia Chi* are two major battles men-

Simultaneously Chingis and the Khitan prince Yeh-lü Hsieh-she, who had just returned from the west, besieged Chi-shih Chou, which they carried by storm. The date is not given, but possibly April was the month, for it was about then that the conqueror moved south. A garrison was left in the town, but soon an epidemic threatened to lay it low. Learning how matters stood, Yeh-lü Ch'u-ts'ai hurried to the scene, and with the help of the medicines he had gathered at Ling Chou, cured the stricken men.[32] Typhus or dysentery suggest themselves, as either could have been occasioned by the slaughter.

After the capture of Chi-shih Chou, Chingis Khan spoke to Hsieh-she thus: " Formerly your father put you under my care as a gauge of his loyalty. Him, I always treated as if he were my younger brother and you I love as a son. Command my troops with my brother Belgutai and live together in close harmony." He then gave the prince permission to return home, but before allowing him to depart, sent him to join the army in front of Chung-hsing as he wished him to have the honor of helping to take the Hsi Hsia capital.[33]

tioned. All other works, except the *Yüan Ch'ao Pi Shih*, which seems to have confused the two battles, report only that arising from the attempted relief of Ling Chou. (For information on Halachar, the Kalajan of Rashid ad-Din; See Yule's *Book of Marco Polo*, Vol. I, pp. 282-283, Note by Cordier.)

Commanding the force beleaguering Chung-hsing was an officer named A-lu-tu (chu)-han. In 1213 he had been no more than a commander of 1,000, when he had been sent with Anchar Noyan to help Yeh-lü Liu-ke against a Chin punitive expedition. Now, victorious over the last Tangut army, he found himself entrusted with the reduction of the enemy capital.

[32] This information is from the *Hsi Hsia Shu Shih*, which also informs us that when Li Hsien learned of the epidemic, he planned to make a surprise attack to retake the place. But it is improbable that the Tangut king, besieged in his own capital, can seriously have contemplated ordering a force to try to break out and recover Chi-shih Chou.

[33] Chingis Khan's words to Hsieh-she and the prince's participation in the sieges of Chi-shih Chou and Chung-hsing are from De Mailla who, however, makes no reference to the conqueror's presence at either place. But the *Yüan Shih* definitely states that he was at the former. As regards the investment of Chi-shih Chou, the *Hsi Hsia Shu Shih* says that Chingis sent, not led, the army to the city, and that it only arrived there during the third month (March 19th to April 17th), but in view of the Mongol operations east and south of the Yellow River from the second month of the year (February 18th to March 18th) on, it is unlikely that the conqueror left Chi-shih Chou unattacked in his rear until so late. Perhaps the discrepancy in the two dates is due to the Mongols having begun the siege in the first month (January 19th to February 17th), and captured the place in the third month of 1227.

The metropolis was now completely isolated, and almost the whole kindom conquered. Only Sha Chou far to the west still held out. In the extreme east, Hsia Chou to the south of the Ordos, had fallen as early as November, 1226.[34] Who took it is not stated, but very likely its reduction was the work of Mongkha Bukha, who, it will be remembered had been left by Boru in the autumn of 1224 to hold the Yin Chou area. As regards the Ordos, it was probably raided into submission by troops sent out by the conqueror while at Yen-ch'uan Chou. This should not have been difficult, for one may suppose that the majority of its fighting men were with Li Hsien at the capital.

With the field forces of the Tanguts virtually destroyed, Chingis could spare troops for a western offensive against the Chin. Before he left for the siege of Chi-shih Chou, he had ordered Subudei to invade the valley of the T'ao River.[35] From a study of the " Meng-wu-erh Shih " and its biography of the general, one gathers that Subudei marched south to Huan Chou and there swung southwest and seized Chen-jung. Thence he moved southward to the Liu-p'an Shan, crossed the range and attacked Lung-te and Te-shun. They proved too strong to take at once so, leaving behind a blockading force, he marched via Hsi-ning, only reduced in March or April, and on through Ting-hsi to the city of Lan Chou.[36] This was captured, and advancing up the T'ao, he arrived before Lin-t'ao. It fell in February or March, so while one part of his army crossed the river and marched west to Ho Chou on the Ta-hsia

---

[34] *Hsi Hsia Shu Shih.*

[35] One is not told when Subudei left Yen-ch'uan Chou, but as the town of Lin-t'ao fell during the second month of the year (February 19th to March 18th, 1227), it would have been impossible for him to have got so far west unless he set out in late January or early in February.

Some writers appear to believe that the conquest of the T'ao valley was carried out by troops that marched from Hsi-liang and crossed the Yellow River at Lan Chou. But the biography of " Subudei " clearly states that on his way west, he attacked Chen-jung and Te-shun before he took Lan-hui (Lan Chou) and the towns of the T'ao.

[36] Neither the towns of Huan Chou or Ting-hsi are mentioned, but both lay on Subudei's line of march.

River, the other went upstream to besiege Min Chou and T'ao Chou. Neither Ho Chou nor T'ao Chou resisted long, perhaps until April, but Min Chou opposed so desperate a defense that a force had to be left before it, and not until late in the year after Chingis Khan's death was it entered. Then the commander, refusing to outlive its loss, committed suicide, with his entire family.[37] His task all but finished, Subudei returned to report to the conqueror, that except for one place, Chin authority in the T'ao valley was no more, and presented him with a gift of 5,000 horses.

As well as this news there came tidings from the west. Sha Chou had at last been taken and April saw the whole of the Shu-lo valley under the heel of the invader. With the exception of Chung-hsing, the once powerful kingdom of Hsi Hsia had ceased to exist.

Toward the end of April or in the first week of May, Chingis Khan advanced south, and going over the Liu-p'an Mountains, laid siege to Lung-te. At the same time one of his generals began the reduction of Te-shun. No specific date is given for their fall, but the Mongols seem to have been in possession of both by the end of June.

While in front of Lung-te, Chingis Khan sent an embassy to the Chin with the astonishing demand that they explain the reason for having sent no tribute.

As the month of June progressed the weather became very hot, so the conqueror repaired to the Liu-p'an mountains. There he ordered Chaghan to go to Chung-hsing to try to negotiate its surrender.

Ever since January the city had stoutly resisted all attempts to take it and at first Li Hsien refused to discuss terms. But at length food began to run short and sickness started to spread among the garrison and inhabitants, so in July or August he and his officers agreed to capitulate. The king also consented to visit the Mongol camp, but before setting out he begged one month's grace in which to prepare some presents. Chingis Khan

[37] For the heroic defence of Min Chou; See Gaubil who took his information from the *Yüan Shih Lei Pien*.

granted this request and at the same time changed the monarch's title to Siduryu, meaning loyal or faithful. But he sent Tolun Cherbi to reside in the city until the allotted time was up.

Haenisch has an interesting explanation for this alteration of Li Hsien's title.[38] In the Mongol language the title borne by all the Tangut rulers was Iluhu Burkhan, i. e., the Exalted or Conquering Buddha, which indicates that the kings of Hsi Hsia were spiritual as well as temporal lords. Although Chingis Khan had resolved to kill Li Hsien, he did not wish to offend the Buddhist church by slaying a Buddha. Consequently he changed the king's name to Siduryu (Faithful) as he could then put Li Hsien to death for having been a rebellious instead of a loyal vassal.

Besides the Tangut representatives, the conqueror also received two peace envoys from the Chin, Wan-yen Ho-ta and Ao-tun A-hu, who reached his camp in the Liu-p'an mountains during July or August. When he had heard the object of their mission he turned to those about him and said: " Since the conjunction of the five constellations we forbade slaughter and plundering; why have you forgotten my commands? Make public my orders to all so that even travellers may know my will." Beyond these words he made no reply to the deputation, and the Chin, mistakenly thinking that he was about to suspend hostilities, called a temporary halt in their collection of taxes for the war.

Chingis Khan had now almost run his course. On the 19th of August he fell ill, and after no more than seven days of sickness the great conqueror died at the age of sixty-one.[39]

---

[38] Haenisch, " Die Letzten Feldzüge Cingis Han's und Sein Tod nach der Ostasiatischen Ueberlieferung"; Asia Major, Vol. IX.

Haenisch also points out that since the Tangut ruler would hardly have borne a Mongol title, the real one may have been the Tibetan equivalent, Sansrgyas-rgyal-ba.

Grousset says that Iluhu was the Mongol equivalent of Srong-btsan meaning just or upright; See Grousset, L'Empire Mongol (1re phase), Histoire Du Monde, Tome VIII, p. 494.

[39] It is from the Yüan Shih that one learns that Chingis Khan's illness lasted no more than seven days.

Concerning the manner and place of his death there are various accounts. The " Yüan Ch'ao Pi Shih " and the " Yüan Sheng Wu Ch'in Cheng Lu " report that he lived to see the end of the war with Hsi Hsia and returned to Mongolia where he died. The " Yüan Shih " says that the end came in Ch'ing-shui Hsien on the Hsi River. The " Sanang Setsen " declares that he died at Durmegei (Ling Chou), and the "Sung Shih " names the Liu-p'an mountains. Since the Mongol records are often inaccurate as regards the details and chronology of Chingis Khan's wars outside Mongolia, the " Yüan Shih" would seem the safest source to follow. So one may assume that he died on the extreme upper reaches of the Hsi River, which is today known as the Ch'ing-shui River. The present Ch'ing-shui Hsien is south, not north of the Liu-p'an Mountains.

The nature of the conqueror's illness is unknown, but the heavy fall he sustained when hunting near Aburkha in November, 1225, may have been the cause of it.

The " Yüan Shih " reports that on his deathbed he outlined a plan for the completion of the war against the Chin. " The best troops of the Chin," he said, " are at T'ung Kuan; to the south they rest on the Lien mountains, on the north they reach the great river (Yellow River).[40] It is not easy to force this position, but if permission can be obtained to march through the dominions of the Sung, our men can be led via Teng and T'ang and go straight to Ta-liang (K'ai-feng). This will place the Chin in a difficult position and compel the withdrawal of many thousand troops from T'ung Kuan. But these, both men and horses, will be exhausted after marching over one thousand li (approximately 330 miles) to the capital, and even if they arrive will be worthless and fall an easy prey to our men."

Juwayni gives an entirely different deathbed speech.[41] According to him, Chingis Khan, having reached Ongu Talan Khutuk, dreamed a dream portending his end. He therefore ordered Yesunggé, the second son of Juchi Khassar, to sum-

[40] The troops in question, the main army of the Chin, numbered 200,000; See *Ch'eng-chi-ssŭ Han* by Feng Ch'eng-chün; also De Mailla, Vol. IX.
[41] See D'Ohsson, pp. 379-381.

mon Ugedei and Tului before him, and sending everyone else from his presence, spoke as follows: " I have almost come to my end. For you I have created this empire. To the north, south, east and west my dominions extend for a year's journey. My last will and testament are these. If you want to retain your possessions and conquer your enemies, you must make your subjects submit willingly and unite your energies to one end, as in that way you may continue to hold your power. When I am gone you must recognize Ugedei as my successor. Further, let each see to his own affairs. During many years I have enjoyed a great name and I die without regrets, but my spirit wishes to return to my native land. Although Jaghatai is not present to hear my words, I do not think that he will disobey my wishes and cause a disturbance. I die in the territory of the enemy and though the ruler of Hsi Hsia has submitted, he has not yet arrived. Hence, after I am dead, conceal my death and kill him when he comes." Having spoken these words, Chingis Khan died.

There can be no doubt that had Chingis lived, a final offensive against the Chin would have started, perhaps that very winter. The primary object of Subudei's conquests west of the Liu-p'an Mountains must have been to prevent the Chin out-flanking the invading army when the attack began. The conqueror's death postponed the day, and not until 1230 did the Mongols resume operations on a large scale. When they did, their plan of campaign included that laid down by Chingis Khan.[42]

His one month's grace at an end, Li Hsien departed for the Mongol camp, where he arrived in September. There he was told that Chingis Khan was ill, and was ordered to make his greetings outside the Imperial quarters. He did this and also

---

[42] T'u Chi, author of the *Meng-wu-erh Shih*, believes that the plan drawn up for the liquidation of the Chin was really the work of Ugedei and his staff, not of Chingis Khan. Whatever the truth may be, the operations put into effect by Ugedei and Tului during the winter of 1231-32, not only included the plan suggested by the conqueror, but closely resembled the abortive campaign of the celebrated Jurchid commanders Jemugor and Wu-chu to recover K'ai-feng from the Sung in 1128.

offered many rich presents: gold and silver basins, golden
Buddha statues, horses, camels and young boys and girls, of
each gift nine, but all availed him nothing. He was bidden to
bow down before the conqueror's tents and three days later
was slain with all his family by Tolun Cherbi.[43]

Simultaneously Chung-hsing was occupied, and the officers of
the besieging army wished to give it over to fire and sword.
But as at Kan Chou, Chaghan interceded, and though the city
was pillaged and many women were raped, the lives of the
people were spared.

Thus ended the most destructive war in the annals of Mongol
history. Having for over two centuries weathered assaults from
Sung, Khitan and Chin, the Kingdom of Hsi Hsia was swept
from the face of the earth by the all-conquering Mongol. In
reality more had been done. The last relics of Tibetan imperialism had been destroyed, for the Tanguts, once refugees
before the successors of Srong-btsan Ganbo, were the real con-
tinuators of their empire and with them went the last of Tibet
as a great power.

The body of Chingis Khan was taken back to his homeland,
whither, according to the biography of Subudei, the cortège was
conducted by the great general himself, but the later and
more fanciful accounts of the " Altan Tobci " and " Sanang
Setsen " say that it was led by Kilugen Baatur the Sunid. Addressing the spirit of the conqueror during the homeward journey, Kilugen wailed: " Yesterday did you not soar in pride
over your people, oh my Khan?

But today, as one dead, a rumbling chariot bears you onward,
oh my Khan!

Have you really abandoned your wife and your children, oh
my Khan?

Have you left all your faithful subjects?

[43] The *Hsi Hsia Shu Shih* and the *Hsi Hsia Chi* both state that the conqueror
left instructions for Li Hsien's murder. The *Yüan Ch'ao Pi Shih*, however, declares that the Tangut King offered his presents to Chingis Khan in person. Three
days later his name was changed to Siduryu, and Tolun Cherbi received orders to
kill him. As seen, I think it more likely that his name was altered before leaving
Chung-hsing and that he arrived with his presents after the great Mongol was dead.

Yesterday did you not wheel in the sky like a falcon, oh my Khan? And today, as an unbroken colt after a wild gallop, have you not stumbled and fallen, oh my Khan?

Or as the new grown grass been uprooted by the tempest? After barely sixty years, and at the very moment when you were about to give to the Nine Banners the joy of repose, have you not been taken from them and remain cast down?"

Again, later in the journey when the funeral cart became stuck in a swamp and refused to move, Kilugen once more called upon Chingis: " Lion of mankind, sent by eternal heaven, son of the spirits; Oh my sacred and divine lord; do you wish to abandon your devoted people? do you wish to leave us? The country of your birth, your noble spouse, your indestructible empire, your laws, your people divided into tens of thousands, all are there. Your well loved wives, your palace tent of felt, your golden abode, your realm founded upon justice; all are there. The place of your birth, the waters where you bathed, the teeming Mongol people, your generals, your princes and your nobles; Deliun-boldak on the Onon, where you were born; all are there. Your standard made from the black tails and manes of bay stallions,[44] your drums, your trumpets, your flutes, the prairies of the Kerulen, the place where you mounted the throne as Khaghan, all are there. Your wife Burte whom you married in your youth, your beautiful land, your great people, your faithful companions, all are there. Because this country is hot, because the Tanguts have been conquered and their queen is beautiful, do you wish to abandon your people, oh my Khan? If we are no longer able to protect your life, we wish at least to convey your body to your birthland, to present it to your wife Burte and to satisfy the vows of your people." [45] No sooner had Kilugen ceased, than the cart started from the swamp and continued on its way unaided.

On arriving north of the desert, Chingis Khan's remains were taken to his camp on the river Kerulen and there his death was

---

[44] In referring to Chingis Khan's great standard the *Yüan Ch'ao Pi Shih* speaks of yak tails, not horse tails.

[45] See Grousset, *Le Conquérant du Monde,*" p. 370-371.

made public. After that his body was buried in the Burkhan Khaldun (an eastern spur of the range today known as the Kentei) where various members of his family were later laid to rest. But up to the present, neither his grave nor theirs have been discovered[46]

Though the princes and many great officers accompanied the body of Chingis Khan back to Mongolia, several thousand troops were left to keep the Chin forces in the valley of the Wei occupied. These took Ch'in Chou, Ch'ing-shui—the town of that name to the south of the Liu-p'an Mountains—Hsi-ho Chou to the south of the Ts'in-ling Mountains and other places. With the beginning of the winter they moved down the river, and after plundering the departments of Feng-hsiang and Ching-chao, January, 1228, found them as far east as Shang Chou, Chu-yang and Lu-shih, all of which were taken and looted. It was perhaps this raid that gave rise to the erroneous report in the " Yüan Shih " that prior to the conqueror's death, Ugedei and Chaghan laid siege to K'ai-feng.

The following summer (1228) some of the same troops, 8,000 strong, were operating in the valley of the Huan in Northern Shensi, but at Ta-ch'ang-yüan, twelve miles to the west of Ning Chou, they were severely defeated by a Chin force.[47] After that the Mongols not only abandoned the basin of the Huan

---

[46] The oft repeated story that Chingis Khan's funeral cortège slew all whom it met comes from Marco Polo and is almost certainly a mistake. Apparently the Venetian was confused by the report of Mongkha Khaghan's last journey to the north, when as many as 20,000 people are said to have been killed by the escorting soldiers.

As regards Chingis Khan's resting place, the accounts of Hsü Ting and Tap-ya, sent north by the Sung on an embassy—1235-36—are of great interest. According to both, who were eye witnesses, the conqueror's tomb was surrounded by a circle of posts 30 li (approximately 10 miles) in circumference and horsemen put there on guard and was located on the Lu-K'ou River. According to Hsü Ting, the Lu K'ou River was the birth place of the conqueror, which would indicate the River Onon, but Lu K'ou may be a variation of Lu-ch'u which is the Chinese name for the Kerulen, so that the tomb may be located on either the Onon or the Kerulen rivers. (For the report of the Sung embassy; See Haenisch, " Die Letzen Feldzüge Cingis Han's und sein Todt nach der Ostasiatischen Ueberlieferung," Asia Major, Vol. IX.)

[47] The name of the victorious Chin general was Wan-yen Ch'eng Ho-sheng, also known as Wan-yen I.

and Ching, but embarked upon no further activities until the great attack of 1230.

From the words spoken by Chingis Khan at Cho'orkhat on the return of his messenger from the Tangut king, it is evident that he had a premonition of approaching death, and throughout the foregoing campaign he was probably a dying man. As related, he had with him two extremely able soldiers, Bugurji, perhaps acting as chief of staff, and the great Subudei. To either he might have delegated the conduct of the war. However, so important did he consider it that, despite illness, he remained at the head of the army until the last.

Having fought the Tanguts before, he knew that the war would be a hard one, and he was not wrong. Except at Hsi-liang, the Tanguts resisted with a determination that excites the highest admiration. But it was a hopeless struggle from the first. When Chingis Khan took the field in the autumn of 1225 the Mongol army was the greatest war machine the world had ever seen. Experienced in campaigns from the Yellow Sea to the Crimea, and possessed of every siege engine known to that age, it was all but invincible.

The Mongol casualties during the war are unknown, but in addition to the loss of their great leader, there also died Bugurji, the conqueror's oldest friend and companion of his early days.[48]

The destruction of Hsi Hsia, though overshadowed by the in-

[48] As regards Bugurji, the *Meng-wu-erh Shih* implies that his death occurred some time between that of Chingis Khan and the great battle fought with the Tanguts on the western side of the Ho-lan Mountains, i. e., at Halachar, but its cause is not given. The *Yüan Ch'ao Pi Shih* refers to his presence with the army, but has not a word to say about his end. This is strange, because he figured prominently in the conqueror's rise to power, which is that part of his career most extensively dealt with by the work.

Although the oldest record extant on Chingis Khan, the *Yüan Ch'ao Pi Shih* is guilty of many such omissions and contains several chronological errors. An outstanding instance occurs in the message delivered by the Mongol envoy to the Tangut king after Chingis Khan's injury at Cho'orkhat. Li Te Wang had ascended the throne only in 1224, yet it is he who is accused of having failed to assist in the Khorezmian war. As already seen, the culprit was his predecessor, Li Tsun-hsiang, but despite shortcomings of this nature, the *Yüan Ch'ao Pi Shih* is invaluable, since it provides information found nowhere else.

vasions of the Chin and Khorezmian empires, was a tremendous undertaking. Never attempted by the Khitans, Jurchids or the Sung, it was accomplished by Chingis Khan. One of the principal events of the thirteenth century, it was also one of the greatest military achievements in a career of conquest unparalleled in the history of war.

# CHAPTER XI

# THE LEGACY AND GREATNESS OF CHINGIS KHAN

CHINGIS KHAN died at the height of his power and glory and lord and master of the largest empire ever created in the lifetime of one man. Leaving to his sons a body of devoted and talented servants, he can have had little fear that the unity of the state would be impaired by his death. As he had wished, Ugedei succeeded him without opposition. Formally elected Khaghan at a great assembly held on the Kerulen during the spring of 1229, he ascended the throne on the 13th of September of the same year. In 1235, however, he set up his capital at Khara Khuren, (Khara Khorum) in the valley of the Orkhon, i. e. in the traditional seat of nomad empire, but to the east, not the west of the river.[1]

The only cloud to mar the conqueror's last days had been the death of Juchi seven months before his own. But from one standpoint even that had contributed to his peace of mind. Ever since the siege of Gurganj in 1221, Juchi had tended to hold aloof from his father and brothers, and after Chingis Khan's return from the west, had begun to show signs of independence, so that his early death was probably as much a relief as it was a source of grief to the old Mongol.

Although the political successor of the Hsiungnu, Juan-juan, Turkish and Uighur empires, the Mongol imperium was in certain respects different. In the first place it was far larger, extending further south, east and west than any previous nomad empire, and second it was eventually to embrace the whole of China and Iran. It is this feature that brings us to a

---

[1] Khara Khuren is not to be confused with Khara Balghasun, the former Uighur and Kirghiz capital of the 8th and 9th centuries, on the western side of the Orkhon. For an account of the ruins of both; See La Coste, *Au Pays Sacré des Anciens Turcs et des Mongols*, Chap. III.

third point which makes the Mongol empire almost unique. Up
to the rise of the Mongols and after their fall, all the nomad
powers to establish themselves as rulers over large areas in the
civilized countries to the south arose in the adjoining border
regions. To mention only a few; the Tabgach and Khitans
originated in southern Mongolia and southwestern Manchuria,
the Jurchids and Manchus on the upper Sungari and Hurka,
while the Khara Khanid and Saljuk empires rose beyond the
Syr Darya, the outpost line of Iran and Islam in Central Asia.
With the exception of the Western Turks of the sixth and early
seventh centuries, who conquered and held Transoxiana, Tukharistan and the Tarim, the Mongols are the only nomads to
have arisen beyond the desert, who while remaining a northern
pastoral power, conquered and governed vast regions to the
South.[2] This was due partly to the power they derived from
Chingis Khan's prodigious military genius, which enabled them
to make conquests far surpassing those of their predecessors,
partly to the policy they inherited from him. As Vladimirtsov
remarks: " The conquest of immense territories and of civilized
nations did not change Chingis Khan's constitutional views,
and they remained what they had been when he had only
succeeded in uniting under his rule ' all the generations that
lived in felt tents.' To the end of his life he regarded the empire
as the property of his clan, where all things were arranged
in such a way that his clansmen and his companions might
extract the greatest amount of advantage for themselves and
make their life enjoyable. He believed that his descendants
and the Mongol aristocracy would certainly live this nomad
life because a nomad life was easier and freer, and because it
was easier for nomads to rule over the sedentary population.

[2] The Hsiungnu, Juan-juan and Oelets of course from time to time controlled
greater or smaller portions of the Tarim and T'ien Shan regions.

  The empire of Khara Khitai, which held sway in these regions, as well as South
of the Syr Darya, was an offshoot of the great Khitan empire, so it properly falls
into the same category as its progenitor. Nevertheless, Wittfogel believes that its
overall administrative system was the pattern upon which that of the Mongol
world empire was fashioned. (See Wittfogel and Feng Chia-sheng, *History of
Chinese Society: Liao* (907-1125), p. 3.)

The sedentary inhabitants of towns and villages were, in his view, the lifelong slaves of their nomad rulers, obliged to toil in order that the latter might live a freer and better life.[3]

His views, coinciding as they did with those of his people and advocated by such a person as Chingis Khan, naturally became almost sacred law, and not until after 1260 did his descendants begin to abandon his ideas and the great empire start to break up. When this happened the various branches of his family were falling under the influence of political, economic, social and cultural forces too strong for them to withstand.[4]

The ideology of Chingis Khan actually attained its final development after the first two years of war against the Chin. Up to 1212, it is very nearly certain that he had little thought of deriving a steady revenue from the permanent occupation of settled areas. As in the expedition against Hsi Hsia during 1209, so in that against the Chin in 1211, he had two main objectives: the destruction of the enemy's military strength and the amassing of a vast booty. It was only after he became more conversant with the great resources of China and also, one may suppose, was urged to the step by the Khitan and Chinese renegades in his service, that he commenced the systematic occupation of Chin territory. This, as seen, occasioned terrible loss of life to the Chinese populace, but despite many appalling massacres for military reasons, and sometimes, as at Chung Tu, because the besieging army got temporarily out of hand, the Mongols warred not against the Chinese people but against the Chin government. Admittedly, there were in the Mongol army many officers who revelled in carnage, but neither in the conquest of China nor in that of Transoxiana and Iran is there any evidence that either Chingis Khan or his successors embarked upon a deliberate policy of extermination. Careless they were of human life and made unlimited use of

---

[3] Vladimirtsov, *The Life of Chingis Khan*, pp. 146-147.

[4] From the time of Kubilai (1260-94) on, when the unity of the empire was broken, the succeeding part empires came more and more to resemble their forerunners in east and west, that of Kubilai its Jurchid predecessor, those in Central Asia and Iran the Khara Khanids and Saljuks of the 11th and 12th centuries.

the local population in sieges, but they never ordered a massacre without some definite aim in mind and rarely indulged in acts of gratuitous cruelty.

The great extent of the dominions conquered by Chingis Khan during the latter years of his life is amply demonstrated by the possessions he bequeathed to his sons and brothers. To Juchi, or rather to his sons, were left the steppes to the west of the Irtish, the present provinces of Turgai and Uralsk, Khwarazm and everything up to the lower Volga. Further, all the country overrun by Jebe and Subudei in 1222 was to be theirs as soon as reconquered. In accordance with Turko-Mongol custom, the house of Juchi, as the eldest branch of the conqueror's family, inherited the dominions most distant from the main Ordus.[5] To Jaghatai was given the Uighur kingdom of the T'ien Shan, the Lake Balkash country, the valleys of the Tarim, Ili, Chu and Taraz (Talas), and Transoxiana. To Ugedei, overlord of the whole empire, there fell the territories watered by the Imil, Khara Irtish, Urungu and Khobuk, and to Tului, the Ochigin or Hearth Prince, the home country of the Onon, Kerulen and Tola. This, as his inheritance of the greater part of the Mongol army proper, was also in accordance with a recognized custom, whereby the youngest son received the paternal homeland. To the conqueror's eldest brother Juchi Khassar went the Hailar and Argun rivers, and also it seems the Nonni; to Temuge Ochigin, the Bur Nor, Khalkha Gol and perhaps the valley of the T'ao-erh beyond the Khing-han. The other members of Chingis Khan's family, e. g., his nephew Aljigidei, his half-brother Belgutai, Kulgan the son of the Mergit princess Kulan, and his adopted sons, Shiki Kutuku and Chaghan, all received dominions of varying size. Directly subject to the Khaghan were the Kirghiz, Oirads, Jalairs, Khon-girads, Onguds and Khitans, as well as the great mass of the Chinese.

Thus, while Ugedei succeeded Chingis as supreme ruler, the empire was the joint property of the whole imperial family,

[5] The Kirghiz, Kem-kemjiuts and neighboring forest tribes, made over to Juchi in 1217, seem to have become directly subject to the Khaghan.

who with the Mongol aristocracy formed its ruling class. As stated by Vladimirtsov; " The idea of a collective domination of a clan was in no way opposed to the idea of the individual authority of the Kagan (Khaghan), for he was primarily the head of his own clan, raised to that rank by the Sky and by all his clansmen. The empire must be one and at its head there must be one emperor. ' Let my rank,' said Chingis, ' be inherited by one of my sons. My words are immutable; I shall not permit them to be infringed.' " [6] " But, continues Vladimirtsov, " as the empire was the property of the whole imperial family, Chingis recognized the old system of partitions, owing to which every member of the dynasty had the usufruct of his share of the common property. The nucleus of each of these part kingdoms (inju) was formed by an Ulus or group of nomad clans capable of producing a given contingent of warriers and provided with sufficient grazing ground (nutuk, yurt) to allow them to live in affluence. Besides this nucleus, the sons, brothers, widows or other kinsmen of the Kagan (Khaghan) could also be assigned appanages consisting of newly-conquered lands with a sedentary population— (e.g., the oasis of the Tarim and Transoxians in Jagahatai's inju.) But a sedentary province did not become part of their inju; its revenues did not go to the prince who camped in its vicinity, but were shared between the Kagan (Khaghan) and all the appanaged rulers, i. e., all the members of the dynasty.[7] On the other hand, each of the appanaged persons received a certain number of skilled workmen, artisans, artists and so on, who were at his entire disposal and whom he might settle where he liked. The civilized provinces were governed by lieutenants (darugachi) responsible to the Kagan (Khaghan), the appanaged princes not being allowed to interfere in the financial or civil administration of the sedentary population . . ." [8] To maintain speedy and efficient

[6] Vladimirtsov, *The Life of Chingis Khan*, p. 147.

[7] After 1260 these injus developed into independent kingdoms. When that happened, little revenue found its way to those members of the family—Kubilai and his descendants—holding the title of Khaghan.

[8] Vladimirtsov, *The Life of Chingis Khan*, pp. 147-148.

communication within these part kingdoms and between them and the Khaghan, and throughout the whole vast empire, a post system (yam) of mounted couriers was organized. Having at their disposal unlimited horses, which made possible a continuous change of mounts, these couriers in certain regions covered over two hundred miles in a day.

Further expressing the idea of collective rule is the kuriltai or the great assembly. At this all matters pertaining to the empire, military and civil, were discussed by the Khaghan, his family and the supporting aristocracy. But if able to voice their opinions in open council, the amount of influence the imperial family and aristocracy were able to exert varied greatly according to circumstances and the personality of the reigning Khaghan. Under Chingis Khan the Kuriltai can have exercised little real power, though on occasions such outstanding individuals as Bugurji and Mukhali swayed him in certain matters.

Vladimirtsov contends that to the end of his days Chingis Khan remained a partisan of Uighur culture and education, which he considered to be that best adapted to the needs of the Mongols. In support of this is the conqueror's adoption of the Uighur alphabet as a model for that which he ordered to be drawn up for his own people. Moreover, realizing that at the time the Mongols were ideologically unfitted for the administration of sedentary peoples—in his day they were also all needed to carry on his military undertakings—he entrusted the government of settled areas to the Uighur, Khitan, Chinese and Moslem officials in his service. Of these the Uighurs and Khitans were certainly his favorites, and it was the latter, with the Chinese, and headed by Yeh-lü Ch'u-ts'ai, who during the reign of Ugedei (1229-41) became paramount in the civil service. " But Chingis," says Vladimirtsov, " thought that the time would soon come when the number of Mongols who had acquired an Uighur education would be so great that the empire would be able to do without the employment of foreigners in the civil administration. He regarded education—at any rate that education without which it was impossible to keep the empire together or to assure its authority over settled and civilized provinces—as quite compatible with nomadic life. He hoped his successors would be able to organize a civil administration similar to that which he had given his army and instilled with spirit of the Jasak (Yasa) . . . ." [9]

Chingis Khan's plan failed because for his people as a whole the combination of pastoral life with even the degree of Uighur culture that he thought sufficient for administrative purposes proved impossible. The members of the imperial family and supporting aristocracy who followed him little more than a generation later, either fell under the glamor of the civilizations of China and Iran and because less pastoral, or shunned them all, Chinese, Iranian and even Uighur. Though by no means the only cause, this cleavage was to be a powerful force in promoting the subsequent disintegration of the Mongol empire. Despite his hopes for the future, almost prophetic of the behavior of those that succumbed to the attractions of China and Iran are the following words of the conqueror from the Bilik. " After us the descendants of our clan will wear gold embroidered garments, eat rich and sweet food, ride fine horses, and embrace beautiful women, but they will not say that they owe all this to their fathers and elder brothers, and they will forget us and those great times." [10]

Favoring the Uighurs as Chingis did it was natural that they should figure prominently in the civil administration of the empire, but, doubtless due to the influence of Yeh-lü Ch'u-ts'ai, the organization of the Mongol provinces in China was left to Khitan and Chinese officals. After the accession of Ugedei, who continued to give Ch'u-ts'ai his unbounded confidence and respect, the great Khitan minister undertook the restoration of prosperity and order in both Manchuria and China, and drew up a fixed scale of taxation. The main features of this were an impost of 1/30 of the value on all commodities essential

---

[9] Vladimirtsov, *The Life of Chingis Khan*, pp. 152-153. For a description of the Yasa; See Chapter IV.

[10] Riasanovsky, *Fundamental Principles of Mongol Law*, p. 88.

to life and 1/10 on luxuries.[11]  In matters of legal procedure, the Yasa applied only to the Mongol and associated nomad troops in China, not to the Chinese, who continued to be judged by the code in force under the Chin.

As shown by Chingis Khan's alteration of the Tangut King's title from Iluhu Burkhan to Siduryu, so as not to offend the Buddhist clergy by the execution of a Buddha, the conqueror was careful to cultivate the support of all religious bodies. Still further illustrating this policy is the edict issued on behalf of the celebrated sage Ch'iu Ch'ang-ch'un in favor of the Taoists, then so powerful in China.  " The holy commandment, the commandment of Chingis Khan to the chiefs of all districts.  Wherever hermitages and ascetic retreats pertain to Tzu Sheng Hsien (Ch'ang-ch'un), let those who daily read the holy scriptures and pray to Heaven, pray also for the longevity of the Khan; let them be free from taxes and duties and tribute great and small, let all hermitages and abodes of monks belonging to Tzu Sheng Hsien in all places be free of taxes, duty and tribute, but if anyone refuses to pay taxes on false pretense of being a monk, let him be denounced to the authorities and punished accordingly.  After the receipt of this order, let no one dare to oppose it." [12]  It goes without saying that such toleration and favor served a useful political purpose and considerably aided the restoration of order after the conquest was over.  Temples, mosques and churches were of course one of the chief objects of plunder to an army such as the Mongol, but the looting of these in no way reflects on imperial policy as regards the religious communities that fell under its authority.

Kulagu's attack on the Caliph, the politico-religious head of Orthodox Islam, was not prompted by any real hostility for the Moslem faith but by the necessity of affirming Mongol authority over the Moslem subjects of the empire. On the

---

[11] De Mailla, *Histoire Générale de la Chine*, Vol. IX.

[12] Riasanovsky, *Fundamental Principles of Mongol Law*, p. 44.  This excerpt Riasanovsky took from Palladius's translation of Ch'iu Ch'ang-ch'un's journey to the west.

other hand the non-millitant Buddhist Sa-skya Pandita of Tibet,[13] with his predominantly spiritual ascendency, was gladly utilized by Kubilai and his successors to promote Mongol authority in Tibet where it was hoped that his ecclesiastical power would militate against the natural turbulence of the people. Hence, in 1270 the Sa-skya Pandita, Phags-pa, was appointed both civil and religious viceroy of the country, a position enjoyed by his successors until 1345 when they were overthrown by the founder of the second Tibetan empire after the Mongol Yüan dynasty had fallen into decay.[13]

East and west Chingis Khan's two most spectacular foreign conquests remained incomplete. The final subjugation of Iran was the work of Ugedei's reign, as was also that of the Chin, while the ultimate conquest of all China did not take place until the reign of his grandson Kubilai Khaghan (1216-94). But in both cases Chingis had achieved the most difficult stage. After the overthrow of the Khwarazm Shah, there was no state in the world of Islam capable of resisting the Mongols. In China things were rather different. The Sung empire, though politically and economically on the decline, was after the Mongol the most powerful state left in the world. Moreover, when the descendants of Chingis Khan undertook its conquest, they were obliged to learn riverine warfare. While their ultimate success was to a great extent due to their employment of Chinese officers conversant with this new technique, the overall plan was Mongol and so a tribute to the military genius of this remarkable people. But despite the length of time required to subdue the south, Chingis Khan's overthrow of Chin power in the north was a far greater feat of arms. Even when beset simultaneously by Mongol, Tangut and Sung, the Jurchid empire exhibited powers of resistance surpassing anything encountered by the Mongols elsewhere. Possessed of the second economic area of China—the lower Yellow River and the Wei—

---

[13] The founder of the second Tibetan imperium was Chang-chub Gyal-tsen; See Sir Charles Bell, *Tibet Past and Present*, p. 32. Further information on the relations of Buddhism with the Mongol Yüan dynasty is to be found in Pelliot's " Les Kouo-cheou maitres du royaume dans le Bouddhisme Chinoise," *T'oung Pao*, 1911, p. 671.

the Jurchids with their powerful army were much stronger
than the Sung, and from start to finish proved an incomparably
more formidable antagonist than the Khorezmian empire, the
strongest state in the world of Islam.

Ralph Fox, in his "Ghenghiz Khan," declares that the
Mongols owed much of their success to the social and economic
decay in the states opposed to them. The empire of Chin he
contends was seething with discontent and unrest and it only
required the Mongol invasion to bring it to a head. He tells
us that once Chingis Khan had broken down the first defenses
of the Chin, he was assisted by widespread risings of peasantry, who called themselves the Red Coats. As seen, this insurrection was largely confined to Shantung, and not until 1215,
i. e., after more than four years of continual war and devastation, did it break out.

As regards the Khorezmian empire, it was political dissension
in the body politic, rather than agrarian and social weakness,
that helped the Mongols in their conquest. Referring to its
collapse and that of the Chin, Fox states that had the Mongols
been opposed to the T'ang and Abbasid dynasties in their hey-
day, neither eastward nor westward could they have achieved
such conquests. Admittedly the Mongols were opposed by a
disunited China, one controlled in the north by two foreign
powers, namely the Jurchids and Tanguts, and ruled in the
south alone by a Chinese dynasty, the Sung, insead of a united
empire backed by the resources of the entire country. They
were therefore faced by a definitely weaker political and
economic situation than in the best days of the T'ang. There
can be no question that in the West too the empire of the first
Abbasids was economically sounder than that of the Khwarazm
Shahs and could have rallied numerically greater military
forces, but it must not be forgotten that the disaffected Shia
element was a constant source of internal weakness which
more than once embarrassed the Caliphs in times of danger.
Argument on the subject can lead to little beyond speculation,
but it is perhaps worth including at least a few words about
the military organization of these two famous powers.

The army of the T'ang from 618 to 738 numbered 616,000 militia. These were divided into twelve corps of 51,000 men, each corps into fifty-one regiments of 1,000, each regiment into five battalions of 200, each battalion into two sections of 100, and each section into ten squads of ten. Military age for all able bodied men was from twenty to sixty. Theoretically each corps was called upon to furnish no more than 7,000 men every month, but in actual practice duty at the capital, frontier service and foreign expeditions meant that a far greater number—anything from 150,000 to 200,000 troops—were frequently under arms for three or more years at a time. Besides this great militia host, the emperor had a picked force of 30,000 men—increased to 120,000 in 723—many of whom were mounted bowmen, and who were kept constantly at the capital. Further, the sons of these men took the places of their fathers when the latter became too aged or unfit for duty.

By the second quarter of the 8th century, the militia establisment was in decay so during 738 it was replaced by a full time professional army. This was stationed in various cantonments along the frontier, where the families of the troops were encouraged to settle. But, except for certain units, notably those under outstanding commanders, this force too deteriorated and proved of little use against the rebel An Lu-shan in 755. From that date on, save for a gleam of glory here and there, the power and military prestige of the T'ang steadily waned.

Throughout its whole tenure of power the dynasty employed considerable numbers of Turkish horse archers, but the majority of its troops were spear and sword wielding infantry who did not use the bow. During the reign of T'ang T'ai Tsung (627-49), Chinese armies penetrated even present Outer Mongolia, but they were fighting a disrupted Turkish Empire. Later, when this was restored by Mo-ch'o (Khapaghan) (691-716),

---

[14] For these particular figures; See Tsui Chi, A Short History of Chinese Civilization, p. 142, but for a detailed description of the T'ang army, Rotour's " Traité des Fonctionnaires et Traité de l'Armée," Vol. I, pp. xiv-lxxii, Bibliothèque de l'Institut des Hautes Etudes Chinoises, Vol. VI.

the T'ang suffered several reverses and saw northern Hopei and Shansi fearfully ravaged. Great soldier though Mo-ch'o was, he was not a Chingis Khan.

The principal standing army of the Abbasids, known as the army of Iraq, numbered 125,000 horse and foot. This was divided into units of 10,000, 1,000, 100, 50 and 10. The equipment of the cavalry consisted of helmet, breast-plate, lance, sabre and battle axe; that of the infantry, who are spoken of as being little better than a rabble, of spear, sword and shield. Archers are mentioned only as being employed to support the army's naptha throwers, so must have been used chiefly at sieges.[15] Against the troops of the Byzantine Empire, the Abbasid army at first more than held its own, but never did it encounter any large forces of mounted bowmen from central or northern Asia.[16]

However, under the preceding dynasty of the Umayyads the Arabs repulsed three attempts by the Turks to re-establish their authority over Transoxiana. In 707 and 712 two armies were sent south by Mo-ch'o, but neither was large enough to accomplish much. A more dangerous attack came in 731 when the Turgesh Khan Sulu (717-38) aided a local revolt and even drove the Arabs over the Amu (Oxus). Not until 738 did the Moslems defeat Sulu and force his withdrawal. After that the Khan was murdered and the Turgesh empire broke up and so put an end to the possibility of another attack.

[15] For the Abbasid army; See Hitti, *History of the Arabs*, p. 327.

The army of Iraq, like the 150,000-200,000 troops stationed near the T'ang capital Ch'ang-an, was not only the largest but the best organized and equipped army in all the dominions of the Caliph. Further, like its counterpart at Ch'ang-an, it controlled the most important combined strategic and economic region in the empire. Hence, so long as the central government was in competent hands, it enjoyed a military and economic advantage over even the largest and all but the most distant provinces of the empire. In China from T'ang times on of course, the most important purely economic area was the lower Yang-tse. (For the history of China's key economic areas; See Chi Ch'ao-ting, *Key Economic Areas in Chinese History*.)

[16] From 651 to 825 the troops of both the Umayyad and Abbasid dynasties had frequent clashes with the Khazars, victory declaring now for one side, now for the other. But though a people of the steppes, the spear rather than the bow was the weapon of the Khazar.

(See Vernadsky, *Ancient Russia*, Vol. 1, pp. 220-222 and pp. 287-289.)

But on none of these occasions were the invading armies
large. That of Sulu on his last and most formidable inroad,
which penetrated Khurasan, the heart of Arab power in the
East, numbered no more than 30,000, a far cry from the
mighty host led south by Chingis Khan in 1219.[17]

By the time that the Mongol conqueror appeared upon the
scene, the empire of the T'ang had long since fallen and the
once vast dominions of the Abbasids had shrunk to little more
than Iraq. With this political change there had also come an
equally great military change. In north China, first the Khitans
and then the Jurchids mustered armies in which mounted
bowmen were employed on a scale not seen since the days of
the T'o-pa or Tabgach and never equalled by their Chinese
predecessors. In the west, throughout the greater part of Asiatic
Islam, the Arab troops and peasant levies of former days had
been largely replaced by Turkish horse archers.[18] First as
mercenaries, then as conquerors, the Turks had become lords
from the River Kama to the Indian Ocean and from the Bay
of Bengal to the Mediterranean. Less numerous than the
territorial levies of days gone by, these new armies not only
saved the state from drawing on the agrarian population for
troops but proved far more effective. Inured to war, and able
to use the bow from the saddle as only the people of the
northern steppes knew how, the Turkish horse archer proved
the most formidable soldier that the world of Islam had ever
seen.

Whatever may have been the political and economic conditions within the Asia of Chingis Khan's day, the military material opposed to him was never surpassed. True, the field
armies of the Chin empire were mishandled through being led by
generals more conversant with warfare in China than on the

---

[17] For the Turkish invasions of Transxonia during the Umayyad dynasty; See
H. A. R. Gibb, *The Arab Conquests in Central Asia*, and René Grousset, *L'Empire
des Steppes*, pp. 165-172.

[18] During the last years of the 11th century, Turkish horse archers were found
even as far west as Mogreb (Morocco) and played an important part in the
Almoravide victory over the Spanish Christians at the battle of Sagrajas in 1086.
(See Ramon Menendez Pidal, *The Cid and His Spain*, pp. 218-219.)

steppes, and the resistance of the Khorezmian empire was impared by the Shah's quarrel with his mother Turkhan Khatun. For all that, they were two of the foremost military states known to Asiatic history. Had Chingis Khan not appeared upon the scene, the Chin would in all probability have lasted for another century, and the Khwarazm Shah Muhammad perhaps have pushed his frontiers to Syria and the Ganges.

It goes without saying that Chingis Khan eclipsed equally his nomad predecessors and successors. Neither the Hsiungnu Mao-tun (Maktur) (209-174 B. C.), who in 201, B. C. surrounded the first Han Emperor Kao Ti (206-194) at Pai-teng in northern Shansi, nor the Turk Mo-ch'o (Khapaghan) (691-716), who defeated the T'ang armies and ravaged Hopei and Shansi, performed feats of arms like those of the Mongol. After him came two outstanding men, Yisun Taiji (1439-55) the Oirad, who defeated and captured the Ming Emperor Ying Tsung (1435-49) [19] at T'u-mu in 1449, and the Tumed Altan Anda Khan (1543-83), who became the first Mongol protector of the Dalai Lama. But after the death of the former in a civil war, the Oirads lost the hegemony of the steppes. Western Mongolia continued in their hands, but the east once more fell under the Borjigin. So great was the prestige that this clan derived from the memory of Chingis Khan that it proved almost impossible for a rival to suplant it. Altan Anda Khan (1543-83), grandson of the Borjigin Dayan (1470-1573), was the last really powerful figure to arise in Mongolia proper,[20] but not only did he recognize the spiritual suzerainty of the Dalai Lama, but his authority in Outer Mongolia was limited to that of a commander-in-chief in time of war. Consequently his power was in no way comparable to that of Chingis after the latter's election on the Onon in 1206, or that of such men as Mao-tun and Mo-ch'o.

It will be noted that neither the Khitan A-pao-chi (907-26) nor the Jurchid Akuda (1113-25) have been included in this

---

[19] Ying Tsung was subsequently released and restored to power and had a second reign lasting from 1457-64.

[20] The Jungar Galdan (1676-97), though a remarkable figure, rose beyond the Altai and enjoyed only a brief period of power in Mongolia proper.

comparison, but like Nurkhachi (1583-1626) the founder of Manchu power, they arose in the border regions to the east of the gobi, so belong to a different category of nomad empire builders. They were, however, as soldiers and statesmen, the equal of any leaders to appear north of the desert before or after Chingis Khan. It might seem that the Tumet Altan Anda Khan was a ruler of the same kind, for the seat of his power was at Kuei-hua Ch'eng or Kuku Khoto. But since he was born in the north and originally came south with other Borjigin princes to settle and rule in Inner Mongolia, I have included him among the northerners. Strictly speaking he belongs to a third class of nomad ruler and can be compared to the Shaybanid Abu'l Khair (1428-68) who had his capital at Sighnak on the lower Syr. Both began in the northern steppes, but both, taking advantage of the very marked decline of the Ming and Timurid empires respectively, moved their headquarters south and so transformed their states into border powers closely resembling those of the more gradually evolved and orthodox type just named.

The only Asiatic figure to challenge comparison with the great Mongol as a conqueror is Timur (1370-1405) and it is worth mentioning that he consciously tried to pattern himself on Chingis. A close rival as a soldier, he was far less successful as a constructive statesman. This is attributable partly to his own personality, partly to the impracticability of his attempt to combine in one state the sedentary world of Iranian Islam and that of pastoral and semi-pastoral Central Asia. A Transoxiana Turk, the power of Timur was inherent in neither world, and death's removal of his strong hand was immediately followed by the secession of the steppe regions of the empire from the more settled areas to the south. As pointed out earlier in this chapter, somewhat similar causes brought down the empire founded by Chingis Khan, but Mongol power, based as it was on a strong nomad nucleus, proved far more stable and took very much longer to collapse than the empire of Timur.[21]

[21] Since I hold this belief, it will not be out of place to refer to quite a different

Among the common people of Asia, the military feats of
Chingis Khan are regarded as superhuman. To the Mongols,
most of whom now have little conception of the extent of his
conquests, he has assumed the proportions of a demi-god, and
is generally referred to as Chingis Bogdo (Chingis the Heaven
Sent). If one speaks of him, they will tell you that his triumphs
were ordained by Heaven and in this they are in agreement
with their ancestors. One of the apocryphal stories illustrating this belief is still current in the Ordos country.
According to it, Chingis Khan was once on the verge of defeat
in a battle with the Chinese, when suddenly he received a sword
from Heaven, and charging upon the enemy, won an overwhelming victory.[22] Among many there is also the Messianic
belief that he will rise again and lead his people to new power
and glory.

Some writers, perhaps reflecting upon utterances made at
the great assembly of 1206, e. g. " The sky has ordered me to
govern all peoples," and upon others made by the conqueror's
successors, seem to feel that Chingis Khan aspired to world
conquest. Unquestionably, as with Alexander and Timur, his
ambition grew with each successive step in his career, but it
is unlikely that, like the Macedonian, whose knowledge of the
world was necessarily far more limited than his own, he thought
it possible to subjugate the earth in a single life-time. Beyond
a doubt, Chingis was not a little surprised at the enormous
success of his arms, and with every fresh triumph planned

one put forward by the celebrated historian A. J. Toynbee. According to him,
the collapse of Timur's empire was due to the tremendous strain imposed on
Transoxiana and Iran by his wars, the first, the primary source of his military
power, and both of the wealth and civilization that stood behind him. Timur,
contends Toynbee, challenged and opposed his proper destiny when he turned his
arms on Iran instead of fulfilling his original role of champion of Iranian civilization against non-Moslem, non-Iranian, pastoralism. It is worth noting, however,
that Timur's whole career shows, that while he was able to appreciate much in
the Iranian world, e. g., its splendid buildings, he was really far more a product
of the pastoral than of the Iranian world. Otherwise was it with his descendant
Barbur who was ideologically much better fitted to play the role that Toynbee
feels should have been adhered to by Timur. (For Toynbee's opinion on the subject;
See *A Study of History*, pp. 491-501.

[22] Van Oost, *Au Pays des Ortos*.

greater and greater projects. Moreover, the territories allocated to the sons of Prince Juchi, as well as his death-bed plan for the final liquidation of the Chin, indicate that he confidently expected the empire to go on expanding after his decease. Nevertheless, it would be very bold to assert that he seriously contemplated the conquest of the world. But if he did not, his successors most certainly did. Quite apart from the series of systematic invasions undertaken by them after 1230, this is borne out by their arrogant attitude toward the rulers of the rest of the world. A revealing instance is afforded by the letter which Mongkha (1251-59) sent to the French king St. Louis (1226-70) by the hand of William of Rubruck.[23] In it he unhesitatingly affirms that Chingis Khan and all his descendents to mount the imperial throne had received Heaven's mandate to rule mankind. Of a like nature was his brother Kulagu's ominous epistle to the Mamluks of Egypt which starts; " These are the words of him (Mongkha) who rules the earth." One might cite other examples, but it is not necessary. It may be fairly assumed that it was largely such declarations that gave birth to the belief that Chingis Khan was a conscious world conqueror. But if universal dominion did not come within his horizon, and if his sons and grandsons failed to subdue the world, between them they created the greatest military power known to history. It goes without saying that the repercussions of their wars were tremendous and that many subsequent developments and trends in the world at large drew their origins from them, but these are matters outside the scope of this work and our story must here end.

---

[23] See Rockhill, *The Journey of William of Rubruck*, pp. 248-251.

# APPENDIX A.

## (The Mongol Invasion of Transoxiana)

The Mongol invasion of the Khorezmian empire has always attracted more attention than any other of Chingis Khan's wars, but it is only comparatively recently that it has come in for study by the military expert. Among those writing in English, the best known is Captain B. H. Liddell Hart, who dealt with the conquest of Transoxiana in his " Great Captains Unveiled." After his book came a series of articles on Chingis Khan contributed to the Canadian Defence Quarterly during the years 1932 and 1933, by Squadron Leader C. C. Walker. Six years later these appeared, revised, and to a certain extent rewritten, in a book called " Jenghiz Khan." Although that part of the work dealing with China suffers from the inadequate authorities on the subject available to Walker, the chapters covering the invasion of Transoxiana, Khurasan and Afghanistan are of great value. Therefore in the following account I shall quote frequently from him.

As seen, the Khwarazm Shah Muhammad declined to give Chingis Khan battle in the open, partly on account of the internal political situation which beset him, partly because of geographical disadvantages. Both D'Ohsson and Barthold inform us that he was at odds with the Moslem clergy and with a large part of the army which was under the influence of the Queen Mother Turkhan Khatun. This, thinks Barthold, had considerable weight in discouraging him from assembling a great host and marching north to meet the invader.[1] The Russian author believes that, even if victorious, the Shah feared a mutiny by a considerable number of his troops, namely those who were Khanghlis, and so bound to his mother who was of the same race.[2] But in addition to this danger there were a number of geographical factors that must have greatly influenced him. Here one cannot do better than turn to Walker.

" In order," he says, " to obtain a clear appreciation of the problem which confronted Mahommed, it is necessary first to describe the land known as Transoxiana from a strategical standpoint."

" Transoxiana, the country between the Oxus (Amu) and Jaxartes

---

[1] Vladimirtsov, see *The Life of Chingis Khan*, also believes that Muhammad feared to assemble a large army lest his generals mutiny.

[2] The Khanghlis were the same people as the Kipchaks the latter name being that often applied to the nomads of southern Russia at this time. To avoid confusion, the name Khanghli is here always used for those of the race subject to the Khwarazm Shah. (For the identification of the two names, see Barthold, *Turkestan down to the Mongol Invasion.*)

(Syr), can be roughly described as a letter H lying on its side, with the populated region limited to the river banks and broad cross bar of the H—the latter formed by the valley of the Zarafshan, in which are Bokhara and Samarkand and, in addition, the oases of Nakshah in which stand Shahri-sabz (Kesh) and Karshi (Nasaf).[3] Between this central densely populated area and the Aral Sea[4] the terrain between the rivers is desert and desert-steppe, called the Kizil Kum or Red Sands. . . ." " East of the belt of agriculture and settlement rise the mountains, and the further east they extend the higher become the peaks and the more difficult the passes, until at last the only means of communication between the Oxus (Amu) and Jaxartes (Syr) is the valley of the Wakhs, which is almost impassable in its upper reaches. . . .[5] "

" It is obvious that the defense of this area against invasion from the north would be as difficult an undertaking as any commander could be called upon to effect. The long line of the Jaxartes (Syr) was served by only one line of communication practicable for an army, i. e., the high-road from Samarkand to Benaket (Banakath). The river and the mountains assist the invader rather than the defense, for if a commander with a view to saving the northern cities, all of which lie on the north bank of the river, decides to meet the enemy on the frontier, he will have to risk fighting with a broad river at his back, with a chance of annihilation if defeated. If, on the other hand, he advances beyond the mountains into the steppes with sufficient force to risk an encounter, he would be limited to one line of supply or retreat, i. e., the Arys Pass."[6]

" On the other hand, if he decides to use the river as his defensive line, he will lose the cities on the north bank."

" One critic of Mahommed's strategy makes a point of the dispersal of his forces, but takes care not to offer a suggestion as to where he should have concentrated them . . . ."

" His defensive plan was this. He placed strong garrisons in the cities north of the Jaxartes (Syr)—Otrar alone was given a force of 50,000— and concentrated the bulk of his army, to the strength of 60,000 Kankalis (Khanghlis) cavalry and 50,000 local infantry, in Samarkand, probably hoping that the Mongols when plundering the surrounding districts, would give him an opportunity for a counter stroke. . . ."

" His plan failed because of the ability of the Mongols to storm the fortresses. Had Jenghiz Khan not appeared on the scene, the ability of Mahommed to conquer and organize an immense empire would have been

---

[3] At the time of the Mongol invasion Shahri-zabz was known as Kesh or Kish, while for Karshi one should read Nasaf, the town of Karshi not having been built until the days of the Jaghatai dynasty (1227-1363).

[4] The Mongols called the Aral Sea the Khara Dengiz. See Cordier, *Histoire Générale de la Chine*, Vol. II, Chap. XIII, p. 207.

[5] During medieval times the Wakhs was known as the Wakhshab. (See Le Strange, *The Lands of the Eastern Caliphate*, pp. 437-439.)

[6] The Shah did this in 1210 during the last days of his war with Khara Khitai, but of course the forces of his opponent the Gur Khan were much inferior to those of Chingis Khan.

seized on by historians as evidence of supernatural genius and superlative
statesmanship, and his treachery and indecision would have been considered wisdom.  So much for the judgment of history."

Leaving Walker for a moment: Chingis Khan, when he saw that he

## Mongol Conquest of Transoxiana

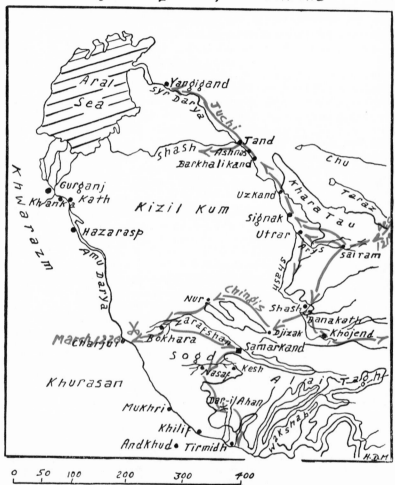

could expect no engagement on the frontier, divided his troops, numbering
some 150,000, into four armies.  One under Jaghatai and Ugedei marched
to Utrar (Otrar), which was probably invested early in December, 1219,
another, with the towns of the lower Syr as its objective, moved northwest
with Juchi along the river, which up to Jand, was then known as the

Shash. At this town it divided, one channel continuing as the Shash to the southeastern end of the Aral Sea, the other as the Syr, to the northeastern end. A third force of 5,000 men laid siege to the towns of Shash and Banakath, and a fourth, the largest of all, perhaps 60,000 strong, remained north of the Arys Pass with the conqueror and his youngest son Tului.[7]

More than one explanation of this arrangement has been offered, but that put forward by Walker seems the most acceptable. To quote him: " It is obvious that before Jenghiz Khan could operate against Samarkand, he would have to clear the Jaxartes (Syr) of the enemy forces holding it; but the scheme he adopted demands attention. The size of the third corps, only a half tuman, under subordinate commanders named Alak, Suketu Cherbi and Tughai, indicates that it had two functions, first to make certain of the river crossing at Benaket (Banakath) where the road to Samarkand met the river, but its second and equally important function was to present a bait to Mahommed in the hope that it would draw him into the open."

" Jenghiz Khan undoubtedly desired to meet his opponent on the battle field, and if Mahommed had been an able soldier, he would have tried to destroy his enemies in detail, so to help him make up his mind, one weak detachment was offered him. If Mahommed had crossed the river, this detachment could have retreated to Otrar, where Jaghatai and Ogdai (Ugedei) were encamped before the walls."

" Owing to the Mongol practice of completely destroying the inhabitants of a locality, Mahommed could have had little knowledge of the army which was waiting patiently north of the pass. From Mahommed's point of view, an engagement at Otrar should have been most desirable, for with his army of 100,000 men advancing from the east, and the other 50,000 composing the garrison of Otrar, he should have thought that it would have been possible to catch Jagatai and Ogdai between two fires. But looking at this situation from Jenghiz Khan's standpoint, we can see the detachment before Benaket (Banakath) retreating to Otrar when threatened, Juji hurrying back from down-river to reinforce Ogdai and Jagatai, and then when battle was joined, Jenghiz and Tule could descend like a thunderbolt on the flank of Mahommet, in a typical Mongol manner. If it be objected that such a scheme depends on accurate timing of widely dis-

---

[7] The 5,000 men despatched to Banakath is the only force for which our authorities give a figure. The numbers of the others are more or less guess work. Modern writers on the subject—the most noteworthy of which are Barthold and Vladimirtsov—believe that the whole army of invasion numbered from 150,000 to 200,000. Considering the forces at Chingis Khan's disposal for this war, I think that 150,000 cavalry is the most he could have taken with him. As regards the strength of the four armies, that under Jaghatai and Ugedei may have numbered some 40,000, Juchi's about the same, that of Chingis and Tului approximately 60,000, the force for Banakath, as already seen, 5,000, while a remaining 5,000 may have been distributed north of the Arys Pass in charge of supply and forwarding depots.

persed forces, it must be remembered that the Mongols made use of this maneuver on many occasions."

The action never took place, but as Walker remarks, the delay of the army under Chingis Khan is difficult to explain, unless one was contemplated.

After waiting from December, 1219, to February, 1220, during which time all but the citadel of Utrar had been taken and Juchi had met with no check, the Mongol Khan decided that it was unlikely the Shah would ever be drawn into a decisive battle. Unable to put his first plan into execution because of Muhammad's inaction, he formed another. Again one cannot do better than follow Walker.

" At the head of 40,000 to 50,00C cavalry and two companies of siege engineers, he marched through the pass and up the river to Benaket (Banakath).[8] There he crossed and directed his force to Djizak or Zernuc, about half way to Samarkand.'

" The road between Benaket (Banakath) and Zernuc crosses an arid region known as the ' famished steppe,' eighty miles in extent, a parched and barren waste. . . .''

" Zernuc submitted with hardly more than a show of resistance; but then, instead of marching on Samarkand, the center of enemy resistance, the Mongol swung out into the desert around the range of hills called the Khrebet Nurata, with Nur as his objective. A Turkeman guided his army to Nur, and the route he took was for long afterwards called ' The Great Khan's Way.' Nur, taken by surprise at the sudden appearance of a great army at its gates, when it believed itself safe from attack through the desert, submitted quietly, and Jenghiz Khan spared the town. From Nur he marched straight on Bokhara, reaching the great city in March, 1220. The garrison, 20,000 strong, defended it for some days, but either disloyalty or Mahommed's inaction had caused such a lowering of morale, that the position was regarded as hopeless; and the cavalry of the garrison deserted and fled. This force reached the Oxus (Amu), but there the Mongols came up and annihilated them.[9] The inhabitants, left without defenders, opened the gates and the Mongols rode in."

" From the steps of the great mosque of Bokhara, Jenghiz Khan ordered his troops to find fodder for their horses, i. e., permission to loot; and for days they indulged in an orgy of rape, plunder and destruction, the wealthier inhabitants being forced to surrender their riches."

" The stroke bespeaks the master. Foiled by Mahommed's inaction from a decisive victory in the field, he read aright his enemy's mind and evolved another plan when the first one failed."

---

[8] Fifty thousand is Walker's highest figure for the army under Chingis Khan and Tului, but considering the great enemy forces of cavalry at Bokhara and Samarkand, I think it likely that the conqueror had with him at least 60,000 men. The Mongol advance guard was commanded by the famous Subudei.

[9] The strength of the garrison is variously estimated; Juzjani puts it at 12,000 cavalry in all, Juwayni at 20,000 in the exterior army alone, i. e., troops other than the garrison proper, and Nasawi at 30,000 inclusive.

(For these figures; see Barthold, *Turkestan down to the Mongol Invasion*, p.409.)

" The capture of Zernuc must have appeared to Mahommed as a prelude to the Mongol's appearance before Samarkand, but before he could gain information to the contrary, Jenghiz Khan had swung through the desert, his flank covered by the hills, and taken Nur. Then came the final catastrophe of the failure of the garrison of Bokhara to hold the Mongols, and the fall of the city."

" Mahommed had put his trust in the strength of his walls, and Jenghiz Khan, having tested out his enemy's desires and seen his plan, had correctly gauged his opponent's mind and had delivered one of the masterstrokes of war. At one blow, as daring in execution as it was simple in conception, he had isolated Samarkand from all hope of eventual victory. Instead of hurling his splendid troops against its impregnable walls, he used his superior mobility to attack the weaker points of his enemy's defensive system; and when they were gone, Samarkand ceased to be of importance."

" Having eliminated Bokhara as a center of resistance, Jenghiz Khan now turned back from the gutted city and directed his forces up the valley of the Zarafshan to Samarkand."

Without quoting Walker further, it remains to be said that simultaneously Jaghatai and Ugedei, who had at last taken the citadel of Utrar (Otrar), moved to join their father before Samarkand. Juchi remained on the Syr until sent against Gurganj in November or December, 1220.

Muhammad did not wait but fled across the Amu (Oxus) with 30,000 Turkish soldiers of the garrison.

Advancing with thousands of captives, who were organized in sections of ten to give them the appearance of being part of the hostile troops, the two converging Mongol armies, which can hardly have exceeded 90,000 effectives, seemed innumerable. On the third day after their arrival the inhabitants made a great sortie from the city. This ended in a terrible disaster, 50,000 to 70,000[10] being left dead outside the walls, and two days later Samarkand and its still large garrison, except for 2,000 men in the citadel, surrendered. Of this remnant, half succeeded in fighting their way through the Mongol lines, but the rest perished when the citadel fell a month afterward—probably late in April, 1220.

Juwayni reports that Samarkand contained 110,000 defenders, 60,000 Turks and 50,000 Tajiks.[11] The Turks were regular troops, but the majority of the garrison were Tajiks who must have been local militia and it is evident that it is they who made the disastrous sortie from the city. When referring to the surrender and subsequent massacre of the Turks, Juwayni says that the latter numbered 30,000, so the Shah must have taken

---

[10] Ibn al Athir says that the citizens making the sortie numbered 70,000, Juzjani 50,000. Both agree that all perished. (See Barthold, *Turkestan down to the Mongol Invasion*, p. 412.)

[11] As regards the numbers of Samarkand's defenders, it should be noted that Nasawi says the army was only 40,000 strong. Ibn al-Athir 50,000, and Juzjani 60,000, including Turks, Tajiks, Ghurs, Khalaj and Kharluks, all under the command of Tughay Khan the brother of Turkhan Khatun. (See Barthold, *Turkestan down to the Mongol Invasion*, p. 411.)

about half of the original 60,000 with him when he left. On reaching the other side of the Amu, two half hearted attempts were made to help the city. First 10,000 men and then 20,000 moved toward Samarkand, but on getting near it dared not approach the Mongol army. After that Muhammad abandoned all hope and fled west.

Smarkand in his hands, Chingis Khan detached two tumans, some say three, in pursuit of the Shah. The generals of the first two were Jebe and Subudei, that of the third Tokuchar who may have left then or later. At the same time, 20,000 troops and 50,000 laborers were sent to help reduce Khojend.\ After capturing Shash and Benekath, the 5,000 men under Alak, Suketu Cherbi and Tughai, marched on this town which was heroically defended by Timur Malik.[12] Only after the arrival of these reinforcements did the place fall, which presumably was followed by the conquest of Farghana. Meanwhile Chingis Khan, leaving two small detachments in occupation of Bokhara and Samarkand, took up his summer quarters at Nasaf in the Nakhshab oasis. From there he sent bodies of troops to reduce the mountains to the South. In September he was again on the move, and marching through the Dar i-Ahan (Iron Gates),[13] reached the Amu and laid siege to Tirmidh. This he took in eleven days but not until the spring of 1221 did he cross the river.

Chingis Khan's march to Bokhara may be thought an extremely hazardous undertaking because of the possibility of an attack by numerically superior forces. As Walker points out in Appendix II of "Jenghiz Khan," he had no more reason than Muhammad to believe that Bokhara would capitulate in a few days. On the contrary, it is reasonable to suppose that he anticipated a long siege which Muhammad would try to raise. Also, one might have expected that an army would come down on him from the province of Khwarazm. In reality the situation was not so dangerous. Had the Shah left Samarkand to relieve Bokhara, Chingis Khan could have refused battle long enough to have given Jaghatai and Ugedei time to come in on Muhammad's rear, which would have been just what he would have liked. At the same time precaution had been taken against a similar move by the enemy from Khwarazm. After Juchi had completed his operations in the north, he ordered Taynal Noyan[14] to take 20,000 men—half of them recently enlisted Turkomens—to advance down the Lower Shash towards Gurganj. The size of the force shows that its intention was not conquest but distraction. The raid failed because the 10,000 Turkomens mutinied and had to be crushed, but the possibility of it being repeated would discourage the Queen Mother, who as we know, was on bad terms with her son, from sending troops to help him. Therefore,

---

[12] Timur Malik escaped down the river to Gurganj and subsequently joined Jalal ad-Din, with whom he remained until the prince's death.
(See D'Ohsson, *Histoire des Mongols.*)

[13] This pass is also known as the Kolugha.

[14] When in January, 1221, the Mongols marched to the conquest of the province of Khwarazm, they numbered 50,000 to 60,000.
(See Barthold, *Turkestan down to the Mongol Invasion*, p. 436.)

Chingis Khan's march on Bokhara was really comparatively safe and the worst he had to fear were two long and obstinate sieges at Bokhara and Samarkand, neither of which materialized.

Much as one admires the conqueror's invasion of the Khorezmian empire, it is obvious that his great success was in part due to the political and geographical disabilities of his opponent. Also Muhammad did not enjoy the large numerical superiority supposed by certain authorities. Of the Shah's reputed 400,000 men,[15] nearly half would be stationed in different parts of his dominions, which meant that he had perhaps rather more than 200,000 with which to meet the Mongols in Transoxiana, not a great superiority, when one bears in mind the defense problem on his hands.[16] Had all his troops been loyal, instead of some being attached to the Queen Mother rather than to himself, he might have saved the country south of the Amu (Oxus). If not a brilliant soldier, he was nevertheless an experienced one and had twice been exposed to adversity in his ultimately successful wars against the Ghurs and Khara Khitans. His behavior in the first of these is perhaps indicative of what might have happened had he been able to rely solidly on the whole of his army. In 1204 the Ghurs, with whom he had been intermittently at war since his accession in 1200, suddenly invaded his dominions with an army of 70,000 men. At the head of this force was Shihab ad-Din Muhammad (1203-6), one of the most able and daring soldiers of his day.[17] Advancing swiftly toward Gurganj, he completely surprised the Shah who was caught at Merv while at the head of no more than 10,000 troops and had to retire southward.[18] Hearing of the enemy's approach, the inhabitants of the threatened city, flooded the surrounding country, but this delayed Shihab ad-Din no more than forty days, and as soon as the waters had subsided, he resumed his advance. Undaunted by their failure, the Khorezmians marched out to meet him, but near Khara Su suffered a crushing defeat and the invading army laid siege to Gurganj.

Meanwhile the Shah had sent in all directions for troops, probably stripping the garrisons of Khurasan and Iraq-i Ajami, and soon marched

---

[15] This figure, which can be no more than a rough estimate, has come down to us from Rashid ad-Din who has been followed by the author of the *Shajrat ul Atrak*, p. 121, and by the Europeans Pétis de la Croix, p. 159, Howorth, part I, p. 75 and Curtin, *The Mongols*, p. 104. However, D'Ohsson, Barthold and Vladimirtsov nowhere commit themselves to an estimate, but merely say that the Shah's army was decidedly superior in numbers to that of Chingis Khan.

[16] Two hundred thousand is also the number given by B. H. Liddell Hart as the approximate strength of the army with which Muhammad was able to meet Chingis Khan.

(See B. H. Liddell Hart, *Great Captains Unveiled*.)

[17] Shihab ad-Din, also known as Muiz ad-Din, conquered the greater part of northern India for his brother Ghiyath ad-Din Muhammad (1180-1203), whom he succeeded in 1203.

[18] The figure for Shihab ad-Din's army and that for the Shah's at Merv are taken from Vambéry's *History of Bokhara*, Chap. III, p. 111.

north with an army also reported to have numbered 70,000.[21] At the same time he successfully appealed for the despatch of a Khara Khitan force.[20] Learning of the approach of both enemies, Shihab ad-Din quickly raised the siege and began to withdraw, but at Hazarasp the Shah came up with him and forced an agreement. The Ghurid Sultan was severely defeated and the victor, leaving the Khara Khitans, just arrived on the scene, to pursue him, returned to his capital. In the last days of September, or at the beginning of October (1204), the Ghurs found themselves surrounded in the neighborhood of Andkhud, and after a two week's battle were compelled to shut themselves up in the town. Fortunately for the Ghurid Sultan, Othman of Samarkand, who was with the Khara Khitan army, interceded for him and he was able to buy his return to his own dominions at the price of a huge ransom.[21]

In this war Muhammad had one important advantage that he did not enjoy against Chingis Khan, namely, the support of a strong ally, the Khara Khitans. As seen, although caught unawares and at first thrown off balance, he quickly recovered. Confident that his capital, then Gurganj and under the still friendly Queen Mother, would fight to the utmost, he remained firm in Khurasan and collected a large army of relief. If on this occasion his opponent was not nearly so powerful as Chingis Khan, his own resources at the time were half of what they were in 1220. But the political situation was comparatively good and the problem of defense far easier. Consequently he could and did put up a much more able and determined fight than against the Mongols. While this does not prove that, even if properly supported by the Queen Mother, he would have defeated Chingis Khan, it does at least show that he was by no means an incompetent soldier and hardly deserves the charges of military ineptitude and cowardice hurled at him by various writers.

---

[19] This is the strength of the army as reported by Barthold, who says nothing about the numbers of the Ghurid force. (See Barthold, *Turkestan down to the Mongol Invasion*, p. 350.)

[20] At the time the Gur Khan of Khara Khitai was the Shah's overlord and continued to receive tribute until Muhammad's rebellion in 1207. (For the Shah's wars against the Khara Khitans and Ghurs; see Barthold, *Turkestan down to the Mongol Invasion*, Chap. III.)

[21] Like the Shah, Othman of Samarkand (1200-12) was a vassal of the Gur Khan and probably pointed out to the Khara Khitans that the destruction of the Ghurs would remove a valuable counterweight to the growing power of the Khwarazm Shah.

# APPENDIX B.

## (The Flight of Ilkha the Kerait to Etsin Gol)

There is an interesting story still current among the Torguts of the Etsin Gol, whose princes believe that they are descended from one of Tughrul the Kerait's brothers, that the now deserted town of Khara Khoto—the Hei-shui Ch'eng and Etsina of Medieval times—was heroically defended against the Chinese by a certain Khara Baatur Janjyn. Pressed by the enemy, he sent to the tribes of the west for help but in vain. At length, by means of magic spells, the Chinese turned the Etsin Gol from its course and forced the town to surrender through lack of water. With only a single donkey for Khara Baatur Janjyn to ride, the defenders were about to leave, but when the hour of departure came a deep sleep descended upon the besieging army and Khara Baatur rode forth without the victors witnessing his shame. But the trees outside Khara Khoto, overcome with pity at the sight of the hero reduced to such straits, bowed down before him and today the dead trunks still lie prostrate in the surrounding sands. See; Henning Haslund-Christensen, *Men and Gods in Mongolia.*

I know of no siege of Khara Khoto by the Chinese and it seems to me that Khara Baatur Janjyn may be one and the same with the Kerait Ilkha, the Sangun or Chiang-chün, while Khara Baatur's appeal to the tribes of the west could be an echo of Ilkha's flight to the Naimans; and the defense and loss of Khara Khoto, a memory of his brief appearance on the Etsin Gol. In point of fact, the Torguts are reckoned a branch of the Oirads and not descendants of the Keraits, but their princes could easily be of Kerait extraction. However, it is very likely that this legend is a confused version of two events; Ilkha's flight to the Etsin Gol, and the defense of Khara Khoto against the Mongols in 1226. In this latter connection, it is also possible that the story owes something to tales about the two desperate sieges of Sha Chou, 300 miles to the southwest. This town, like Khara Khoto, was a Tangut possession and was besieged by the Mongols, once during 1224 and again from August, 1226 to April, 1227. On the first occasion it escaped capture but on the second fell, though not until the commander and garrison had put up one of the finest defenses in Tangut history, a longer one by far than that of Khara Khoto.

# APPENDIX C.

## (The Battle of Huan-erh-tsui)

Since the battle of Huan-erh-tsui is such an outstanding event, and as I have taken it upon myself to reconstruct it in outline, the curious may be interested in the sources with which I have supplemented the " Yüan Sheng Wu Ch'in Cheng Lu." The most important of these has been the " Meng-wu-erh Shih," which is itself largely based on the " Yüan Sheng Wu Ch'in Cheng Lu," but which has also made use of the biographies of Mukhali in the " Ssǔ Ch'ao Pieh Shih " and the " Yüan Ch'ao Ming Ch'en Shih Liao." According to it, when news reached the Chin that the Mongols were pillaging Fu Chou, two Khitan officers of the staff, Pa-ku-shih and Sang-ch'en, advised Chih-chung to order his mounted troops to try a surprise attack. But Chih-chung thought the plan too hazardous and decided upon a ranged battle in which he could employ both cavalry and infantry. The next day, while Chingis Khan was still at his morning meal, the Chin began to advance. He thereupon rose and commanded the armies of the center and left-wing to meet the onset at Huan-erh-tsui, and there before the conflict began, a Chin officer, Shih-mo Ming-an, surrendered.

Impressed with the great numerical superiority of the enemy, Mukhali turned to Chingis Khan and said: " the soldiers of the Chin are far more numerous than our own and unless we fight to the utmost we shall be defeated." He then charged with the troops of the left-wing army, who drove into the enemy with their lances. The onslaught was at once supported by the central army under Chingis Khan, and the Chin were so heavily defeated that the bodies of the slain strewed the countryside. The victorious Mongols then pressed on to attack Wan-yen Hu-sha's army, which was overtaken at Hui-ho Pao and almost annihilated."

From the above mentioned biography of Mukhali in the " Yüan Ch'ao Ming Ch'en Shih Liao," one learns that the general charged the first line of the enemy—undoubtedly the cavalry—whereupon Chingis Khan attacked with the rest of the army and before noon the Chin were completely overthrown and pursued to the Hui Ho. So great was the carnage that the dead were scattered over 100 li (approximately 33 miles) and all the crack soldiers of the Chin slain.

The biography of Ch'a-han (Chaghan), though brief, provides an interesting piece of information not found elsewhere. When Ting Hsüeh's arrival at the Yeh-hu Ling became known, Chingis Khan sent Chaghan to reconnoitre. On his return the officer reported that there was no need to fear the enemy as they seemed disorganized. Chingis Khan forthwith gave orders for an advance and won an overwhelming victory.

As regards Wan-yen Hu-sha, his biography informs us that when he heard that the Mongols were in the Yeh-hu Ling, he fell into a panic and returned to Hsüan-p'ing. There the officers of the garrison begged him to stay and make a stand, but he could think only of retreat and in the night took the road for Hsüan-te Chou. Before he got there he was overtaken by the Mongols at Hui-ho Pao and so badly defeated that he himself barely escaped to the city.

Concerning Chih-chung's flight from Huan-erh-tsui to Hui-ho Pao, the only work that definitely states that he joined Hu-sha at Hui-ho Pao is a rather unsatisfactory account in the "Sung Yuan T'ung-chien Ch'uan-pien." " Chingis Khan," it reports, " attacked Wu-sha Pao and Wu-yüeh ying, whereupon Wan-yen Hu-sha and Tu-chi Ch'ien-chia-nu retired to the Hui Ho. There they were joined by Hu-sha-hu (Chih-chung) and resisted the Mongols three days, but when Chingis Khan led (sent) 3,000 picked troops to An-ting (presumably a mistake for Ting-an) Hu-sha-hu unexpectly quit the field with 7,000 chosen men and the Chin were severely beaten and pursued all the way to the Ts'ui-p'ing K'ou." The pass here referred to is evidently that southeast of Hsi Ching, not the one in the Yeh-hu Ling.

Despite this excerpt and that from the " Yüan Sheng Wu Ch'in Cheng Lu," there is considerable confusion regarding the part played by Chih-chung in opposing Chingis Khan. The biography of Yeh-lü T'u-hua (Tukha), like that of Chih-chung himself, merely records the action fought near Ting-an. The " Meng-wu-erh Shih " mentions the presence of the general at both Huan-erh-tsui and Ting-an, but makes no reference to his joining Hu-sha at Hui-ho Pao. Completely at variance with all other sources are the " Chin Shih " and the " Li-tai T'ung-chien Chi-lan." According to both, Chih-chung was besieged by the Mongols in Hsi Ching, not beaten in battle at Huan-erh-tsui, which the latter dates in the 9th. month (Oct. 9th-Nov. 6th.). More detailed than the "Chin Shih," the " Li-tai T'ung-chien Chi-lan " asserts that during the 8th month (Sept. 12th Oct. 8th.) the Mongols defeated the Chin at Wu-sha Pao. Following up the victory, Chingis Khan took Pai-teng Ch'eng and laid siege to Hsi Ching. After seven days, Hu-sha-hu began to fear for his safety and broke through the Mongol lines with a body of chosen troops. Chingis Khan forthwith despatched 3,000 cavalry in pursuit and the fugitives were overtaken, defeated and driven down the Ts'ui-p'ing K'ou—here the defile to the S. E. of Hsi Ching—while the city fell. The " Chin Shih " makes no reference to the capture of the place, and the biography of Mo-jan Chin-chung implies that it remained untaken. Since the " Yüan Sheng Wu Ch'in Cheng Lu " is more reliable for the first years of the Mongol invasion than either the " Chin Shih " or the " Li-tai T'ung-chien Chi-lan," it is safe to assume that Chih-chung was at Huan-erh-tsui and not at Hsi Ching. Perhaps the " Li-tai T'ung-chien Chi-lan " has been led into error by Chih-chung's position as commander of Hsi Ching and the existence of two Ts'ui-p'ing K'ou, one in the Yeh-lu Ling, and another southeast of Hsi Ching. Further confusion has also doubtless arisen from Chingis Khan's unsuccessful siege of the city in 1212.

# APPENDIX D.

## (The First Appearance of jhe Mongols in Korea)

Since the mutiny in Yeh-lü Liu-ke's army played an important part in the Khitan prince's reign, a brief account of the mutineer's doings in Korea may be of interest. After Ch'i-nu-ya-erh's expulsion from Ch'eng Chou, he and his followers found themselves unable to continue in Liao-tung, and crossing the Yalu, probably early in November 1216, fell upon that part of Korea still nominally subject to the Chin. There they looted the towns of Sak Ju, Chung Ju[1] and Jung Ju, after which they divided their forces and over-ran all the country between the mouth of the Yalu and the Korean capital Song Do. In December (1216) they were brought to battle near the latter by 30,000 Koreans, but were victorious and forced the beaten army to retire to Ta-fu Ying.

Soon after the beginning of 1217, the rebel leader Ch'i-nu-ya-erh was murdered by Chin-shan, one of his officers, who led the insurgents north. Marching down the frozen Ta-t'ung Chiang, the new leader attacked Huang Ju, which was taken in February and all the inhabitants put to the sword. Chin-shan survived this atrocity but a short time and was in his turn killed by T'ung-ku-yü, formerly Yeh-lü Liu-ke's chief of staff. But T'ung-ku-yü was also assassinated. The succeeding Khitan leader Han-she then moved south and Song Do was again menaced, but though the Yellow Bridge within five li (2½ miles) of it was burned, the capital was too strong to attack. Once more the invaders turned north and laid siege to Pyong-yang. The town fell, but this was almost the last Khitan success. Again marching down the Ta-t'ung Chiang, by this time open, they were severely beaten by the Koreans at P'u-t'a-chin to the south of the river's mouth and forced to retreat to Pei Kuan. The identity of both these places is uncertain, but P'u-t'a-chin may be the same as old Chu-chin, the Hik Kiori of today, and Pei Kuan, if the Pei-an of Yüan times, identical with present An Ju, forty-five miles to the north of Pyong-yang. At the latter the Khitans were compelled to assist the Jurchids, probably the authorities of P'o-ssŭ Lu in their May expedition against P'u-hsien Wan-nu, but subsequently they returned south. At Pak-chün, Han-she was attacked by a Korean army, but though defeated was able to advance on Kang-dong which he captured and where, as related, he was eventually overthrown by Yeh-lü Liu-ke in February, 1218. (See the "*Meng-wu-erh Shih*," biog. of "Yeh-lü Liu-ke"; Yanai, *Ken Dai Kyo Ryako Tohoko* and Nakaba Yamada, *Ghenko*.)

(All places have been identified from the *Karte von Ost China*, section on "Pyong-yang"; Yanai's *Tōyō Dokushi Chizu*, p. 15, "map of Korea under the Yüan dynasty" (1260-1368), and Lu T'ung's *Chung Hua Ming Kuo Li Ssŭ I Chan Cheng Hsing Shih Ch'uan T'u* (Maps and explanations of China's wars with the barbarians), maps, 7 and 18.

---

[1] Sak Ju is 33 miles northwest of Wi Ju, and Chung Ju 50 miles to the southeast; See *Karte von Ost China*.

# BIBLIOGRAPHY

## CHINESE, JAPANESE AND MONGOL

*Altan Tobci*, written in 1604, and the *Sanang Setsen*, written in 1662, are purely Mongol works. The former was first translated into Russian in 1858, the latter into German during 1829.

*Ch'eng-Chi-Ssŭ-Han*, by Feng, Ch'eng-chün, published 1934.

*Chin Shih*, a historical text including biographies of a number of Chin commanders; first brought out during the Yüan dynasty (1260-1368) and photostated in 1932.

*Chung Hua Min Kuo Li Shih Ssu I Chan Cheng Hsing Shih Ch'uan T'u* (Maps and explanations of China's warfare and strategy with the barbarians), by Lu, T'ung, published 1911.

*Chung Hsi Hui Shih Jih Li* (Calendar of Chinese, Christian and Moslem dates), by Ch'en, Yüan, published in Peking, 1926.

*Chung-kuo Ku-chin Ti-ming Ta-tzu-tien* (A dictionary of Chinese geographical names, past and present), Shanghai, 1931.

*Hoku Shina Chizu* (Map of North China), published in Dairen, 1936.

*Hsi Hsia Chi*, by Tai, Hsi-chang, published in 1924. The main works used by the author have been the Wu Tai Shih, Sung Shih, Liao Shih, Chin Shih, Yüan Shih of Sung, Lien, Meng-wu-erh Shih and the Hsi Hsia Shu Shih.

*Hsi-Hsia Chi Shih Pen-mo*, by Chang, Chien-ch'ung, published in 1884.

*Hsi Hsia Shu Shih*, by Wu, Kuang-ch'eng, published in 1825. The principal sources consulted in the writing of this work have been the Shu T'ung-chien, Shu Kang-mu, T'ung-chien Ch'ang-pien by Li T'ao, the Tung Tu Shih Liao, Hsi Hsia Shu Chih, Hsia Ku Kai-yao and the Sung Shih.

*Hsin Yüan Shih*, by K'e, Shao-ming, published 1920.

*Ken Dai Kyo Ryako Tohoko* by Yanai, Watari, Tokyo.

*Li-tai T'ung-chien Chi-lan*, by Fu, Heng, Shanghai, 1872.

*Li-tai Yu-ti Yen-ke Hsien-Yao-T'u* (A historical atlas of China under her successive dynasties), by Yang, Shou-ch'ing, published 1898.

*Meng Ta Pei Lu*, compiled in the 13th century by the Sung general Meng Hung and with annotations by Wang, Kuo-wei, published 1927-28, Shanghai.

*Meng-wu-erh Shih*, by T'u, Chi, main text and biographies. This is an unofficial history compiled between 1875 and 1911, and is the most extensive and critical work written on the Mongols in Chinese. Not only have all the standard and official records on the subject been consulted, but also a multitude of other and little known sources.

*Sui-yüan Sheng Fen-hsien Tiao-ch'a Kai Yao* (The Survey of the History of the province of Suiyuan), published 1934.

*Ssu Ch'ao Pieh Shih*, a supplementary record to the official histories of the Liao, Sung, Chin and Yuan dynasties compiled by Shao, Yüan-p'ing and corrected by Hsi Shih-ch'en.

*Sung Shih*, brought out during the Yüan dynasty (1260-1368) and photostated in 1926.

*Sung Yüan T'ung-chien Ch'uan-pien*, first published during the Ming dynasty (1368-1644). Though of questionable value, it contains odds and ends of information found nowhere else.

*Tōyō Dokushi Chizu*, by Yanai, Watari (A historical atlas of China and her neighbors, Korea in particular detail), Tokyo, 1931.

*Yüan Ch'ao Ming Ch'en Shih Liao*, by Ssu, T'ien-chiao, first published in the reign of Kubilai Khaghan (1260-94) and republished in 1899.

*Yüan Ch'ao Pi Shih* (The Secret or Official History of the Mongols), was written in Mongol in 1240 and first translated into Chinese at the end of the 14th century. This was published in 1847 and was translated into Russian by Palladius during 1866. During 1908 a photostatic copy was made of the Chinese version. Since then two excellent translations have been completed by Pelliot and Haenisch.

*Yüan Sheng Wu Ch'in Cheng Lu*, a work also based on Mongol tradition, covers the same period as the Yuan Ch'ao Pi Shih, and was translated by Palladius in 1872. A new edition of the Chinese text was brought out by Wang, Kuo-wei in 1926.

*Yüan Shih*, published in 1371, was brought out by Sung, Lien, of the Historical Commission, and is a re-collection of material formerly collected during the Yüan Dynasty (1260-1368), but lost after its fall. In 1936 a photostatic copy was made of this work.

*Yüan Shih Chi Shih Pen-mo*, published in 1606.

*Yüan Shih Ping Chih* (Military organization of the Yüan Dynasty).

*Yüan Shih I Wei Ch'eng Pu*, by Hung, Chün, published 1894.

*Yüan Shih Hsin Pien*, by Wei, Yuan, published 1905.


## OCCIDENTAL WORKS CONSULTED

Abu'l Ghazi Bahadur Khan. "*History of the Turks, Mongols and Tartars*, London, 1730.

Barthold, W., *Turkestan Down to The Mongol Invasion*, E. J. W. Gibb, Memorial New Series V, London, 1928.

Barthold W., " Bishbaligh," *Encyclopaedia of Islam*, Vol. I
" Bulghar "            "            "      Vol. I
" Cagatai "           "            "      Vol. I
" Cingis Khan "       "            "      Vol. I
" Kara Khitai "       "            "      Vol. II
" Turks "             "            "      Vol. IV

Beazley, *The Journey of Friar John Plano Carpini*, Hakluyt Society, London, 1900.

Bell, Sir Charles, *Tibet Past and Present*, Oxford, 1924.

Bouvat, L., *L'Empire Mongol*, Paris, 1927.

Bretschneider, E., *Mediaeval Researches From Eastern Asiatic Sources*, Vols. I and II, London, 1888.

――――, *Recherches Archéologiques et Historiques sur Pekin et ses environs*, Paris, 1879.

British General Staff Map, Sheet 22 (Mongolia), London, 1931, Sheet 23 (China), London, 1926.

Byron, R., *The Byzantine Achievement*, London, 1929.

Cahun, Léon, *Introduction a l'Histoire de l'Asie; Turcs et Mongols des Origines à 1405*, Paris, 1896.

Carruthers, Douglas, *Unknown Mongolia*, Vols. I and II, London, 1913.

*Chinese Year Book, 1938-39*, Shanghai, 1939.

Chi, Ch'ao-ting, *Key Economic Areas in Chinese History*, London, 1936.

Cordier, H. *Histoire Générale de la Chine et ses Relations avec les pays étrangers*, Vol. II, Paris, 1920.

Courant, M., *L'Empire Kalmuk ou l'Empire Manchu*, Paris, 1912.

Creel, H. G., *The Birth of China*, Chap. X (Ref. to bows in China and England), London, 1936.

Cressey, G. B., *China's Geographic Foundations*, New York, 1934.

Curtin J., *The Mongols*, Boston, 1908.

Dames, Longworth, " Afghanistan," *Encyclopaedia of Islam*, Vol. I.

Debevoise, N. C., *A Political History of Parthia*, Chicago, 1938.

De Harlez, *L'Histoire de l'Empire du Kin* (Trans. from the Aisin Gurun), Paris, 1888.

Diehl, Charles, " Le Monde Oriental de 395-1081," " Histoire de Moyen Age," Tome III, *Histoire Générale*, Paris, 1944.

DeMailla, J.,*Historie Générale de la Chine*, Vol. IX, compiled from the T'ung-chien Kang-mu and other sources), Paris, 1779.

D'Ohsson, Mouradgea, *Histoire des Mongols depuis Tchinguiz Khan jusqu'a Timur Béc*, Vol. I, II, Amsterdam, 1834-35.

Donner, Kai, *La Sibérie*, trans. from the Finnish by Léon Froman, Paris, 1946.

Douglas, R. K., *The life of Jenghiz Khan* (Main sources were the Yüan Shih, Yüan Shih Lei Pien, and the Shih Wei), London, 1877.

Erdmann, *Temudschin der Unerschutterliche*, Leipsig, 1862.

Ferrero, Gulielmo, *The Life of Julius Caesar*, trans. by A. E. Zimmern, New York, 1933.

Ferishta, *The History of Hindostan* (Trans. by Alexander Dow, published in London, 1770).

Fox, Ralph, *Genghis Khan*, New York, 1936.

Gaubil, *Histoire de Gentchiscan et toute la dynastie des Mongous ses successeurs conquérants de la Chine.* (A translation of the first ten Chapters of the Yüan Shih Lei Pien, which is an abstract of the Yüan Shih plus material from a number of other sources.)

Gibb, H. A. R., *The Arab Conquests in Central Asia*, London, 1923.

Gibbon, Edward, *The Decline and Fall of the Roman Empire*, annotated by J. B. Bury, Vol. VI, London, 1902.

Gibert, L., *Dictionnaire Historique et Géographique de la Mandchourie,* Hongkong, 1934.

Goodrich, L. C., *A Short History of the Chinese People,* New York, 1943.

Grenard, Fernand, *Baber Fondateur de l'Empire des Indes,* Paris, 1930. This book contains an interesting note on the armies of conquerors.

——, *Gengis-Khan,* Paris, 1935.

Grousset, René, *Histoire de l'Extreme-Orient,* Vols. I and II, Paris, 1929.

——, *L'Empire des Steppes,* Paris, 1938.

——, *L'Asie Orientale,* Vol. X, Histoire Générale, Paris, 1941.

——, *L'Empire Mongole* (1 ère phase), Histoire du Monde, tome VIII, Paris, 1941.

——, *Le Conquérant du Monde,* Paris, 1944. This work is particularly valuable for the early days of Chingis Khan and has derived much from the labours of Haenisch and Pelliot on the Yüan Ch'ao Pi Shih (Secret or Official History of the Mongols).

——, *Histoire Des Croisades,* Vol. III, Paris, 1936.

Haenisch, E. *Die Letzen Feldzüge Cingis Han's und Sein Tod Nach der Ostasiatischen Ueblieferung,* Asia Major, Leipsiz, Vol. IX, 1932. This contains translations of the last years of Chingis Khan as related by the Yüan Ch'ao Pi Shih, Yüan Sheng Wu Ch'in Cheng Lu, Yüan Shih, Altan Tobci, and the Sanang Setsen.

Haslund, Henning, *Men and Gods in Mongolia,* New York, 1935.

Hitti, P. K., *History of the Arabs,* London, 1940.

Haig, Sir Wolseley, "Turks and Afghans," *The Cambridge History of India,* Vol. III, Cambridge, 1928.

Hartman, Martin, "China," *Encyclopaedia Islam,* Vol. I. This contains an interesting résumé on the overland trade between China and the world of Islam.

Hart, Liddell, *Great Captains Unveiled* (Chap. 1 on Jenghiz Khan and Sabutai), Edinburgh and London, 1927.

Howorth, H. H., *History of the Mongols,* London, 1876-88.

——, "The Kireis and Prester John," *Journal of the Royal Asiatic Society,* London, 1889.

Husain, Dr. Mahdi, *The Rise and Fall of Muhammad Bin Tughluk,* London, 1938.

Herrmann, A., *Atlas of China,* Harvard, 1935.

Julien, Stan., "Ethnographie des Peuples Étranges a la China." This was translated from the work on the subject by the 13th century encyclopaedist Ma Tuan-lin and appeared in the *Journal Asiatique,* Genève, 1876-83.

Kervyn, L. M., *L'Empire Chinois et les Barbares,* Peiping, 1933.

*Karte Von Ost-China,* "Pyong-yang," (Korea), Landesaufnahme, 1909.

Lacoste, *Au Pays Sacré des Ancien Turcs et des Mongols,* Paris, 1911.

Lamb, H., *Tamerlane,* New York, 1928. This book contains a valuable note on bows in the East and West.

Lattimore, Owen, "Caravan Routes of Inner Asia," *Geog. Journal,* London, 1928.

———, " The Geographical Factor in Mongol History," *Geog. Journal*, London, 1938.

———, *The Desert Road to Turkestan*, Boston, 1930.

———, *High Tartary*, Boston, 1930.

———, " Prince, Priest and Herdsman in Mongolia," *Pacific Affairs*, New York, 1935.

———, Review of Fernand Grenard's " Gengis Khan," *Pacific Affairs*, New York, 1937.

———, *Inner Asian Frontiers of China*, New York, 1940.

———, *Mongol Journeys*, New York, 1941.

Le Strange, *The Lands of the Eastern Caliphate*, Cambridge, 1930.

Li, Chi, *Manchuria in History*, Peiping, 1932.

Mabel Ping-hua Lee, *The Economic History of China*, New York, 1921.

Lukinich, Imre, *A History of Hungary*, Budapest, 1937; London, n. d.

Martin, H. D., " Preliminary Report on Nestorian Remains North of Kuei-hua, Sui-yüan," *Monumenta Serica*, Peiping, 1937.

———, " The Mongol Wars with Hsi Hsia," *J. R. A. S.*, parts 3 and 4, London, 1942.

———, " The Mongol Army," *J. R. A. S.*, parts 1 and 2, London, 1943.

———, " Chinghiz Khan's First Invasion of the Chin Empire," *J. R. A. S.* parts 3 and 4, 1943.

Mullie, J., " Les Anciens Villes de L'Empire des Grands Leao au royaume Mongol de Barin," *T'oung-Pao*, Leiden, 1922.

Murdoch, J., *A History of Japan*, Vol. I, London, 1925. Chapter XVI of this work contains some very revealing facts about the power of the Mongol bow.

Muir, Sir William, *The Mameluke or Slave Dynasty of Egypt*, London, 1896.

Oman, Charles, *A History of the Art of War in the Middle Ages*, London, 1924.

Oost, P. Van, *Au Pays Des Ortos*, Paris.

Parker, E. H., *China*, London, 1917.

———, *A Thousand Years of the Tartars*, London, 1895. 2nd Edition, New York, 1926.

Pelliot, P., " Chrétiens d'Asie Centrale et d'Extrême Orient," *T'oung Pao*,

———, " Notes sur le Turkestan," *T'oung Pao*, Vol. XXVII, Leiden, 1930.

———, *Histoire Secrète Des Mongols*, Paris, 1949.

Pétis de La Croix, *The History of Genghizcan the Great* (English trans.), London, 1722.

Pidal, Ramon, *The Cid and His Spain*, trans. by H. Sunderland, London, 1934. (An interesting reference to the Turkish archers in the Almoravide army.)

Poole, S. Lane, *The Mohammadan Dynasties*, Paris, 1925.

Prasad, Ishwari, *History of Medieval India*, Allahabad, 1920.

Rawlinson, G., *The Sixth Great Oriental Monarchy*, London, 1873.

Rémusat, Abel, *Nouveaux Mélanges Asiatiques*, Paris, 1829.

Riasanovsky, V. A., *Fundamental Principles of Mongol Law*, Tientsin, 1937.

Rockhill, W. W., *The Journey of William Rubruck*, London, 1900.

Rotours, Robert, Des, " Traité des Fonctionnaires et Traité de L'Armée T'ang," Vol. I, *Bibliothèque de l'Institut des Hautes Etudes Chinoises*, Vol. VI, Leyden, 1947.

Saeki, *The Nestorian Documents and Relics in China*, Tokyo, 1937.

Schlegal, " The Invention of Gun-powder and Fire-arms in China prior to the Arrival of Europeans," *T'oung Pao*, Leiden, 1902.

Sirén, Osvald, *The Walls and Gates of Peking*, London, 1924.

Shirokogorov, S. M., *Social Organization of the Northern Tungus*, Shanghai, 1929.

Stein, Rolf, " Leao-Tche," trans. by Stein, *T'oung Pao*, Vol. XXXV, Leiden, 1939.

Spaulding, Nickerson and Wright, *Warfare*, Wahington, 1924.

Stevenson, W. B., *The Crusaders in the East*, Cambridge, 1907.

Sykes, P. M., Brigadier, *A History of Persia*, Vol. I, London, 1915.

Tarn, W. W., *Hellenistic Military and Naval Developments*, Cambridge, 1930.

Toynbee, Arnold J., *A Study of History*, London, 1934-39.

" The Great Tatar Invasion of Europe," *Slavonic Review*, Vol. V, London, 1926-27.

Tsui, Chi, *A Short History of Chinese Civilization*, London, 1942.

Ulugh Beg, *Shajrat ul Atrak*, trans. by Col. Miles, London, 1838.

Vambéry, A., *History of Bokhara*, London, 1873.

――――, *Story of Hungary*, New York, 1886.

Vernadsky, G., *A History of Russia*, Vol. I, *Ancient Russia*, Yale, 1943.

――――, " The Scope and Contents of Chingis Khan's Yasa," *Harvard Journal of Asiatic Studies*, 1938.

Vladimirtsov, B. Ya., *The Life of Chingis-Khan*, trans. by Prince Mirsky, London, 1930.

Waddel, L. A., *The Buddhism of Tibet*, London, 1934.

Waley, A., *Ch'ang-Ch'un*, London, 1931.

Walker, C. C., *Jenghiz Khan*, London, 1939.

Wilcken, U., *Alexander the Great*, trans. by G. C. Richards, London, 1932.

Wittfogel, K. A., " Dynasties of Conquest," *China*, University of California, 1946.

Wittfogel, K. A., and Feng Chia-sheng, *History of Chinese Society: Liao (907-1125)*, brought out by the American Philosophical Society, Philadelphia, 1949.

Yamada, Nakaba, *Genko, The Mongol Invasion of Japan*, London, 1916. This work contains a brief account of the Mongol conquest of Korea.

Yule, Sir Henry, *The Book of Marco Polo*, ed. H. Cordier, London, 1921.

――――, *Cathay and The Way Thither*, London, 1876.

# INDEX

345